RETHINKING INVESTMENT INCENTIVES

RETHINKING INVESTMENT INCENTIVES

Trends and Policy Options

Ana Teresa Tavares-Lehmann,
Perrine Toledano, Lise Johnson,
and Lisa Sachs, Editors

COLUMBIA UNIVERSITY PRESS
NEW YORK

Columbia University Press
Publishers Since 1893
New York Chichester, West Sussex
cup.columbia.edu

Library of Congress Cataloging-in-Publication Data
Names: Tavares, Ana Teresa, editor. | Toledano, Perrine, editor.
Title: Rethinking investment incentives :
trends and policy options / Ana Teresa Tavares-Lehmann,
Perrine Toledano, Lise Johnson, and Lisa Sachs, eds.
Description: New York, NY : Columbia University Press, 2016. |
Includes bibliographical references and index.
Identifiers: LCCN 2015048049 | ISBN 9780231172981
(cloth : alk. paper)
Subjects: LCSH: Investments. | Investments, Foreign—Government
policy. | Investments, Foreign—Taxation—Law and legislation. |
International business enterprises—Government policy.
Classification: LCC HG4521 .R477 2016 | DDC 332.6—dc23
LC record available at http://lccn.loc.gov/2015048049

Columbia University Press books are printed
on permanent and durable acid-free paper.

Printed in the United States of America
c 10 9 8 7 6 5 4 3 2 1

Cover design: Noah Arlow

CONTENTS

Foreword vii
Theodore H. Moran

1. Introduction 1
Ana Teresa Tavares-Lehmann, Lisa Sachs, Lise Johnson, and Perrine Toledano

PART I Invesment Incentives: An Introduction

2. Types of Investment Incentives 17
Ana Teresa Tavares-Lehmann

3. Definitions, Motivations, and Locational Determinants of Foreign Direct Investment 45
Sarianna M. Lundan

PART II A Global Overview of Investment Incentives

4. The Use of Investment Incentives: The Cases of R&D-Related Incentives and International Investment Agreements 63
Christian Bellak and Markus Leibrecht

5. Incentives in the European Union 94
Philippe Gugler

6. Incentives in the United States 122
Charles Krakoff and Chris Steele

7. Tax Incentives Around the World 153
Sebastian James

PART III Designing Incentives Programs to Get Value for Money and Achieve Intended Goals

8. A Holistic Approach to Investment Incentives 179
Louis Brennan and Frances Ruane

9. Investment Incentives for Sustainable Development 204
James Zhan and Joachim Karl

10. Cost-Benefit Analysis of Investment Incentives 228
Ellen Harpel

PART IV Reducing Incentives Competition: Regulatory Efforts to Limit "Races to the Bottom"

11. Regulation of Investment Incentives: National and Subnational Efforts to Regulate Competition for Investment Through the Use of Incentives 251
Kenneth P. Thomas

12. Regulation of Investment Incentives: Instruments at an International/Supranational Level 264
Lise Johnson

13. Conclusions: Outstanding Issues on the Design and Implementation of Incentives Policies 323
Lise Johnson, Perrine Toledano, Lisa Sachs, and Ana Teresa Tavares-Lehmann

Acknowledgments 329
Contributors 331
Index 335

FOREWORD

Policy makers and theorists have had more than two centuries—since the times of Adam Smith and David Ricardo—to investigate the dynamics of trade flows, and to explore the intricacies of trade policy. It should not be surprising, therefore, that we are still in the formative stage of coming to grips with analytical challenges and policy quandaries associated with today's much more complicated realm of trade-and-investment.

Over the past three and a half decades, foreign direct investment has become the principal vehicle to deliver goods and services across borders. World nominal GDP has increased four times, and world bilateral trade flows have grown more than sixfold, while the stock of foreign direct investment has swelled by roughly 20 times from an already reasonably large base in 1980. Today the global sales of the foreign affiliates of multinational corporations equal roughly two times the amount of total world exports, making foreign investors considerably more important than trade in provision of goods and services around the globe.

Within the realm of trade, 80 percent of all flows across borders take place as internal transactions within multinational firms or through supply chains supervised by them. MNCs account for about half of the world's total R&D expenditure and more than two-thirds of the world's business R&D. The bulk of technology flows between countries takes place within the confines of multinational investor production systems.

What is the role of incentives in helping to direct—or redirect—flows of foreign direct investment? Fundamental questions abound: How should investment incentives be defined? How should different kinds of investment incentives be classified? How can their impact on FDI flows be measured? What are the pro's and con's of various incentives, and how can their costs and benefits be measured?

To what extent are investment incentives in competition with each other? Is there a destructive race-to-the-bottom in incentive competition, via bidding wars to attract the same companies? Might there sometimes be races to the top, with competition across borders in public expenditures on infrastructure improvements, vocational skill-building initiatives, and regulatory institutions? What is the relationship—if any!—between the provision of incentives at the local or state level and the provision of incentives at the national level? How might incentive competition be regulated? What have been the results of past attempts to regulate incentive competition?

These are only a few of the many questions investigated in this volume. Encyclopedic in scope, the chapters gathered here feature a virtual who's-who of experts across this broad span of topics. This will certainly be a foundational work for researchers and policy makers alike.

What role do investment incentives play in the larger development strategies of emerging market governments? Can investment incentives be designed to change the profile of investor operations, not just the location of such operations—a question of increasing importance as host governments in the developing world try to use foreign direct investment to upgrade and diversify their production and export base? How might developed and developing countries join in harmonizing policies to attract multinational investors?

These issues are of pressing concern to both developing and developed countries in today's era of ever-expanding globalization. This volume is the place to start!

Theodore H. Moran
Marcus Wallenberg Professor of International Business and Finance
Georgetown University
Nonresident Senior Fellow, Peterson Institute for International Economics
Nonresident Senior Fellow, Center for Global Development

RETHINKING INVESTMENT INCENTIVES

CHAPTER 1

Introduction

Ana Teresa Tavares-Lehmann, Lisa Sachs, Lise Johnson, and Perrine Toledano

In July 2015, the government of Ethiopia hosted the Third International Financing for Development Conference, bringing together world leaders from governments, businesses, and international organizations to chart a course for financing the post-2015 development agenda. That agenda includes the most critical challenges facing society—ending extreme poverty, eradicating preventable diseases, and halting global warming, among others. Achieving the resulting sustainable development goals (SDGs) by 2030 will require mobilizing and harnessing substantial resources from both the public and the private sectors. At the conference, the global leaders recognized that "private business activity, investment and innovation are major drivers of productivity, inclusive economic growth and job creation" and that "private international capital flows, particularly foreign direct investment, along with a stable international financial system, are vital complements to national development efforts" (UN 2015, para. 35).

Indeed, now more than ever, investment has an important role to play in sustainable development through the injection of capital, generation of employment, and transfer of technology and know-how. Many governments have increasingly recognized that role: recent decades have seen a dramatic increase in the array of government incentives offered to attract such investment—and, in particular, foreign direct investment (FDI)—and to increase its contribution to sustainable development. In fact, the Addis Ababa Action Agenda adopted at the conference recognized that "incentives can be an important policy tool" (UN 2015, para. 27) in financing sustainable development. Well-designed investment incentives can attract and channel resources so as to develop renewable energy technologies, enable wider access to energy and other infrastructure, train human resources, and strengthen health systems—all of which can support sustainable development (UNCTAD 2014).

Understanding how, when, where, and why governments use incentives to attract and guide investment is critically important if we are to assess whether and how society benefits from incentives. It is increasingly apparent, however, that the use and impact of incentives are not well understood—including by the policy makers who use them. Incentives are often quite costly for governments, and yet they are only rarely designed to strategically meet sustainability or development objectives. It is widely acknowledged that companies may seek—and governments may offer—incentives beyond those that may be needed to attract an investment, whereas other investments or more general policies that would be more effective at attaining SDGs are underutilized or poorly designed or implemented.

Although the use of incentives by both national and subnational governments around the world is ubiquitous, with few exceptions, little is known about their prevalence, distribution, effectiveness, and impacts. Due largely to a lack of transparency regarding these measures, the use of investment incentives has thus far largely escaped systematic monitoring, reporting, or analysis.

But this may be changing. Some government entities, including, most notably, the European Union (EU), are imposing broad transparency requirements and strengthening their monitoring and evaluation. Along with improvements in understanding the use of these measures, there have been developments in terms of hard or soft regulation. International organizations and experts are increasingly discouraging certain types of fiscal, financial, or regulatory incentives for a number of reasons, one of which is that they might be wasteful and inefficient. This concern is particularly pressing as subnational and national jurisdictions competing for capital engage in "bidding wars" that can drive those jurisdictions to increase the types and generosity of incentives they offer in order to attract new investments and even lure coveted existing investments away from other jurisdictions. In the latter case, such incentives are inefficient in a regional or global sense, as the result is simply to reallocate investment within or across regions rather than generating new investments. Other concerns are that locational or behavioral incentives might be unduly costly (with costs outweighing their benefits) and might have harmful distributional impacts, resulting in increased inequality rather than inclusive growth.

Investments and investment incentives have potentially large costs and benefits for national and subnational jurisdictions. This volume advances our understanding of the role that incentives have played in attracting and retaining investment from foreign and domestic sources, the policy rationales supporting or discouraging various types of incentives, the strategies that may be more effective at achieving the objectives of host governments, and the potential for future coordinated action on competition for capital and other issues.

The book is structured as follows: Part I sets the scene, providing a crucial introduction to the main concepts, definitions, and types of incentives. Part II gives a global overview of the use of investment incentives across geographic regions. Part III provides practical guidance for designing, administering, and monitoring the use of incentives in order to optimize their impacts on sustainable development. Part IV focuses on current and potential future governance of incentives from multilateral to subnational levels.

DEFINING INVESTMENT INCENTIVES

Before beginning an analysis of the use and effects of incentives, it is necessary to define what types of measures are included as investment incentives in this book. In fact, there are a number of different, well-accepted definitions of investment incentives. An often-cited definition of investment incentives is provided by the OECD (2003, 12): "measures designed to influence the size, location or industry of a foreign direct investment project by affecting its relative cost or by altering the risks attached to it through inducements that are not available to comparable domestic investors." Another commonly used definition is that suggested by UNCTAD (1996, 11): "measurable advantages provided by government to particular companies or group of companies with a goal to force them to behave some way." For Thomas (2007, 11), investment incentives represent "a subsidy given to affect the location of investment. The goal may be to attract new investment or to retain an existing facility."[1] Wells et al. (2001, vii) refine this perspective of investment incentives as subsidies by stating that "incentives can be direct subsidies (including cash payments or payments in kind, such as free land or infrastructure) or indirect subsidies (tax breaks of various sorts or protection against competition from rival firms, including import protection, for example)." Using an illustration of a fiscal incentive, they further note that "to be considered an investment incentive, however, a tax break must not be available to all investors but, rather, must be tailored to specific investors or types of investors" (vii).

The definition of investment incentives is important not just from an academic perspective. When assessing the practical policy implications of investment incentives, it is crucial, in the first place, to be clear on what measures are being analyzed. Because different authors may use the term in different ways, they may come to varying conclusions about the appropriateness or effectiveness of particular incentives. For instance, the first definition is focused on FDI incentives, assuming that the entity that decides on the incentives can discriminate against domestic investors. Much of the literature and policy is expressly directed at FDI incentives because of the particular advantages FDI can bring in terms of capital, technology, and other transfers;[2] the distinct challenges countries may face in attracting that investment; and the issues that may arise when granting incentives to foreign or multinational companies. However, not all investment incentives are geared toward attraction of FDI; indeed, many investment incentives schemes do not distinguish between investors based on their nationality. Thus, the policy rationales and implications of incentives specific to FDI may not apply to general incentives that are available to domestic investors as well.

Some chapters of this book focus on strategies for using incentives to attract and benefit from FDI (e.g., chapter 8 by Brennan and Ruane), whereas other chapters discuss incentives given to domestic and foreign firms alike (e.g., chapter 6 by Krakoff and Steele). In general, most of the policy implications drawn from the chapters of this volume apply to incentives generally, whether targeted at foreign investments or at all investments.

A second important aspect of the definitions above is the notion of specificity—that is, as set out in the revised OECD Benchmark Definition of FDI (OECD 2008), investors (companies or individuals) are given such incentives or advantages when they carry out specific investment projects. Similarly, Wells et al. (2001) note that incentives—to qualify as such—must be tailored to specific investors or types of investors. Thus, under these definitions, incentives are not given to every project or investor. Rather, they are attached to certain priorities or characteristics of the investment project—for example, investment in a certain sector, in a certain territory (e.g., a low-density area or a poorer region), of a certain financial magnitude, or attached to a target such as employment or technological content.

A definition of investment incentives limited to such specific measures typically excludes general policies and host-state characteristics that are attractive for investors, such as the quality of a jurisdiction's physical infrastructure and its general legal and regulatory climate. Nevertheless, as Gugler and Johnson discuss in chapters 5 and 12, respectively, the line between specific and general measures is not always easy to draw. And, as is illustrated by Bellak and Leibrecht (chapter 4), in the context of evaluating governments' efforts to attract and keep FDI, more general policies and practices, such as those enshrined in international investment treaties, are often considered as part of the investment incentives mix.

A third element introduced in the definitions above is the notion that the advantages provided should be measurable. Although this is important, the value of incentives is not always easy to identify, much less to quantify, in practice.[3] Of course, this presents substantial challenges when assessing the costs, benefits, and effectiveness of incentives policies, as discussed throughout the chapters in this volume.

A final issue raised by the definitions above and highlighted by Thomas in chapter 11 is the focus on incentives as subsidies geared toward altering the *location* of an investment. This is a somewhat narrow definition of incentives, as incentives may be aimed at inducing other outcomes, such as altering the amount of the investment, the value-added characteristics, the technological content, or even the sectoral focus (as the first definition by the OECD notes). However, by focusing more narrowly on (re)location incentives (and excluding, e.g., incentives to overcome market failures that result in underinvestment in public goods and incentives to induce more development-oriented outcomes), we may more readily isolate the especially problematic measures that drive wasteful interjurisdictional competition for capital and identify governance strategies aimed at addressing those issues.

For the purposes of this volume, we employ the following definition, merging the most important (in our perspective) aspects from the above definitions:

> Investment incentives are targeted measures designed to influence the size, location, impact, behavior, or sector of an investment project—be it a new project or an expansion or relocation of an existing operation.

Investment incentives are most frequently financial, fiscal, and regulatory measures, but they can also include information and technical services (specifically provided to certain investors) as a particular type of incentive (see chapter 2 for a complete overview of incentive types).

THE EFFECTIVENESS AND EFFICIENCY OF INCENTIVES

Many of the incentives analyzed in this volume are those used by jurisdictions to influence the location decisions of investors, based on the belief that incentives may compensate for market failures[4] or otherwise tip the balance in favor of a specific jurisdiction to which an investor would otherwise not come. Inward investment incentives have been around for over a century (Sbragia 1996; Thomas 2007). However, only in the late twentieth century can a generalized use of incentives by most countries in the world be observed, together with a considerable diversification in terms of types and subtypes of incentives (Thomas 2007). Jurisdictions compete in what have been called beauty contests (OECD 2001), bidding wars (Oman 2000), and locational tournaments (Mytelka 2000) in order to look more appealing to investors.

In the last two decades, "red carpets replaced red tape" (Sauvant 2012), and there has been a widespread use of investment incentives aimed at making regions and countries look more attractive to increasingly mobile and global businesses.[5] In the global race for investment, incentives are used as "anabolic steroids" (Oxelheim and Ghauri 2004).

A major question underlying the chapters in this volume is whether incentives are in fact effective at attracting investment.[6] There is little doubt that *some* incentives may contribute to luring *some* investors to *some* jurisdictions, but effectiveness depends on what is being offered, to what type of investment project, and by what location. Some investors, such as strategic asset–seeking investors and resource-seeking investors, do not seem to be readily swayed by incentives when making investment decisions; others, including more "footloose," efficiency-seeking investors, may value them more (UNCTAD 2015; chapter 3 in this volume).

It is very difficult to empirically assess the redundancy of incentives—that is, whether investors would have come even without the incentives. Some of the chapters in this volume explore this question directly and others implicitly; nevertheless, there is evidence that the risk of redundancy is quite high. Surveys undertaken in many jurisdictions by the World Bank's Facility for Investment Climate Advisory Services (FIAS) showed an average redundancy ratio (the share of investors that would have invested even without investment incentives) of 77 percent and a positive answer to the question of whether the fiscal incentive influenced the decision in only 16 percent of cases, on average. Those positive answers were generally observed (1) in the case of efficiency-seeking FDI whose strategy is only to minimize costs of exported products, (2) when the investor had to decide among similarly attractive jurisdictions, and (3) when the incentive matched the need of the investor in a particular phase of the project cycle. In all the other cases, it has been regularly shown that the role of fiscal incentives is rather marginal (CCSI 2015).

Even though incentives may tip the balance, or be "the cherry on top of the cake," particularly when a short list of similar locations is being evaluated (CCSI 2015), incentives cannot fully compensate for the absence of certain fundamentals, such as the existence of a relevant market, the availability of adequate human resources, and political stability, among other factors. In particular, it has been argued that incentives often fail to make up for unattractive business climates and investment environments characterized by poor infrastructure, legal and economic instability, weak governance, and small markets (CCSI 2015). Many factors (or determinants) affect the investor location decision: the distance to major markets, the proximity of raw materials, the size of the local market, the quality of the infrastructure,[7] the state of property rights, the existence and enforcement of contract laws, the extent of corruption, the skills of the workforce, the costs of complying with regulations and other government procedures, the barriers to international trade, the macroeconomic and political stability of the country, and whether capital and profits can be repatriated without restrictions. All of this enters into the business plan of the investor and is highly dependent on the level of development of the country.[8] Given the importance of these factors, there are reasons to question whether incentives are indeed effective in influencing investors' locational decisions.

Even if incentives may play some role in influencing investment decisions, the "million-dollar" question in this regard concerns their efficiency (about which very little is known). This fundamental question, explored implicitly throughout the volume, is whether the potential benefits of offering incentives justify the costs. Even if incentives are not redundant, they can be extremely costly (Krakoff and Steele give some numerical accounts in chapter 6), highlighting how important (though notably rare) sophisticated cost-benefit analysis is. Although establishing a comprehensive approach to conducting such analysis is beyond the aspirations of this volume, a series of three chapters (chapters 8, 9, and 10) does provide guidance on performing, on a case-by-case basis, appropriate assessments of costs and benefits.

REINING IN A RACE TO THE BOTTOM

The potential high costs of incentives are not limited to the jurisdiction offering them. When jurisdictions compete through grants of incentives, they can create market distortions (motivating firms to locate in territories that are less suitable than others), cause allocative inefficiency, and generate interjurisdictional competition and tensions. Thomas (2007) notes that subnational (e.g., state or municipal level) competitions tend to be particularly inefficient, lead to intracountry bidding wars, and should be avoided. Krakoff and Steele, in chapter 6 of this volume, also delve into aspects related to the offering of incentives at national and subnational levels.

This escalation of incentives has been permitted by ever-increasing liberalization of investment flows and a persistent lack of comprehensive regulatory frameworks governing the ability of jurisdictions to use incentives to try to capture a share of those investments. Whereas specialists converge in a consensus that governments should cooperate with each other in order to reduce incentives competition (while also potentially providing special flexibilities to small or developing economies), governments are reluctant to surrender their "sovereignty" in determining what to offer to investors. This is akin to a Prisoners' Dilemma situation (Guisinger [1985] was the first author to analyze location incentives as a case of Prisoners' Dilemma; see also Thomas [2007] and chapter 11 in this volume). Most jurisdictions end up doing whatever they deem fit, generating considerable deadweight losses, and eroding their bargaining power vis-à-vis prospective investors.

For all of these reasons, locational incentives are among the most controversial topics in investment literature and policy. Politicians are often more convinced of their importance than are investors and academics.

Yet it is worth digging further into this theme, and this volume does exactly that, clarifying several conceptual issues; providing empirical evidence; discussing the thorny issue of what aspects enter into a cost-benefit analysis; and reflecting on regulatory regimes, so obviously needed but difficult to develop and implement in practice. This book has a further advantage, compared to extant single-discipline volumes: it offers a holistic and multidisciplinary perspective, integrating contributions from law and economics as well as from political economy, sustainable development, geopolitics, and other fields.

STRUCTURE AND SUMMARY OF THE BOOK

This volume is structured in four parts.

Part I sets the scene for the rest of the volume, providing an introduction to the key definitions, types of incentives, and main concepts related to investment promotion.

In chapter 2, Ana Teresa Tavares-Lehmann, following the working definition and considerations set out in this introductory chapter, explores the various types and subtypes of investment incentives, including not only the usually considered financial, fiscal, and regulatory incentives but also the less studied but very often used information and technical services offered by investment promotion agencies that can target specific industries and potential investors and have proved to be particularly influential in shaping investment decisions.

Sarianna Lundan in chapter 3 discusses the differences among market-seeking, resource-seeking, efficiency-seeking and strategic asset–seeking investments, each of which has different implications for governments seeking to attract FDI, particularly through the use of incentives. In particular, she discusses the growth of market-seeking investment in emerging markets and the rise of market- and asset-seeking investment from emerging markets, in terms of their impact on investment attraction and the use of incentives.

Part II gives an overview of the global use of investment incentives in various jurisdictions and for various types of investment. Christian Bellak and Markus Leibrecht (chapter 4) provide an in-depth look at two types of investment incentives used globally: international investment agreements as broadly available regulatory incentives to *attract* FDI and fiscal and financial research and development (R&D) incentives as measures to encourage establishment and expansion of certain types of investment activities. The following two chapters then take us to particular regions to explore the use of incentives in a regional context. In chapter 5, Philippe Gugler looks at how the EU and its individual Member States are using incentives as one strategy to strengthen the attractiveness for FDI. Importantly, he also describes in depth the strong regulatory framework that the EU has established to govern the use of State aid and to prevent EU Member States from entering into destructive competition. Nevertheless, as he also highlights, the European Commission policy on State aid has become increasingly flexible, allowing the increased use of incentives by Member States, particularly for regional development and R&D promotion.

Chapter 6, by contrast, portrays the relatively unregulated use of investment incentives by states and municipalities in the United States; Charles Krakoff and Chris Steele describe the "veritable cornucopia of exemptions, allowances, and credits" offered to investors. They illustrate how state and municipal governments use beggar-thy-neighbor policies to lure investments away from neighboring or competing states or cities; in the end, the authors contend, the only winners are the companies, as the incentives become so generous that the benefits do not outweigh the fiscal costs and that in fact there is no clear correlation between the incentives granted and the outcomes achieved by the governments granting them.

In chapter 7, Sebastian James presents a global picture, looking, in particular, at fiscal incentives and how they are granted and administered in various high-, middle-, and low-income jurisdictions around the world. Moreover, he looks at how these diverse uses of investment incentives have evolved over time, their effectiveness at achieving policy objectives, and implications for governance.

Part III looks at strategies for designing optimal incentives programs to ensure that governments achieve their policy objectives and get value for their money. In chapter 8, Louis Brennan and Frances Ruane argue that locations should adopt a holistic approach to the design of their FDI policy (including any incentives) and that their rationale for promoting, or not promoting, FDI should be fully embedded in their broader economic development strategy. Accordingly, the authors explain the principles of incentives design that locations should adopt to ensure that any incentives offered are grounded not only within the FDI policy but also, importantly, within an overall development framework.

James Zhan and Joachim Karl go a step further in chapter 9, suggesting that incentive schemes should be redesigned according to a location's sustainable development objectives and the potential contributions of FDI toward sustainable development. Not only will this help to avoid wasteful or inefficient incentives, they argue, but also, by promoting sustainable development through incentive programs, governments could improve the viability of important investments (such as in electricity, water supply, and health and education services), making those services more accessible and affordable for the poor and the jurisdiction a more attractive investment destination.

In chapter 10, Ellen Harpel gives practical suggestions for how (and why) governments should undertake cost-benefit analyses in the design of investment incentives. Drawing on relevant case studies and examples from various jurisdictions, she illustrates the risks of failing to do proper cost-benefit analyses and offers examples of how such analyses are being undertaken.

Given the pervasive use of investment incentives around the world and the tendency for ineffective and destructive regional and global incentives competition to create a "race to the bottom," the fourth and final part of this volume looks at global regulatory efforts to avoid such zero-sum outcomes. In chapter 11, Kenneth Thomas delves into particular regulatory mechanisms in three countries—Australia, Canada, and the United States—evaluating their effectiveness in controlling harmful incentives bidding. Those three case studies describe efforts to control the use of incentives to relocate existing investments or facilities within the country—that is, from one subregion to another. The author draws three conclusions from these case studies: first, that the subsidy process must be transparent, as accountability relies on the availability of information; second, that voluntary agreements among jurisdictions have been too weak in practice, so national governments should impose mandatory "no raiding" agreements on their subnational units; and, finally, that a dialogue is needed globally and among diverse stakeholders with a view toward developing consensus for more comprehensive controls on incentives.

Building on these themes, in chapter 12 Lise Johnson looks at instruments that are used at an international or supranational level to help govern the use of investment incentives. She looks both at the extent to which those instruments overregulate investment incentives that are designed to achieve sustainable development objectives, such as incentives to encourage investment in R&D for clean technologies, and at the extent to which they underregulate more wasteful location incentives.

Chapter 13 synthesizes some of the main conclusions of the book and highlights the need for further research and collaborative dialogue in order to optimize the impact of incentives for sustainable development.

NOTES

1. These definitions of incentives are often cited in the literature and in review articles on incentives—for instance, that by Cedidlová (2013).

2. The rationale for offering investment incentives packages is often grounded on the argument that the investment it seeks to stimulate generates positive externalities or spillovers (horizontal/intraindustry and vertical/interindustry) to local enterprises. Moran (2014) mentions the positive impacts of FDI in terms of economic growth, domestic productivity, transfer and cocreation of technology, employment, exports, domestic entrepreneurship, human capital formation, backward and forward linkages, cluster formation, structural change, and access to global supply chains, among other variables. Despite the fact that recent empirical evidence using state-of-the-art methodologies and firm-level data suggests that FDI tends to generate positive spillovers to local companies, particularly in the supplying industries (Javorcik 2004; Blalock and Gertler 2008; Javorcik and Spatareanu 2011), there is no consensus that such positive spillovers from FDI will materialize (Tavares and Young 2005; for comprehensive reviews, including relevant case studies, see Meyer 2008 and Moran 2014).

3. See chapter 2 in this volume for an account of several econometric studies quantifying distinct aspects of incentives.

4. In addition to the argument of market failure, other rationales may be pertinent to understand incentives provision by government—notably, and already mentioned, the existence of externalities in the form of horizontal and vertical spillovers. See chapter 4 in this volume for a detailed explanation of the different rationales and arguments (economic and political economy focused) for investment incentives.

5. Even if it is true that in the last couple of decades most regulatory changes were geared to making the investment climate more welcoming, there has been a more nuanced approach recently (Sauvant 2012; UNCTAD 2014), with relatively more restrictive measures than before—even if there is still a majority of "welcoming" measures.

6. Indeed, there has been considerable empirical analysis on the topic (as noted by, for instance, Guisinger 1992; Brewer and Young 1997; and Oxelheim and Ghauri 2004). Chapter 2 in this volume refers to a host of econometric studies that dealt with this theme.

7. For instance, in an experimental study analyzing the FDI outflows to Central and Eastern European countries from Western Europe and the United States, Bellak, Leibrecht, and Damijan (2009) revealed that infrastructure is a more relevant locational factor for FDI than taxes and that, among the various infrastructure types, information and communication infrastructure is more determinant than transport and power infrastructure. The study also finds that the negative effect of high taxes is negated by good infrastructure endowment, contributing to the higher productivity of the multinational enterprises.

8. For instance, according to Bellak, Leibrecht, and Stehrer (2008), the United States and Western Europe would get more FDI inflows if they reduced the share of low-skilled workers and the labor costs, whereas countries in Eastern Europe would mostly gain by focusing on the infrastructure and R&D policies.

REFERENCES

Bellak, C., M. Leibrecht, and J. Damijan. 2009. "Infrastructure Endowment and Corporate Income Taxes as Determinants of Foreign Direct Investment in Central and Eastern European Countries." *World Economy* 32 (2): 267–90.

Bellak, C., M. Leibrecht, and J. Stehrer. 2008. "The Role of Public Policy in Closing Foreign Direct Investment Gaps: An Empirical Analysis." *Empirica* 17 (1): 19–46.

Blalock, G., and P. J. Gertler. 2008. "Welfare Gains from Foreign Direct Investment Through Technology Transfer to Local Suppliers." *Journal of International Economics* 74 (2): 402–21.

Brewer, T., and S. Young. 1997. "Investment Incentives and the International Agenda." *World Economy* 20 (2): 175–98.

CCSI. 2015. "Investment Incentives: The Good, the Bad and the Ugly." *2013 Columbia International Investment Conference Report.* New York: Columbia Center on Sustainable Investment.

Cedidlová, M. 2013. "The Effectiveness of Investment Incentives in Certain Foreign Companies Operating in the Czech Republic." *Journal of Competitiveness* 5 (1): 108–20. Accessed May 2, 2015, http://dx.doi.org/10.7441/joc.2013.01.08.

Guisinger, S. E. 1985. "A Comparative Study of Country Policies." In *Investment Incentives and Performance Requirements,* by S. E. Guisinger and Associates. New York: Praeger.

Javorcik, B. S. 2014. "Does FDI Bring Good Jobs to Host Countries?" World Bank Policy Research Working Paper No. 6936. Washington, DC: World Bank.

Javorcik, B. S., and M. Spatareanu. 2011. "Does It Matter Where You Come From? Vertical Spillovers from Foreign Direct Investment and the Origin of Investors." *Journal of Development Economics* 96 (1): 126–38.

Meyer, K., ed. 2008. *Multinational Enterprises and Host Economies.* Cheltenham, UK: Edward Elgar.

Moran, T. 2014. "Foreign Investment and Supply Chains in Emerging Markets: Recurring Problems and Demonstrated Solutions." Working Paper 14–12, Peterson Institute of International Economics, Washington, DC.

Mytelka, L. K. 2000. "Locational Tournaments for FDI: Inward Investment Into Europe in a Global World." In *The Globalization of Multinational Enterprise Activity and Economic Development,* ed. N. Hood and S. Young, 278–302. Basingstoke, UK: Palgrave MacMillan.

OECD. 2001. "Corporate Tax Incentives for Foreign Direct Investment." OECD Tax Policy Studies No. 4. Paris: Organisation for Economic Cooperation and Development.

——. 2003. *Checklist for Foreign Direct Investment Policies.* Paris: Organisation for Economic Cooperation and Development.

——. 2008. *Benchmark Definition of Foreign Direct Investment.* 4th ed. Paris: Organisation for Economic Cooperation and Development.

Oman, C. 2000. *Policy Competition for Foreign Direct Investment: A Study of Competition Among Governments to Attract FDI.* Paris: Organisation for Economic Cooperation and Development.

Oxelheim, L., and P. Ghauri, eds. 2004. *European Union and the Race for Foreign Direct Investment.* Oxford, UK: Elsevier.

Sauvant, K. 2012. "The Times They Are A-changin'—Again—in the Relationships Between Governments and Multinational Enterprises: From Control, to Liberalization to Rebalancing." Columbia FDI Perspective No. 69. New York: Columbia Center on Sustainable Investment.

Sbragia, A. 1996. *Debt Wish: Entrepreneurial Cities, U.S. Federalism, and Economic Development.* Pittsburgh, PA: University of Pittsburgh Press.

Tavares, A. T., and S. Young. 2005. "FDI and Multinationals: Patterns, Impacts and Policies." *International Journal of the Economics of Business* 12 (1): 3–16.

Thomas, P. K. 2007. *Investment Incentives: Growing Use, Uncertain Benefits, Uneven Controls.* Geneva: Global Subsidies Initiative. Accessed May 2, 2015, http://www.iisd.org/gsi/sites/default/files/gsi_investment_incentives.pdf.

UN. 2015. "Addis Ababa Action Agenda of the Third International Conference on Financing for Development," Addis Ababa, Ethiopia, July 13–16, 2015. Accessed July 30, 2015, http://www.un.org/ga/search/view_doc.asp?symbol=A/CONF.227/L.1.

UNCTAD. 1996. *Incentives and Foreign Direct Investment.* Current Studies, Series A, No. 30. New York: United Nations Conference on Trade and Development.

——. 2014. *World Investment Report 2014—Investing in the SDGs: An Action Plan.* New York: United Nations Conference on Trade and Development.

——. 2015. *World Investment Report 2015-Reforming International Investment Governance.* New York: United Nations Conference on Trade and Development.

Wells, L. Jr., N. Allen, J. Morisset, and N. Pirnia. 2001. "Using Tax Incentives to Compete for Foreign Direct Investment." FIAS Occasional Paper No. 15. Washington, DC: Foreign Investment Advisory Service.

PART I

Investment Incentives: An Introduction

CHAPTER 2

Types of Investment Incentives

Ana Teresa Tavares-Lehmann

This chapter clarifies the types of incentives that territories can use to attract or influence the behavior of investors, drawing on the definitions of incentives and on the considerations found in chapter 1. It does not purport to evaluate the different types of incentives in terms of their efficiency (Are their costs compensated for by appropriate benefits?), effectiveness[1] (Are they successful?), and other criteria; several chapters in this volume address these questions (see, for instance, chapter 9, which suggests the importance of aligning investment incentives with sustainable development goals). Nor does it purport to explain the economic rationale for the provision of incentives (chapter 4 develops that issue, presenting reasons to adopt incentives, such as market failure and spillovers).

First, this chapter reflects on factors relevant to understanding why certain types of incentives are adopted, addressing the key trade-offs and the pros and cons of different approaches or decisions. Then, at its core, it explains some of the types (and subtypes) of incentives that are used to attract or influence the behavior of investors. The definition of each type and subtype is supplemented by illustrative examples. Finally, the chapter offers some concluding remarks on the issues tackled herein.

WHAT ARE INCENTIVES FOR? POLICY MAKERS' KEY STRATEGIC DECISIONS AND INHERENT TRADE-OFFS

Incentives are increasingly multifaceted, and this happens for many reasons: they serve different purposes, and there are many ways of designing and administering them, depending on the beliefs and objectives of policy makers.

Policy makers are thus confronted by complex choices when formulating policies or making decisions regarding the use of incentives, and there are no simple guidelines for them to follow. They frequently do not have the means, the ability, or even the interest to estimate the full impact of adopting different incentives policies and packages. Furthermore, in many cases, they would probably not implement incentives policies if others were not doing the same—because everyone is providing incentives, they believe they have to be in the "race" if they want investment to be located within their jurisdictions (Oxelheim and Ghauri 2004; Young and Tavares 2004; chapter 11 in this volume).

To give a flavor of their multidimensionality and the complexity inherent to their use, incentives can be distinguished according to the following characteristics.

- *Purpose*: Are incentives meant to attract new investors or to retain/deepen/impact the commitment of existing investors—that is, are they geared to stimulating initial, sequential, or specific types of investment? It is commonly thought that most investment in developed countries comes from existing investors, those that already know the host economy. This sequential investment can take the form of accruals to the equity of the company, reinvested earnings,[2] or intracompany loans (Dunning and Lundan 2008). So the question for policy makers is whether they should bet on what is more "near" and what they already know best or try to get newer—yet less known—players. It is a matter of deepening versus widening the array of investors, of betting on the same (probably more reachable) actors versus diversifying (and opening new areas, new sectors, etc.). There is no simple answer as to which choice is better, although it is likely that going after investors already present in the territory increases the likelihood of obtaining new investment projects for that location—and often ones with deeper commitment in terms of value-added functions (as extant investors do not face the same asymmetry of information as new investors and have already been convinced of the merits of investing in that location). This likelihood depends on several variables: for instance, in the case of foreign direct investment (FDI), it depends on factors such as the strategic role the multinational enterprise (MNE) subsidiary located in that economy has in the MNE group (Is it a subsidiary with a critical importance to the group? Is it demanding an expansion?) and the power local subsidiary managers may have within the MNE group (if these are influential, they may be likely to convince the group to locate more value-added activities—thus sequential investment—in that host territory).

• *Level of targeting or level of discrimination*: How narrowly are incentives tailored and eligibility criteria defined? Examples of targeting criteria follow (note that some of these are closely related):

- according to the sector
- according to the home country of the investor
- according to the type of parent company (by size/turnover, perceived technological and industry positioning, market share in the relevant sector and in key markets, etc.)
- in the case of FDI, according to the type of MNE subsidiary to be attracted, usually depending on the market, technological, and value-added scope of the subsidiary (White and Poynter 1984)[3]
- according to the type of activity (research and development [R&D], production, sales, etc.)
- according to the size/magnitude of the investment project (number of jobs, pecuniary amount of the investment, or other performance criteria)
- according to the level of compliance of the investment project with state-of-the-art environmental or labor standards
- according to the extent to which the investment project promotes sustainable development goals (SDGs) (see chapter 9 in this volume)

• With respect to targeting, Ireland is a case in point: fine sectoral targeting (e.g., in microelectronics and later in tradable services like financial services), aligned with considerable development of local capabilities in the relevant areas, yielded a significant amount of FDI in the desired activities, with a high incidence of U.S. MNEs.

• The case of Singapore shows how integrating incentives with clear targeting of specific investors or particular types of activities can have positive effects (Oman 2000)—for instance, in the targeting and attraction of regional headquarters (HQs). Through its consistent incentives policy, integrating tax incentives and other measures (such as grants and loans)—coupled with other economic policies (including human capital formation), state-of-the-art infrastructure, political stability, and other conditions (good schools, a safe environment, etc.)—Singapore attracted thousands of MNEs' HQs for the Asia Pacific region.

• In the Netherlands, HQs were also lured with a very favorable tax regime. The same happened in Ireland and Luxembourg. As Braunerhjelm (2004) notes, HQs are firms' strategic centers, so their attraction can be particularly desirable, especially when they are not mere financial operations and include other influential functions involving skilled workers, like strategic planning and control.

- *Level of discretion*: Is administration of incentives rule-based and automatic or negotiated individually on an ad hoc basis? Are all the conditions and amounts or percentages applicable to incentives specified (e.g., in an investment code), or are incentives negotiable on a case-by-case basis? Whereas the former presents advantages in terms of simplicity of administration and savings on transaction (information and bargaining) costs and is undoubtedly more transparent, the latter allows for more flexibility and "calibration" regarding the perceived merit of the investment (see also chapter 7 in this volume). Nevertheless, there may be suspicion regarding how objectively and thoroughly merit is assessed.

Costa Rica, for instance, has all the conditions specified in its investment code, and every investor knows in advance how much they can get in terms of incentives. Portugal, by contrast, has a contractual regime that involves individual negotiation of large investment projects, hence opening the door to case-by-case negotiations of incentives packages. However, even in the case of a relatively discretionary regime such as that in Portugal, there are limits to incentive concessions (dictated by European Union rules, as described in chapter 5 in this volume) and also general guidelines and principles, so it may be argued that there is "bounded discretion."

- *Timing*: Are incentives ex ante or ex post, sometimes called front-loaded and back-loaded (CCSI 2015), respectively? Incentives may be offered before the investment is made or after the investment has produced effects. Ex ante provision of incentives is based on the expectation of future, and thus unconfirmed, performance. Investors tend to like this type of incentive, as it is given without the investor having any burden of proof of a certain performance. Such incentives also enable better financial management, as they represent financing that is anticipated. Yet they can be counterproductive, attracting opportunistic, "footloose," or less successful investors that will not deliver the expected results (see also chapter 7 in this volume).
- *Basis*: Are incentives tied to performance or unconditionally offered? This issue is related to that of ex ante or ex post incentives. If incentives are tied to performance, they can be given ex ante with provisions for clawbacks, or they can be given on an ex post basis, after the verification of the key performance indicators (KPIs), which may be defined in terms of export targets, employment targets, the establishment of certain activities like R&D, or other objectives. If incentives are given ex ante, even with provisions for clawbacks, there may be problems with enforcing penalties or getting back the incentives provided in case KPIs are not met. Conceptually, there tends to be a wide literature in favor of the former (CCSI 2015).

Still, performance requirements bear the disadvantage of being costly from an administrative point of view (as noted in James 2009) and have often been subject to controversy—for instance, in terms of obligating investments to fulfill local content requirements (Christiansen, Oman, and Charlton 2003). CCSI (2015) considers that incentives tied to performance criteria constitute a best practice but need to be accompanied by adequate mechanisms for monitoring and enforcement.

- *Format*: Are incentives provided as a one-off payment or in installments? This also relates to the issues of timing and basis, discussed immediately above, and the same types of arguments arise.

Overall, all of these choices (ex ante or ex post; tied to performance or unconditionally offered; and provided as a one-off payment or in installments) need to be pondered in the light of critical principles and issues like the importance of merit assessment, transparency, simplicity, and administrative burden. There is an evident trade-off between merit or performance evaluation, on the one hand, and transparency and administrative cost, on the other hand. Whenever incentives packages are not defined in a general law and are developed on a case-by-case basis, involving performance assessments that are seldom 100 percent objective, opportunities for rent seeking and corruption arise. The administrative burden also increases exponentially, as there must be relevant merit and performance analyses for each case, often implying costly data collection and other inputs for these assessments to be viable. The administrative burden is thus related to the costs and time necessary to implement the incentives policies or measures. Costs here generally mean transaction costs related to information acquisition, bargaining or negotiating, monitoring, and the like.

TYPES AND SUBTYPES OF INVESTMENT INCENTIVES

There is a considerable array of types and subtypes of incentives. Very often governments offer a mix, or a package, of different types of incentives. This mix or package of measures varies greatly among countries and even subnational jurisdictions. This will be addressed when referring to individual incentive types.

This section employs a broad conception of incentives. Very often the discussions about incentives are more narrowly focused, considering only financial and fiscal incentives. Between these, fiscal incentives are those that capture more attention in both the theoretical and the empirical literatures (CCSI 2015).

We define and provide illustrative cases of the usually considered financial, fiscal, and regulatory incentives (OECD 2003), but we also include and develop two other measures that help to attract investment or stimulate the location of a certain investment in a particular territory: information and technical services and inward investment agencies. The rationale for including these is explained in the respective section in which each is discussed.

FINANCIAL INCENTIVES

Financial incentives include the provision of grants, subsidies, loans, wage subsidies, and job training subsidies; creation of new, targeted infrastructure; and support for expatriation costs. As resource-constrained governments find it harder to pay money than to forego receipt of money, financial incentives are less common in developing countries than developed (CCSI 2015).

Direct financial assistance—like loans and grants provided to the investing firm when making an initial or a subsequent investment—tends to be particularly relevant for companies when financing will not be easy to obtain. Financial incentives can be nonreimbursable or may need to be partially or totally reimbursed, with or without interest or extra costs. As already noted, given that these incentives represent direct financial advantages, investors tend to like them, especially if they are received as a one-off ex ante payment.

Grants are a form of financial support that provides firms with cash or subsidies for certain eligible expenses. They may reach stratospheric amounts. For instance, in 1996, a Dow Chemical investment project in Germany is estimated to have received $800,000 for each of the 2,000 jobs created; in 1997, Shintech (an electronics company), $500,000 for each of the 250 jobs created in the United States; in 1993, GM, $300,000 for each of the 213 jobs created in Hungary; and in 1991, Ford-VW, $255,000 for each of the 1,900 jobs created in Portugal (Oxelheim and Ghauri 2004, 11 (table 3); more examples can be found in chapter 6 in this volume).

According to Oxelheim and Ghauri (2004), grants were one of the most important incentives offered by the European Union (EU) and European Free Trade Organization (EFTA) countries in the 1980s and 1990s and were used, in particular, to subsidize capital formation. They have been especially applied in manufacturing projects and in the automotive, electronics, and semiconductor industries.

Loans are another type of financial incentive and can be concessional or nonconcessional. Concessional loans are direct loans provided on more favorable terms than market conditions (e.g., subject to lower interest rates, longer grace periods, or a mix of both). Usually, they involve protocols with banks. Nonconcessional loans are loans provided at market rates, with conditions identical to those offered by commercial lenders. When credit is not widely available, they can be especially relevant to small and medium-sized enterprises (SMEs) without a sound capital structure or large assets to guarantee loans. According to Perera (2014, 5), "Loans were widely used during the 1990s and 2000s but have declined in importance in the EU and U.S.A. as a result of sovereign debt-related reforms." Burger, Jaklic, and Rojec (2012) offer the interesting case of the Slovenian FDI Co-financing Grant Scheme, in which loans (covering part of the investment, in a cofinancing perspective) are provided to qualifying investors in Slovenia.

In addition to the very frequently used categories of grants and loans, financial incentives (mainly in the form of specific subsidies) include the following.

- *Job training subsidies*: Such measures, for instance, support trainees in the firm or offer training subsidies to newly recruited employees (more common due to incremental employment impact) or to already established staff of the firm; in the EU, these measures are very often used in regions having low per capita income or undergoing structural change or industrial reconversion. A considerable part of the EU structural funds is geared to this type of subsidy; the European Social Fund (ESF) administers the subsidies that are designed to stimulate training.
- *Infrastructure subsidies*: These subsidies are one of the preferred ways of increasing the attractiveness of a location. Here, to act as an investment incentive, they have to be related somehow to a particular investor and not be offered to all investors. They may, however, be shared by other actors (e.g., in the case of an improved road in the location of the supported new investment). They can include the provision of physical infrastructure (such as roads, harbors, or railways) or the concession of land and several types of infrastructure improvements. The European Regional Development Fund (ERDF) supports several infrastructure developments, especially in "cohesion" or economically depressed areas, but these are supposed to be used to improve the general competitiveness and welfare of the region, not to help a specific investor. In many cases, however, under this generally accepted de jure argument, governments

may de facto bias the provision of infrastructure to benefit specific investors or groups of investors (e.g., those that set up their operations in a new industrial park; those that benefit from improved roads, ports, airports, etc., serving specifically the territory where they are located).

It should be noted that subsidies that enhance the level of qualifications of the workforce or the caliber of infrastructure (via job mobility or the sharing of improved infrastructure) tend to have a more beneficial impact in the host economy than do measures that are geared only to one firm and that cannot spill over or produce positive externalities to other actors.

- *Money to organize missions*: These funds enable investors to visit the markets in which they want to operate or intend to deepen their commitment. They also support reverse missions, in which business leaders or opinion makers visit the host country. In the EU, very often this money comes from European funds aimed at increasing the competitiveness and internationalization of industries, but it is usually given to collective initiatives to avoid problems with state aid legislation (chapters 5 and 12 in this volume address State Aid in more detail).
- *Government equity participation*: This measure has been used, for instance, in Austria in the 1980s and is often disguised as a joint venture (Oxelheim and Ghauri 2004). It is considered to involve a subsidy when "the rate of return demanded by the government falls below that demanded by private capital markets" (27).
- *Loan guarantees*: Guarantees on loans can be a form of subsidy. These measures were common in France, Iceland, and Sweden (Oxelheim and Ghauri 2004) and help companies to leverage debt from lending institutions that may not be willing to lend, or may be willing to lend only at higher rates, absent such guarantees.

FISCAL INCENTIVES

Fiscal incentives are tax provisions tailored to qualified investment projects that represent a favorable deviation from general tax laws and regulations (Fletcher 2002) and aim to increase the rate of return of a certain investment or reduce its risks and costs by reducing the tax burden (OECD 2000). Fiscal incentives include both lower taxation and outright exemptions from taxation. From the point of view of the host government, they amount to revenues foregone or deferred. For this reason, they have been called "tax expenditures" in the literature (Anderson 2008; OECD 2010).

As already mentioned, fiscal incentives they are often considered the most commonly used type of investment incentive (CCSI 2015; chapter 7 in this volume), as they are popular in both developed and developing countries.[4] Very often, in developing economies, they are the only type of incentive being offered, as these countries do not have the financial resources to provide outright financial incentives that their developed counterparts do.

Tax policy has thus been used as a tool for attracting and benefiting from investment (Tavares-Lehmann, Coelho, and Lehmann 2012), and it implies reductions in, exemptions from, or deferrals of taxes payable in the host country and arising from income sources such as profits, dividends, and royalties. Such incentives may also take the form of tax credits.

What is clear is that differences in tax rates may lead to profit shifting between jurisdictions with different levels of tax burden, affect the amount of dividends subsidiaries repatriate to HQs, and, most importantly, influence the allocation of MNEs' investments (Hines 1999). Whereas this is evident in the case of FDI allocation among countries, as MNEs can arbitrate among different national tax jurisdictions, tax rate differences may also influence intracountry investment where subnational jurisdictions can impose different tax burdens (e.g., in the United States, as Hines [1996] has shown empirically).

Fiscal incentives include the following subtypes (UNCTAD 2000; Fletcher 2002; Morisset 2003; Tavares-Lehmann, Coelho, and Lehmann 2012; CCSI 2015; chapter 7 in this volume).

- *Tax havens* suppress direct income taxes and rely on consumption-related taxes. This is probably the most generous fiscal framework for investors. Those territories considered tax havens include Panama in Latin America, Luxembourg and the Channel Islands in Europe, and Turks and Caicos and several other Caribbean destinations.

There are some nuances, as tax haven is a designation that encompasses very different realities. For instance, in some territories, nonresidents enjoy specific tax advantages vis-à-vis residents; in others, the tax advantages apply only to income received from activities in other markets; and in still other cases, packages are even negotiated with one investor or group of investors (e.g., see the contentious case of Google in Luxembourg).

- *Tax holidays* are a type of measure in which qualifying newly established firms are exempt from paying corporate income taxes during a certain period. These holidays have the advantage of simplicity, with a low compliance burden for investors and low administrative costs for tax officials.[5] Their danger is that they may reward footloose industries that rapidly move to another jurisdiction once the holiday expires. Tax holidays are among the most controversial and criticized tools, as they are considered very blunt.

Providing outright tax exemptions, or tax holidays, is a widespread practice in export-processing zones (EPZs) and special economic zones (SEZs), which are very common in several low- and middle-income countries.

An example of targeting and tax holidays is Colombia's regime for investments in tourism, which provides a thirty-year income tax exemption: "The exemption takes effect once service delivery begins for hotels that are built, remodeled and/or expanded between 2003 and December 2017" (ProExport Colombia 2014, 1).

- *Reduced corporate income tax rates* result in more favorable rates for qualifying investors. Hong Kong, Cambodia, Malaysia, Ireland, Estonia, Costa Rica, and many other locations have used this type of measure, and it is one of the incentives used by Singapore to attract the regional HQs of MNEs.
- *Investment tax credits* can be flat (credits earned as a fixed percentage of the investment made in a certain year) or incremental (credits earned as a fixed percentage of the expenditures made in excess of a certain threshold, or level, or moving average). The investor thus has an incentive to make extraordinary expenditures that would not occur in the absence of the relief, leading to potential overinvestment that is not necessarily needed or strategic. Investment tax credits are often used to encourage investment in R&D (as described in chapter 4 in this volume) and to stimulate exports.
- *Loss carryforwards* allow losses to be carried forward or backward a specified number of years. They are useful for investors that have losses in the first years as they penetrate markets or increase production.
- *Investment allowances* are deductions from taxable income that are based on a percentage of the investment (depreciation). Because they reduce taxable income, their value to investors depends on the corporate tax rate applicable to the tax base. Eligible investors are provided with faster or more generous write-offs. As Bellak and Leibrecht note in chapter 4 in this volume, investment allowances are commonly applied to R&D investment.
- *Accelerated depreciation* is a type of investment allowance whereby firms are able to write off capital costs in a shorter period than dictated by the capital's useful economic life.

- *Enhanced deduction* is another type of investment allowance whereby firms are able to claim deductions that are a multiple of the actual capital cost.
- *Reduced tax rates on dividends and interest paid abroad* decreases the taxes paid on dividends and interest remitted abroad by investors. This measure is particularly relevant for investors coming from countries that have a worldwide taxation system, like the United States.
- *Preferential treatment of long-term capital gains* allows gains from capital retained over a certain minimum period to be taxed at a lower rate than short-term capital gains. This benefits investors that are present in the territory for longer periods, to the potential disadvantage of start-ups.
- *Zero or reduced tariffs* are measures that eliminate or reduce tariffs on equipment or spare parts needed for the investment project or (even though this is not a measure intended for investors, but a "mirror measure" to decrease the competitiveness of competitors that do not invest in that host territory) that increase tariffs on imports of finished goods. These are often used in EPZs and in the extractive industry sector, and they are very common in Southeast Asia. However, the legitimacy of such measures under World Trade Organization (WTO) rules is disputed.

Governments (national and subnational) usually employ a mix of the above types of fiscal incentives in order to attract and/or alter the behavior of certain investments. Lowering corporate income tax rates has been the most common incentive (Becker and Fuest 2009). Figures show that the average statutory corporate tax rate in the OECD countries was about 50 percent in the early 1980s, then dropped to under 35 percent in 2000 (Devereux, Griffith, and Klemm 2002), and reached around 26 percent in 2009 (OECD 2010). These averages, however, conceal considerable diversity and discrimination among types of investors.

Empirical evidence of tax competition comes from all over the world (Yao and Zhang 2008; chapter 6 in this volume). Such competition is present both between counties (Davies and Voget 2008; Hansson and Olofsdotter 2008) and within countries, as can be seen in the case of states in the United States (Oates 2002; Gurtner and Christensen 2008; chapter 11 in this volume) and states in Brazil (Christiansen, Oman, and Charlton 2003).

The use of tax incentives in Ireland is very well documented. Since the 1950s, the Irish government has implemented a policy of attracting FDI using important tax incentives. Until 1982, it applied a full-fledged tax holiday to all new sales by foreign export–focused manufacturing subsidiaries. After that year, and until 2002, such companies benefited from an automatic preferential corporate tax rate of 10 percent on all manufacturing profits, independent of the place where these profits were generated (Oxelheim and Ghauri 2004). From 2002 onward, and after pressure from the EU, Ireland established a corporate tax rate of 12.5 percent applicable to all activities. The EU has continued to press the country to abandon such favorable rates.

In the United States, Delaware and Nevada are among the most cited cases of aggressive tax policies. Due in part to its favorable tax rules, applicable not only to foreign entities but also to domestic corporations, Delaware is the legal home of almost a million business entities, including more than 50 percent of all U.S. publicly traded firms and 60 percent of Fortune 500 companies.[6] This is clearly an across-the-board measure whose fit with a narrow, discriminatory view of incentives (within a jurisdiction) may be questioned, but there is little or no doubt that favorable taxation in these states (when compared to other jurisdictions) has impacted considerably the *magnitude* of investments they receive. Chapter 6 in this volume analyzes tax incentives provided by different states within the United States in more depth.

Coming back to the example of the location of corporate HQs, this complex and multidimensional process is affected by different factors. The HQs location decision is sensitive to the incentives governments can offer (Boddewyn and Brewer 1994), and distinct incentives may have an impact (Braunerhjelm 2004). Tax packages are the incentives most used to lure the location of HQs. As noted above, HQs are interesting to host countries, as they are usually the strategic center of the MNE for a region or for global markets. There are, however, HQs that have a mere financial role, so how "productive" these incentives are will depend on the type of functions the HQs perform. Singapore, Ireland, and the Netherlands (the last being probably the most debated case in Europe lately) are examples of countries with a clear targeting strategy vis-à-vis HQs, relying mainly on tax incentives and secondarily on financial incentives, as explained above.

A host of survey-based and econometric studies have delved into the issue of how effective fiscal incentives are in attracting investment (for reviews, see De Mooij and Ederveen 2001, 2008; Raudonen 2008; Tavares-Lehmann, Coelho, and Lehmann 2012). The literature on the effectiveness of fiscal incentives is ambiguous, although there is clearly a division between older studies (which tend to be more qualitative and survey-based and, when quantitative, tend to use now-dated proxies for tax incentives, such as simple corporate tax rates) and newer studies (which are more rigorous econometrically and use more-encompassing proxies for taxation, such as bilateral effective average tax rates [BEATRs]). Whereas most of the former (an exception being Guisinger [1985]) tend to find fiscal incentives irrelevant or of little importance to investment location decisions, the latter overwhelmingly find taxation a significant factor impacting FDI attraction. The turning point appears to have been the use of effective average tax rates (EATRs) by authors like Devereux and Griffith (1998); Altshuler, Grubert, and Newlon (1998, 2000); and Grubert and Mutti (2000). An interesting nuance is provided by Mutti and Grubert (2004), whose empirical estimates indicate that investment geared to export markets is particularly sensitive to host country taxation and that this sensitivity appears greater in developing countries than in their developed counterparts and is becoming greater over time.

More recent studies—such as those by Bellak, Leibrecht, and Römisch (2007); Egger, Loretz, and Pfaffermayr (2008); and Bellak, Leibrecht, and Damijan (2009), all using the BEATR as a proxy for measuring taxes—have found that FDI inflows are significantly and negatively related to taxes. Nevertheless, most of these studies are focused mainly on developed countries, and it remains to be proven that the tax incentives so widely used in the developing world are effective. Moreover, even if effectiveness is proven, the question remains as to whether they are worth the costs and trade-offs they imply (e.g., they may be diverting funds from much-needed reforms—in areas like basic infrastructure and education; in terms of the national budget, when tax income is lower, expenditures may have to be lower, too). The effect on sustainability may also be questioned (for more details on the need to incorporate SDGs in the incentives equation, see chapter 9 in this volume).

This overview of some commonly cited econometric studies puts in evidence two undeniable facts: the difficulty (due to opacity and lack of transparency, or simply due to the non-disclosure of organized and detailed information) of finding "fine-grained" data on investment incentives (understood as targeted/selective measures directed at particular types or groups of investors according to the definitions presented in chapter 1) and also the complexity of measuring investment. In most cases, when trying to assess the relevance of tax incentives for investment attraction and for relocation or change in investment characteristics and patterns, such incentives are proxied by more macro measures than would be desirable—usually indicators of general taxation or tax rates, from statutory tax rates to BEATRs, and often even containing a mix of several such measures. For example, Buettner and Ruf (2005) test the predictive power of marginal, statutory, and effective average tax rates for location decisions. They also raise a very important concern: "The scarcity of evidence on the impact of taxation on location decisions might be due to the fact that the corresponding analysis cannot be done using aggregate FDI data, but requires data on individual cross-border direct investments, which are usually difficult to obtain" (1).[7] This statement highlights clearly the way in which the terms *taxation*, *tax rates*, and *tax incentives* are used interchangeably in a great deal of the literature (although they are in terms of rigor different concepts) and the deficiencies in generally available data on both tax incentives and measures of investment (it must be noted that Buettner and Ruf's [2005] paper focuses only on FDI, whereas the present volume adopts a wider view related to foreign as well as domestic investment incentives).

This interchangeable use of distinct concepts leads to broad-based econometric works using large-scale datasets that often employ proxies for tax incentives that are more general than what would be desirable if the objective was to uncover the impact of targeted tax incentives. Another aspect that might be at play is that in some of these studies the concept of tax incentives is broader than the one used in this volume, including low general tax rates as investment incentives.[8]

Despite these limitations, a greater number of empirical (econometric) studies exist for tax incentives than for other types of incentives. And these broad-based econometric studies have the merit (versus works that deal exclusively with particular cases) of not being based only on individual situations and pure (yet often interesting) anecdotal evidence that would impede generalizations. Albeit imperfect, these large-scale studies based on econometric models are useful, as they highlight general trends and provide some sense of the impact of tax measures on the investment variable. For the other types of incentives (e.g., financial), the difficulty in finding appropriate data is even more pronounced,[9] making broad-based studies often not viable. This highlights the need for better firm-level data on incentives offered to specific companies and for further and more relevant econometric research using data both on targeted incentives and on particular investments done by the firms that do and do not receive them.[10]

REGULATORY INCENTIVES

Regulatory incentives are "policies of attracting . . . enterprises by means of offering them derogations from national or sub-national rules and regulation" (OECD 2003, 17). In practice, these derogations have often meant "easing the environmental, social and labour-market related requirements placed on investors" (17). They may include, for instance, relaxing the standards for labor conditions (social dumping, in pejorative terms) and/or for the environmental responsibility of the firm (often labeled environmental dumping).

Regarding labor standards, competition for inward investment on the basis of flexibility of employment contracts and reduced nonwage labor costs has characterized the OECD economies (and states' policies within the United States) for some decades (OECD 2001). The OECD (2001, 7) also suggests that developing countries have sectors that are more vulnerable to the potential lowering of labor standards—for instance, those intensive in low-skill employment that tend to attract more footloose industries like textiles and clothing. The International Labor Organization (ILO; 1998) argues that the strongest evidence for regulatory competition is probably the establishment of free trade zones (FTZs) that offer looser labor regulations in order to attract light industry such as electronics, clothing, and footwear. FTZs are especially pervasive in Southeast Asia.

However, the empirical evidence leads to no clear conclusions on whether a regulatory "race to the bottom" in fact exists (Brown 2000; UNCTAD 2001; OECD 2003). There is also no robust indication that demanding or strict environmental or labor standards are negatively associated with investment inflows (OECD 2001, 10).

One way that such derogations are granted is through stabilization provisions included in investor-state contracts. These provisions purport to excuse investors from having to comply with changes in the law that increase their costs of doing business either for a set term or for the length of the contract. They can be drafted to cover any change in the law but most commonly apply to changes in the fiscal framework. Regulatory incentives may also be granted through various other channels, including provisions in investor-state contracts that give investors greater rights or protections than would otherwise be available under domestic law. Depending on the processes used in the negotiation of these contracts, there may be an abundance of discretion and an absence of transparency, raising concerns of efficiency and accountability, among others highlighted elsewhere in this volume.

Regulatory incentives may also be provided through laws. As alluded to above, the laws establishing FTZs or other special economic zones, for example, may provide that the general legal framework regarding labor, taxation, or other issues does not apply within the FTZ, thereby offering an incentive to invest in those areas. Additionally, investment laws, which are more common in developing than developed countries, are often drafted to provide foreign investors special substantive or procedural rights.

A third channel is through international treaties. International investment agreements (IIAs), for instance, are arguably a regulatory incentive in that they provide foreign investors legal protections beyond those that are available under the domestic law of the host state (discussed further in chapters 4 and 12).

There is an important distinction between regulatory incentives, as described here, and other investor-friendly elements of the broader regulatory framework (just as there is a distinction between fiscal incentives and a favorable fiscal regime and between infrastructure incentives and general investments in supportive infrastructure). As noted above, there is little evidence that lowering environmental or labor standards actually leads to increased investment.[11] But there is also little doubt that a fair, transparent, and predictable regulatory framework is attractive to investors. Indeed, certain aspects of the regulatory framework, such as the strength of property law protections and corporate law principles, are often fundamental to investors' location and behavioral decisions. Nevertheless, a system of laws and procedures that is generally applicable to all investors (as opposed to laws and procedures established for particular investment zones or for designated industries or firms) does not fall within our definition of investment incentives.

INFORMATION AND TECHNICAL SERVICES

Considering the definition of incentives adopted in chapter 1 ("investment incentives are targeted measures designed to influence the size, location, impact, behavior, or sector of an investment project—be it a new project or an expansion or relocation of an existing operation"), information and technical services can act as investment incentives.

Although this measure is of a different nature than the previous three types (financial, fiscal, and regulatory), the provision of information and business intelligence, as well as various technical support services, can undoubtedly stimulate investment (Oxelheim and Ghauri 2004) and influence investment location patterns and related investor behaviors (e.g., amount invested, decisions about recruitment and supply linkages; Spar's [1998] work on the investment of Intel in Costa Rica highlights these aspects). Even if its influence on the project's rate of return is not direct or immediate, this measure is likely to influence that rate of return indirectly or over a longer time frame (e.g., by motivating investors to choose more efficient suppliers, to establish linkages with better local actors such as centers of excellence or universities, or to obtain market information for free or in a cheaper way).

The purpose of offering such a measure is to reduce the information asymmetry arising from investors' lack of familiarity with the host economy; notably, they lack information about market conditions, the legal and judiciary system, ways of doing business, the business culture, potential partners, and so on. Foreign investors face "costs of foreignness" (Hymer 1976) when going abroad, which puts them, all other factors constant, at a disadvantage vis-à-vis local investors. All these factors that lead to information asymmetry and "liability of foreignness" (Zaheer 1995) are adequately encapsulated in the concept of "psychic distance" (Johanson and Vahlne 1977) and increase costs and risks.[12] Therefore, any targeted measure that effectively reduces information asymmetries and leads a certain investor (or group of investors) to maneuver more successfully in the host economy can reduce such costs and risks, hence impacting the rate of return of the project.

The rationale for the provision of information is twofold (Buckley et al. 2010; Sundaresh 2012): (1) as information has public-good characteristics, a market failure usually materializes in the underprovision of such information by the private sector; and (2) the government enjoys economies of scale in the production of information and in the provision of technical services (Copeland 2008), which eliminates the duplication of resources that occurs when private firms have to generate this information by themselves.

As already noted, filling these information gaps reduces the risks faced by investors by allowing such investors to better assess the parameters of their business plans. Ceteris paribus, these measures tend to be more important for SMEs and for inexperienced investors than for large (i.e., more resourceful) and more globalized MNEs.

Information/business intelligence and technical services may be provided for free or on a fee basis. The more specific the information or the service, the higher the probability that there will be copayment by the investor (e.g., in Portugal, general information about markets is provided freely to the investor, but specially designed training courses may be cofunded by the investor or subject to the payment of a fee).

Information and technical services can be provided in different phases of the investment project: (1) in the planning phase—that is, before the investment is made, or even before a specific opportunity is identified or the investment is decided; (2) during the implementation or setup phase of the investment project; and (3) after the investment project has been implemented (at which time they are referred to as after-care or corporate development services).

Examples of *investment-related information and business intelligence* that may be provided by governments or, more usually, by agencies on their behalf include access to

- databases, reports, and publications on various themes relevant for the investment process—such as the investment climate; macroeconomic context; industry/sector-related data; market characteristics; legislation; investment opportunities; and partnership opportunities with suppliers, clients, universities/research centers, or funding sources; and
- seminars, webinars, training sessions and programs, workshops, conferences, and other events.

In terms of *investment-related technical services*, often called technical assistance, examples include

- advice or consulting (e.g., technical assessments and surveys, particularly important for investment in natural resources or in infrastructure; financial analysis; market evaluations; due diligence services; feasibility/viability studies; and advice on investment procedures);
- preparatory and ongoing services (e.g., legal and accounting services);
- organization of missions (e.g., short trips, visits to markets, site visits for prospective investors) and reverse missions (e.g., visits to the host economy by journalists and opinion makers in order to disseminate the advantages of investing in that location);
- matchmaking services (e.g., identifying partners and putting investors in contact with them or with other actors and key players relevant to the investment process);
- lobbying with international organizations/entities;
- business facilitation, or reduction of bureaucracy and hassle costs;

- after-care services (e.g., generating investment leads, increasing the value of the investment to the host country, and helping to "embed" MNEs by stimulating linkages and supply chain development strategies or by supporting reinvestment by existing investors [Loewendahl 2001]).

There are numerous examples of the provision of business services by governments and the agencies to which they delegate investment attraction. Virtually all agencies offer information in some form (e.g., Kotra in South Korea offers a very comprehensive array of publications and seminars, as do IDA Ireland and many others).

After-care services may be crucial (Young and Hood 1994) but are often overlooked—creating missed opportunities, given that it is commonly accepted that most investment projects come from existing investors. There are proactive and reactive approaches to after-care. Whereas the latter represent the ability to "be there" and help only when investors ask, the former involve the provision of more dynamic and attentive, initiative-driven services. The rational for after-care services is similar to that for after-sales services (Loewendahl 2001). They can be strategic, informational, general supply-side services (Young and Hood 1994; Loewendahl 2001) and can be quite diverse.

The main difficulty with after-care programs is that they represent a challenging and resource-intensive set of activities. They involve continuity (not always easy to guarantee, given electoral calendars and institutional changes), the credibility of the provider, consistency in the quality of services (as they involve a great deal of trust), and the employment of considerable human and financial resources. Ireland's National Linkage Program (implemented since the mid-1980s) is commonly regarded as a successful example. Its aim is to improve the linkages between subsidiaries of MNEs and domestic firms or entities (via the supply of raw materials or components, the provision of services, links with universities and research centers, and so forth). Linkage programs have also been developed in other countries, such as Malaysia and Brazil (Giroud and Delane 2008).

THE ROLE OF INVESTMENT PROMOTION AGENCIES IN ATTRACTING INVESTMENT

The institutional environment for investment attraction, particularly for FDI, has been highlighted in the literature (Henisz 2000; Morisset 2003). The availability of a one-stop shop or single point of contact for the interaction with inward investors has been seen as a stimulating factor for investment in its own right (Morisset 2003). The existence of such an institution is often correlated with one of its key tasks—namely, investment promotion. The activity of investment promotion agencies (IPAs) may qualify as an incentive, according to the definition we advanced in chapter 1, when such activity is focused on or targets certain types of investments and investors.

Several studies have analyzed the role played by IPAs in attracting investors and investments. In an attempt to examine empirically the effectiveness of IPAs across countries, Morisset (2003) studied fifty-eight countries and concluded that IPAs are effective in influencing the decision to invest. However, this happens as a complement to critical factors such as the quality of the investment climate and the country's market size. He found that investment promotion tends to be more effective in countries with a relatively high level of development and a good investment climate. In countries where the investment climate is poor, promotion can even be counterproductive. He also concluded that the effectiveness of IPAs is influenced by the scope of the activities or functions they undertake. These activities or functions may differentiate among investors, in which case there is little doubt that IPAs provide information- and services-related incentives.

Wells and Wint (2001, 4) define investment promotion as "activities that disseminate information about, or attempt to create an image of the investment site and provide investment services for the prospective investors." According to Morisset (2003), this definition evokes the two most relevant analytical justifications for IPAs: (1) communicating and disseminating information (which, we add, when targeted and specific, may act as an investment incentive); and (2) coordinating the majority of activities geared to improving the business climate in the host country. Hence, information and coordination issues are the foremost justifications for the creation of an IPA, and a facilitating and competent entity can be an extra motive that persuades investors to locate or acquire certain activities in the host economy.[13]

Previous research synthesized in Moran (2014) has very effectively highlighted the relevance that proactive efforts by IPAs to market a territory can have in terms of FDI attraction (a fact also highlighted by Wells and Wint [2001] and Morisset and Andrews-Johnson [2003]). Harding and Javorcik (2011) provide empirical evidence for this phenomenon. Analyzing a sample of 109 countries with an IPA and 31 without such an organization, they find support for a positive and significant impact of the IPA on FDI inflows—particularly in the sectors targeted by the IPA.[14]

In a later but related paper, Harding and Javorcik (2012) suggest again that investment promotion leads to higher FDI flows, particularly to territories where information asymmetries are severe and bureaucracy is complex. They also argue that investment promotion is more relevant for developing countries than for their developed counterparts. However, Harding and Javorcik (2011) consider FDI promotion to be a rather uncontroversial component of any FDI attraction measures package and a very cost-effective type of measure; they even perform what they call a "back-of-the-envelope" cost-benefit calculation that leads them to conclude that "a dollar spent on investment promotion leads to $189 of FDI inflows" (1447) and that the cost per job created (in investment promotion) is $78.

CONCLUSION

Incentives are means to achieve ends; that is, they act as carrots to entice investors to a particular sector or location or to induce particular investor behaviors. They come in many types and flavors, and these were reviewed in detail in this chapter. Often countries choose to offer a package of incentives, combining different types of measures to attract and benefit from investment. However, incentives do not work unless certain fundamentals are in place (macro and enabling conditions, such as political, economic, and social stability and a minimum threshold of institutional quality), along with other, more tangible investment determinants, such as market-related or other factors, that reflect the multiplicity of motivations for investment (this multiplicity of motivations is developed in chapter 3).

It is not obvious that all incentives are effective (as the empirical work on Indonesia by Wells and Allen [2001] shows[15]) and even less obvious that they are efficient. However, countries do choose to give them because nowadays everybody is in the "race" and offers them proactively. A new direction being explored consists of trying to connect incentives to SDGs (UNCTAD 2014; chapter 9 of this book). There have also been some discussions on the advantages of agreeing on at least a minimum set of basic principles in order to level the incentives-policy playing field, but as described in part 4 of this book, efforts so far have not been very successful.

NOTES

1. Although it is not the core of this chapter, the effectiveness of certain types of investment incentives (e.g., fiscal) has not been forgotten, as econometric studies of such effectiveness are explicitly mentioned in the chapter.

2. As mentioned in UNCTAD (2013, 33), "One third of inward FDI income is retained within host countries as reinvested earnings that are a major component of global FDI inflows."

3. Three main subsidiary types can be considered in this regard (White and Poynter 1984; Pearce 1999; Tavares-Lehmann 2007): replica/multidomestic subsidiary (host market–oriented—not so common nowadays); rationalized subsidiary (exporter, efficiency seeker—usually less autonomous and high value-added but can be important in terms of employment and export volume, i.e., in terms of a quantitative criterion); creative subsidiary/product mandate (exporter, develops products or innovates products and processes to international markets—quite a desirable subsidiary type if the quality of the investment is a priority).

4. This is not beyond dispute. As noted in chapter 1 in this volume, the other candidate for most popular measure to stimulate FDI location is information and technical services, but its use is hard to prove.

5. It may be argued that they require the same government administration to be in place to avoid costs being shifted into the tax period.

6. According to the *New York Times*, "1209 North Orange . . . is the legal address of no fewer than 285,000 separate businesses. Its occupants, on paper, include giants like American Airlines, Apple, Bank of America, Berkshire Hathaway, Cargill, Coca-Cola, Ford, General Electric, Google, JPMorgan Chase, and Wal-Mart. These companies do business across the nation and around the world. Here at 1209 North Orange, they simply have a dropbox. . . . And, at last count, Delaware had more corporate entities, public and private, than people—945,326 to 897,934." Accessed November 14, 2014, http://nytimes.com/2012/07/01/business/how-delaware-thrives-as-a-corporate-tax-haven.html?pagewanted=all&_r=1&.

7. James (2009, 4) reinforces this fact specifically in the case of developing countries and highlights other important aspects/data limitations:

> Changes in incentive policy are generally made at the same time as other changes that affect investment behavior (such as macroeconomic restructuring). This simultaneity makes analysis challenging because it is difficult to attribute changes in investment to changes in incentives. But by carefully selecting the incentive reforms studied, it is possible to address some of these issues. Another significant problem for econometric studies on investment in developing countries involves the measurement of investment. A lack of good data on investment in these countries makes it hard to estimate the effects of incentives in general and tax incentives in particular. Gross domestic capital formation is especially poorly measured, though FDI is measured better. The best data on investment come from firms, but such data are rare in developing countries.

8. Klemm and Van Parys (2009) test whether countries compete over tax incentives in the same way they do over tax rates. These authors conclude, for the sample

of developing countries studied in their work, that specific tax holidays and general corporate income tax rates are subject to the same kind of effects in terms of their impact on investment. They also state clearly that "data on tax incentives are difficult to collect" (4).

9. This is probably due to the fact that governments do not want, in general, to disclose how much was given in grants and preferential loans to specific investors. We argue that the controversy potential of these financial handouts leads to the nontransparent practices of those who provide the incentives.

10. Albeit with a broader reach, the OECD (2014, 2) corroborates impressions expressed in several chapters in this volume with this important statement:

> Despite the widespread use of tax incentives for investment, in general there is inadequate analysis of their costs and benefits in a national context to support government decision-making. There is limited data collected on granted tax incentives, qualifying investments made, direct (and indirect) benefits to the host economy, and the cost of these tax incentives in terms of foregone revenue. Moreover, even information that should be more readily available—lists of tax incentives and beneficiaries—is not always collected or reported. This sums up very well the state of relevant data availability and substantiates a plea for more transparency and better data availability for researchers in order to inform policy.

11. There is, however, a suggestion that in some cases the lowering of such standards can increase investment. For instance, less stringent pollution standards may appeal to certain companies whose current technologies do not enable them to avoid polluting activities or whose need to lower operating costs leads them to less environmentally friendly but cheaper practices, and lower labor standards may attract some investors that are focused mainly on reducing costs—in this case, labor-related ones.

12. Psychic distance can be defined as all factors that impede or make difficult the flow of information between the company and the market (e.g., differences among home and host countries—language, culture, political system, education level, industrialization level, etc.). Psychic distance increases costs and risks for investors, leading them to be more likely to internationalize first to geographically or culturally close countries.

13. Agencies like IDA Ireland, Locate in Scotland, UK Trade and Investment, Singapore's EDB, Costa Rica's CINDE, Thailand's BOI, and Malaysia's MIDA are commonly regarded as successful IPAs.

14. Here it is worth citing the excellent summary by Moran (2014, 5–6) of the Harding and Javorcik paper:

> Torfinn Harding and Javorcik provide rigorous econometric backing for this proposition (Harding and Javorcik 2011). Comparing data from 109 countries with an IPA and 31 without, they find that the presence of an IPA is correlated with higher FDI inflows, in particular higher FDI inflows into those sectors targeted by the IPA. They compare FDI inflows into targeted sectors, before and after targeting, with FDI inflows into nontargeted sectors during the same time period, and find that active IPA targeting doubles FDI inflows. They control for changes in host country business environment by including country-year fixed effects, for heterogeneity of sectors in different locations by including country-sector fixed effects and for shocks to supply of FDI in particular sectors by

adding sector-time fixed effects. In checking for reverse causality, they find no evidence that targeting took place in sectors with relatively high or low inflows in the years preceding targeting. I am grateful to Theodore Moran for noting the relevance of this aspect.

15. Based on their empirical work on Indonesia, particularly studying the impact of eliminating tax holidays in that country, Wells and Allen (2001, 15) concluded: "In summary, the experiment in Indonesia provides strong evidence that a country can attract growing amounts of foreign direct investment without offering tax holidays, at least if its general income tax rate differs little from that of its neighbors."

REFERENCES

Altshuler, R., H. Grubert, and T. S. Newlon. 1998. "Has U.S. Investment Abroad Become More Sensitive to Tax Rates?" NBER Working Paper No. 6383. Washington, DC: National Bureau of Economic Research.

——. 2000. "Has U.S. Investment Abroad Become More Sensitive to Tax Rates?" In *International Taxation and Multinational Activity*, ed. J. R. Hines Jr., 9–38. Chicago: University of Chicago Press.

Anderson, B. 2008. "Tax Expenditures in OECD Countries." Presentation to the Fifth Annual Meeting of OECD–Asia SBO. Accessed November 9, 2014, http://www.oecd.org/governance/budgeting/39944419.pdf.

Becker, J., and C. Fuest. 2009. "Optimal Tax Policy When Firms Are Internationally Mobile." Working Paper No. 907, Oxford University Centre for Business Taxation.

Bellak, C., Leibrecht, M. and R. Römisch. 2007. "On the Appropriate Measure of Tax Burden on Foreign Direct Investment to the CEECs." *Applied Economics Letters*, 14(8): 603–6.

Bellak, C., Leibrecht, M. and J. Damijan. 2009. "Infrastructure Endowment and Corporate Income Taxes as Determinants of Foreign Direct Investment in Central and Eastern European Countries." *World Economy*, 32 (2): 267–90.

Boddewyn, J. J., and T. Brewer. 1994. "International-Business Political Behavior: New Theoretical Directions." *Academy of Management Review* 19 (1): 119–43.

Braunerhjelm, P. 2004. "Heading for Headquarters? Why and How the Location of Headquarters Matters Among the EU Countries." In *European Union and the Race for Foreign Direct Investment*, ed. L. Oxelheim and P. Ghauri. Oxford: Elsevier.

Brown, D. K. 2000. "International Trade and Core Labor Standards: A Survey of Recent Literature." OECD Occasional Papers WD(2000)4. Paris: Organisation for Economic Cooperation and Development.

Buckley, P. J., L. J. Clegg, A. R. Cross, and H. Voss. 2010. "What Can Emerging Countries Learn from the Outward Direct Investment Policies of Advanced Countries?" In *Foreign Direct Investment from Emerging Markets: The Challenges Ahead*, ed. K. P. Sauvant, W. A. Maschek, and G. McAllister, 243–76. Basingstoke, UK: Palgrave.

Buettner, T., and M. Ruf. 2005. "Tax Incentives and the Location of FDI: Evidence from a Panel of German Multinationals." Discussion Paper Series 1: Economic Studies No. 17/2005, Deutsche Bundesbank, Frankfurt.

Burger, A., A. Jaklič, and M. Rojec. 2012. "The Effectiveness of Investment Incentives: The Slovenian FDI Co-financing Grant Scheme." *Post-Communist Economies* 24 (3): 383–401.

CCSI. 2015. "Investment Incentives: The Good, the Bad and the Ugly." *2013 Columbia International Investment Conference Report.* New York: Columbia Center on Sustainable Investment.

Christiansen, H., C. Oman, and A. Charlton. 2003. "Incentives-Based Competition for Foreign Direct Investment: The Case of Brazil." OECD Working Papers on International Investment, 2003/01. Paris: OECD Publishing.

Copeland, B. 2008. "Is There a Case for Trade and Investment Policy?" In *Trade Policy Research 2007*, ed. D. Ciuriak, 1–64. Ottawa: Foreign Affairs and International Trade Canada.

Davies, R. B., and J. Voget. 2008. "Tax Competition in an Expanding European Union." Working Paper 8/30, Oxford University Centre for Business Taxation. Accessed November 9, 2014, http://www.sbs.ox.ac.uk/sites/default/files/Business_Taxation/Docs/Publications/Working_Papers/Series_08/WP0830.pdf.

De Mooij, R. A., and S. Ederveen. 2001. "Taxation and Foreign Direct Investment: A Synthesis of Empirical Research." CESifo Working Paper Series No. 588, CESifo Group, Munich.

——. 2008. "Corporate Tax Elasticities: A Reader's Guide to Empirical Findings." *Oxford Review of Economic Policy* 24 (4): 680–97.

Devereux, M. P., and R. Griffith. 1998. "Taxes and the Location of Production: Evidence from a Panel of US Multinationals." *Journal of Public Economics* 68 (3): 335–67.

Devereux, M., R. Griffith, and A. Klemm. 2002. "Corporate Income Tax Reforms and International Tax Competition." *Economic Policy* 17-35 (October): 451–94.

Dunning, J. H., and S. Lundan. 2008. *Multinational Enterprises and the Global Economy.* Cheltenham, UK: Edward Elgar.

Egger, P., S. Loretz, M. Pfaffermayr, and H. Winner. 2009. "Bilateral Effective Tax Rates and Foreign Direct Investment." *International Tax and Public Finance* 16 (6): 822–49.

Fletcher, K. 2002. *Tax Incentives in Cambodia, Lao PDR, and Vietnam.* Hanoi: IMF Conference on FDI: Opportunities and Challenges for Cambodia, Lao PDR, and Vietnam.

Giroud, A., and B. Delane. 2008. "Policies Promoting MNEs Linkages in Host Economies: A Comparison Between Brazil and Malaysia." Paper presented at the OECD Global Forum on International Investment, March 27–28, Paris. Accessed November 16, http://www.oecd.org/investment/globalforum/40408228.pdf.

Grubert, H., and J. Mutti. 2000. "Do Taxes Influence Where US Multinational Corporations Invest?" *National Tax Journal* 53 (4): 825–39.

Guisinger, S. E. 1985. "A Comparative Study of Country Policies." In *Investment Incentives and Performance Requirements* by S. E. Guisinger and Associates. New York: Praeger.

Gurtner, B., and J. Christensen. 2008. "Race to the Bottom: Incentives for New Investment?" Tax Justice Network, accessed November 9, 2014, http://www.taxjustice.net/cms/upload/pdf/Bruno-John_0810_Tax_Comp.pdf.

Hansson, A., and K. Olofsdotter. 2008. "Foreign Direct Investment in Europe: Tax Competition and Agglomeration Economies." Department of Economics, Lund University, Sweden, accessed November 9, 2014, http://www.etsg.org/ETSG2008/Papers/Olofsdotter.pdf.

Harding, T., and B. Javorcik. 2011. "Roll Out the Red Carpet and They Will Come: Investment Promotion and FDI Inflows." *Economic Journal* 121 (557): 1445–76.

——. 2012. "Roll Out the Red Carpet and They Will Come: Investment Promotion and FDI Inflows." Columbia FDI Perspective No. 72, Columbia Center on Sustainable Investment, New York.

Henisz, W. 2000. "The Institutional Environment for Multinational Investment." *Journal of Law, Economics and Organization* 16 (2): 334–64.

Hines, J. R. Jr. 1996. "Altered States: Taxes and the Location of Foreign Direct Investment in America." *American Economic Review* 86 (5): 1076–94.

——. 1999. "Lessons from Behavioral Responses to International Taxation." *National Tax Journal* 52 (2): 305–22.

Hymer, S. H. 1976. *The International Operations of National Firms: A Study of Foreign Direct Investment.* Cambridge, MA: MIT Press (1960 doctoral thesis submitted posthumously for publication by C. P. Kindleberger).

ILO. 1998. *Labour and Social Issues Relating to Export Processing Zones.* Geneva: International Labour Organisation. Accessed November 9, 2014, http://www.ilo.org/public/libdoc/ilo/1998/98B09_223_engl.pdf.

James, S. 2009. "Incentives and Investments: Evidence and Policy Implications." World Bank Group, Washington, DC. Accessed November 9, 2014, https://www.wbginvestmentclimate.org/uploads/IncentivesandInvestments.pdf.

Johanson, J., and J.-E. Vahlne. 1977. "The Internationalization Process of the Firm: A Model of Knowledge Development and Increasing Foreign Market Commitments." *Journal of International Business Studies*, 8 (1): 23–32.

Klemm, A., and S. Van Parys. 2009. "Empirical Evidence on the Effects of Tax Incentives." IMF Working Paper 09/136. Washington, DC: International Monetary Fund.

Loewendahl, H. 2001. "A Framework for FDI Promotion." *Transnational Corporations* 10 (1): 1–42, reprinted in S. Young, ed. 2004. *Multinationals and Public Policy*, 279–320. Cheltenham, UK: Edward Elgar.

Moran, T. H. 2014. "Foreign Investment and Supply Chains in Emerging Markets: Recurring Problems and Demonstrated Solutions." Working Paper 14–12, Peterson Institute for International Economics, Washington, DC.

Morisset, J. 2003. "Does a Country Need a Promotion Agency to Attract Foreign Direct Investment? A Small Analytical Model Applied to 58 Countries." FIAS Policy Research Working Paper No. 3028, World Bank Group, Washington, DC.

Morisset, J., and K. Andrews-Johnson. 2003. "The Effectiveness of Promotion Agencies at Attracting Foreign Direct Investment." Foreign Investment Advisory Service (FIAS) Occasional Papers, 16. Washington D.C.

Mutti, J., and H. Grubert. 2004. "Empirical Asymmetries in Foreign Direct Investment and Taxation." *Journal of International Economics* 62 (2): 337–58.

Oates, W. E. 2002. "Fiscal and Regulatory Competition: Theory and Evidence." *Perspektiven der Wirtschaftspolitik* 3 (4): 377–90.

OECD. 2000. *Tax Burdens, Alternative Measures.* Paris: Organisation for Economic Cooperation and Development.

——. 2001. *Regulatory Investment Incentives.* Paris: Organisation for Economic Cooperation and Development. Accessed November 9, 2014, http://www.oecd.org/industry/inv/investmentstatisticsandanalysis/2510459.pdf.

——. 2003. *Checklist for Foreign Direct Investment Incentive Policies.* Paris: Organisation for Economic Cooperation and Development.

——. 2010. *Tax Expenditures in OECD Countries.* Paris: Organisation for Economic Cooperation and Development.

——. 2014. "Principles to Enhance the Transparency and Governance of Tax Incentives for Investment in Developing Countries." OECD, accessed September 24, 2015, http://www.oecd.org/ctp/tax-global/transparency-and-governance-principles.pdf#page=1&zoom=auto,-135,726.

Oman, C. 2000. *Policy Competition for Foreign Direct Investment: A Study of Competition Among Governments to Attract FDI.* Paris: Organisation for Economic Cooperation and Development.

Oxelheim, L., and P. Ghauri, eds. 2004. *European Union and the Race for Foreign Direct Investment.* Oxford: Elsevier.

Pearce, R. D. 1999. "The Evolution of Technology in Multinational Enterprises: The Role of Creative Subsidiaries." *International Business Review* 8 (2): 125–48.

Perera, O. 2014. *Rethinking Investment Incentives.* Winnipeg: International Institute for Sustainable Development.

ProExport Colombia. 2014. "Top Ten Reasons to Invest in Tourism." ProExport Colombia, accessed November 12, 2014, http://www.investincolombia.com.co/Adjuntos/Ten_Reasons_Invest_Tourism_Infrastructure.pdf.

Raudonen, S. 2008. "The Impact of Corporate Taxation on Foreign Direct Investment: A Survey." Working Paper No. 182, Tallinn School of Economics and Business Administration, Tallinn University of Technology, Estonia.

Spar, D. 1998. "Attracting High Technology Investment: Intel's Costa Rican Plant." FIAS Occasional Paper No. 11. Washington, DC: Foreign Investment Advisory Service.

Sundaresh, M. 2012. "Home Country Measures for Outward Foreign Direct Investment—Lessons for India from the Republic of Korea and Canada." Unpublished manuscript, Columbia University, New York.

Tavares-Lehmann, A. T. 2007. "Public Policy, FDI Attraction and Multinational Subsidiary Evolution: The Contrasting Cases of Ireland and Portugal." In *Multinationals on the Periphery,* ed. G. R. G. Benito and R. Narula. Basingstoke, UK: Palgrave.

Tavares-Lehmann, A. T., A. Coelho, and F. Lehmann. 2012. "Taxes and Foreign Direct Investment: A Literature Review." In *New Policy Challenges for European Multinationals,* ed. R. Van Tulder, A. Verbeke, and L. Voinea, 89–117. Bingley, UK: Emerald Group.

UNCTAD. 2000. *Tax Incentives and Foreign Direct Investment: A Global Survey.* ASIT Advisory Studies No. 16. New York: United Nations Conference on Trade and Development.

——. 2001. *World Investment Report 2001: Promoting Linkages.* New York: United Nations Conference on Trade and Development.

——. 2013. *World Investment Report 2013: Global Value Chains: Investment and Trade for Development*. New York: United Nations Conference on Trade and Development.

——. 2014. *World Investment Report 2014: Investing in the SDGs: An Action Plan*. New York: United Nations Conference on Trade and Development.

Wells, L. Jr., and N. Allen. 2001. "The First Experiment: Eliminating Tax Holidays." In L. Wells Jr., N. Allen, J. Morisset, and N. Pirnia, "Using Tax Incentives to Compete for Foreign Investment: Are They Worth the Costs?" FIAS Occasional Paper No. 15, 5–20. Washington, DC: Foreign Investment Advisory Service.

Wells, L. Jr., and A. Wint. 2001. "Marketing a Country, Revisited." FIAS Occasional Paper No. 13. Washington, DC: World Bank Group.

White, R. E., and T. Poynter. 1984. "Strategies for Foreign-Owned Subsidiaries in Canada." *Business Quarterly* (Summer): 59–69.

Yao, Y., and X. Zhang. 2008. "Race to the Top and Race to the Bottom: Tax Competition in Rural China." Discussion Paper No. 799, International Food Policy Research Institute, Washington, DC.

Young, S., and N. Hood. 1994. "Designing Developmental After Care Programmes for Foreign Direct Investors in the European Union." *Transnational Corporations* 3 (2): 45–72.

Young, S., and A. T. Tavares. 2004. "Multilateral Rules on FDI: Do We Need Them? Will We Get Them? A Developing Country Perspective." *Transnational Corporations* 13 (1): 1–16.

Zaheer, S. 1995. "Overcoming the Liability of Foreignness." *Academy of Management Journal* 38 (2): 345–63.

CHAPTER 3

Definitions, Motivations, and Locational Determinants of Foreign Direct Investment

Sarianna M. Lundan

This chapter examines the different motivations for foreign direct investment (FDI) as well as the economic and institutional determinants of location choice for foreign investment. It concentrates on what determines the extent of cross-border activity by multinational enterprises (MNEs) based on the fundamentals of the interplay between the location and firm-specific determinants of investment. Because investment incentives seek to influence the decision to invest and location choice for MNEs, an understanding of the fundamental determinants is essential to evaluating which incentives are likely to be effective in influencing investment decisions.

The chapter also discusses some of the policy challenges related to investment attraction arising from the changing landscape of FDI. In particular, it discusses the growth of market-seeking investment in emerging markets and the rise of market- and asset-seeking investment from emerging markets in terms of their impact on investment attraction and the use of incentives.

We pay specific attention to greenfield investment and to mergers and acquisitions. However, we also contrast these modes of entry with other cross-border engagement strategies that can substitute for foreign investment. In so doing, we highlight and emphasize the heterogeneity of investors and the varying impact that investment has on the host countries. The impact of incentives on decisions with respect to these various entry modes should be considered in the design of investment policy, including the design and evaluation of investment incentives.

FOREIGN DIRECT INVESTMENT

Traditionally, the territorial expansion of a firm's productive capacity outside its national boundaries has been achieved through FDI. Such direct investment is different from foreign portfolio (or indirect) investment in that the former involves the transfer of a package of assets or intermediate products, which includes financial capital, management and organizational expertise, technology, entrepreneurship, incentive structures, values and cultural norms, and access to markets across national boundaries. The latter involves the transfer only of financial capital. For those reasons, most governments have undertaken a number of policies, including those that offer various investment incentives, to attract FDI and its associated package of assets.

Some cross-border capital flows reflect distortions in the market rather than real economic activity. This is the case with the so-called round-tripping investment between China and Hong Kong and between Russia and Cyprus, for example, which is designed to take advantage of incentives offered to foreign investors. It is also the case with FDI undertaken via holding companies in countries such as the British Virgin Islands, Bermuda, the Netherlands, and Luxembourg, which are used as tax havens by MNEs (Beugelsdijk et al. 2010; Desai, Foley, and Hines 2006; UNCTAD 2006). The revised OECD Benchmark Definition of FDI, which came into effect in late 2014, is aimed at separating the flows related to such special-purpose entities from genuine FDI that is related to employment and value added (OECD 2008). Round-tripping investment is important for governments to understand as they design investment incentives, as companies may simply be restructuring so as to take advantage of the incentive without creating any additional benefits for the host government; in such a case, the incentives will be a net cost for the government.

MOTIVATIONS

Before we move on to consider the factors influencing location choice, it is important to outline the different motivations for FDI—namely, resource-seeking, market-seeking, efficiency-seeking, and strategic asset–seeking investment. These are not always mutually exclusive because they influence the MNE's sensitivity to incentives.[1]

RESOURCE-SEEKING INVESTMENT

There are three main types of resource seekers. First, there are MNEs seeking physical location–bound resources of one kind or another. These include investors that seek fossil fuels like oil, coal, and gas; metals like copper, tin, and zinc; diamonds; and agricultural products such as rubber, tobacco, sugar, bananas, pineapples, palm oil, coffee, and tea. One feature of this first kind of resource-intensive MNE activity is that it usually involves significant capital expenditure. Moreover, once the investment has been made, it is relatively location-bound. Some FDI in service activities is also intended to exploit specific location-bound resources. Examples include tourism, car rentals, oil drilling, construction, and medical and educational services.

The second group of resource-seeking MNEs comprises those seeking plentiful supplies of cheap unskilled or semiskilled labor. Most of this type of MNE activity has been found in the more advanced industrializing developing countries such as Mexico, Taiwan, and Malaysia. Within Europe, there has been some labor-seeking investment in Southern, Central, and Eastern European countries. However, as labor costs have risen, investment has shifted to other countries, such as China, Vietnam, Turkey, Morocco, and Mauritius. Frequently, in order to attract such production, host countries have set up free trade or export processing zones. This kind of resource-seeking investment is quite different from the first kind. A plentiful supply of relatively unskilled labor can be seen as a location-bound "natural" resource, but it is seldom a unique resource. However, investments to improve the training and skill level of the labor force can transform it into a "created" resource, more likely to attract efficiency-seeking investment by mature MNEs.

The third type of resource-seeking MNEs are those that need to acquire technological capability, management or marketing expertise, and organizational skills that are highly specialized and not readily available in the home country. Examples include executive search subsidiaries set up by U.S. firms in the United Kingdom and research and development (R&D) listening posts established by UK chemical companies in Japan and French pharmaceutical companies in the United States. Some of this type of investment can turn into strategic asset–seeking investment if the MNE moves to acquire foreign firms in order to augment or enhance its own capabilities.

MARKET-SEEKING INVESTMENT

Market-seeking investment may be undertaken to sustain or protect existing markets or to exploit or promote new markets. Apart from market size and the prospects for market growth, there are five main reasons why firms would engage in market-seeking investment. The first is that their main suppliers or customers have set up foreign production facilities and, to retain their business, they need to follow them overseas. In services, cross-border mergers and acquisitions among accounting, auditing, law, and advertising firms are a case in point.[2]

Second, products quite frequently need to be adapted to local tastes, language, business customs, legal requirements, and marketing procedures. Third, the production and transaction costs of serving a local market from an adjacent facility are much lower than when supplying it from a distance.

The fourth, and increasingly important, reason for market-seeking investment is that an MNE may consider it necessary to have a physical presence in the leading markets served by its (oligopolistic) competitors. Such investment might be undertaken for defensive or strategic reasons. For example, the sheer size of the potential market in China has attracted unprecedented inflows of foreign investment, some of which has followed the investments made by key customers, whereas some of it has followed the moves made by industry leaders.

Finally, market-seeking investment can be the result of host government policies that discourage imports by imposing tariffs or other import controls.

EFFICIENCY-SEEKING INVESTMENT

Usually, the efficiency-seeking investors are experienced, large, and diversified MNEs producing fairly standardized products. In order for efficiency-seeking foreign production to take place, cross-border markets must be both well developed and open, and, consequently, it flourishes in regionally integrated markets. Efficiency-seeking FDI enables a more fine-grained slicing of the value chain and is generally of two kinds. The first is designed to take advantage of differences in the availability and relative cost of traditional factor endowments in developed and developing countries. This includes the ability of mature MNEs to access low- to medium-skilled labor at the lowest possible cost, which requires not only investment to improve the skill level of the labor force but also some investment in the supporting infrastructure. Thus, both resource- and efficiency-seeking types of investment may benefit from access to relatively low-cost labor; in the case of resource-seeking investment, the benefits mainly arise from the simple substitution of labor for capital, whereas efficiency-seeking investment requires the ability to effectively integrate activities in the firm's value chain across borders without necessarily changing the capital/labor ratio of production.

The second kind of efficiency-seeking investment takes place between developed countries with broadly similar economic structures and income levels and is designed to take advantage of the economies of scale and scope and the differences in consumer tastes and supply capabilities. Here traditional factor endowments play a less important role in influencing FDI, whereas "created" competences and capabilities, including a highly skilled labor force and the availability of good-quality supporting institutions, play a more important role.

STRATEGIC ASSET–SEEKING INVESTMENT

The fourth group of MNEs comprises those that engage in FDI by acquiring the assets of foreign companies to promote their long-term strategic objectives. The investing firms include both established MNEs pursuing an integrated global or regional strategy and first-time foreign direct investors seeking to access or to buy some kind of competitive strength in an unfamiliar market. The motive for strategic asset–seeking investment is less to exploit specific cost (technological) or marketing advantages over the acquiring firm's competitors and more to enhance its global portfolio of physical assets and human competences. Increasingly, the strategic- and efficiency-seeking types of FDI tend to go hand in hand as firms restructure their assets to meet their objectives. Importantly, strategic asset–seeking investment is also increasingly undertaken by MNEs from emerging economies in order to gain both market access and knowledge-intensive assets, such as R&D facilities.

LOCATIONAL DETERMINANTS

The choice of location for foreign investment projects has country-specific and firm-specific components. The country-specific determinants are dependent on the motivation for the investment and include traditional factors from economic geography such as the size of the market, the level of development (GDP per capita), natural resources, labor costs, transportation, energy, and information infrastructure. They also include institutional factors such as political stability and economic openness as well as "soft" institutional factors such as generalized trust, which tends to lower transaction costs (Dunning and Lundan 2008b). For a firm with a given investment motivation, we would expect that it would value the same parameters roughly equally.

The firm-specific factors have to do with the accumulated ownership advantages of the investing firm—particularly its own experience with investment—as well as its ability to gather knowledge concerning the risk factors related to foreign investment projects (Belderbos, Olffen, and Zou 2011; Forsgren 2002). The search for information is filtered by cumulative experience at the level of the firm and specifically among its top management. This includes direct first-hand knowledge of prior investment projects as well as seemingly irrational biases for disregarding particular locations (Schotter and Beamish 2013). It also includes management decisions concerning the value of agglomeration benefits and the signaling value that investments by competitors represent.

For resource-seeking investment, the general locational determinants are fairly easy to summarize, as they consist of access to the location-bound (natural) resources, which has traditionally been gained as a result of negotiations with the government (Grosse 2005). Owing to its special nature, resource-seeking investment is typically quite impervious to poor governance and the kinds of institutional deficits that normally would increase transaction costs and drive investors away (UNCTAD 2007). In negotiating for access, the government wants to ensure broader benefits from the investment, whereas the investor is trying to protect its investment against expropriation and renegotiation. In general, traditional investment incentives will not be determinative of resource-seeking investment. Although MNEs may take advantage of any incentives that are available, it is the negotiated terms of access that will influence the location choice and duration of resource-seeking investment. This has important policy implications for resource-rich host governments, as traditional incentives may be costly and ineffective at attracting foreign investors.

For market-seeking investment, it is clear that the size of the market and the rate of GDP growth are relevant factors. The level of development and transaction costs also play more important roles than with resource-based investment. Opaque administrative systems such as in Japan, lack of intellectual property enforcement such as in China, and frequent policy reversals such as in India are all factors that discourage long-term investors. That being said, the very populous emerging markets—and China, in particular—are an exception, as foreign investors seem to have been tolerant of substantial deviations from good governance in order to secure their position in these markets.

Efficiency-seeking investment is driven by factor price differentials across markets—particularly low labor costs for semiskilled labor as well as more-skilled workers such as engineers and programmers. These cost differentials form the backbone of the global factory (Buckley 2011). Efficiency seeking is about the ability to fine-slice the value chain by relocating activities or tasks to the location where they can be performed at the lowest cost. That being the case, when countries experience rapid economic growth and rising incomes, their attractiveness for lower-level assembly tasks tends to go down, and efficiency-seeking investment will be redirected to locations where the cost differentials are more pronounced. The relative ease of location shifting makes such activities suitable targets for incentive policies that seek to attract new investment.

Strategic asset–seeking investment is in some sense infinitely location specific, as the aim of the firm is to acquire specific assets in specific locations. The availability of this mode of foreign engagement is curtailed, however, by the availability of suitable targets. Out of this set of possibilities, the choice will be dependent on a number of factors related to the digestibility of the assets, the willingness of the seller, and general market conditions (Harzing 2002; Hennart and Reddy 2000; Slangen and Hennart 2008). Such cases, of course, represent a change in ownership rather than additional investment, but they may be seen as necessary in order to ensure the future of both the investing and the acquired enterprises and to allow them to better access the growth markets in the global economy.

Strategic asset–seeking investment can be combined with a market-seeking motivation when the firm to be acquired will help the investing firm to enter an unfamiliar market. Many acquisitions by established MNEs in emerging markets have been of this kind (Uhlenbruck 2004). However, strategic asset–seeking acquisitions can also enable the investing firm to add to its other intangible advantages, such as technology. Acquisitions by Chinese and Indian MNEs in the United States and Europe have often been directed at adding technological as well as market-related capabilities (Alon, Fetscherin, and Gugler 2012; Sauvant et al. 2011).

LOCATION CHOICE AND AGGLOMERATION

It is well known that investment projects tend to cluster in terms of both time and space. There is herding or follow-the-leader behavior, when one investment is fairly rapidly followed by others in the same industry

(Knickerbocker 1973). There is also evidence of more-classical agglomeration patterns, where firms with a particular specialization profile concentrate around each other. In addition, there is likely to be some signal value to new foreign investment, particularly in an emerging market where the initial investment is used as a signal of a positive cost-benefit calculus. Incentives can be used either to enhance an existing pattern of concentration (building on already successful industries or regions) or to encourage investment in less successful areas.

The spatial concentration of investment is visible at the country level, so if we use FDI as a proxy for the activities of MNEs, they are concentrated in a relatively small number of countries. If we go to the subnational level, the same pattern is repeated: in most countries, a few regions absorb a great deal of the FDI. Incentives can be influential in terms of either increasing or decreasing the geographic concentration of investment. On the one hand, incentives can be used to induce clustering by promoting sectoral targeting and thus influencing sectoral concentration. On the other hand, incentives can be used to attempt to distribute investments more evenly across a territory. This is not to say that the incentives necessarily are worth the cost paid for them but that investment policies have the potential to both increase and decrease this pattern of concentration.

Traditional location theory following Marshall (1920) was mainly concerned with the firm's need to achieve economies of scale while simultaneously minimizing cross-border and other transportation costs. Although this model still accounts for the location decisions of much of resource-seeking and market-seeking activity by MNEs, efficiency-seeking and asset-augmenting investment require adjustments to these explanations. In particular, the transportation costs of the classic location model are often better interpreted as the costs of communication relating to the transfer of intangible goods such as knowledge and institutional practices.

If we then try to incorporate the importance of colocation (and spillovers) into a model of location choice, we get three broad categories of factors that influence the location of MNE investment. These have been described by Dunning and Lundan (2008a) as endowment effects, agglomeration effects, and policy-induced effects. Endowment effects are drawn from trade theory and explain why particular economic activity would be "naturally" drawn to a given location. Endowment effects are thus the factors that draw resource-seeking investment, such as agricultural growing conditions (e.g., in the wine industry), mineral or oil deposits, or the availability of cheap electricity (e.g., in the early nineteenth-century relocation of aluminum producers near large hydropower facilities at Niagara Falls). They can include the presence of a large low-cost labor force. However, they also include the created or knowledge-based endowments that form the basis for the competitiveness of most developed economies.

To the extent that the ability to exploit a particular resource is not restricted to a single firm (such as in the case of a mineral concession), firms will locate in the proximity of the geographically bound resource—and consequently in proximity to each other. Colocation will be beneficial until diseconomies in the form of congestion or overexploitation set in. Such diseconomies might include the bidding up of the price of a nonrenewable resource, an increase in pollution, or excessive depletion of the resource. Additionally, minimum efficient scale (and consequently market structure) in a given industry limits the number of possible competitors that can colocate when using the same natural resource. If the minimum efficient scale is very large, it may be possible for only one or two firms to exploit the resource in a given location. If the minimum efficient scale is smaller, more firms can colocate, but they may still do so in spite of the presence of each other rather than because of it.

The second type of effects influencing location choice is agglomeration effects, which, following Marshall (1920), may be classified as arising from three sources: the availability of specialized labor, easy and cost-effective access to other specialized inputs, and knowledge spillovers. The key to agglomeration effects, as distinct from endowment effects, is that the attraction of one firm will generally make it more attractive for another firm to colocate. Although the self-reinforcing tendency related to agglomeration effects can be due to simple imitation, it is more likely to arise because the presence of other firms signals that some external economies are present in a given location.

In reality, spatial clustering is often the result of a combination of endowment and agglomeration effects. Spatial colocation can result from MNE affiliates simply locating their activities where important customers are located (an endowment effect), but the resulting agglomeration might also draw other firms to the area because of the potential for linkages and spillovers (an agglomeration effect). In industries where interpersonal relationships are important to competitiveness, for example, the benefits from clustering are likely to be based mainly on knowledge spillovers, such as in the case of the financial services in

London or New York City, but even in these cases, traditional locational factors continue to play a role. The attractiveness of large cities in general to investment is due to both the availability of specialized labor and agglomeration effects (Acs 2002; Goerzen, Asmussen, and Nielsen 2013; McCann, Arita, and Gordon 2002).

THE ROLE OF POLICY

The heterogeneity of the investors in terms of their ownership, motivation, degree of multinationality, decentralization, and financial and technological resources makes it clear that when one considers the possible combinations of different types of foreign investors operating in different sectors of the economy, a number of different outcomes are possible. As a result, it is generally recognized that a dollar of investment does not have the same impact everywhere and that policy interventions, including through the use of investment incentives, should target both the quantity and the quality of incoming investment.

As mentioned by Tavares-Lehmann in chapter 2 in this volume, the relevant policies fall into two main categories, policies on investment attraction (preestablishment) and policies on investment retention and performance (postestablishment), that aim to maximize the net benefits from investment. We distinguish among three types of preestablishment policies:

1. Policies focused on private-sector development (e.g., education and training, absorptive capacity building, and institutional upgrading)
2. Policies concerning economic openness (e.g., trade and investment liberalization and specifically the provisions contained in international investment agreements and regional trade agreements)
3. Policies specifically aimed at attracting foreign investment (e.g., investment incentives, facilitation, promotion, and matchmaking)

A narrow definition of investment policy would include only the third category, but the other two policy areas are likely to be equally relevant for both domestic and foreign investment. Indeed, a range of policies aimed at private-sector development contributes to good governance and socially and environmentally sustainable development.

Whereas the preestablishment policies seek to meet investor expectations concerning what is being offered by the host country, the postestablishment policies reflect the host country's expectations of investor performance. The postestablishment policies include the following:

1. Policies to enhance linkages and spillovers (e.g., matchmaking, intellectual property rights protection, and technology transfer)
2. Policies on public procurement and local sourcing (e.g., trade-related investment measures policies)
3. Policies to encourage investment retention and reinvestment in the host country (e.g., participation in local R&D consortia and repatriation taxes)

Although a range of policies thus helps to shape the attractiveness of a specific location for investors, particular attention has been directed by both academics and the media to the financial or fiscal incentives that have been offered specifically to influence the choice of location. In addition to the attempts that have been made to identify the conditions under which such incentives are likely to increase the flow of inward direct investment (Oxelheim and Ghauri 2004), attention is increasingly being paid to appraising the benefits resulting from the incentives and their opportunity cost (Young and Tavares 2004).

If countries were able to make credible commitments not to distort locational competition based on the fundamentals (i.e., factor costs, effective institutions, and an adequate social and economic infrastructure), they would probably not need to offer additional financial or fiscal incentives to attract FDI. The end result would be a distribution of investment based on competitive conditions. However, in the absence of the (collective) ability to make a credible commitment and in the presence of information asymmetries between the host country and the investor (which tend to be frequent), governments may be tempted to offer financial inducements to get MNEs to locate in the area. This then puts pressure on other locations to reciprocate by offering their own incentives, and the end result is a situation where everyone offers inducements, albeit to a different degree.

A common justification for financial and fiscal incentives is that due to the performance (productivity) gap between MNEs and local firms, it is worth more to attract FDI than it is to stimulate the development of local firms. This assumption has come under scrutiny in recent years by scholars such as Bellak (2004), who argues that the existence of a performance gap between foreign investors and domestic firms needs to be investigated and established empirically before any such incentives are contemplated. Furthermore, a realistic assessment of the expected spillovers (and the absorptive capacity of domestic firms) is required to establish the upper bound for any incentives paid (Blomström and Kokko 2003; Van Biesebroeck 2010).

One reason incentives continue to be popular policy instruments is that examples exist where fiscal and other financial incentives seem to have worked to attract considerable amounts of investment, such as in Ireland, Switzerland, and Singapore (see also chapters 2 and 8 in this volume). However, these examples illustrate situations in which the incentives were only one part of a coordinated policy to attract FDI (Mathews 1999; Monaghan 2012) that also included, for example, substantial investments in human capital and infrastructure (e.g., Ireland and Singapore) or in which efforts were made to improve locational competitiveness and competitive conditions for all firms, whether domestic or foreign (e.g., Switzerland). Another reason for the popularity of incentives policies is that, as Rondinelli and Burpitt (2000) point out, from the point of view of elected public officials, a policy of upgrading educational facilities or physical infrastructure over the long term will not produce results quickly enough and may seem unduly passive, particularly if other states or regions are offering financial or fiscal inducements.

A firm that is attracted to a particular location because of the fundamentals (e.g., a combination of factor costs, institutional quality, and infrastructure) might become better integrated (or more embedded) into the local economy (Blömstrom and Kokko 2003; Cantwell and Mudambi 2005). This embeddedness of the local subsidiary, in turn, would serve to increase the costs of divestment over time, given the greater linkages established with the host environment (Andersson, Forsgren, and Holm 2002). By contrast, a firm attracted by financial or fiscal incentives might be less committed to the region and might make fewer subsequent investments in the area while remaining responsive to inducements offered in other locations. Furthermore, firms attracted by financial or fiscal incentives might not draw in more firms that make their investment decisions based on the fundamentals. Consequently, there is reason to believe that an adverse selection problem may arise as a consequence of the use of incentives. There is, however, very little systematic evidence linking investment duration and incentives, although some studies comparing the effectiveness of specific incentives schemes are available (Burger, Jaklič, and Rojec 2012; Mallya, Kukulka, and Jensen 2004; Mudambi 1998).

In general, financial or fiscal incentives to attract foreign investment are more likely to be warranted if the resources and capabilities used by MNEs (such as labor) are in elastic supply, if MNEs are not expected to crowd out local firms in the market, and if local firms benefit from productivity spillovers (Görg and Greenaway 2003; Hanson 2001). As we have already discussed, it is quite likely that only one or none of these conditions holds in practice. This is, of course, not to say that countries could not or should not do anything to ensure that their economies offer a suitable platform for foreign production. Coordinated investments in infrastructure and education and the provision of information to enable MNEs to make well-informed choices have yielded positive results, but subsidizing foreign investment without encouraging the absorptive capacity of local firms to engage with MNEs is unlikely to produce the desired results.

CONCLUSION

This chapter has reviewed the different motivations for investment and how these are linked to cross-border location choice. It has also reviewed the basic policy options for governments wishing to attract MNE investment and the circumscribed role for the use of financial and fiscal incentives. Its focus has been on traditional equity-based investment, as that continues to be highly valued and sought after by policy makers.

However, offshoring and the fine-slicing of global value chains are transforming the kinds of cross-border relationships that are required for the value-adding activities of MNEs to take place, and as a result, the location calculus of investment is changing. Investors that put their own equity on the line are naturally conservative and cautious, and it is not surprising that they have a pattern of investment that is concentrated in the known "good" locations.

It is evident that success in attracting FDI cannot be measured by simple dollar amounts; its measurement has to include an assessment of the kind of investment that is attracted. There is also a growing need to more systematically track the ability to attract activities (i.e., expand the market for domestic output) rather than investment (i.e., foreign ownership of productive assets), as these can be substitutes. A comprehensive and holistic view of the impact of foreign investment and nonequity forms of MNE activity is required to craft intelligent investment policy. Investment policy is relevant to both domestic and foreign investors and should aim to create a stable long-term environment with low transaction costs that is conducive to investment. This involves policy coordination in multiple areas and at multiple policy levels and is not solely limited to foreign investment.

NOTES

1. This section is based on Dunning and Lundan (2008a).

2. Investment in services and investment in manufacturing now account for roughly equal proportions of FDI flows (UNCTAD 2013). Services cover a very heterogeneous group of activities from business process services to contract research, tourism, and financial services, and the locational determinants are quite different between tradable services and those services that need to be produced in the location where they are consumed. In some business services, there are scale economies similar to those in manufacturing. In others, however, the operations are less amenable to scale, but some type of coproduction with the clients is necessary, such as in many industrial services. In financial services, deregulation and regulatory harmonization across borders have created more opportunities for cross-border expansion.

REFERENCES

Acs, Z. J. 2002. *Innovation and the Growth of Cities.* Cheltenham, UK: Edward Elgar.

Alon, I., M. Fetscherin, and P. Gugler, eds. 2012. *Chinese International Investments.* Houndmills, UK: Palgrave.

Andersson, U., M. Forsgren, and U. Holm. 2002. "The Strategic Impact of External Networks: Subsidiary Performance and Competence Development in the Multinational Corporation." *Strategic Management Journal* 23: 979–96.

Belderbos, R., W. V. Olffen, and J. Zou. 2011. "Generic and Specific Social Learning Mechanisms in Foreign Entry Location Choice." *Strategic Management Journal* 32 (12): 1309–30.

Bellak, C. 2004. "How Performance Gaps Between Domestic Firms and Foreign Affiliates Matter for Economic Policy." *Transnational Corporations* 13 (2): 29–55.

Beugelsdijk, S., J. F. Hennart, A. Slangen, and R. Smeets. 2010. "Why and How FDI Stocks Are a Biased Measure of MNE Affiliate Activity." *Journal of International Business Studies* 41 (9): 1444–59.

Blomström, M., and A. Kokko. 2003. "The Economics of Foreign Direct Investment Incentives." NBER Working Paper 9489. Washington, DC: National Bureau of Economic Research.

Buckley, P. J. 2011. "International Integration and Coordination in the Global Factory." *Management International Review* 51 (2): 269–83.

Burger, A., A. Jaklič, and M. Rojec. 2012. "The Effectiveness of Investment Incentives: The Slovenian FDI Co-financing Grant Scheme." *Post-Communist Economies* 24 (3): 383–401.

Cantwell, J. A., and R. Mudambi. 2005. "MNE Competence-Creating Mandates." *Strategic Management Journal* 26: 1109–28.

Desai, M. A., C. F. Foley, and J. R. Hines. 2006. "The Demand for Tax Haven Operations." *Journal of Public Economics* 90 (3): 513–31.

Dunning, J. H., and S. M. Lundan. 2008a. *Multinational Enterprises and the Global Economy.* 2nd ed. Cheltenham, UK: Edward Elgar.

——. 2008b. "Institutions and the OLI Paradigm of the Multinational Enterprise." *Asia Pacific Journal of Management* 25 (4): 573–93.

Forsgren, M. 2002. "The Concept of Learning in the Uppsala Internationalization Process Model: A Critical Review." *International Business Review* 11 (3): 257–77.

Goerzen, A., C. G. Asmussen, and B. B. Nielsen. 2013. "Global Cities and Multinational Enterprise Location Strategy." *Journal of International Business Studies* 44 (5): 427–50.

Görg, H., and D. Greenaway. 2003. "Much Ado About Nothing: Do Domestic Firms Really Benefit from Foreign Direct Investment?" IZA Discussion Paper No. 944. Bonn: IZA-Institute for the Study of Labor.

Grosse, R. 2005. "The Bargaining View of Business-Government Relations." In *International Business and Government Relations in the 21st Century,* ed. R. Grosse, 273–90. Cambridge: Cambridge University Press.

Hanson, G. H. 2001. "Should Countries Promote Foreign Direct Investment?" G-24 Discussion Paper No. 9, UNCTAD, New York.

Harzing, A. W. 2002. "Acquisitions Versus Greenfield Investments: International Strategy and Management of Entry Modes." *Strategic Management Journal* 23 (3): 211–27.

Hennart, J.-F., and S. B. Reddy. 2000. "Digestibility and Asymmetric Information in the Choice Between Acquisitions and Joint Ventures: Where's the Beef?" *Strategic Management Journal* 21 (2): 191.

Knickerbocker, F. T. 1973. *Oligopolistic Reaction and Multinational Enterprise.* Cambridge, MA: Harvard University Press.

Mallya, T. J. S., Z. Kukulka, and C. Jensen. 2004. "Are Incentives a Good Investment for the Host Country? An Empirical Evaluation of the Czech National Incentive Scheme." *Transnational Corporations* 13 (1): 109–48.

Marshall, A. 1920. *Principles of Economics.* 8th ed. London: Macmillan.

Mathews, J. A. 1999. "A Silicon Island of the East: Creating a Semiconductor Industry in Singapore." *California Management Review* 41 (2): 55.

McCann, P., T. Arita, and I. R. Gordon. 2002. "Industrial Clusters, Transactions Costs and the Institutional Determinants of MNE Location Behaviour." *International Business Review* 11 (6): 647.

Monaghan, S. 2012. "Attraction and Retention of Foreign Direct Investment (FDI): The Role of Subnational Institutions in a Small, Highly Globalised Economy." *Irish Journal of Management* 31 (2): 45–61.

Mudambi, R. 1998. "The Role of Duration in Multinational Investment Strategies." *Journal of International Business Studies* 29 (2): 239–62.

OECD. 2008. *Benchmark Definition of Foreign Direct Investment.* 4th ed. Paris: Organisation for Economic Cooperation and Development.

Oxelheim, L., and P. Ghauri, eds. 2004. *European Union and the Race for Foreign Direct Investment in Europe.* Oxford, UK: Elsevier.

Rondinelli, D. A., and W. J. Burpitt. 2000. "Do Government Incentives Attract and Retain International Investment? A Study of Foreign-Owned Firms in North Carolina." *Policy Sciences* 33 (2): 181–205.

Sauvant, K. P., J. P. Pradhan, A. Chatterjee, and B. Harley, eds. 2011. *The Rise of Indian Multinationals: Perspectives on Indian Outward Foreign Direct Investment*. Houndmills, UK: Palgrave.

Schotter, A., and P. W. Beamish. 2013. "The Hassle Factor: An Explanation for Managerial Location Shunning." *Journal of International Business Studies* 44 (5): 521–44.

Slangen, A. H. L., and J. F. Hennart. 2008. "Do Multinationals Really Prefer to Enter Culturally Distant Countries Through Greenfields Rather than Through Acquisitions? The Role of Parent Experience and Subsidiary Autonomy." *Journal of International Business Studies* 39 (3): 472–90.

Uhlenbruck, K. 2004. "Developing Acquired Foreign Subsidiaries: The Experience of MNEs in Transition Economies." *Journal of International Business Studies* 35 (2): 109–23.

UNCTAD. 2006. *World Investment Report 2006: FDI from Developing and Transition Economies: Implications for Development*. New York: United Nations Conference on Trade and Development.

——. 2007. *World Investment Report 2007: Transnational Corporations, Extractive Industries and Development*. New York: United Nations Conference on Trade and Development.

——. 2013. *World Investment Report 2013: Global Value Chains: Investment and Trade for Development*. New York: United Nations Conference on Trade and Development.

Van Biesebroeck, J. 2010. "Bidding for Investment Projects: Smart Public Policy or Corporate Welfare?" *Canadian Public Policy* 36: S31–S47.

Young, S., and A. T. Tavares. 2004. "Multilateral Rules on FDI: Do We Need Them? Will We Get Them? A Developing Country Perspective." *Transnational Corporations* 13 (1): 1–29.

PART II

A Global Overview of Investment Incentives

CHAPTER 4

The Use of Investment Incentives

THE CASES OF R&D-RELATED INCENTIVES AND INTERNATIONAL INVESTMENT AGREEMENTS

Christian Bellak and Markus Leibrecht

Investment incentives, broadly defined as governmental provisions that lead to money-valued advantages for investors, have increased in importance over the last three decades (e.g., CCSI 2015). They are granted to both domestic and foreign firms and have taken on an increasing variety of forms (see chapter 2 in this volume). Some investment incentives are general in nature. Others are very specific and are granted only in case of a particular type of investment. Investment incentives frequently take the form of higher public expenditures or lower tax revenues. They also can be public guarantees (e.g., loan guarantees) and are encapsulated in specific legal stipulations (e.g., investment agreements or environmental regulations). Furthermore, information provided to investors—for example, through investment promotion agencies—with the aim of reducing transaction costs can be seen as a specific type of investment incentive (as also explained in chapter 2).

Due to the broad range of investment incentives, this chapter is necessarily selective. It has a narrow focus on fiscal and financial investment research and development (R&D) incentives and on international investment agreements (IIAs) as a particular type of regulatory incentive. IIAs are policy tools to attract foreign direct investment (FDI) in general, whereas fiscal and financial R&D incentives are selective and are designed to encourage and support a particular type of investment.[1]

The aim of this chapter is twofold: first, to give a brief overview of the basic rationales for granting investment incentives and, second, to provide empirical evidence for the growing use of IIAs and R&D investment incentives.

RATIONALES AND WELFARE IMPACTS OF INVESTMENT INCENTIVES

The rationale for granting investment incentives could be the desire of benevolent governments to maximize social welfare by influencing the location (Where?), scale (How much?), type (What?), timing (When?), and mode (How?) of firms' investments. Alongside or instead of those motives, the underlying rationale for granting investment incentives could be the desire of decision makers to maximize their private welfare. In particular, various political economy arguments suggest that politicians and bureaucrats use taxes and public expenditures to increase their reelection probability or to maximize their own status and influence in political decision making, respectively. Promoting firms' investment for social welfare purposes is then of second-order importance.[2]

The first rationale, based on a benevolent government, poses the question of whether, in a market economy, investment incentives can be justified from a normative economic viewpoint. Answers resort to distributional-, macro stabilization–, and allocation-related arguments (e.g., Musgrave 1957). The distribution-related justification for investment incentives can be seen in society's wish to speed the catch-up process for particular geographical regions by diverting investment to those areas via, for example, regional tax breaks or subsidies. Clearly, regional investment incentives can also be seen as grounded in an allocation-related justification, as their goal is to increase the region's rate of economic growth by reallocating capital-stock across space. The macro stabilization–related justification is grounded in the political will to smooth business cycle volatility via, for example, granting incremental investment tax credits or premiums in economic downturns.

Allocation-based arguments for investment incentives rest on the theory of market failure. According to this approach, markets fail if they do not deliver a Pareto-efficient outcome. Market failures are caused by factors like nonexcludability and information and transaction costs as well as bargaining failures (Gravelle and Rees 2004).[3] Market failure manifests itself in different ways (see, e.g., Gruber 2013, 321ff.): too few market transactions due to monopolies or oligopolies, too few market transactions due to positive technological external effects or too many transactions due to negative effects, too many market transactions due to common property resources, no market transactions in the case of pure public goods, and too few market transactions due to asymmetric information (adverse selection and moral hazard). In these cases, government intervention to correct market outcomes might increase a nation's welfare.[4]

However, to correct market failures via investment incentives, higher tax revenues may be required, or other public expenditures may need to be curbed due to budget constraints. As increased taxes or reduced public expenditures usually distort private decisions, market failures are not sufficient to justify government interventions even from a pure allocation-related perspective. Government intervention is not a "free lunch." Moreover, market failure is the norm rather than the exception. This "pervasiveness of market failure . . . makes the analysis of the appropriate role of government far more difficult; the issue becomes not one of identifying market failures, . . . but of identifying *large* market failures where there is scope for welfare-enhancing government intervention" (Stiglitz 1989, 38f; italics in original).

Hence, rational investment promotion policy is based on comprehensive cost-benefit or cost-effectiveness analyses, which, inter alia, consider factors like the size of the market failure, distortions caused by higher tax rates (How can incentives be financed?), a nation's level of development (Will the level and/or quality of public goods available decrease if investment incentives are provided?), and a nation's endowment with natural resources (see, e.g., James 2013 on cost-benefit analysis [particularly table 10]).

With respect to FDI promotion, allocation-related arguments favoring investment incentives are dominant (e.g., James 2013). According to Blomström (2002), the "most powerful arguments in favor of such [investment] incentives are based on the prospect for knowledge spillovers" (165). By virtue of the OLI (Ownership-Location-Internalization) paradigm, a multinational enterprise (MNE) must have an ownership advantage to service a foreign market (e.g., Dunning 2000). Ownership advantages enable MNEs to compete with local firms in the latter's home markets. These advantages comprise diverse aspects like managerial capabilities, scale advantages or superior production technology, and patents (Blomström 2002). Ownership advantage–related know-how may spill over to local upstream and downstream firms via forward and backward linkages or to local competitor firms, leading to increased productivity of the concerned firms.

MNEs typically will not include these positive external effects in their FDI decisions. Thus, a particular type of FDI that would be socially favorable for the host country may not be undertaken at all (extensive margin of FDI) or only to an inefficient amount (intensive margin of FDI) due to relatively low private returns. Investment incentives aim to narrow the gap between social and private returns from investment (Blomström 2002). The recent meta-analysis of Havranek and Irsova (2012) finds empirical support for positive spillover effects from FDI on the productivity of domestic firms through backward linkages (i.e., spillover to domestic supplier firms). These authors find that a 10-percentage-point increase in FDI (in "foreign presence") is associated with a 1.2 percent increase in the productivity of domestic supplier firms. In contrast, other types of spillover effects seem to be of negligible magnitude (1389).

Differences in social and private rates of return due to spillover effects are also frequently used to justify investment incentives that support firms' R&D investments (e.g., OECD 2010b). Empirical studies in fact find "social rates of return to R&D to be substantially above private rates of return" (Griffith 2000, 1). MNEs are important in worldwide R&D activity. Furthermore, MNEs increasingly internationalize their R&D investments (e.g., UNCTAD 2005). This internationalization of R&D opens new possibilities for host countries to enhance their growth performance via promotion of R&D-related FDI. In addition, R&D-related FDI decisions frequently are decisions to upgrade existing FDI by moving up the value chain (Guimón 2013; Wellhausen 2013). Hence, in addition to attracting FDI, R&D incentives can be an important means of making existing FDI sustainable (as defined in endnote 1).

As a result of uncertainty about the business environment in a foreign country, potential investors may be confronted with elevated transaction costs (e.g., high search and bargaining costs or high monitoring costs). High transaction costs may prevent MNEs from investing in a foreign country even though the FDI would be desirable from a welfare viewpoint. Investment incentives for MNEs may reduce these costs. For instance, the level of the tax rates on corporate income may signal the quality of the business environment in a foreign location.[5] And IIAs, which aim to secure a certain vector of policies toward FDI, may reduce transaction costs by providing MNEs the possibility of effectively enforcing their property rights. Moreover, IIAs might also be one means to alleviate the "hold-up problem," which arises when part of the return on an agent's relationship-specific investments can be expropriated ex post by the trading partner (Che and Sákovics 2008). When investors anticipate this behavior by host country governments, otherwise efficiency-enhancing FDI may not take place.[6]

From a positive economic viewpoint, the distribution-, macro stabilization–, and allocation-related justifications for investment incentives may not fully explain when investment incentives *actually* are granted. Political economy considerations like the reelection concerns of incumbent governments (including the "claim credit and deflect blame" argument), rent-seeking behavior of interest groups, or desire of decision makers to receive "political income" suggest that investment incentives are granted in the absence of large market failures or distributional and macro stabilization needs.[7] Importantly, these political economy considerations imply that the primary rationale for granting investment incentives is maximizing the private welfare of decision makers. In addition, even in the case of a purely "benevolent" decision maker, limited information may result in incentives for investments that would have taken place in the absence of the government intervention. Pure windfall gains for firms arise in this case. Thus, due to the inability or unwillingness of decision makers to act primarily in the interest of citizens ("government failure"; see, e.g., Gravelle and Rees 2013, 341ff.; Gruber 2013, 242ff.), investment incentives may lead to an inefficient and welfare-decreasing allocation of resources.

The preceding remarks imply that the many investment incentives observed empirically are of two types: those granted because normative reasons for investment incentives exist and those granted despite the absence of any normative justification. In addition, one can imagine cases where government intervention in the market process is justified from a normative viewpoint but governments do not correct the market failure. Specifically, one way to attract certain forms of FDI is via lax environmental regulations or lax enforcement of de jure restrictive regulations (e.g., Kukenova and Monteiro 2008). That is, FDI is attracted by noninternalization of negative environmental externalities despite environmental externalities being a textbook case in favor of government intervention.

CONCLUDING REMARKS ON THE GENERALIZED USE OF INVESTMENT INCENTIVES

To sum up, one rationale for granting investment incentives is grounded in the promotion of firms' investment as means to increase social welfare. The public and welfare branches of economics offer a range of arguments that, in principle, justify investment incentives to firms. However, in reality, investment incentives may be used much more often than justified by this traditional economic reasoning. The sole rationale for granting investment incentives might not be the promotion of investment and social welfare. Rather, depending on the institutional environment, politicians and bureaucrats might use these policy instruments to secure reelection or to increase their own status and political influence. Yet even if the sole rationale for granting investment incentives is the promotion of investment and social welfare, investment incentives could be paired with negative welfare consequences (e.g., due to the noninternalization of negative external effects or the need to finance investment incentives by distorting taxes).

With respect to promoting FDI, one has to bear in mind that financial and fiscal investment incentives are neither the sole nor the most important drivers of many types of FDI. The bulk of the literature shows that investment incentives—for example, in the form of low effective tax rates—are positively correlated with FDI.[8] Yet these studies also imply that a country's own market size and the size of nearby markets, the availability and costs of production factors, and general institutional and economic fundamentals (e.g., macroeconomic and political risk as well as administrative barriers) have a decisive role in shaping an MNE's location decision. Some of these fundamentals are in the realm of public decision makers and need to be of a certain quality before governments should consider fiscal or financial incentives for FDI as policy tools. FDI driven mainly by fiscal and financial investment incentives probably is of a "footloose" and "cherry-picking" nature. As stressed by Blomström and Kokko (1996, 27), footloose FDI implies that little physical capital is "nailed down," which enables firms to easily and quickly relocate their investments to a more favorable environment.

Furthermore, to internalize positive spillover effects from MNEs' investments, local firms require a certain level of absorptive capacity. They must also be financially able to adapt new technologies or to hire higher-skilled workers to realize productivity gains. Thus, when granting fiscal or financial investment incentives for FDI, policy makers have to consider how to ensure that local firms are able to realize possible productivity gains from the presence of foreign MNEs; that is, incentives must be geared to enhancing the absorptive capacity of domestic companies.

These remarks suggest that investment incentives are by no means a panacea for spurring investments. However, once general institutional and economic fundamentals are of a certain quality, investment incentives can be one element of a broader national development strategy.

INVESTMENT INCENTIVES TARGETED AT SPECIFIC ACTIVITIES: FISCAL AND FINANCIAL INCENTIVES FOR R&D

R&D investment is not just an important driver of innovation, technological progress, and economic growth, according to the new growth theory (e.g., Romer 1990). R&D also seems to be positively correlated with economic growth empirically, even if country-specific factors (e.g., the institutional environment) play a decisive role in the precise effects (e.g., Pessoa 2010).

As sketched above, the most important justification for public investment incentives for R&D is grounded in the positive discrepancy between social and private returns to R&D, which leads to an underprovision of R&D investment by profit-maximizing firms. R&D investment incentives intend to correct this inefficiency and, in turn, to increase long-run growth performance. Several additional arguments in favor of R&D investment incentives are put forward in the literature (see OECD 2010b; Mohnen 2013):

1. R&D investments are risky and partly irreversible and may have payoffs only over a rather long time period. Given asymmetric information, it is therefore likely that R&D-intensive young firms, which cannot rely on retained earnings as a source of finance, are credit-constrained. Public support, for instance in the form of direct grants or loan guarantees, is then justified to overcome credit constraints.[9] Furthermore, the long payback period might discourage myopic managers from investing in R&D. Fiscal measures, like the possibility of carrying loss forward and/or backward over extended periods of time, might stimulate investments of this kind.

2. Information problems and transaction costs may lead to coordination failure. For instance, asymmetric information or high transaction costs may lead to a shortage of skilled labor, a complementary input in R&D. Easing immigration procedures for high-skilled foreign workers or providing incentives for collaboration in R&D between firms and universities may help in this respect.

3. Knowledge generated by R&D has characteristics of a pure public good (nonrivalry in consumption and nonexcludability). Nonexcludability leads to free riding and—in extreme cases—to zero private investment in R&D. Securing intellectual property rights, for instance via temporary patenting, might help to overcome this type of market failure. Costs of

patenting might be reduced by financial and fiscal investment incentives (Guimón 2009).[10]

4. Moreover, as stressed by the OECD (2010b), tax and financial R&D incentives are possible policy instruments to increase investment during times of macroeconomic crisis.

Thus, the various arguments advanced for granting R&D incentives are consistent with the view that fiscal and financial incentives are especially relevant for internalizing positive spillover effects, for easing credit constraints, and for fine-tuning the macroeconomic situation (also see Mohnen 2013).

EMPIRICAL EVIDENCE

How important are fiscal and financial R&D incentives in terms of their prevalence, size, and effectiveness?

It is well documented that R&D expenditures as a share in GDP (gross expenditure in R&D—GERD) have been increasing over the past decade in many countries (see, e.g., the data provided by OECD's Main Science and Technology Indicators database and Eurostat database as well as by European Commission 2012).[11] Comparable data for the importance of R&D investment incentives are scarce.[12]

The OECD (2013) provides an indication of the volume of tax and financial R&D investment incentives granted by central governments[13] in a broad sample of countries. Figure 4.1 includes the data for 2011. R&D investment incentives range from a low of 0.01 percent of GDP (Mexico) to about 0.40 percent (Russia). All OECD countries offer direct (financial) incentives (via subsidies, loans, and government procurement) for R&D.[14] In contrast, not all countries included in figure 4.1 grant fiscal incentives. Two OECD countries, Mexico and New Zealand, abolished fiscal incentives for R&D in 2006; however, other countries have started to grant fiscal incentives recently or are debating their introduction (e.g., Poland, Finland, and Germany; see OECD 2011, 2013; Deloitte 2014). It is worth mentioning that in addition to China several European countries (Ireland as early as 1973 and Belgium, Luxembourg, France, the Netherlands, Spain, Switzerland, and Great Britain since 2005; see Cardinal Intellectual Property 2014) have recently introduced preferential Patent Box regimes, which allow companies to apply a reduced statutory corporate income tax to profits accrued from patents.[15] These regimes are

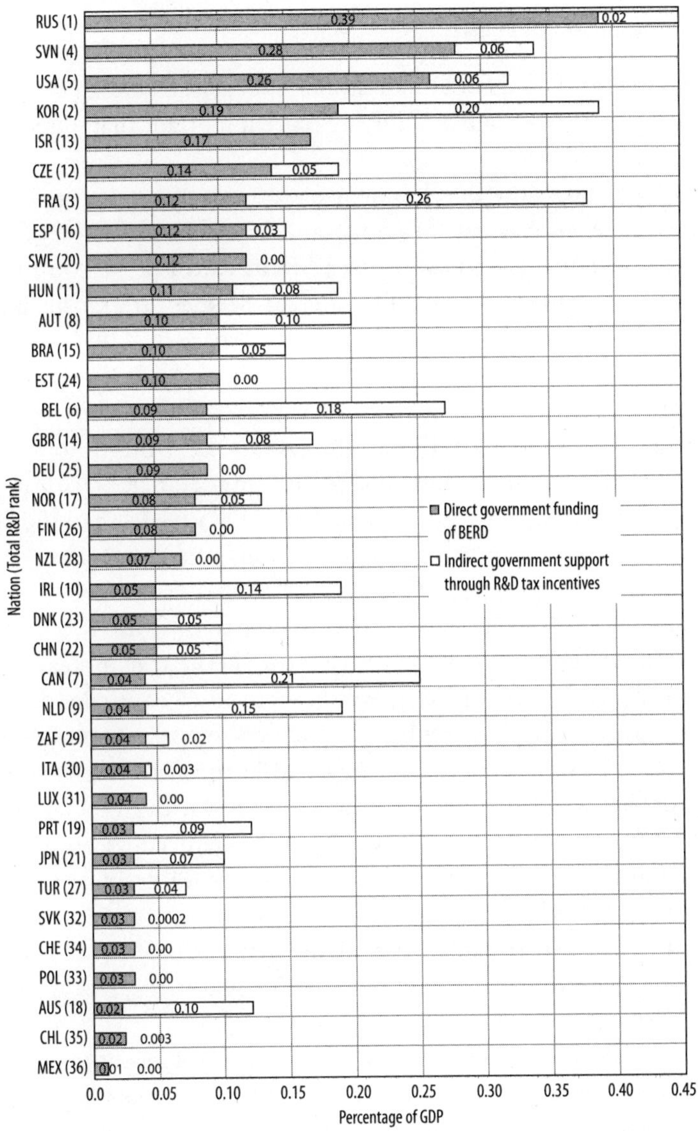

Figure 4.1 Direct government funding of business R&D and tax incentives for R&D, 2011.

Source: OECD 2013.

Notes: In (rank). Values are generally for 2011; for CHL, AUS, IRE, BEL, BRA, and ISR, values are for 2010; for LUX, ZAF, and CHN, values are for 2009; and for CHE, value is for 2008. BERD = Business expenditure on R&D; direct (central) government funding of R&D is the amount of BERD funded by the government (as reported by firms). Direct government funding comprises the sum of various components (procurement, loans, grants/subsidies); tax incentives measure revenues foregone (by the central government due to R&D tax credits, R&D allowances, and reductions in R&D workers' wage taxes and social security contributions as well as accelerated depreciation of capital used for R&D [see OECD 2013 for details]). No data for tax incentives are available for Israel. According to the OECD (2013), the indicator shown is experimental in nature; international comparability may thus be limited. For further details and specific country notes, consult http://www.oecd.org/sti/rd-tax-stats.htm.

mainly targeted toward R&D-intensive FDI. Finally, according to figure 4.1, fiscal incentives as a share of GDP are more important than direct incentives in ten countries.

Table 4.1 shows the development of volume and structure of R&D investment incentives between 2007 and 2011 for a subset of countries included in figure 4.1. In both years, South Korea is the country with the largest incentives for R&D, whereas Mexico offers the smallest amounts of fiscal and direct incentives (as a share of GDP). The mean increase (measured in percentage points) in fiscal incentives is bigger than the corresponding mean increase in direct incentives. Direct incentives as a share of GDP are largest in the United States (both in 2008 and 2011), not least due to the importance of competitive R&D contracts (OECD 2010a). The United States also had the largest increase in direct incentives over the period considered. Fiscal incentives are most important in Canada (2007) and France (2011). France also had the largest increase in fiscal incentives from 2007 to 2011. Furthermore, France is the country with the largest increase in the total share of investment incentives granted. Five countries decreased the total share of R&D incentives from 2007 to 2011, with Japan being in the lead. Japan's reduction of total R&D incentives rests solely on the decreasing importance of fiscal incentives. Besides Japan, two additional countries (Denmark and Canada) reduced fiscal incentives. Canada did so starting from a relatively high value in 2007. Seven countries reduced their share of direct incentives in terms of GDP. Overall, we see from table 4.1 that investment incentives for R&D increased somewhat in importance, with fiscal incentives gaining in relative importance.

From a theoretical point of view, direct and fiscal incentives for R&D involve different economic effects and implications (see OECD 2010b; Busom, Corchuelo, and Martinez Ros 2012; Tanayama 2012; Mohnen 2013):

1. Direct incentives provide funding up front, whereas fiscal incentives are based on profits or tax liabilities due to an investment; thus, in the case of fiscal incentives, firms must be able to fund the project initially (Busom, Corchuelo, and Martinez Ros 2012).

2. Due to their up-front characteristics, subsidies are better suited to support credit-constrained (young, small) firms; put differently, profit-based fiscal incentives favor mature and large companies over young and potentially dynamic and creative firms (e.g., Mohnen 2013).

Table 4.1 Development of volume and structure of investment incentives for R&D

2011 or ()	Direct	Fiscal	Sum	2007 or ()	Direct	Fiscal	Sum	Diff direct	Diff fiscal	Diff sum
MEX	0.01	0.00	0.01	MEX	0.01	0.00	0.01	0.00	0.00	0.00
AUS (2010)	0.02	0.10	0.12	AUS (2006)	0.05	0.05	0.09	−0.03	0.05	0.03
POL	0.03	0.00	0.03	POL	0.02	0.00	0.02	0.01	0.00	0.01
SVK	0.03	0.00	0.03	SVK (2008)	0.03	0.00	0.03	0.00	0.00	0.00
TUR	0.03	0.04	0.07	TUR	0.03	0.00	0.03	0.00	0.04*	0.04
JPN	0.03	0.07	0.10	JPN	0.03	0.12	0.15	0.00	−0.05	−0.05
PRT	0.03	0.09	0.12	PRT	0.02	0.06	0.08	0.01	0.03	0.04
LUX (2009)	0.04	0.00	0.04	LUX	0.05	0.00	0.05	−0.01	0.00	−0.01
ITA	0.04	0.003	0.04	ITA	0.04	0.00	0.04	0.00	0.003*	0.003
NLD	0.04	0.15	0.19	NLD	0.02	0.08	0.10	0.02	0.07	0.09
CAN	0.04	0.21	0.25	CAN (2008)	0.02	**0.22**	0.24	0.02	−0.01	0.01
DNK	0.05	0.05	0.10	DNK (2008)	0.05	0.06	0.11	0.00	−0.01	−0.01
IRE (2010)	0.05	0.14	0.19	IRE	0.05	0.09	0.13	0.00	0.05	0.06
NZL	0.07	0.00	0.07	NZL	0.05	0.00	0.05	0.02	0.00	0.02
FIN	0.08	0.00	0.08	FIN	0.09	0.00	0.09	−0.01	0.00	−0.01
NOR	0.08	0.05	0.13	NOR (2008)	0.09	0.04	0.12	−0.01	0.01	0.01
DEU	0.09	0.00	0.09	DEU	0.08	0.00	0.08	0.01	0.00	0.01
GBR	0.09	0.08	0.17	GBR (2008)	0.08	0.06	0.14	0.01	0.02	0.03
BEL (2010)	0.09	0.18	0.27	BEL	0.07	0.14	0.22	0.02	0.04	0.05
AUT	0.10	0.10	0.20	AUT	0.10	0.09	0.19	0.00	0.01	0.01
HUN	0.11	0.08	0.19	HUN	0.05	0.08	0.13	0.06	0.00	0.06
SWE	0.12	0.00	0.12	SWE	0.11	0.00	0.11	0.01	0.00	0.01
ESP (2010)	0.12	0.03	0.15	ESP	0.12	0.03	0.15	0.00	0.00	0.00
FRA	0.12	**0.26**	0.38	FRA (2008)	0.15	0.08	0.23	−0.03	**0.18**	**0.15**
CZE	0.14	0.05	0.19	CZE	0.13	0.03	0.16	0.01	0.02	0.03
KOR	0.19	0.20	**0.39**	KOR (2008)	0.15	0.19	**0.34**	0.04	0.01	0.05
USA	**0.26**	0.06	0.32	USA (2008)	**0.18**	0.05	0.23	**0.08**	0.01	0.09
Mean	0.08	0.07	0.15		0.07	0.05	0.12	0.01	0.02	0.03
Median	0.07	0.05	0.12		0.05	0.05	0.11	0.00	0.00	0.01
MIN	0.01	0.00	0.01		0.01	0.00	0.01	−0.03	−0.05	−0.05
MAX	**0.26**	**0.26**	**0.39**		**0.18**	**0.22**	**0.34**	**0.08**	**0.18**	**0.15**

Sources: OECD 2010a, 2013.

Notes: Mean and median represent unweighted values; data for 2007 are available only for a subset of countries included in figure 4.1; Switzerland is excluded, as different OECD sources provide different data for 2008 (OECD 2010a, 2013).

*Italy and Turkey provided fiscal incentives in 2007, but the OECD (2010a) does not quantify their costs; the displayed change in fiscal credits in these two countries may thus exaggerate true change.

3. Similarly, for macroeconomic fine-tuning in times of crisis, investment subsidies or premiums may be a better option than profit-based tax incentives.

4. Compliance costs are lower for fiscal incentives (e.g., Tanayama 2012); yet one may argue that large, mature firms are better able to cope with complicated tax structures; thus, the compliance-cost advantage of fiscal incentives over direct funding might be higher for mature firms (Mohnen 2013).

5. Direct incentives are less neutral and more targetable, as public officials, not firms, decide on the exact R&D projects on which money is spent (e.g., Mohnen 2013; Tanayama 2012). On the one hand, this implies that a "benevolent social planner" can pick the socially most valuable projects by using direct incentives; on the other hand, direct incentives are easier to use to satisfy the decision maker's clientele. Furthermore, the information required for a benevolent public official to pick the most valuable R&D projects is often absent in practice; under these considerations, less distorting fiscal incentives, granted for investment in certain high-innovation sectors and in an incremental form (to reduce the likelihood of pure windfall gains for firms), may be the preferred option.

6. Direct incentives may be a means to reduce asymmetric information; receiving R&D subsidies implies screening by public officials, which, in turn, might act as a signal for financial institutions (certification effect; Takalo and Tanayama 2010; Busom, Corchuelo, and Martinez Ros 2012).

7. The size of a government is frequently measured by indicators like government outlays over GDP or tax revenues over GDP. Direct incentives increase the size of government, whereas tax incentives reduce it; thus, even if direct and tax incentives have an equal impact on the overall public budget, the visibility of government intervention to the general public is higher with direct incentives.

8. According to the OECD (2010b), tax credits mostly encourage short-term applied research, whereas direct incentives foster more long-term basic research.

The differences across countries shown in figure 4.1 in the structure of R&D incentives granted can be taken as an indication that different types of firms and different types of R&D are targeted. Countries that predominately rely on fiscal incentives, ceteris paribus, favor large and mature companies over young and small firms as well as short-term applied research over long-term basic research.

Table 4.1 implies that fiscal and financial investment incentives for R&D (as a share in GDP) have gained in importance over time. At the same time, internationalization of R&D activities by MNEs has soared.[16] Among the important reasons why MNEs start to abandon the "home bias" in R&D are the needs to "adapt foreign technologies to local markets, to access skilled research personnel and to learn from foreign lead markets and customers" (UNCTAD 2005, 159). Cost issues and the availability of research manpower gain importance at high speed (159). Thus, by providing cost-reducing public R&D programs—including R&D investment incentives—countries are increasingly able to attract R&D activities of foreign MNEs (or to keep R&D activities of domestic MNEs at home).

On the one hand, this ability to promote R&D-intensive FDI clearly paves the road for horizontal competition for FDI via incentives (incentive competition).[17] On the other hand, the internationalization trend opens the possibility that emerging economies not only will attract R&D FDI[18] but also will make existing, non-R&D-related FDI sustainable. Indeed, according to Guimón (2013), due to intracorporate competition to attract R&D, "R&D-intensive FDI normally unfolds by upgrading existing subsidiaries, rather than through completely new investments" (3). Thus, R&D incentives are, in principle, of particular importance for making FDI sustainable.

As fiscal incentives favor large and mature firms, one can hypothesize that R&D tax credits and enhanced allowances are especially relevant for attracting and sustaining R&D-intensive FDI from the dominant players in a certain industry. Direct subsidies, which can be targeted to specific firms and projects, are especially useful to make investments of smaller but highly innovative foreign firms financially sustainable. Put differently, direct investment incentives might be the preferred option to help smaller and younger foreign firms move up their value chain toward R&D-intensive products and services.

From a host country policy perspective, a key question is whether R&D investment incentives are indeed capable of promoting R&D-intensive FDI. Empirical evidence on this issue, based on a broad sample of countries, is scarce—not least due to the lack of comparable data on R&D investment incentives. The existing literature points to the minor importance of fiscal and financial incentives in promoting R&D-intensive FDI.

Wellhausen (2013) tests two hypotheses: (1) R&D FDI is an upgrading decision, and (2) fiscal and financial incentives are not capable of promoting R&D-intensive FDI. She uses data for R&D FDI emerging from the United States to various developed and developing countries over several years. Host country coverage and years considered vary over the hypotheses tested. Notably, hypothesis 1 is tested on a sample of eleven developing host countries over the years 1985–2005. Wellhausen finds empirical support for both of her hypotheses.

Thursby and Thursby (2006) present results from a survey of 200 MNEs across fifteen industries dealing with the factors that influenced the MNEs' decisions on where to conduct R&D. The majority of included MNEs have their headquarters either in the United States or in Western Europe. The results are structured along the developed–emerging economies divide. The authors find only weak relevance of tax breaks to the location of R&D-intensive FDI. For developing economies (thereof 51 percent are located in China and India), the authors state: "One can reasonably reject the argument that tax breaks and/or direct government assistance are luring firms to establish R&D facilities in developing or emerging economies" (24). They conclude that "regardless of where companies locate R&D, four factors stand out: output market potential, quality of R&D personnel, university collaboration, and intellectual property protection" (1).

Evidence for a rather minor importance of R&D incentives in increasing the R&D activity of established foreign firms is provided by Görg and Strobl (2007). Their analysis is based on plant-level data for the manufacturing sector in the Republic of Ireland over the years 1999–2002. They consider financial investment incentives (grants) in their analysis. For foreign plants, they find evidence neither for additionality nor for crowding-out effects of R&D incentives. Thus, R&D investment incentives have no effect on the intensive margin of R&D-related FDI.

Cantwell and Mudambi (2000) ask whether investment incentives as a location factor are on par with firm- and other location-specific variables, whether they have incremental importance, or whether they are totally unimportant in MNEs' R&D decisions. "Incremental" is defined as having importance after other location factors have already been allowed for. The authors consider fiscal incentives (e.g., tax credits) as well as financial incentives (e.g., loans and loan guarantees). Based on firm-level data (derived by a mail survey) for foreign firms with engineering and engineering-related operations in the Midland region of the United Kingdom, they find an incremental effect of tax credits on MNEs' R&D location decisions but no direct effect. Thus, investment incentives are dominated by firm- and other location-specific factors. Yet they may have an impact on the margin. Cantwell and Mudambi conclude that "in a decision between locations in which major firm and location parameters are very similar, investment support will play a key role" (136).

CONCLUDING REMARKS ON THE USE OF R&D INVESTMENT INCENTIVES

This section of the chapter concludes that from a welfare perspective one should be skeptical about active strategies for investment incentives in general and for FDI in particular. It underscores this point from an empirical perspective. Fiscal and financial investment incentives are of second-order importance for promoting R&D-intensive FDI, especially in developing countries. Instead, developed and developing countries alike should make efforts to continuously improve the educational system, as availability of research manpower is essential for R&D FDI. Furthermore, there is a need to adapt telecommunication infrastructure, as R&D activity requires communication and exchange of ideas. And, of course, countries need to establish and credibly secure the institutions needed by MNEs to conduct R&D-intensive FDI. Securing intellectual property rights is of high importance in this respect, as technology leaders' fears of technology theft are one reason for the home-country bias in R&D investment (e.g., Belderbos, Leten, and Suzuki 2013). Put differently, countries must acquire and/or maintain the relevant threshold level of technological as well as infrastructure- and institution-related capabilities to be considered for MNEs' R&D activities (UNCTAD 2005; Guimón 2013).

BROADLY AVAILABLE INVESTMENT INCENTIVES FOR FOREIGN INVESTORS: INTERNATIONAL INVESTMENT AGREEMENTS

Since the 1960s, bilateral investment treaties (BITs) have been used to protect foreign investments not only between high-income and low-income countries but also increasingly between pairs or groups of high-income countries and between pairs or groups of low- and middle-income countries. Over time, the range of countries concluding BITs has changed to include less risky countries, but the goal of BITs has been remarkably stable: capital exporters seek protection, and capital importers signing the treaties seek FDI. Additionally, governments have increasingly concluded IIAs on a regional level, mostly by including investment provisions in regional trade agreements like NAFTA. It is by now common knowledge that IIAs (which include BITs and free-trade agreements with investment provisions) attempt to promote FDI directly through their protection function and indirectly through their signaling function. Less commonly recognized is the possibility that IIAs may enhance the effects on FDI of other location factors, including FDI incentives. For example, BIT provisions dealing with indirect expropriation can strengthen the effect of a favorable intellectual property rights regime, and BIT provisions like umbrella clauses can provide an additional incentive for investors to enter public-private partnerships. Accordingly, this section first provides a review of the question of how policy intervention in the case of IIAs can be justified. This is followed by empirical evidence on the extent to which BITs, as the most important type of IIAs by number, promote inward FDI and increase the impact of other location factors on FDI.

ECONOMIC RATIONALE FOR IIAS

The rationale for IIAs is discussed here in light of the obsolescing bargain; that is, "once a firm undertakes a foreign direct investment, some bargaining power shifts to the host country government, which has an incentive to change the terms of the investment to reap a greater share of the benefits" (Büthe and Milner 2008, 743).

The economic justification of IIAs is also derived from instances of market failure, which leads to the fact that government promises lack credibility. As a consequence of this lack of credibility, an efficient investment, which would otherwise have taken place, is not carried out or is carried out in an inefficiently low amount in the absence of an IIA. More specifically, the lack of credibility pertains to the existence of two types of market failure: adverse selection and time inconsistency, which is also known as the hold-up problem (e.g., Tomz 1997; Guzman 1998). It is noteworthy at the outset that the hold-up problem is neither a necessary nor a sufficient condition for the credibility problem to arise, as there need not be intent to deceive on the part of the host. Rather, adverse selection and time inconsistency aggravate the obsolescing bargain (Vernon 1971).

Adverse selection refers to the fact that information about the true intentions of a government may be private as "when observers lack information about the beliefs and values that are motivating a government to pursue" a certain policy, such as liberalizing capital flows (Tomz 1997, 2). This type of market imperfection can be even more pronounced if the government in question administers a country that lacks credible institutions, like some developing countries. Inducement of the policy change may be internal or external.

Time inconsistency refers to the fact that host country governments will always have "in the short run incentives to change the terms of existing foreign investments when the short-run benefits exceed the long-term costs" (Büthe and Milner 2008, 743). Short-term welfare maximization may dominate long-term welfare maximization/efficiency and takes various forms, all of which are concerned with shifting the surplus of FDI in favor of the host country government. Among agreements changing the division of surplus are "concessions and commitments on the part of each party. For example, the host might agree to offer certain tax advantages to the investor, agree to allow the repatriation of profits, and waive certain import restrictions. The firm, on the other hand, might bind itself to providing a certain level of employment, certain transfers of technology, local content/value-added etc." (Guzman 1998, 661). It should be noted that the time-inconsistency problem remains even if the information asymmetry is completely avoided—that is, if all information is public.

Problems in the division of surplus are likely to exist between domestically owned firms and the local government, but they may be aggravated in developing countries if foreign-owned firms are the main source of surplus. Moreover, as Büthe and Milner (2008, 743) argue, "resource-strapped developing country governments may have an even greater incentive than governments in advanced industrialized countries to discount the long term." Tomz (1997) lists a number of reasons why a government could be prompted to seek protectionism in trade policy ex post, even though free trade was superior ex ante: "For example, a program of commercial liberalization could conflict with the objective of fiscal retrenchment" (4). A similar problem could be a deteriorating current account. Tomz concludes: "Thus, the temptation for 'true' reformers to escalate tariffs may prove irresistible once investors have committed themselves. This type of reasoning can easily be transferred to the realm of investment policy: For example, a government could aim to liberalize capital flows and free transfer of funds, but could revert to capital controls later on in times of economic crisis; or raise tariffs on reexported goods and intermediate services, despite a liberalizing policy approach in general" (4).[19]

Given the likelihood that both types of market failure exist simultaneously, how can they be addressed by IIAs? Kerner (2009) argues that there are two possibilities: ex ante costs (signals) and ex post costs (commitments). The interplay between these two is important: "In a setting of imperfect information, all commitments are signals but not all signals are commitments" (Tomz 1997, 5). Signaling in the case of IIAs and FDI may be defined as "sending a broadly received 'signal' that a country is trustworthy" (Kerner 2009, 74). In other words, investors' doubts about the true intentions of the host country government—stemming from the information asymmetry—can be reduced as they update their beliefs when the host country signs/ratifies an IIA.

When IIAs "present significant ex-post costs to signatory states that violate the agreement," they tie the hands of ratifying host states (Kerner 2009, 74). In this view, an IIA is a commitment device.[20] Because an IIA includes a number of commitments between two sovereign governments, violating an IIA "constitutes a breach of international commitments, which should make those commitments *more costly to break*" (Büthe and Milner 2008, 744; italics added).[21] Both the signaling function and the commitment function may ultimately contribute to FDI promotion.

It is important to note that these conceptual arguments relate to single bilateral or regional treaties, yet they disregard the fact that IIAs are part of a system of these agreements. Once a systemic view is taken (see Poulsen 2011, Poulsen and Aisbett 2013), a lack of coherence in BIT standards as well as in the application of BITs (by arbitration tribunals) is revealed. This implies that the above arguments need to be qualified in light of a more systemic view. For example, based on a large number of interviews, Poulsen (2011) reports a severe lack of knowledge among host country authorities about the actual application of treaties. For instance, it is often uncertain and can require lengthy and costly litigation to determine if a government's decision to alter a tax policy or incentive regime actually does constitute a breach of the BIT. And different tribunals may come up with different answers based on the same set of facts. Such evidence shows clearly that BITs may not be able to automatically solve both types of market failures. It is therefore questionable from a conceptual point of view whether the host country goals of BITs will be met.

EMPIRICAL EVIDENCE

The World Bank's (2014) World Governance Indicators show that the number of countries with the lowest estimates for (1) political stability,[22] (2) regulatory quality,[23] or (3) the rule of law[24] is large, and progress toward improvement has been very slow over time. Political risk remains a decisive deterrent for FDI.

Investment policies, both in developing and in developed states, have increasingly included IIAs, and, consequently, they have grown substantially over time (UNCTAD 2013, 101ff.; see figure 4.2). Recently, the growth rate of IIAs has been decreasing. As of the beginning of 2014, there were 3,196 IIAs in place, 2,857 of which were BITs. The difference between these two numbers is mainly explained by free-trade agreements—most notably, regional agreements with investment provisions included.

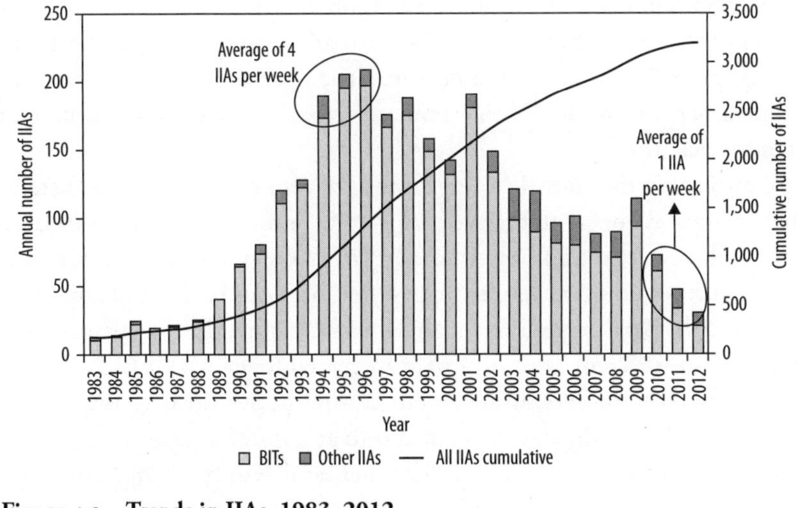

Figure 4.2 Trends in IIAs, 1983–2012.

Source: UNCTAD 2013, 102.

Notes: left-hand scale: Annual number of IIAs, dark gray; right hand scale: cumulative number of IIAs, black line

The number of investor-state dispute settlement (ISDS) cases grew along with the number of IIAs (see UNCTAD 2014; Chaisse 2013). Since the 2000s, the number of cases initiated by investors has grown at a faster pace. As of 2013, there were about 568 known ISDS cases, and 56 cases were initiated during 2013 alone. It is noteworthy that almost half of the 2013 cases were filed against developed states and 45 of the 56 cases were brought by investors from developed states. This suggests that such claims are not purely the developed–developing country game they were in the early periods of BIT making.

On the question of whether IIAs increase inward FDI, most authors state that empirical evidence is mixed (see, e.g., Sauvant and Sachs 2009). Yet a meta-analysis may provide an objective quantitative literature review on the subject and reveal the size of the publication bias.[25] The crucial measure used to compare the impact of BITs on FDI across empirical studies is semi-elasticity, which is defined as the percentage change in FDI upon a unit change in BITs (an increase of the total stock of BITs by one BIT or the emergence of a new BIT between a certain country pair). Preliminary results based on a meta-analysis (Bellak 2015a, 2015b) of about thirty-five empirical studies on the impact of BITs on inward FDI flows show a semi-elasticity of FDI with respect to BITs on the order of 8.2 (79 observations; significant at the 1 percent level) when BITs are measured by a dummy variable and 2.3 (110 observations; significant at the 1 percent level) when cumulated BITs are used. In both cases, the most precise estimates of the semi-elasticity are close to zero. (Note that precision is based here on the size of the standard error of a coefficient estimate in an empirical study.)

Concerning the statistical significance of results, Aisbett (2009) states that "countries appear to believe that the FDI-promoting abilities of BITs outweigh . . . legal and policy costs. I find no evidence to support this belief. Furthermore, my results suggest that previous findings of a positive impact of BIT participation . . . are almost certainly due to misspecification and insufficient attention paid to the endogeneity of BIT participation" (421). However, more recent studies derive positive impacts of BITs even when endogeneity is taken into account. Some of these studies (Büthe and Milner 2014; Busse, Königer, and Nunnenkamp 2010) are cited in the following paragraphs.

Although it would be important to distinguish between short-term and long-term effects, as the hypothesis would be that enhancing the credibility via IIAs may take time, this has hardly been done in empirical studies. An exception is Egger and Merlo (2007), but they use outward rather than inward FDI stocks. Peinhardt and Todd (2012) perform a time-series intervention analysis and find that out of thirty-two countries, "only three appear to experience an increase in US FDI flows after implementing BITs" (771). Büthe and Milner (2014) do not find a significant long-term effect of BITs in force on inward FDI. On the basis of this evidence, one may conclude that the conceptually plausible time-consuming process of gaining credibility on the part of host country governments does not find empirical support and that positive and significant long-run effects of BITs on FDI have hardly been established so far.

On the basis of such evidence, one cannot conclude that BITs are an important means to attract FDI. Moreover, although their indirect effects on FDI attraction by signaling to investors from other countries may be important, research reported by Poulsen, Bonnitcha, and Yackee (2013) suggests convincingly that these effects may be limited due to systemic features of international investment law. Yet, this lack of evidence sustaining the effects of BITs on FDI attraction does not imply that BITs are irrelevant for such attraction. One of the arguments is that, through their FDI protection function, BITs may contribute substantially to the sustainability of FDI. An important aspect is that BITs allow investors to take legal action against the host country government not only during the often long-term existence of the BIT but also after the BIT has expired (by termination, by elapse of time, etc.), as the rights enshrined in BITs are guaranteed for a certain period by survival clauses.

On the question of whether IIAs have an impact on other determinants of FDI, empirical evidence is still scarce but growing. The main argument is that IIAs may enhance the impact of other fundamentals, location factors, and incentives on FDI because IIAs address the hold-up problem, which affects all areas of government policy. For example, because the previous section dealt with R&D incentives, assume that a host country government is providing R&D incentives to all firms for a certain period but suddenly, due to budgetary constraints, raises the threshold of access to R&D incentives for foreign investors.[26] Foreign investors may invoke one or more BIT clauses (e.g., the fair and equitable treatment standard or the national treatment standard) to challenge such changes in policy. The threat of invoking BIT clauses may have a disciplining effect on the host government, which may, as a consequence, decide not to raise the threshold at all or to raise it less than originally planned. More generally, the commitments enshrined in BITs may strengthen the effects of investment incentives on FDI by tying the government's hands because investors covered by BITs may evoke BIT provisions in case of policy changes, including changes in investment incentives schemes (see endnote 23 for an example).

Several studies model interaction effects with governance factors like political stability (Neumayer and Spess 2005; Busse, Königer, and Nunnenkamp 2010), government stability (Neumayer and Spess 2005), law and order (Neumayer and Spess 2005), risk (Tobin and Rose-Ackerman 2005, 2011), market size (Tobin and Rose-Ackerman 2011), interest rate and money supply (Tortian 2007), capital account openness (Busse, Königer, and Nunnenkamp 2010), quality of domestic institutions, and quality of interstate political relations (Desbordes and Vicard 2009). Yet the main difficulty in establishing the empirical relevance of this argument is that most of these studies do not show the statistical significance of the combined effect of the constitutive terms. This would require establishing the significance of the coefficient on the BIT variable and the interaction effect with the BIT variable combined, which is not automatically produced by standard software; thus, their statistical significance cannot be established ex post. Unfortunately, so far no incentives measure has been interacted with the BIT variable, and, therefore, no empirical evidence on the incentive-magnifying hypothesis can be reported here.

CONCLUDING REMARKS ON THE USE OF IIAS

Against the rather skeptical view developed earlier on the use of investment incentives in general and with regard to FDI attraction in particular, this section has discussed the virtues of IIAs as a tool to promote FDI. On the one hand, IIAs act as a kind of governmentally guaranteed insurance against political risk and may thus help to attract FDI; yet, on the other hand, existing empirical evidence that their effect on investment flows is large, or even exists, is not very convincing, once empirical results are corrected for publication bias. In line with econometric results, Poulsen (2014, 3) argues on the basis of interviews that the diffusion of modern IIAs can best be explained by a bounded rationality framework and reports feedback from developing country officials that reflects the ex post unjustified hopes of negotiators. He concludes that national economic benefits have been overestimated and national costs ignored.

However, the lack of empirical evidence may be an artifact, as IIAs are heterogeneous and this heterogeneity has hardly been taken into account in earlier empirical studies. None of the empirical studies surveyed in the meta-analysis of Bellak (2015b), with the exception of Busse, Königer, and Nunnenkamp (2010) and Neumayer and Spess (2005), has claimed that IIAs are able to substitute for the lack of institutional factors conducive to FDI (such as a developed legal system or sound monetary and fiscal policies). In other words, although IIAs may unfold their protection effect best in environments where institutional factors are problematic, the combination of insufficient infrastructure and IIAs cannot be a successful FDI attraction policy. It should also be mentioned that empirical studies using aggregate FDI data and aggregate numbers of BITs face the problem of treaty shopping—that is, the common and accepted practice of routing an investment in the host country through a third country in order to secure the protection of that third country's BIT with the host country. This problem has increasingly been addressed by studies using bilateral FDI data. Nevertheless, the poor measurement of FDI itself limits the importance and relevance of empirical studies in this field.[27] Moreover, causality is an issue here, as many BITs also cover investments made before a BIT has been concluded.

In summary, for the time being, strengthening domestic institutions in order to minimize political risk seems to be a necessary and promising option for host governments, in parallel with the provision of insurance against political risk created ultimately by themselves. This conclusion is important, as political scientists like Jandhyala, Henisz, and Mansfield (2011) have claimed convincingly on the basis of empirical evidence that "as the density of BITs among peer countries increased, more countries signed them in order to gain legitimacy and acceptance without a full understanding of their costs and competencies" (1047).

CONCLUSION

Investment incentives are growing in importance. Incentives for R&D and IIAs are no exception. Most arguments favoring their welfare-improving role rest on the theory of market failure. However, the presence of market failure is sufficient neither for granting investment incentives from a normative viewpoint nor for explaining their generalized use. Like any other economic policy measure, an investment incentives policy should be based on thorough cost-benefit analysis on the domestic level. And it should consider unintended consequences like the fueling of harmful incentives competition for mobile capital, an issue that may ultimately be tackled only on the multilateral level. Also, it should be noted that the policies discussed throughout this chapter need to reflect the specific country context, as the economic effects of incentives differ across countries. These issues are dealt with in more depth in chapters 9 and 10 in this volume.

NOTES

1. Sustainability is understood here in the sense of keeping operations of MNEs in the country, yet possibly changing their type (e.g., upgrading from a pure manufacturing plant to one that also provides R&D services).

2. The possibility of using taxes and public expenditures to increase status and influence depends not least on the power dispersion within the bureaucracy. In particular, if budgetary institutions grant significant decision-making power to the finance minister, the opportunities for other government entities to use investment incentives to increase their private welfare may be severely constrained.

3. According to Inman (1987), there is one common reason for market failure: markets cannot enforce cooperative behavior of utility- or profit-maximizing agents. This leads to Prisoners' Dilemma situations.

4. Musgrave (1957) also introduces the concept of merit goods or merit wants. In contrast to public goods or externalities, where preferences of individual actors are accepted as the base of decision making (consumer sovereignty), the merit goods perspective is a paternalistic one. If one accepts the existence of merit goods, investment incentives might also be justified, for instance, due to a "too short" planning horizon of firms' managers.

5. Yet investment incentives targeted toward foreign capital may induce incentives competition for mobile capital between independent jurisdictions, with potentially negative welfare consequences. Horizontal tax competition for mobile capital, due to the noninternalization of positive fiscal externalities, may lead to an inefficient provision of public consumption goods (e.g., Sinn 2004).

6. In principle, monopolies, pure public goods, and common property resources may form the base for justifying investment incentives for FDI as well. Investment incentives can make locally monopolized markets contestable by reducing sunk costs or by increasing competition via the easing of credit constraints. The problem of nonexcludability may be reduced by moderating exclusion costs via grants.

7. Political income occurs when officeholders grant favorable treatment (in the form of, e.g., excess payments to factors of production, tax loopholes, and favorable economic legislation) to specific groups in exchange for benefits (in the form of, e.g., campaign contributions or promises of future employment) (Barro 1973). The "claim

credit and deflect blame" argument rests on the perception that reelection-oriented politicians grant investment incentives for FDI so that they are able "to take credit for investment flowing into their districts and to minimize the political fallout when investors choose to locate elsewhere" (Jensen et al. 2010, 1). The "claim credit and deflect blame" rational for granting FDI incentives seems to have a clear political payoff (see Jensen and Malesky 2010 for a brief outline).

8. Low effective tax burdens arise from many different tax policy measures, including low statutory tax rates and narrow tax bases due to the exemption of certain types of income in general or for a certain period of time from taxation (see, e.g., Devereux, Elscher, Endres, and Spengel 2009; Botman, Klemm, and Baqir 2008). The underlying policy rationale for these measures is not always known, but statements concerning corporate tax policy almost never leave out the effect on attracting FDI.

9. As stressed by Takalo and Tanayama (2010), receiving a public subsidy for R&D investments may provide an informative signal to financial institutions, which, in turn, ease their credit conditions.

10. Market failures due to positive spillover effects and those due to public good characteristics are clearly closely interrelated. To avoid free riding, measures must be taken to reduce knowledge leakage, which, in turn, reduce the speed and extent of knowledge spillover. Both arguments assume a certain degree of absorptive capacity in local firms.

11. Many EU countries increase GERD not least due to targets set by the Europe 2020 Strategy, which succeeds the Lisbon Strategy and sets out the EU's prime economic targets. EU2020 GERD targets range between 0.5 percent of GDP (Cyprus with 0.46 in 2012) and 4 percent of GDP (Sweden with 3.41 in 2012; Finland with 3.55 in 2012). For comparison, GERD/(target GERD) for the United States, Japan, South Korea, and China is 2.67/(3), 3.25/(4), 3.74/(5), and 1.76/(2.5) percent, respectively (European Commission 2012; Eurostat database [latest available data May 2014]).

12. Data on R&D incentives specifically/exclusively granted to foreign MNEs are—to the best of our knowledge—completely lacking. Data of this kind would provide useful information on the extent to which countries compete for R&D investments of foreign firms using specific fiscal tools or on the issue of whether investment incentives policies discriminate against domestic or foreign firms.

13. For federal countries like Germany or the United States, these figures probably underreport the true volume of R&D incentives as a share of GDP.

14. Greece and Iceland are not covered by figure 4.1. Yet both countries offered direct grants in 2009 (Greece) and 2008 (Iceland), according to the OECD (2011).

15. Moreover, the German government plans to introduce a Patent Box regime (December 2015).

16. Guimón (2013, 1) includes some descriptive evidence. For instance, annual R&D investments by foreign firms more than doubled in the OECD between 1997 and 2007, reaching about US$89 billion in 2007.

17. See chapters 11 and 12 in this volume on initiatives to regulate the use of investment incentives.

18. For risks paired to R&D-intensive FDI for host countries, see Guimón (2013). Importantly, R&D-intensive FDI might crowd out innovative efforts of local firms due to fiercer competition in input markets.

19. There are many ways in which the host country government can shift the distribution of surplus/profit from the investor to the host state: raising tax levels, raising tariff levels, changing regulations, adding fees, selectively enforcing the law, imposing new labor requirements, and so on. The most extreme ones involve expropriation (Guzman 1998, 661). Compared to the earlier discussions about direct expropriations (importantly concerning resource-seeking FDI), the phenomenon of the increasing international division of value chains has decreased the likelihood of direct expropriation: FDI that is part of a firm's global production chain leaves an expropriating government with essentially worthless assets, as Büthe and Milner (2009) argue. In addition, the host country government's competence to run an expropriated production facility may be low.

20. How do commitments raise ex post costs? According to Büthe and Milner (2008, 745), formal agreements, such as treaties, make these commitments more visible. For example, most BITs can easily be downloaded from the Web. In addition, organizations like UNCTAD publish reports on investment policies of some of their Member States. Also, MNEs that benefit from BITs have an incentive to make violations of BITs public. Reasons like these make commitments more credible and hence should lead to more FDI. Yet the most important reason, by far, that BITs make commitments more credible is that they have a mechanism that makes it easier "to bring costly pressure on governments if they do not carry through on those promises" (Büthe and Milner 2008, 746). This is the investor-state dispute settlement mechanism.

21. Note the difference between the first and the second arguments; this is due to the fact that the first argument refers to all investors, including those not covered by the BIT in question, whereas the second refers only to investors covered by the BIT.

22. Political stability reflects perceptions of the likelihood that the government will be destabilized or overthrown by unconstitutional or violent means, including politically motivated violence and terrorism.

23. Regulatory quality reflects perceptions of the ability of the government to formulate and implement sound policies and regulations that permit and promote private-sector development.

24. The rule of law reflects perceptions of the extent to which agents have confidence in and abide by the rules of society and, in particular, of the quality of contract enforcement, property rights, the police, and the courts as well as the likelihood of crime and violence.

25. See Stanley and Doucouliagos 2012, 61.

26. This is not an entirely theoretical issue: according to the Investment Arbitration Reporter (June 18, 2013), Spain has been sued under the Energy Charter Treaty for actions relating to cuts in the incentives it had offered investors in order to promote diffusion of renewable energy.

27. For example, Venezuela has no BIT with the United States; yet ExxonMobil was covered under the Venezuela-Netherlands BIT because it opened a post office box in The Hague. Many investors, regardless of their parent nationality, invest through a Dutch holding company and hence benefit from a BIT between the Netherlands and the respective host country. Therefore, a researcher is unlikely to know whether investments are covered or not.

REFERENCES

Aisbett, E. K. 2009. "Bilateral Investment Treaties and Foreign Direct Investment: Correlation Versus Causation." In *The Effect of Treaties on Foreign Direct Investment*, ed. K. P. Sauvant and L. E. Sachs, 395–435. Oxford, UK: Oxford University Press.

Barro, R. J. 1973. "The Control of Politicians: An Economic Model." *Public Choice* 14 (1): 19–42.

Belderbos, R., B. Leten, and S. Suzuki. 2013. "How Global Is R&D? Firm-Level Determinants of Home-Country Bias in R&D." *Journal of International Business Studies* 44: 765–86.

Bellak, C. 2015a. "Survey of the Impact of Bilateral Investment Agreements on Foreign Direct Investment." In *Current Issues in Asia Pacific Foreign Direct Investment*, 71–78. Melbourne: Australian APEC Study Centre, RMIT University. http://mams.rmit.edu.au/cwgz1keqt2r8.pdf.

——, C. 2015b. "Economic Impact of Investment Agreements." Department of Economics Working Paper Series, 200, WU Vienna University of Economics and Business, Vienna. https://ideas.repec.org/p/wiw/wiwwuw/wuwp200.html.

Blomström, M. 2002. "The Economics of International Investment Incentives." In *International Investment Perspectives*, ed. OECD, 165–83. Paris: Organisation for Economic Cooperation and Development.

Blomström, M., and A. Kokko. 1996. "The Impact of Foreign Investment on Host Countries: A Review of the Empirical Evidence." Stockholm School of Economics. Mimeo.

Botman, D., A. Klemm, and R. Baqir. 2008. "Investment Incentives and Effective Tax Rates in the Philippines: A Comparison with Neighboring Countries." IMF Working Paper 08–207, Washington, DC.

Busom, I., B. Corchuelo, and E. Martinez Ros. 2012. "Tax Incentives or Subsidies for R&D?" UNU-Merit Working Paper 2012–056, United Nations University–Maastricht Economic and Social Research Institute on Innovation and Technology, Maastricht, The Netherlands.

Busse, M., J. Königer, and P. Nunnenkamp. 2010. "FDI Promotion Through Bilateral Investment Treaties: More than a Bit?" *Review of World Economics* 146 (1): 147–77.

Büthe, T., and H. Milner. 2008. "The Politics of Foreign Direct Investment Into Developing Countries: Increasing FDI Through International Trade Agreements?" *American Journal of Political Science* 52 (4): 741–62.

——. 2009. "Bilateral Investment Treaties and Foreign Direct Investment: A Political Analysis." In *The Effect of Treaties on Foreign Direct Investment*, ed. K. P. Sauvant and L. E. Sachs, 171–224. Oxford, UK: Oxford University Press.

——. 2014. "Foreign Direct Investment and Institutional Diversity in Trade Agreements: Credibility, Commitment, and Economic Flows in the Developing World, 1971–2007." *World Politics* 66 (1): 88–122.

Cantwell, J., and R. Mudambi. 2000. "The Location of MNE R&D Activity: The Role of Investment Incentives." *Management International Review* 40 (1): 127–48.

Cardinal Intellectual Property. 2014. "The Patent Box." Cardinal IP, IP News & Strategy. http://www.cardinal-ip.com/ip-news-strategy/the-patent-box/, accessed December 28, 2015.

CCSI. 2015. "Investment Incentives: The Good, the Bad and the Ugly." *2013 Columbia International Investment Conference Report.* New York: Columbia Center on Sustainable Investment.

Chaisse, J. 2013. "Assessing the Exposure of Asian States to Investment Claims." *Contemporary Asia Arbitration Journal* 6 (2): 187–225.

Che, Y. K., and J. Sákovics. 2008. "Hold-Up Problem." In *The New Palgrave Dictionary of Economics Online Edition*, ed. S. N. Durlauf and L. E. Blume. Palgrave Macmillan, accessed May 27, 2014. http://www.dictionaryofeconomics.com/article?id=pde2008_H000171, accessed December 28, 2015.

Deloitte. 2014. "2014 Global Survey of R&D Tax Incentives." Amsterdam, The Netherlands.

Desbordes, R., and V. Vicard. 2009. "Foreign Direct Investment and Bilateral Investment Treaties: An International Political Perspective." *Journal of Comparative Economics* 37 (3): 372–86.

Devereux, M. P., Elschner, C., Endres, D., and C. Spengel. 2009. "Effective Tax Levels Using the Devereux/Griffith Methodology." TAXUD/2008/CC/099, Centre for European Economic Research, Mannheim, Germany.

Dunning, J. H. 2000. "The Eclectic Paradigm as an Envelope for Economic and Business Theories of MNE Activity." *International Business Review* 9 (2):163–90.

Egger, P. H., and V. Merlo. 2007. "The Impact of Bilateral Investment Treaties on FDI Dynamics." *World Economy* 30 (10): 1536–49.

European Commission. 2012. "Europe 2020 Targets: Research and Development." Brussels: European Commission.

Görg, H., and E. Strobl. 2007. "The Effect of R&D Subsidies on Private R&D." *Economica* 74 (4): 215–34.

Gravelle, H., and R. Rees. 2004. *Microeconomics.* 3rd ed. Essex, UK: Pearson Education.

Griffith, R. 2000. "How Important Is Business R&D for Economic Growth and Should Government Subsidizes It?" IFS Briefing Note 12, Institute for Fiscal Studies, London.

Gruber, J. 2013. *Public Finance and Public Policy.* 4th ed. New York: Worth.

Guimón, J. 2009. "Government Strategies to Attract R&D-Intensive FDI." *Journal of Technology Transfer* 34 (4): 364–79.

——. 2013. "National Policies to Attract R&D Intensive FDI in Developing Countries." Innovation Policy Platform Policy Brief, World Bank, Washington, DC.

Guzman, A. T. 1998. "Why LDCs Sign Treaties That Hurt Them: Explaining the Popularity of Bilateral Investment Treaties." *Virginia Journal of International Law* 38: 639–88.

Haftel, Y. Z. 2007. "The Effect of U.S. BITs on FDI Inflows to Developing Countries: Signaling or Credible Commitment?" Paper presented at the Annual Meeting of the Midwest Political Science Association, Chicago, April 12.

——. 2010. "Ratification Counts: US Investment Treaties and FDI Flows Into Developing Countries." *Review of International Political Economy* 17 (2): 348–77.

Havranek, T., and Z. Irsova. 2012. "Survey Article: Publication Bias in the Literature on Foreign Direct Investment Spillovers." *Journal of Development* Studies 48 (10): 1375–96.

Inman, R. P. 1987. "Markets, Governments, and the 'New' Political Economy." In *Handbook of Public Economics*, ed. A. J. Auerbach and M. Feldstein, 2: 647–777. Oxford: Elsevier.

James, S. 2013. "Tax and Non-tax Incentives and Investments: Evidence and Policy Implications." World Bank, Washington, DC.

Jandhyala, S., W. J. Henisz, and E. D. Mansfield. 2011. "Three Waves of BITs: The Global Diffusion of Foreign Investment Policy." *Journal of Conflict Resolution* 55 (6): 1047–73.

Jensen, N. M., and E. J. Malesky. 2010. "FDI Incentives Pay—Politically." Columbia FDI Perspectives on Topical Foreign Direct Investment Issues 26, Vale Columbia Center on Sustainable International Investment, New York.

Jensen, N. M., E. J. Malesky, M. Medina, and U. Ozdemir. 2010. "Pass the Bucks: Investment Incentives as Political Credit-Claiming Devices Evidence from a Survey Experiment." Prepared for presentation at the International Political Economy Society Annual Meeting, Harvard University, Cambridge, MA, November 15.

Kerner, A. 2009. "Why Should I Believe You? The Costs and Consequences of Bilateral Investment Treaties." *International Studies Quarterly* 53 (1): 73–102.

Kukenova, M., and J. A. Monteiro. 2008. "Does Lax Environmental Regulation Attract FDI When Accounting for Country Effects?" MPRA Paper 11321, University Library of Munich.

Kydland, F., and E. Prescott. 1977. "Rules Rather than Discretion: The Inconsistency of Optimal Plans." *Journal of Political Economy* 85: 473–90.

MIGA. "World Investment and Political Risk Report 2013." Washington, DC: Multilateral Investment Guarantee Agency.

Mohnen, P. 2013. "R&D Tax Incentives, European Commission, Innovation for Growth." I4G Policy Brief 25, I4G, Bristol, UK.

Musgrave, R. A. 1957. "A Multiple Theory of Budget Determination." *Finanzarchiv* 17 (3): 333–43.

Neumayer, E., and L. Spess. 2005. "Do Bilateral Investment Treaties Increase Foreign Direct Investment to Developing Countries?" *World Development* 33 (10): 1567–85.

OECD. 2010a. "Investing in Innovation—Firms Investing in R&D." In *Measuring Innovation: A New Perspective*, 76–77. Paris: Organisation for Economic Cooperation and Development.

——. 2010b. "R&D Tax Incentives: Rationale, Design, Evaluation." In *OECD Innovation Platform*. Paris: Organisation for Economic Cooperation and Development. www.oecd.org/innovation/policyplatform.

——. 2011. "Tax Incentives for Business R&D." In *OECD Science, Technology and Industry Scoreboard 2011*. Paris: Organisation for Economic Cooperation and Development. http://dx.doi.org/10.1787/sti_scoreboard-2011–48-en.

——. 2013. "R&D Tax Incentives." In *Science, Technology and Industry Scoreboard 2013: Innovation for Growth*. Paris: Organisation for Economic Cooperation and Development. http://dx.doi.org/10.1787/sti_scoreboard-2013–16-en.

——. 2014. "Science and Technology Outlook 2013." Paris: Organisation for Economic Cooperation and Development.

Peinhardt, C., and A. Todd. 2012. "Failure to Deliver: The Investment Effects of US Preferential Economic Agreements." *World Economy* 35: 757–783.

Pessoa, A. 2010. "R&D and Economic Growth: How Strong Is the Link?" *Economics Letters* 107 (2): 152–54.

Poulsen, L. N. S. 2011. "Sacrificing Sovereignty by Chance: Investment Treaties, Developing Countries, and Bounded Rationality, Thesis Submitted to the Department of International Relations of the London School of Economics and Political Science." London: London School of Economics and Political Science.

——. 2014. "Bounded Rationality and the Diffusion of Modern Investment Treaties." *International Studies Quarterly* 58 (1): 1–14.

Poulsen, L. N. S., and E. Aisbett. 2013. "When the Claim Hits: Bilateral Investment Treaties and Bounded Rational Learning." *World Politics* 65 (2): 273–313.

Poulsen, L. N. S., J. Bonnitcha, and J. W. Yackee. 2013. "Costs and Benefits of an EU-USA Investment Protection Treaty." LSE Enterprise, London.

Romer, P. 1990. "Endogenous Technological Change." *Journal of Political Economy* 98 (5): 71–102.

Royal Swedish Academy of Sciences. 2004. "Finn Kydland and Edward Prescott's Contribution to Dynamic Macroeconomics: The Time Consistency of Economic Policy and the Driving Forces Behind Business Cycles." Royal Swedish Academy of Sciences, Stockholm.

Sauvant, K. P., and L. E. Sachs. 2009. *The Effect of Treaties on Foreign Direct Investment*. Oxford, UK: Oxford University Press.

Sinn, H.-W. 2004. "The New Systems Competition." *Perspektiven der Wirtschaftspolitik* 5 (1): 23–38.

Stanley, T. D., and H. Doucouliagos. 2012. *Meta-regression Analysis in Economics and Business*. London: Routledge.

Stiglitz, J. 1989. "On the Economic Role of the State." In *The Economic Role of the State*, ed. A. Heertje., 11–85. Oxford, UK: Basil Blackwell.

Takalo, T., and T. Tanayama. 2010. "Adverse Selection and Financing of Innovation: Is There a Need for R&D Subsidies?" *Journal of Technology Transfer* 35 (1): 16–41.

Tanayama, T. 2012. "Overview of R&D Tax Incentives." In *Yearbook for Nordic Tax Research: Tax Expenditures*, ed. J. Bolander, 185–96. Copenhagen: DJOF.

Thomas, K. 2007. "Investment Incentives: Growing Use, Uncertain Benefits, Uneven Controls." Global Subsidies Initiative of the International Institute for Sustainable Development, Geneva.

Thursby, J., and M. Thursby. 2006. *Here or There? A Survey of Facts in Multinational R&D Location*. Washington, DC: National Academies Press.

Tobin, S., and J. Rose-Ackerman. 2005. "Foreign Direct Investment and the Business Environment in Developing Countries: The Impact of Bilateral Investment Treaties." Research Paper 293, Yale Law School, New Haven, CT.

——. 2011. "When BITs Have Some Bite: The Political-Economic Environment for Bilateral Investment Treaties." *Review of International Organizations* 6 (1): 1–32.

Tomz, M. 1997. "Do International Agreements Make Reforms More Credible? The Impact of NAFTA on Mexican Stock Prices." Harvard University, accessed May 24, 2014, http://www.stanford.edu/~tomz/working/credible.pdf.

Tortian, A. Z. 2007. "International Investment Agreements and Their Impact on Foreign Direct Investment: Evidence from Four Emerging Central European

Countries." Thèse pour le Doctorat en Sciences Economiques, Université Paris I, Panthéon-Sorbonne, Paris.

UNCTAD. 2005. *World Investment Report 2005: Transnational Corporations and the Internationalization of R&D*. New York: United Nations Conference on Trade and Development.

——. 2013. *World Investment Report 2013: Global Value Chains: Investment and Trade for Development*. New York: United Nations Conference for Trade and Development.

——. 2014. "Investor-State Dispute Settlement: An Information Note on the United States and the European Union." IIA Issues Note, Geneva.

Vernon, R. 1971. *Sovereignty at Bay: The Multinational Spread of U.S. Enterprises*. New York: Basic Books.

Wellhausen, R. L. 2013. "Innovation in Tow: R&D FDI and Investment Incentives." *Business and Politics* 5 (4): 467–91.

World Bank. 2014. "World Governance Indicators." World Bank, retrieved May 22, 2014, http://info.worldbank.org/governance/wgi/index.aspx#reports.

CHAPTER 5

Incentives in the European Union

Philippe Gugler

Both the European Union (EU) and its individual Member States deploy many strategies to strengthen the attractiveness of their business environment. Fostering investment and innovation is seen as a necessary step to increase competitiveness. Competition for investment occurs at the global level (OECD 2013; Guimón 2007) and between Member States within the EU (Oxelheim and Ghauri 2004). State incentives are among the numerous measures adopted by a country (or jurisdiction within it) to increase its attractiveness to investors. State aid is governed by a strong regulatory framework within the EU that is aimed at limiting destructive competition for investment. The "Treaty on the Functioning of the European Union" (TFEU; European Commission 2008) prohibits State aid but also creates some specific exemptions. This chapter illustrates the application of these rules by identifying and analyzing the incentives granted within the EU under those exemptions.

This chapter comprises seven sections. The first section presents a brief overview of the EU regulatory framework on State aid, the second describes the evolution of the EU policy on State aid, and the third identifies the main types of State aid granted within the EU. The fourth and fifth sections are dedicated to the two main types of State aid that are of particular importance within the scope of this book: aid for regional development and aid for research and development (R&D) and innovation, respectively. The sixth section focuses on the EU policy regarding tax incentives. The final section discusses the effectiveness of State aid regulation within the EU.

EU REGULATORY FRAMEWORK

The incentive policies of EU Member States are governed by the EU's law and policy on State aid. According to the EU, "State aid is defined as an advantage in any form whatsoever conferred on a selective basis to undertakings by national public authorities" (AEA 2012, 1). The regulatory framework on State aid is based on a complex package of treaty provisions, communications, and guidelines (table 5.1).

The core provisions on State aid are contained in Articles 107, 108, and 109 of the TFEU (reproduced in the appendix to this chapter). Article 107(1) prohibits "any aid granted by a Member State or through State resources in any form whatsoever which distorts or threatens to distort competition by favouring certain undertakings or the production of certain goods . . . in so far as it affects trade between Member States." Article 107 then stipulates exemptions to this prohibition according to two categories of aid: Article 107(2), aid that is considered "compatible with the internal market," and Article 107(3), aid that "may be considered as compatible with the internal market." Aid that is considered compatible includes measures responding to social concerns or to exceptional events, such as natural disasters, as well as aid granted in some areas of Germany as a result of the former division of the country. Aid that "may be considered as compatible" encompasses different types of measures related to economic development, the adoption of important projects within the EU, the facilitation of certain economic activities, and the promotion of culture, among other types of measures.

Article 108 covers the procedural mechanisms regarding the EU policy on State aid, and Article 109 empowers the European Council to "make any appropriate regulations for the application of Articles 107 and 108 and . . . determine the conditions in which Article 108(3) shall apply and the categories of aid exempted from this procedure."[1]

Since the end of the 1990s, State aid procedures have been simplified (European Commission 2007). One of the major steps was achieved in 1998 with the adoption of the "General Block Exemption Regulation" (GBER; European Commission 1998a, 1–4), the provisions of which were amended in 2013 (European Commission 2013d, 11). According to the GBER, the European Commission (EC) may decide to consider the following categories of aid to be compatible with the treaty (with no prior

Table 5.1 EU regulatory framework on State aid: Main regulations

Regulation	Main content
Art. 107 para. 1 TFEU	Prohibits State aid that "distorts or threatens to distort competition by favouring certain undertakings or the production of certain goods . . . in so far as it affects trade between Member States."
Art. 107 para. 2 TFEU	Lists the types of State aid that "shall be compatible with the internal market": 1. "Aid having a social character, granted to individual consumers, provided that such aid is granted without discrimination related to the origin of the products concerned" 2. "Aid to make good the damage caused by natural disasters or exceptional occurrences" 3. "Aid granted to the economy of certain areas of the Federal Republic of Germany affected by the division of Germany, in so far as such aid is required in order to compensate for the economic disadvantages caused by that division. Five years after the entry into force of the Treaty of Lisbon, the Council, acting on a proposal from the Commission, may adopt a decision repealing this point"
Art. 107 para. 3 TFEU	Lists the types of State aid that "may be considered to be compatible with the internal market" (the European Commission has discretionary power to decide which aid may be considered as compatible): 1. "Aid to promote the economic development of areas where the standard of living is abnormally low or where there is serious underemployment, and of the regions referred to in Article 349, in view of their structural, economic and social situation" 2. "Aid to promote the execution of an important project of common European interest or to remedy a serious disturbance in the economy of a Member State" 3. "Aid to facilitate the development of certain economic activities or of certain economic areas, where such aid does not adversely affect trading conditions to an extent contrary to the common interest" 4. "Aid to promote culture and heritage conservation where such aid does not affect trading conditions and competition in the Union to an extent that is contrary to the common interest" 5. "Such other categories of aid as may be specified by decision of the Council on a proposal from the Commission"
Art. 108 TFEU	Provides procedures regarding the EU policy on State aid.
Art. 109 TFEU	Empowers the European Council to "make any appropriate regulations for the application of Articles 107 and 108 and . . . in particular determine the conditions in which Article 108(3) shall apply and the categories of aid exempted from this procedure."
General Block Exemption Regulation	Exempts (with no prior notification necessary) certain categories of State aid regarding SMEs, R&D, innovation, environmental protection, employment and training, culture, natural disaster, some types of infrastructure, transport in some regions, and agriculture, fisheries and forestry issues.
De Minimis Regulation	Exempts (with no prior notification necessary) State aid under a certain threshold (200,000 euros) over a three-year period and provides several simplification procedures—in particular, those regarding SMEs.

Sources: http://eur-lex.europa.eu/LexUriServ/LexUriServ.do?uri=OJ:C:2008:115:0047:0199:en:PDF; European Commission 1998a, 1–4; 2006a; 2013d, 11.

notification necessary): measures in favor of small and medium-sized enterprises (SMEs), R&D, environmental protection, employment, and training (Article 1 of Council Regulation 994/98 of May 7, 1998). The GBER amendments adopted in 2013 introduce new categories of aid, including measures in favor of "innovation, culture, natural disasters, sport, certain broadband infrastructure, other infrastructure, social aid for transport to remote regions and aid for certain agriculture, forestry and fisheries issues."[2]

According to the EC: "In the future, 3/4 of today's aid measures and about 2/3 of total aid amounts granted by Member States could be covered by the new GBER. This could even extend to up to 90% of all aid measures, if Member States use the GBER to the full extent by designing their measures in order to fit its requirements" (European Commission 2014). Thus, the Commission will scrutinize "ex ante" only aids with a significant potential to harm competition. These latter will have to be notified (European Commission 2014).

Furthermore, the EC has introduced a de minimis regulation, easing rules on grants of State aid under a certain threshold (Article 2). The de minimis regulation has been revised several times. The 2006 revision increased the threshold from 100,000 euros to 200,000 euros per undertaking over a period of three years.[3] However, the threshold of 200,000 euros was maintained in the 2013 revision (European Commission 2013e). These revisions also simplified procedures and introduced the possibility that aid to firms confronting financial difficulties might fall under the de minimis scope.[4] It must be noted that the concept of firms confronting financial difficulties is rather vague and not clearly defined.

EVOLUTION OF THE EU POLICY ON STATE AID

In 2005, the EC adopted the "State Aid Action Plan" (SAAP), which reflected a new economic approach—called a "strengthening economic approach"—regarding State aid policy (European Commission 2005). As highlighted by Heimler and Jenny (2012), rather than focusing on new economic tools dedicated to the distortion of competition created by State aid, the document focuses on the beneficial aspect of State aid in case of market failures: "the strengthening economic approach should only help the Commission in its exemption capacity" (356). The EC applies the so-called "balancing test." This test examines the goals of the aid as well as whether the project is an appropriate means by which to achieve the goals and whether other measures that may be less harmful to competition could achieve the same goals. The test also considers the expected results of the aid in terms of positive effects on the aid's targets and negative effects on competition (OECD 2010a, 21). As observed by the OECD (2010), "State aid control in the European Union has progressively shifted from a purely legalistic approach towards an effects approach" (23). This approach reflects a new policy orientation toward more flexibility and openness regarding State aid that may contribute, according to the EC, to achieving important goals regarding economic growth, competitiveness, innovation capabilities, and regional development.

A major example of this new orientation is the modernization of the EU State aid regulation that has been adopted in view of the "Europe 2020 Strategy", as stated in a 2010 communication (European Commission 2010b). This strategy promotes "three mutually reinforcing priorities": "smart growth," "sustainable growth," and "inclusive growth" (5). This communication indicates that "State aid policy can also actively and positively contribute to the Europe 2020 objectives by promoting and supporting initiatives for more innovative, efficient and greener technologies, while facilitating access to public support for investment, risk capital and funding for research and development" (21). Among the measures foreseen at the EU level (EC level) and at the Member State level, the communication identifies many types of support measures implying State aid. For example, in the field of measures to promote innovation, the communication mentions measures to be taken at the Member State level "to prioritise knowledge expenditure, including by using tax incentives and other financial instruments to promote greater private R&D investments" (13). Regarding the promotion of industrial policy measures, the communication recommends promoting "the restructuring of sectors in difficulty towards future oriented activities, including through quick redeployment of skills to emerging high growth sectors and markets and support from the EU's State aids regime and/or the Globalisation Adjustment Fund" (17). The 2012 Communication on "EU State Aid Modernisation" (SAM) clearly indicates a policy change toward facilitation of the Europe 2020 Strategy, ensuring "that public support stimulates innovation, green technologies, human capital development, avoids environmental harm and ultimately promotes growth, employment and EU competitiveness. Such aid will best contribute to growth when it targets a market failure and thereby complements, not replaces, private spending" (European Commission 2012a, 4).

TYPES OF STATE AID IN THE EU

Figure 5.1 presents the volume of State aid registered in the EU in 2012, and figure 5.2 indicates the types of measures used. State aid is divided into two categories: "non-crisis-related State aid" and "crisis-related State aid." The first category comprises "horizontal aids" and "sectoral aids" and encompasses, inter alia, "tax reduction", "equity participation", and "soft loans." The main subsidies granted in the context of "crisis-related State aid" are "recapitalization measures, guarantees, asset relief intervention, and liquidity measures other than guarantees" (European Commission 2012c). Most of the non-crisis-related aid is concentrated in industry and services, and the main measures are grants and tax reductions (table 5.2). We observe an overall decline in the amount of non-crisis-related aid within the EU over the period 1992–2011 (figure 5.3). As highlighted by table 5.3, we see the same trend with respect to the total

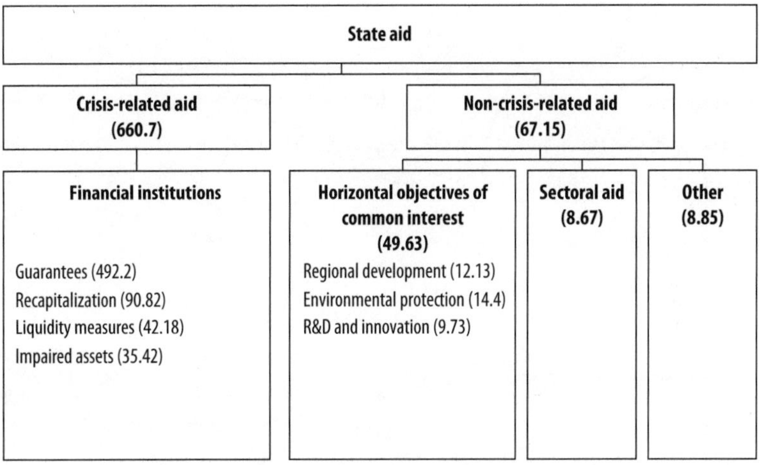

Figure 5.1 State aid in the EU, 2012 (Billions of euros).

Source: State Aid Scoreboard, http://ec.europa.eu/competition/state_aid/scoreboard/non_crisis_en.html.

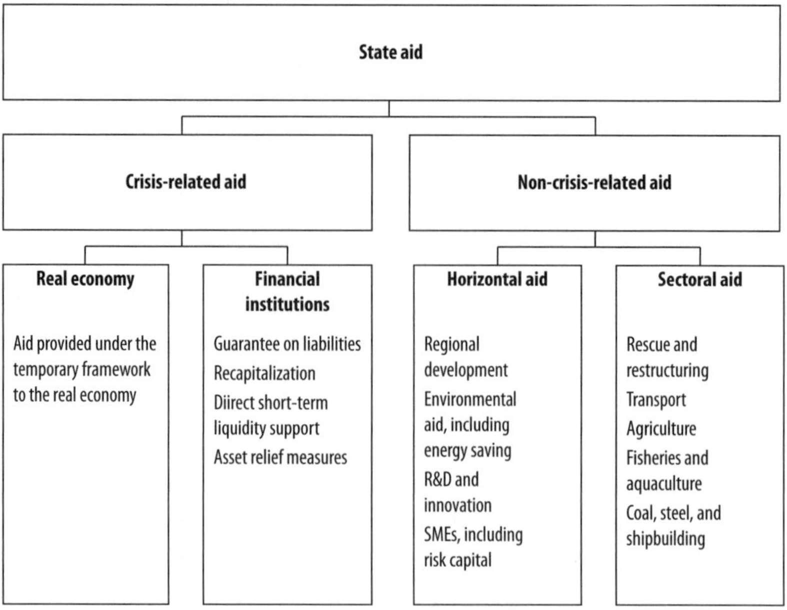

Figure 5.2 Types of State aid in the EU.

Source: Adapted from http://ec.europa.eu/competition/state_aid/scoreboard/index_en.html; http://ec.europa.eu/competition/state_aid/scoreboard/financial_economic_crisis_aid_en.html.

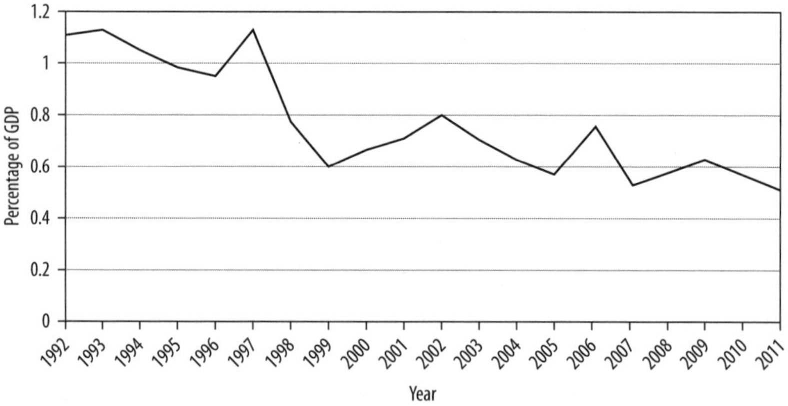

Figure 5.3 Total non-crisis-related State aid (less railway) (EU-27), 1992–2011 (% of GDP).

Source: http://ec.europa.eu/competition/state_aid/studies_reports/expenditure.html#5.

Table 5.2 Non-crisis-related aid to industry and services by aid instrument and by Member State, 2009–2011 (Annual average in millions of euros)

	Grants	Tax reduction (includes tax deferral)	Equity participation	Soft loans	Guarantees
EU-27	32,393	23,903	602	1,895	1,255
Belgium	981	625	9	61	1
Bulgaria	18	7	0	0	0
Czech Republic	753	113	0	6	100
Denmark	1,139	60	6	9	1
Germany	8,245	5,289	29	201	76
Estonia	13	3	0	0	0
Ireland	325	439	2	30	0
Greece	825	117	0	0	1,013
Spain	2,498	984	0	740	7
France	4,971	6,458	14	328	14
Italy	3,147	383	20	226	11
Cyprus	84	2	0	0	0
Latvia	36	15	1	1	0
Lithuania	95	13	1	0	0
Luxembourg	90	0	0	1	0
Hungary	803	488	1	24	5
Malta	38	98	0	0	0
Netherlands	1,461	315	6	18	10
Austria	1,407	222	2	54	12
Poland	1,777	747	17	38	1
Portugal	190	2,603	14	19	0
Romania	219	2	4	3	0
Slovenia	308	6	1	2	0
Slovakia	115	106	0	0	0
Finland	550	294	19	34	3
Sweden	442	2,356	2	5	0
United Kingdom	1,863	2,157	452	96	1

Source: http://ec.europa.eu/competition/state_aid/studies_reports/expenditure.html#3 (Accessed March 15, 2014).

amount of non-crisis-related aid as a percentage of GDP over the period 2001–2011. The main part of non-crisis-related State aid comes from aid granted for horizontal objectives of common interest—and particularly for regional development, R&D and innovation, and environmental protection. Regarding the geographical distribution of non-crisis-related State aid, the main grant providers were France and Germany (together constituting 40 percent of the total amount). Six countries together registered 60 percent of the total amount (France, Germany, Italy, United

Table 5.3 Non-crisis State aid to industry and services, 2001–2011 (% of GDP)

	2001	2002	2003	2004	2005	2006	2007	2008	2009	2010	2011
EU-27	0.55	0.63	0.59	0.49	0.45	0.46	0.41	0.47	0.51	0.48	0.42
Belgium	0.32	0.36	0.24	0.24	0.25	0.29	0.32	0.35	0.51	0.54	0.34
Bulgaria	n.a.	0.45	0.56	0.25	0.11	0.12	0.09	0.04	0.08	0.04	0.05
Czech Republic	1.85	3.79	2.74	0.35	0.44	0.54	0.6	0.73	0.51	0.64	0.76
Denmark	0.77	0.71	0.6	0.7	0.67	0.63	0.67	0.69	0.88	0.31	0.35
Germany	0.85	1.18	0.86	0.71	0.7	0.72	0.57	0.6	0.62	0.57	0.48
Estonia	0.12	0.13	0.08	0.09	0.13	0.08	0.06	0.09	0.07	0.1	0.11
Ireland	0.51	0.43	0.29	0.29	0.39	0.44	0.39	0.49	0.48	0.6	0.43
Greece	0.43	0.22	0.19	0.22	0.2	0.21	0.27	0.56	0.76	0.77	1.01
Spain	1.1	0.73	0.62	0.52	0.52	0.38	0.37	0.42	0.44	0.39	0.35
France	0.34	0.39	0.34	0.42	0.42	0.41	0.41	0.55	0.63	0.64	0.52
Italy	0.41	0.43	0.4	0.34	0.36	0.38	0.26	0.28	0.3	0.19	0.18
Cyprus	2.45	2.68	2.1	1.05	1	0.49	0.4	0.46	0.38	0.52	0.54
Latvia	0.41	0.22	0.27	0.15	0.19	0.16	1.4	0.2	0.12	0.41	0.29
Lithuania	0.16	0.41	0.32	0.15	0.14	0.21	0.16	0.15	0.3	0.3	0.4
Luxembourg	0.16	0.24	0.23	0.15	0.14	0.14	0.13	0.14	0.26	0.19	0.19
Hungary	1.01	1.05	1.16	0.87	1.16	1.1	0.96	1.86	1.41	1.74	0.86
Malta	4.22	4.38	2.1	3.34	3.14	2.4	2.01	1.71	1.61	1.14	1.43
Netherlands	0.16	0.23	0.22	0.22	0.24	0.28	0.24	0.25	0.3	0.32	0.3
Austria	0.3	0.28	0.42	0.4	0.39	0.7	0.36	0.48	0.58	0.63	0.5
Poland	0.63	0.44	2.98	1.05	0.39	0.46	0.42	0.71	0.72	0.74	0.58
Portugal	2.18	2.02	2.15	1.34	0.86	0.87	1.26	0.91	0.96	0.87	1.02
Romania	n.a.	1.83	2.22	2.56	0.52	0.63	0.24	0.19	0.14	0.15	0.21
Slovenia	0.83	0.47	0.59	0.51	0.45	0.47	0.35	0.46	0.79	0.78	0.91
Slovakia	0.35	0.3	0.39	0.48	0.5	0.37	0.37	0.44	0.36	0.37	0.23
Finland	0.27	0.29	0.36	0.36	0.36	0.37	0.34	0.42	0.47	0.44	0.56
Sweden	0.21	0.2	0.39	0.78	0.88	0.87	0.83	0.81	0.8	0.75	0.72
United Kingdom	0.16	0.2	0.18	0.21	0.19	0.18	0.23	0.22	0.27	0.28	0.24

Sources: http://ec.europa.eu/competition/state_aid/studies_reports/expenditure.html#5; http://epp.eurostat.ec.europa.eu/tgm_comp/table.do?tab=table&plugin=1&language=en&pcode=comp_ncr_12.

https://open-data.europa.eu/fr/data/dataset/UEYFD8fgvaXP5irAcOsWQ/resource/8b3724a8-dc6e-4339-b50e-1d5ce2745b0e

Note: n.a. = data not available.

Kingdom, Spain, and Sweden).[5] As far as tax reductions are concerned, France and Germany granted together almost half of the tax reductions registered over the period 2009–2011 (table 5.2). Non-crisis-related aid has decreased over the period 2006–2011 (figure 5.4)

As illustrated in table 5.4, crisis-related State aid has decreased significantly since 2009: from 27.6 percent of GDP in 2008, it dropped to 4.6 percent in 2009, 3.1 percent in 2010, and 2.2 percent in 2011, whereas it increased in 2012 (3.4% of GDP)

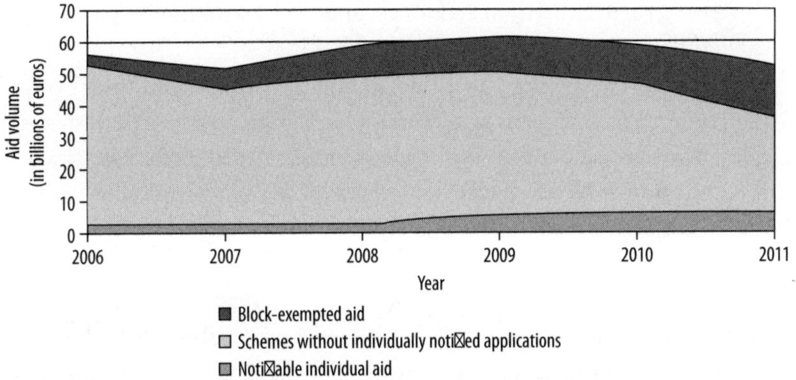

Figure 5.4 Trends in the types of non-crisis-related aid measure used (EU-27), 2006–2011 (Billions of euros).

Source: http://ec.europa.eu/competition/state_aid/studies_reports/expenditure.html#5.

REGIONAL STATE AID

The EC considers regional State aid as a specific category of horizontal aid (i.e., aid that is not sector specific and is aimed at achieving objectives of common interest in the EU): "The objective of geographical development distinguishes regional aid from other forms of aid, such as aid for research, development and innovation, employment, training, energy or for environmental protection, which pursue other objectives of common interest in accordance with Article 107(3) of the Treaty" (European Commission 2013a, 1). Member States may grant regional State aid in accordance with the provisions of Article 107(3a) or 107(3c) of the TFEU:

- Article 107(3a) states that "aid to promote the economic development of areas where the standard of living is abnormally low or where there is serious underemployment, and of the regions referred to in article 349,[6]

Table 5.4 Financial crisis–related aid (EU-27): Approved amount, 2008–1/10/2012 (Billions of euros)

Period	Amount	As % of
2008	3457.49	27.6% as of 2008 GDP
2009	541.66	4.6% as of 2009 GDP
2010	383.55	3.1% as of 2010 GDP
2011	273.70	2.2% as of 2011 GDP
2012	429.54	3.4% of 2011 GDP
2008-30/09/2012	5085.95	40.3% of 2011 GDP

Source: Adapted from http://ec.europa.eu/competition/state_aid/studies_reports/expenditure.html#.

in view of their structural, economic and social situation" "may be considered to be compatible with the internal market."

- Article 107(3c) stipulates that "aid to facilitate the development of certain economic activities or of certain economic areas, where such aid does not adversely affect trading conditions to an extent contrary to the common interest" "may be considered to be compatible with the internal market."

The EC defines the criteria and conditions used to assess whether a specific form of aid "may be considered compatible with the internal market." Regarding regional State aid, these conditions are stated in the GBER, the "Regional Aid Guidelines" (RAG), and the 2009 "Communication Concerning the Criteria for an In-Depth Assessment of Regional Aid to Large Investment Projects" (European Commission 2009a, 2013b, 7). A Member State may grant aid without any prior notification to the EC if the aid fulfills the conditions stated in the GBER. In other situations, a Member State must notify the EC of its intent to grant specific aid. In those cases, the EC assesses the compatibility of such grants according to the provisions established in the RAG and—if the aid project relates to large investments—in the 2009 communication mentioned above (European Commission 2013b, 7).

As a general principle, the EC stipulates that "regional aid can only be found compatible with the internal market, if it has an incentive effect." According to the EC, an incentive effect is observed if (1) the recipient firm engages in additional tasks that contribute to the economic development of the region and (2) the recipient firm would not have been engaged in this additional activity without the aid (European Commission 2013b, 14).

The RAG is periodically reviewed by the EC to modify, withdraw, or add new rules. The current guidelines are valid for the 2014–2020 period and replaced the guidelines adopted for the 2007–2013 period. Sectors are excluded from these guidelines where the EC has adopted sector-specific State aid guidelines (e.g., aid granted to airports or to the energy sector) (European Commission 2013b, 3).

With regard to the assessment of the application of the RAG for the 2007–2013 period, Ramboll and Matrix (2012, 2) confirm that to obtain approval by the EC, regional aid should comply with several criteria: the aid needs to be targeted to the objectives; to be proportionate to the issue; and to create positive impacts outweighing the potential negative ones.

The RAG sets, inter alia, ceilings on regional State aid to prevent Member States from entering into competition with one another and creating competition distortions (Ramboll and Matrix 2012, 1).

STATE AID FOR R&D AND INNOVATION

The promotion of R&D and innovation is an important objective of the "common interest" of the EU (European Commission 2006b, 4), and, therefore, aid for that purpose is another type of horizontal State aid that may be permitted under EU law. Article 163 of the EC Treaty states the following: "The Community shall have the objective of strengthening the scientific and technological bases of Community industry and encouraging it to become more competitive at [*sic*] international level while promoting all the research activities deemed necessary."

The 2006 Communication on the "Community Framework for State Aid for Research and Development and Innovation" stipulates that "the objective is through State aid to enhance economic efficiency and thereby, contribute to sustainable growth and jobs" (European Commission 2006b, 4). State aid promoting R&D and innovation may be granted according to the exemption provisions established in Articles 107(3b) and 107(3c). State aid granted to individual firms does not enter into the field of the GBER. In a case in which State aid for R&D is proposed for an individual firm, the EC applies a balancing test to decide if this aid is permitted or forbidden. The communication of 2006 indicates that "for a block exemption regulation, the State aid is compatible if the conditions laid down are fulfilled. . . . However, for the individual aid measures which may have a high distortive potential due to high aid amounts, the Commission will make an overall assessment of the positive and negative effects of the aid based on the proportionality principles" (5). Several types of aid measures for R&D and innovation have been identified as compatible with Article 107(3c):

- "aid for projects covering fundamental and industrial research and experimental development"
- "aid for technical feasibility studies"
- "aid for industrial property rights costs for SMEs"
- "aid for young innovative enterprises"
- "aid for process and organisational innovation in services"
- "aid for advisory services and innovation support services"

Table 5.5 Maximum aid allowed for R&D projects

	Small enterprise	Medium-sized enterprise	Large enterprise
Aid for R&D Projects			
Fundamental research	100%	100%	100%
Industrial research	70%	60%	50%
• Subject to collaboration between undertakings (for large undertakings, cross-border or with at least one SME) or between an undertaking and a research organization; or • Subject to dissemination of results	80%	75%	65%
Experimental development	45%	35%	25%
• Subject to collaboration between undertakings (for large undertakings, cross-border or with at least one SME) or between an undertaking and a research organization; or • Subject to dissemination of results	60%	50%	40%
Aid for Feasibility Studies	50%	50%	50%
Aid for Construction and Upgrade of Research Infrastructures	50%	50%	50%
Innovation Aid for SMEs	50%	50%	—
Aid for Process and Organizational Innovation	50%	50%	15%
Aid for Innovation Clusters			
Investment aid	50%	50%	50%
Operating aid	50%	50%	50%

Source: European Commission 2013f, 36.

- "aid for the loan of highly qualified personnel"
- "aid for innovation clusters"

The aid measures granted for R&D projects are considered compatible with the provisions of Article 107(3) if they comply with several conditions and are under the thresholds (set as percentages of net costs) stipulated according to the different types of activities that benefit from incentives (table 5.5).

TAX INCENTIVES

Data on State aid granted within the EU demonstrate that most non-crisis-related aid is channeled into the area of industry and services and that tax incentives are among the main measures adopted by the Member States (see figure 5.2). State aid in the form of tax incentives is one of the main instruments adopted by countries to attract new investment, particularly foreign investment (European Commission 2010a). This is not particular to EU countries (WEF 2013). Most countries, such as the United States, adopt tax incentives to attract foreign investment. Not all such fiscal incentive measures fall within the EU framework of State aid. According to Hey (2002, 8), "Art. 107, para. 1 of the EC Treaty is not sufficient to tackle all manifestations of unfair tax competition. The measure has to be specific in terms of offering preferential treatment only to enterprises in certain industrial sectors or regions. Tax incentives offered to foreign investors in general hardly fulfil the selective criteria." Each Member State does apply its own fiscal policy (fiscal sovereignty). The EC is of the view that there is no room to foresee tax harmonization within the EU. This creates a *marge de manoeuvre* for EU Member States. The line between measures understood as State aid according to Article 107 of TFEU and those that do not fall within this article is unclear. There is no "one size fits all" policy on this matter. The jurisprudence regarding each individual case that has been challenged indicates the circumstances under which a tax incentive may be permitted or not. It must be noted that Member States often have not disclosed in detail tax incentives that may have been granted to specific firms. The final deals are the result of bargaining between the authorities and the potential investors.

However, the distinction between State aid and general measures provides some criteria with which to determine whether a tax incentive should be classified as State aid. According to the EC, "tax measures of a purely technical nature" and measures "pursuing general economic interest" are not considered as State aid, "provided that they apply without distinction to all firms and to the production of all goods" (European Commission 1998c, para. 13).

When competing to offer the best locational advantages to new investments, Member States may entice potential investors with attractive tax conditions and enter into a competitive race for foreign direct investment (FDI). The EC adopted a 2009 Communication on Promoting Good Governance in Tax Matters (European Commission 2009b). The main aim of the communication is to improve good governance within the EU and to promote international co-ordination of practices within the EU as well as within other fora (e.g., the UN and the OECD).

The Council of Economics and Finance Ministers (ECOFIN) adopted a "code of conduct for business taxation" in 1997 (ECOFIN 1997). The document identifies sixty-six tax incentives considered "harmful tax competition" (Schön 2003, 10). It also addresses, inter alia, tax advantages granted to nonresident investors. However, the code of conduct is not a legally binding document. As underlined by Hey (2002, 6), "There are no legally enforceable means to deter other Member States from offering tax privileges other than the State aid provisions of the EC-Treaty." It is common for countries to negotiate with multinational enterprises on tax issues ("Brussels Probes Multinationals' Tax Deals" 2013). Furthermore, with respect to tax avoidance practices, the potential benefit to some MNEs from having a location in Europe may also be considered an incentive to invest in the European countries where such practices are tolerated. Recent cases such as Apple in Ireland and Starbucks in the United Kingdom have raised concerns within the EC.

THE EFFECTIVENESS OF EU POLICY REGARDING INCENTIVES

Although the EU does have a specific regulatory framework designed to prevent certain types of State aid, the exemption regime may apply to a wide range of new investments as long as the State aid measure's potential negative effects on competition are compensated for by positive spillovers in the host countries according to the objectives specified in the regulatory framework on State aid. The analysis of the EC policy on State aid applied thus far highlights important features characterizing the types of investments that may benefit from State aid within the EU. A specific issue is the distinction between "variable cost aid (VCA)" and "fixed cost aid (FCA)" (Marinello 2013, 273). An example of FCA is aid that is granted to a start-up to lower its entry costs. The EC considers FCA to be less distortive than VCA (273). This approach is clearly reflected in the case of Ryanair–Charleroi (Official Journal of the EU 2004 L137/1, February 12, 2004, cited in Marinello 2013, 274). Charleroi Airport, a publicly controlled entity, granted some benefits to Ryanair with the aim of developing new routes to Charleroi. According to the EC, some of the subsidies were considered compatible with the EU's State aid regime because they were related to the opening of new routes and to the development of the depressed Charleroi region. However, the EC decided that the subsidies granted to reduce Ryanair's variable costs (for example, low borrowing rates) were not compatible with EU rules and therefore needed to be returned (274). This case highlights the general approach of the

EC in determining whether aid granted for initial investment may be considered compatible, whereas aid granted to decrease the operating costs of enterprises is prohibited (275).

State aid cases require analysis on a case-by-case basis. It is therefore difficult to draw general conclusions regarding the EC's policy enforcement in this matter. However, it is interesting to note—compared to the past practice—the more frequent use of some economic tools to review specific cases. Indeed, the EC's competition policy—including its State aid policy—is increasingly adopting a so-called "more economic-based approach." The EC relies on economic tools to balance the negative impact of a specific aid on competition against its positive effects (e.g., a positive contribution to support a common objective project). This type of assessment is based on the "effects approach" and the "balancing approach" (Frideriszick, Röller, and Verouden 2008, 648–649). More specifically, three economic tests are applied to assess whether a measure is compatible under State aid rules: the "private investment test," the "private creditor test," and the "net additional cost test" (EEMC 2014).

The "private investment test" applies when the government is acting as an economic actor, as opposed to a public authority exercising its regulatory powers. It asks whether a measure generates a rate of return for the government that is at least equal to the income that would have been demanded by a private company for the same investment. If the test is positive, the State measure is not unlawful. This test has been applied in several cases, including, in particular, those involving the airlines sector. The first case employing this test in the airlines sector is the above-mentioned case of Ryanair at Charleroi Airport in Belgium, in which the EC declared that two agreements—one between Ryanair and Brussels South Charleroi Airport (BSCA) and the other between Ryanair and the Walloon Region—were unlawful (European Commission 2004b). According to the EC, the private investment test applied to test the legitimacy of the BSCA's actions but did not apply to the Walloon Region because the latter was acting in its regulatory capacity when, inter alia, indemnifying Ryanair for losses suffered as a result of future changes in certain government regulations. The decision was challenged and nullified in a decision of the Court of First Instance of the European Communities (Ryanair v. Commission, Case T-196/04). In that decision, the court determined that the EC should have applied the private investment test to the actions of both the Walloon Region and the BSCA.

The "private creditor test" was used in several cases, again including the airlines sector. In a decision regarding State aid to Olympic Airways (European Commission 2002), the EC indicated inter alia that to be considered as a State aid, "The payment facilities accorded must also be clearly greater than those which would have been accorded by a private creditor in a comparable situation in regard to his debtor (. . .)."[7]

The "net additional cost test" is applied in the assessment of measures taken for "services of general economic interest" (SGEI; e.g., postal services, energy supply, telecommunications, public transport, and social services). Its aim is to scrutinize the "compensation" granted to the supplier of SGEI to determine if it is reasonable or excessive: "the compensation must not exceed what is necessary for the undertaking to perform the service—allowing for a reasonable profit" (BIS 2011, 49). For example, in a case regarding Radiotelevisione Italiana (RAI) in Italy, the EC concluded that the government support of the public broadcasting company was not excessive and therefore was not unlawful. The decision is supported by a deep econometrical analysis (European Commission 2004a).

The ability of Member States to grant incentives to undertakings is governed by the TFEU provisions on State aid. The goals and interests of individual Member States are not always consistent with the "orthodoxy" of the EC in this respect (Collie 2000). It is outside the scope of this chapter to compare the EU regulatory framework with the different rules on State aid worldwide. However, it is important to address several points. According to the EC, in comparison to other jurisdictions, the "EU State aid rules offer a more transparent, coherent and growth-oriented framework, while allowing comparable levels of aid" (European Commission 2012a, 5). The EC supports its statement by referring to a WTO study (WTO 2006) that "suggests that the level of aid granted by EU Member States is comparable to the levels granted by the EU's main trading partners (subsidies as a percentage of GDP)" (European Commission 2012a, 5).

The EU regulatory framework on State aid differs from the WTO provisions on subsidies with respect to the mechanisms, definition, and objectives that they pursue (Luengo Hernandez de Madrid 2008; Heimler and Jenny 2012). The EU mechanisms are applied ex ante and ex post, whereas the WTO rules are applied only ex post (OECD 2010, 9). The EU regulatory framework states that a Member State must declare when any project is to receive State aid—except when the State aid is covered by a block exemption or granted pursuant to a preapproved aid scheme—and must wait for EC approval to grant this aid. The EC also controls and reviews existing aid (ex post procedures). The WTO regulations include some requirements on disclosure but foresee only ex post procedures that allow a Member State to contest the aid granted by another Member State (WTO 2006).

The EU framework on State aid and the WTO agreements on subsidies are not based on the same definitions (Luengo Hernandez de Madrid 2008, 3–6). One of the main differences is the WTO agreements' stipulation that "subsidies are prohibited only when they directly aim at distorting international trade as strictly defined" (Heimler and Jenny 2012, 362). In contrast, the EU scope refers only to trade between Member States. In other words, aid that does not affect trade within the internal market but distorts competition worldwide can be accepted by the EC but could be challenged at the WTO level. A famous example is the Airbus case. The EC's Aerospatiale decision (European Commission 1998b) determined that aid granted by France to Aerospatiale for Airbus was not covered by Article 107(1) of the TFEU because that aid "did not affect trade between the EC Member States" (Luengo Hernandez de Madrid 2008, 18). In the WAM case (Court of First Instance 2006), the Court of Justice annulled a prohibition decision of the EC for the following reason: "The mere observation that WAM participates in intra-community trade is insufficient to conclude on trade affectation or distortion of competition, and an in-depth analysis of the effects of aids is necessary" (cited by OECD 2010, 22).

Article 107(3) stipulates a large but not exhaustive list of exemptions. This provision gives room for the EC to grant exemptions for other types of aid (Heimler and Jenny 2012, 354). Furthermore, within the framework of the economic and social policy of the EC and of the Member States, some aid may be permitted, as indicated above, if its positive effects on the different objectives pursued can compensate for the distorting effect on competition (Luengo Hernandez de Madrid 2008, 19–20; Friederiszick, Röller, and Verouden 2008, 625–627). Therefore, the criterion for ultimately accepting incentives granted to firms by Member States is quite "elastic."

Heimler and Jenny (2012, 351) note that "Europe is one of the few jurisdictions in the world that has introduced binding provisions regulating State aid." We must recognize that the EU's detailed data on State aid (European Commission 2012b) reflect a strong willingness to ensure transparency. However, despite the notification procedures and data publication, we observe that the data do not capture all incentives provided by Member States or all incentives granted by the EU's institutions. We can also argue that EU regulations allow a *marge de manoeuvre* to the EC and to the Member States in granting aid to companies. The exemption regime established, inter alia, in paragraphs 2 and 3 of Article 107 and in the GBER provides discretionary power to the EC to permit aid to companies. As reported in table 5.4, for example, crisis-related State aid granted over the period January 1, 2008–September 30, 2012, was significant, representing 40.3 percent of the EU GDP registered in 2011. However, since 2008, the largest amount of crisis-related aid was granted in 2009, representing 4.6 percent of the 2009 GDP. The application modalities, such as the "balance test," also allow some discretion for accepting aid and "closing one's eyes" when it appears that an incentive would be necessary for policy reasons. According to an econometric study (Aydin 2007) quoted by the OECD, the propensity to grant horizontal or sectorial incentives may depend on the political system of each Member State: "the more a country's political system makes the provision of targeted aid politically profitable (e.g., in countries with small electoral constituencies, little ideological distance between parties, and little party unity), the greater the share of aid to firms that is indeed targeted ('sectorial', in EU parlance), as opposed to 'horizontal'. This suggests that the provision of support to specific sectors may be based, to some extent, on electoral considerations—despite strict control by the European Commission" (OECD 2010, 35).

Regarding the State aid granted by Member States, one of the most important questions involves assessing its real impact (Combes and Ypersele 2013). The 2012 Communication on the"Modernisation of EU State Aid Policy" addressed this issue and called for actions on both the EC and the Member State levels (European Commission 2012a). An issue paper from the EC clearly indicates the following: "The Commission's monitoring exercise of 2011/2012 identified deficiencies in the implementation of a significant number [of] aid schemes, thus the Member States and the Commission must step-up their efforts to better comply with State aid rules" (European Commission 2013c, 4). Several Member States as well as the EC are already assessing the effectiveness of some aid, as in the case of the EU Structural Funds scheme (European Commission 2012c, 5). However, the urgent aim of the EC is to conduct a systematic review of the overall EU policy on State aid that would allow it to do the following (European Commission 2012c, 6–7):

- "to verify that the assumptions underlying the approval of the scheme on the basis of an ex ante assessment are still valid"

- "to assess whether the scheme is effective in achieving the direct objective for which it was introduced"
- "to cater for unforeseeable negative effects, in particular the potential aggregated effect of a large scheme"

Overall, we may argue that the EU is more effective than other jurisdictions in regulating investment incentives. As stated by Ehlermann and Goyette (2006, 695), this is because the "European Union is unique among the members of the WTO in applying a stringent internal subsidies regime." Moreover, experts consider that the EU restrictions on State aid are more constraining and stricter than the WTO regime on subsidies (695, 714). The main determinant of the more stringent effect of the EU regime on State aid is the ex ante control of subsidies that is not applied under the WTO framework. Nevertheless, as also noted above, the definition of State aid under EU law is narrower than the definition of subsidies under WTO law, creating a risk that in a few cases some measures covered under the multilateral system are not subject to the EU's State aid control (695, 717).

More specific conclusions regarding the scope and effectiveness of EU State aid controls are difficult to draw for a number of reasons. There are currently no instruments to broadly measure the effectiveness of the EU regime on State aid in regulating or limiting the use of incentives or, even more broadly, its effectiveness in achieving the regime's policy goals. Undertaking such an analysis would require greater transparency concerning the State aid sought by firms and granted or denied by EU Member State governments and broader disclosure of the decisions of EU authorities on the consistency of specific measures with State aid rules in particular cases. Efforts by the EC to increase both transparency and evaluation of State aid will therefore be crucial to better understanding the effectiveness of this regime.

CONCLUSION

Within the EU, a complex regulatory framework regarding State aid governs certain incentive policies. The TFEU prohibits State aid that utilizes state resources, creates or threatens to create competition distortions, favors specific firms or production, and affects trade between Member States (see the appendix to this chapter). However, the TFEU, as well as subsequent communications and guidelines, stipulates the conditions under which exemptions are allowed. This "exemption umbrella" provides the framework for Member States to grant incentives. The EC policy on State aid has shifted toward greater flexibility and openness for State aid whose positive effects on competitiveness, productivity, growth, and innovation may compensate for competition distortions. The main non-crisis-related State aid provided within the EU primarily includes horizontal measures in the area of industry and services. These measures are largely grants or tax reductions. With regard to incentives affecting investment and, in particular, FDI, the types of State aid most frequently allowed are in the fields of regional development and R&D and innovation. The EC regularly provides an updated scoreboard of the State aid granted within the EU. Of course, these data do not capture all incentives that may be granted, such as "hidden" State aid and EU institutional measures. However, the degree of "opacity" may be considered lower than in many other jurisdictions.

Of course, Member States' incentives must comply with WTO rules on subsidies. As highlighted in this chapter, the EU and WTO frameworks are quite different. State aid that is allowed within the EU may be challenged according to the WTO agreements, particularly when measures that do not affect trade within the EU may affect trade of third countries.

Overall, although conclusions regarding the effectiveness of the EU's State aid regime are difficult to draw, prospects for more illuminating analysis will improve if the EC increases transparency and evaluation of State aid practices and policies.

NOTES

1. For a detailed analysis of Articles 108 and 109, see Buts, Jegers, and Joris 2001, 401–405.

2. http://europa.eu/rapid/press-release_IP-13-728_en.htm.

3. European Commission 2006a; http://europa.eu/rapid/press-release_IP-13-1293_en.htm.

4. http://europa.eu/rapid/press-release_IP-13-1293_en.htm.

5. http://ec.europa.eu/competition/state_aid/scoreboard/non_crisis_en.html.

6. Article 349 of the TFEU states that, inter alia,

> taking account of the structural social and economic situation of Guadeloupe, French Guiana, Martinique, Réunion, Saint-Barthélemy, Saint-Martin, the Azores, Madeira and the Canary Islands, which is compounded by their remoteness, insularity, small size, difficult topography and climate,

> economic dependence on a few products, the permanence and combination of which severely restrain their development, the Council, on a proposal from the Commission and after consulting the European Parliament, shall adopt specific measures aimed, in particular, at laying down the conditions of application of the Treaties to those regions, including common policies. Where the specific measures in question are adopted by the Council in accordance with a special legislative procedure, it shall also act on a proposal from the Commission and after consulting the European Parliament.

7. Citation taken from http://curia.europa.eu/juris/document/document.jsf;jsessionid=9ea7d2dc30db496ec9324e574bbea45bec2099e0cfed.e34KaxiLc3qMb40Rch0SaxuLc390?text=&docid=67548&pageIndex=0&doclang=en&mode=lst&dir=&occ=first&part=1&cid=1354818.

APPENDIX TO CHAPTER 5

Core Provisions of the Treaty on the Functioning of the European Union on State Aids: Articles 107, 108, and 109

ARTICLE 107

1. Save as otherwise provided in the Treaties, any aid granted by a Member State or through State resources in any form whatsoever which distorts or threatens to distort competition by favouring certain undertakings or the production of certain goods shall, in so far as it affects trade between Member States, be incompatible with the internal market.

2. The following shall be compatible with the internal market:

(a) aid having a social character, granted to individual consumers, provided that such aid is granted without discrimination related to the origin of the products concerned;

(b) aid to make good the damage caused by natural disasters or exceptional occurrences;

(c) aid granted to the economy of certain areas of the Federal Republic of Germany affected by the division of Germany, in so far as such aid is required in order to compensate for the economic disadvantages caused by that division. Five years after the entry into force of the Treaty of Lisbon, the Council, acting on a proposal from the Commission, may adopt a decision repealing this point.

3. The following may be considered to be compatible with the internal market:

(a) aid to promote the economic development of areas where the standard of living is abnormally low or where there is serious underemployment, and of the regions referred to in Article 349, in view of their structural, economic and social situation;

(b) aid to promote the execution of an important project of common European interest or to remedy a serious disturbance in the economy of a Member State;
(c) aid to facilitate the development of certain economic activities or of certain economic areas, where such aid does not adversely affect trading conditions to an extent contrary to the common interest;
(d) aid to promote culture and heritage conservation where such aid does not affect trading conditions and competition in the Union to an extent that is contrary to the common interest;
(e) such other categories of aid as may be specified by decision of the Council on a proposal from the Commission.

ARTICLE 108

1. The Commission shall, in cooperation with Member States, keep under constant review all systems of aid existing in those States. It shall propose to the latter any appropriate measures required by the progressive development or by the functioning of the internal market.

2. If, after giving notice to the parties concerned to submit their comments, the Commission finds that aid granted by a State or through State resources is not compatible with the internal market having regard to Article 107, or that such aid is being misused, it shall decide that the State concerned shall abolish or alter such aid within a period of time to be determined by the Commission.

If the State concerned does not comply with this decision within the prescribed time, the Commission or any other interested State may, in derogation from the provisions of Articles 258 and 259, refer the matter to the Court of Justice of the European Union direct.

On application by a Member State, the Council may, acting unanimously, decide that aid which that State is granting or intends to grant shall be considered to be compatible with the internal market, in derogation from the provisions of Article 107 or from the regulations provided for in Article 109, if such a decision is justified by exceptional circumstances. If, as regards the aid in question, the Commission has already initiated the procedure provided for in the first subparagraph of this paragraph, the fact that the State concerned has made its application to the Council shall have the effect of suspending that procedure until the Council has made its attitude known.

If, however, the Council has not made its attitude known within three months of the said application being made, the Commission shall give its decision on the case.

3. The Commission shall be informed, in sufficient time to enable it to submit its comments, of any plans to grant or alter aid. If it considers that any such plan is not compatible with the internal market having regard to Article 107, it shall without delay initiate the procedure provided for in paragraph 2. The Member State concerned shall not put its proposed measures into effect until this procedure has resulted in a final decision.

4. The Commission may adopt regulations relating to the categories of State aid that the Council has, pursuant to Article 109, determined may be exempted from the procedure provided for by paragraph 3 of this Article.

ARTICLE 109

The Council, on a proposal from the Commission and after consulting the European Parliament, may make any appropriate regulations for the application of Articles 107 and 108 and may in particular determine the conditions in which Article 108(3) shall apply and the categories of aid exempted from this procedure.

REFERENCES

AEA. 2012. "Integrating Resource Efficiency and EU State Aid: An Evaluation of Resource Efficiency Considerations in the Current EU State Aid Framework." Report for the European Commission. EA/R/ED575151.

Aydin, U. 2007. "Politics of State Aid in the European Union: Subsidies as Distributive Politics." Unpublished, Political Science Department, University of Washington, Seattle.

BIS. 2011. "The State Aid Guide: Guidance for State Aid Practitioners." London: Department for Business, Innovation, and Skills.

"Brussels Probes Multinationals' Tax Deals." 2013. *Financial Times*, September 11.

Buts, C., M. Jegers, and T. Joris. 2011. "Determinants of the European Commission's State Aid Decisions." *Journal of Industry, Competition and Trade* 11: 399–426.

Collie, D. R. 2000. "State Aid in the European Union: The Prohibition of Subsidies in an Integrated Market." *International Journal of Industrial Organization* 18: 867–84.

Combes, P.-P., and T. Ypersele. 2013. "The Role and Effectiveness of Regional Investment Aid: The Point of View of the Academic Literature." Luxembourg: European Commission.

Court of First Instance (EU). 2006. Italy and WAM SpA v. Commission. Case T 304/04, September 6.

ECOFIN. 1997. "Conclusions of the ECOFIN Council Meeting on December 1, 1997 Concerning Taxation Policy." 98/C 2/01, Council of the European Union, Brussels.

EE&MC. 2014. "State Aid and the More Economic Based Approach," accessed May 9, 2014, http://www.ee-mc.com/uploads/media/State_Aid_03.pdf.

Ehlermann, C.-D., and M. Goyette. 2006. "The Interface Between EU State Aid Control and the WTO Disciplines on Subsidies." *European State Aid Law Quarterly* 4: 695–718.

European Commission. 1998a. Council Regulation (EC) No 994/98 of 7 May 1998 on the Application of Articles 92 and 93 (Now 87 and 88 Respectively) of the Treaty Establishing the European Community to Certain Categories of Horizontal State Aid. Official Journal L 142, 14.05.1998.

——. 1998b. Commission Decision of 22 December 1998 Concerning Aid No 369/98, France, Repayable Advance to Aerospatiale for the Airbus A340–500/600. Official Journal C 52, 23.2.1999.

——. 1998c. Commission Notice on the Application of the State Aid Rules to Measures Relating to Direct Business Taxation. Official Journal C 384, 10.12.1998.

——. 2002. Commission Decision 2003/372/EC of 11 December 2002 on Aid Granted by Greece to Olympic Airways (Notified Under Document Number C[2002] 4831). Official Journal L 132, 28.05.2003.

——. 2004a. Commission Decision 2004/339/EC of 15 October 2003 on the Measures Implemented by Italy for RAI SpA. Official Journal L 119, 23.04.2004.

——. 2004b. Commission Decision 2004/393/EC of 12 February 2004 Concerning Advantages Granted by the Walloon Region and Brussels South Charleroi Airport to the Airline Ryanair in Connection with Its Establishment at Charleroi (Notified in Document Number C[2004] 516). Official Journal L 137, 30.4.2004.

——. 2005. State Aid Action Plan—Less and Better Targeted State Aid: A Roadmap for State Aid Reform 2005–2009. Consultation document, COM(2005)107 final, 7.6.2005.

——. 2006a. Commission Regulation (EC) No 1998/2006 of 15 December 2006 on the Application of Articles 87 and 88 of the Treaty to De Minimis Aid. Official Journal L 379, 28.12.2006.

——. 2006b. Community Framework for State Aid for Research and Development and Innovation. Official Journal C 323, 20.12.2006.

——. 2007. Amendments to the Treaty on European Union and the Treaty Establishing the European Community, Notice 207/C306/92, General Provisions 157 and 158. Official Journal C 306, 17.12.2007.

——. 2008. Treaty on the Functioning of the European Union—Consolidated Version, Articles 206–207. Official Journal C 115, 9.5.2008.

——. 2009a. Communication from the Commission Concerning the Criteria for an In-Depth Assessment of Regional Aid to Large Investment Projects. Official Journal C 223, 16.9.2009.

——. 2009b. Communication from the Commission to the Council, the European Parliament and the European Economic and Social Committee Promoting Good Governance in Tax Matters. COM(2009)201 final, 28.4.2009.

——. 2010a. Communication from the Commission to the Council, the European Parliament, the European Economic and Social Committee and the Committee of the Regions: Towards a Comprehensive European International Investment Policy. COM(2010)343 final, 7.7.2010.

——. 2010b. Communication from the Commission: Europe 2020: A Strategy for Smart, Sustainable and Inclusive Growth. COM(2010)2020 final, 3.3.2010.
——. 2012a. Communication from the Commission to the European Parliament, the Council, the European Economic and Social Committee and the Committee of the Regions: EU State Aid Modernisation (SAM). COM(2012)209 final, 8.5.2012.
——. 2012b. Commission Staff Working Document: Facts and Figures and State Aid in the EU Member States—2012 Update. COM(2012)778 final.
——. 2012c. Report from the Commission, State Aid Scoreboard: Report on State Aid Granted by the EU Member States. SEC(2012)443 final, 21.12.2012.
——. 2013a. Guidelines on Regional State Aid for 2014–2020. Official Journal C 209, 23.7.2013.
——. 2013b. Impact Assessment, Accompanying the Document Communication from the Commission, Guidelines on Regional State Aid for 2014–2020. C(2013)3769.
——. 2013c. Issues Paper, Evaluation in the Field of State Aid. 12.4.2013. Accessed May 21, 2014, http://ec.europa.eu/competition/state_aid/modernisation/evaluation_issues_paper_en.pdf.
——. 2013d. Council Regulation No 733/2013 of 22 July 2013 Amending Regulation (EC) No 994/98 on the Application of Articles 92 and 93 of the Treaty Establishing the European Community to Certain Categories of Horizontal State Aid. Official Journal L 204, 31.07.2013.
——. 2013e. Commission Regulation (EC) No 1407/2013 of 18 December 2013 on the Application of Articles 107 and 108 of the Treaty on the Functioning of the European Union to De Minimis Aid. Official Journal L 352, 24.12.2013.
——. 2013f. Paper of the Services of DG Competition Containing a Draft Framework for State Aid for Research and Development and Innovation. 19.12.2013.
——. 2014. Memo, State Aid: Commission Adopts New General Block Exemption Regulation (GBER). 21.05.2014. Accessed May 21, 2014, http://europa.eu/rapid/press-release_MEMO-14-369_en.htm.
Friederiszick, H. W., L. H. Röller, and V. Verouden. 2008. "European State Aid Control: An Economic Framework." In *Handbook of Antitrust Economics*, ed. P. Buccirossi. Cambridge, MA: MIT Press.
Guimón, J. 2007. "Government Strategies to Attract R&D-Intensive FDI." ICEI Working Paper 03/07, Madrid.
Heimler, A., and F. Jenny. 2012. "The Limitations of European Union Control of State Aid." *Oxford Review of Economic Policy* 28 (2): 347–67.
Hey, J. 2002. "Tax Competition in Europe: The German Perspective." EATLP Conference, Lausanne.
Luengo Hernandez de Madrid, G. E. 2008. "Conflicts Between Disciplines of EC State Aids and WTO Subsidies: Of Books, Ships and Aircraft." *European Foreign Affairs Review* 13: 1–31.
Marinello, M. 2013. "Should Variable Cost Aid to Attract Foreign Direct Investment Be Banned? A European Perspective." *Journal of Industry, Competition and Trade* 13: 273–308.
OECD. 2010. "Roundtable on Competition, State Aids and Subsidies." Paris: Organisation for Economic Cooperation and Development.

——. 2013. *Checklist for Foreign Direct Investment Incentive Policies*. Paris: Organisation for Economic Cooperation and Development.

Oxelheim L., and P. Ghauri, eds. 2004. *European Union and the Race for Foreign Direct Investment in Europe*. Oxford, UK: Elsevier.

Ramboll and Matrix. 2012. "Ex-post Evaluation of Regional Aid Guidelines, 2007–2013." Luxembourg: European Commission.

Schön, W. 2003. "Tax Competition in Europe General Report." Max Planck Institute, Munich, http://www.eatlp.org/uploads/Members/GeneralReportSchoen.pdf.

World Economic Forum. 2013. "Foreign Direct Investment as a Key Driver for Trade, Growth and Prosperity: The Case for a Multilateral Agreement on Investment." Geneva: World Economic Forum.

WTO. 2006. *World Trade Report 2006: Exploring the Links between Subsidies, Trade and the WTO*. Geneva: World Trade Organization.

CHAPTER 6

Incentives in the United States

Charles Krakoff and Chris Steele

This chapter explores federal, state, and county/municipal investment incentives in the United States. It examines data on specific investments and incentives awards as well as macro-level data on investments by state and metropolitan area, with a view to gauging the correlations, if any, between the incentives granted and the investment outcomes achieved, as measured in total investment, employment creation, higher wages, and/or sustainability of investment, among other factors. In addition to looking at the value of incentives, we seek to evaluate the relative effects of different kinds of incentives, such as exemptions from property taxes or income taxes, accelerated depreciation allowances, training grants, and free or subsidized land and utilities. We do not undertake any rigorous statistical analysis of the data, though this chapter could be considered an invitation to other researchers to do so in order to test the validity of our conclusions. This chapter does, however, refer to several empirical studies that evaluate the effectiveness of specific incentives programs in the United States, mainly at the subnational level. Finally, we attempt to judge the relative effectiveness of general incentives available to all investments that satisfy certain predetermined criteria and of those negotiated on a case-by-case basis.

Paradoxically for a country that vaunts its adherence to free-market principles, the U.S. tax code is a veritable cornucopia of exemptions, allowances, and credits for business investment. To be sure, no company, foreign or domestic, invests in the United States mainly because of fiscal or other incentives. As the largest consumer market in the world and one of the leading centers for innovation and research and development (R&D) in many advanced technology sectors, and possessing a favorable business environment, sophisticated capital markets, and strong intellectual property protection, the United States offers many other inducements to investors. Nevertheless, the federal government, together with state and municipal governments, offers a wide range of fiscal and financial incentives aimed at attracting or retaining both domestic and foreign direct investment.

The federal government itself undertakes relatively little in the way of international investment promotion and offers none of the incentives such as tax holidays that many other countries provide. Instead, at the federal level, investment incentives tend to be targeted to specific industries or sectors or to depressed urban areas by means of tax credits, depreciation allowances, and similar mechanisms embedded in the tax code that tend to grant equal treatment to all investors, both foreign and domestic, in a given category.

At the state and municipal levels, however, it is a different story. Though they rarely, if ever, discriminate between foreign and domestic investors, state and municipal governments have a long history of ratcheting up the value of incentives to snatch prize investments such as automotive plants away from competing jurisdictions. State and local governments spend an estimated $50 billion a year on tax incentives for investors (Davis 2013). These tactics have come to be known as beggar-thy-neighbor policies, though not infrequently it is the winners of these bidding wars that turn out to be the losers, having awarded incentives so generous that even the most ambitious calculations of multiplier effects cannot undo a net economic loss.[1]

FEDERAL INVESTMENT INCENTIVES

For all that major corporations are accused of buying favorable treatment by federal tax authorities, almost 90 percent of the nearly $1.3 trillion in annual federal "tax expenditures"—defined by the Budget Act of 1974 in section 3(3) as "revenue losses attributable to provisions of the federal tax laws which allow a special exclusion, exemption, or deduction from gross income or which provide a special credit, a preferential rate of tax, or a deferral of tax liability"—go to individuals and families. In 2012, these individuals and families received more than $1.1 trillion in tax expenditures, compared to $156 billion for corporations (Joint Committee on Taxation 2013).

Of course, the distinction between corporate and individual tax expenditures is not always clear-cut. The largest single line item in the tally for individuals is the reduced tax rate on capital gains and dividends, worth $108 billion in 2012, a significant portion of which is the "carried interest"[2] earned by hedge fund or private equity fund managers.

Not all tax expenditures, even for corporations, are investment incentives. One could argue, for example, that the deferral of taxation on foreign earnings of U.S. corporations is an investment disincentive because it prevents or delays repatriation of foreign earnings, which might otherwise be invested in the United States and may indeed act as an incentive to U.S. companies to invest overseas instead. What we often think of as "corporate welfare"—which includes various credits and deductions for renewable energy and energy-efficient products such as hybrid vehicles, appliances, and windows, as well as other preferences for manufacturers, the housing industry, and credit unions—amounts to only about 3 percent of annual tax expenditures (Joint Committee on Taxation 2013).

On the other hand, tax expenditures are far from the only federal incentive for corporations. From 1995 to 2012, the federal government spent $292.5 billion on agriculture subsidies, more than three-fourths of which went to the top 10 percent of recipients, who received an average of $463,000 apiece (EWG 2013). Most of these were not family farmers but huge agro-industrial businesses such as Riceland Foods, Inc., of Stuttgart, Arkansas, a co-op owned by 9,000 rice growers in Arkansas, Louisiana, Mississippi, Missouri, and Texas, which bills itself as the world's largest rice miller and marketer and which raked in $554 million in federal subsidies from 1995 to 2012 (Krakoff 2012).

The federal government provides direct grants to a wide range of industries via more than 200 programs (GSA 2014), which include the following:

- Department of Energy loan programs, with a total loan portfolio of $32.4 billion, which includes the Clean Energy Loan Guarantee Program, with $10 billion in loans for nuclear power and another $10 billion for wind and solar, and the Advanced Technology Vehicle Manufacturing (ATVM) Loan Program, which has total funding of $25 billion and has made awards of as much as $5.9 billion to beneficiaries that include Ford, Nissan, Tesla, and Fisker (DOE 2014)
- Department of Commerce Fisheries Finance Program, which provides long-term financing for the cost of construction or reconstruction of fishing vessels and aquaculture facilities in the Northwest halibut/sablefish and Alaskan crab fisheries (NOAA 2014)

- Department of Transportation grant and loan programs, such as the Railroad Rehabilitation & Improvement Financing (RRIF) Program, authorized to provide direct loans or loan guarantees to railroad companies to rehabilitate or build new railway or intermodal facilities (FRA 2014)
- Department of Housing and Urban Development employment credits to companies investing in Renewal Communities and Empowerment Zones (HUD 2014)
- Exim Bank's roughly $20.5 billion per year of pre-export financing, export credit insurance, and loan guarantees and direct loans (buyer financing) to support U.S. exports, of which approximately 40 percent went to Boeing, by far the Exim Bank's largest beneficiary (Akhtar 2015; de Rugy 2015)

This is a fairly small sample of the 226 federal grant and loan programs available to businesses (GSA 2014). For the most part, these programs are nondiscretionary: that is, they are available to all applicants that meet predefined criteria, subject to overall spending limits. Their nondiscretionary character, however, is no guarantee that they accomplish their intended objective of stimulating productive investment. The connection, if any, between the incentives offered and the dollars invested, jobs created, technology developed, carbon emissions decreased, or any other performance indicator would be exceedingly difficult to measure, especially given that at least one program—the agricultural conservation subsidy, which pays farmers around $2.3 billion a year not to grow certain crops—is an incentive not to invest.

State and municipal incentives, as the next section illustrates, are different from federal programs in that they are defined by their largely discretionary character and often by their lack of predefined spending limits.

STATE AND MUNICIPAL INCENTIVES

As we will argue, the estimated $50 billion (Peters and Fisher 2004) to $80 billion (Story 2012) of fiscal incentives (e.g., tax credits and exemptions) and financial incentives (e.g., subsidies/grants, loans, and loan guarantees) offered annually by state and municipal governments play a much greater part than federal incentives in corporate investment location decisions.

The conventional wisdom is that incentives do not matter very much or matter only in specific circumstances, for certain industries, or within a specific market and that other factors such as infrastructure, worker skills, and market size and access are generally more important to investors (Morisset and Pirnia 1999; Wells et al. 2001; UNCTAD 2004; Whyte 2012). A substantial body of research, much of it conducted by or on behalf of international organizations like UNCTAD and the World Bank, supports this view, according to which investment incentives, at most, figure at the margin, where, if all other elements are equal, an incentive may tip the balance in favor of one location over another. In practice, however, and especially when implemented by states and municipalities, incentives appear to matter a great deal. But a closer examination of the evidence yields a more mixed view.

A review of some of the larger incentives awards supports the hypothesis that incentives matter a great deal, as illustrated in a recent report (Mattera and Tarczynska 2014) that identifies nearly 300 "megadeals"—defined as incentive packages worth $75 million or more and amounting, in aggregate, to more than $87 billion in grants or foregone tax revenues—awarded by state and municipal governments in forty-one states over the past thirty-five years. Though Mattera and Tarczynska (2014) are highly critical of incentives on the grounds that they subsidize wealthy corporations and individuals and create little lasting economic or social benefit, they do not dispute the influence of these incentives on investment location decisions.

Many of the negotiations between investors and state or municipal governments have been extensively documented (several of them are summarized below), leaving little doubt that corporations negotiate aggressively, often playing one jurisdiction against another to extract the most generous incentives package, and that state and local authorities frequently compete with one another in the belief that they need to offer the best incentives package to secure a given investment. Sometimes incentives bidding wars between states or municipalities clearly do tip the balance in favor of the location offering the more generous package. But the preponderance of the evidence does not seem to support the common belief that governments offering insufficiently generous incentives will always or most often lose out. For every investor manifestly lured by incentives to relocate from one location to another, there appear to be many others that would probably have gone ahead in the same location, even with fewer competitive incentives or none at all. The specific type and structure of incentives also matter a great deal.

For one thing, state and local income and property taxes together amount to about 1.1 percent of total input costs (income taxes at 0.8 percent and property taxes at 0.3 percent) in the manufacturing sector, compared to 21.8 percent for labor and 2.7 percent for energy (Kenyon, Langley, and Paquin 2013, 6). It therefore seems unlikely that property tax exemptions—one of the incentives most favored by municipal governments—could be a decisive factor. For another, "a large majority of the investment that occurs in a state or locality offering subsidies or tax cuts will occur for reasons that have nothing to do with those subsidies or taxes; this investment will not be induced but will receive the subsidies anyway. . . . There is substantial evidence that in many of these cases businesses negotiated for incentives after making their decision" (Fisher 2004, i–ii). Fisher goes on to cite two specific examples. The first is a package of $75 million in tax breaks offered by the Nebraska state government to induce the Union Pacific Railroad to move 1,038 jobs from St. Louis to Omaha. "While UP told Nebraska officials that they would not move the jobs without the incentives, they were telling a different story in St. Louis, where company officials stated that the move was motivated by 'critical strategic considerations, not tax incentives'" (6). The second occurred in Iowa in the early 1990s: "when citizens took county supervisors to court over a subsidy to a planned IPSCO steel plant, the company was asked if they would reverse their decision to locate in Iowa if the lawsuit were successful; they said they would not. They admitted publicly that the incentives made no difference" (6).

In another case, the pharmaceutical company Sepracor in 2008 began negotiations with the Marlborough, Massachusetts, city government for a property tax reduction on a new building on which it had already begun construction. With its headquarters and 600 existing employees in Marlborough and its new building already in progress, it would seem unlikely that Sepracor's decision to expand there rather than in another location had anything at all to do with the relatively modest tax incentives offered. But "businesses have a clear motivation to exaggerate the importance of tax incentives since they are unlikely to receive tax breaks unless policy makers believe the incentives will sway their location decision" (Kenyon, Langley, and Paquin 2013, 5).

The incentives in table 6.1 are more concentrated than is apparent from the listing. For example, New York, which offered by far the largest number and value of megadeals, gave $5.6 billion—nearly half of its total amount—to one company, Alcoa, in the form of a thirty-year discounted

Table 6.1 Megadeals by state, 1988–2012

State	Total cost	Number of deals
NY	$11,377,331,907	23
MI	$7,101,236,000	29
OR	$3,515,500,000	7
NM	$3,375,000,000	5
WA	$3,244,000,000	1
LA	$3,169,600,238	11
TX	$3,104,800,000	12
TN	$2,509,900,000	11
AL	$2,406,100,000	10
MS	$2,308,000,000	8
PA	$2,100,000,000	3
MN	$1,781,000,000	4
MO	$1,740,000,000	8
NC	$1,569,600,000	8
SC	$1,556,800,000	6
OH	$1,533,300,000	12
NJ	$1,362,335,785	10
KY	$1,346,100,000	10
FL	$1,336,100,000	7
IL	$1,159,937,000	7
IN	$1,130,500,000	6
GA	$914,800,000	5
CT	$820,500,000	6
KS	$577,000,000	5
CA	$490,000,000	2
AK	$330,000,000	2
IA	$326,500,000	2
ME	$317,000,000	2
ID	$276,000,000	1
WV	$225,800,000	2
AR	$224,250,000	2
RI	$215,000,000	2
UT	$210,000,000	2
AZ	$179,400,000	2
NE	$160,000,000	1
WI	$123,000,000	1
MD	$107,000,000	1
MA	$99,500,000	1
VA	$98,000,000	1
NV	$89,000,000	1
DC	$84,000,000	1

Sources: Mattera and Tarczynska 2013.

electricity deal for an aluminum plant. A small number of companies benefited disproportionately: in addition to Alcoa, whose single deal was worth more than the aggregate amount given to any other company, major beneficiaries included Boeing, with four deals worth $4.4 billion; Intel, with six deals worth $3.6 billion; General Motors, with eleven deals worth $2.7 billion; Ford, with nine deals worth $2.1 billion; and Nike, with a single deal worth $2 billion.

Mattera and Tarczynska (2013) include only completed deals in their tally, but other deals reported in a subsequent update and shown in table 6.2 (Mattera and Tarczynska 2014) dwarf even the Alcoa incentives package; for example, in November 2013, Washington State added $5.4 billion to an existing $3.3 billion incentives package for Boeing as an inducement for the company to build the new 777X aircraft in the Seattle area. In March 2012, Royal Dutch Shell PLC put an end to a three-way incentives bidding war between Pennsylvania, Ohio, and West Virginia with its announcement of plans to build a $2 billion ethane cracker in Beaver County, Pennsylvania in response to the Pennsylvania state government's offer of a tax credit of $2.10 per gallon of ethylene the plant would produce, an incentive valued at $1.65 billion over 25 years (Detrow 2012; Sheehan 2015; Woods 2015).[3] The South African company SASOL has begun construction of a $9.1 billion ethane cracker in Calcasieu Parish, Louisiana, part of a planned $22 billion industrial complex that will also include a gas-to-liquids plant, after Governor Bobby Jindal approved a $115 million grant to fund the purchase of land, and an exemption from local property taxes that could be worth between $2 billion and $3 billion (Thompson 2014; Area Development 2015).

This kind of competition remains vibrant. Iowa's legislature in 2011 approved a $37 million incentives package for Orascom, an Egyptian company, to build a fertilizer plant in the town of Wever; however, state officials, trying to ward off a competing bid by Illinois, added another $110 million in tax credits and reimbursement of construction costs, and the county government then sweetened the pot with an additional twenty years of tax breaks worth $130 million.

In another megadeal, 38 Studios, a Massachusetts-based video-game venture started by Boston Red Sox pitching hero Curt Schilling, in 2010 moved its entire operation to neighboring Rhode Island after negotiating a $75 million loan guarantee with the Rhode Island state government; the Massachusetts government declined to match the offer, saying it would not get into a bidding war. In order to fund the guarantee, Rhode Island agreed

Table 6.2 30 largest megadeals, 1988–2013

Rank	Company	Subsidy Value	Year	State	Description
1	Boeing	$8,700,000,000	2013	WA	Aircraft manufacturing facilities
2	Alcoa	$5,600,000,000	2007	NY	Aluminum plant
3	Boeing	$3,244,000,000	2003	WA	Aircraft manufacturing facility
4	Sempra Energy	$2,194,868,648	2013	LA	LNG export facility
5	Nike	$2,021,000,000	2012	OR	Retention of major sportswear company
6 (tie)	Intel	$2,000,000,000	2004	NM	Computer chip plant
6 (tie)	Intel	$2,000,000,000	2014	OR	Semiconductor manufacturing facility
8	Cheniere Energy	$1,689,328,873	2010	LA	Sabine Pass natural gas liquefaction plant
9	Royal Dutch Shell	$1,650,000,000	2012	PA	Ethane cracker plant
10	Cerner Corp.	$1,635,152,242	2013	MO	Office development for a health-care technology company
11	Chrysler	$1,300,000,000	2010	MI	Automobile assembly plant
12	Tesla Motors	$1,287,000,000	2014	NV	Electric-car battery factory
13	Nissan	$1,250,000,000	2000	MS	Automobile assembly plant
14	Advanced Micro Devices (AMD); later Global Foundries	$1,200,000,000	2006	NY	Computer chip plant
15	ThyssenKrupp	$1,073,000,000	2007	AL	Steel plant
16	General Motors	$1,015,500,000	2009	MI	Automobile assembly plant
17	Ford Motor	$909,000,000	2010	MI	Various automotive facilities
18	Boeing	$900,000,000	2009	SC	Aircraft assembly plant
19	Northwest Airlines (now part of Delta Air Lines)	$838,000,000	1991	MN	Aircraft maintenance facility and engine repair base
20	Nebraska Furniture Mart	$802,000,000	2011	TX	Furniture megastore and surrounding development
21	IBM	$660,000,000	2000	NY	Computer chip plant
22	Intel	$645,000,000	1993	NM	Computer chip plant
23 (tie)	Pyramid Companies	$600,000,000	2002	NY	Expansion of shopping mall
23 (tie)	Texas Instruments	$600,000,000	2003	TX	Computer chip plant

Table 6.2 *(Continued)*

Rank	Company	Subsidy Value	Year	State	Description
25	Mayo Clinic	$585,000,000	2013	MN	Health-care campus expansion
26	Intel	$579,000,000	2005	OR	Computer chip plant expansion/ retention
27	Volkswagen	$554,000,000	2008	TN	Automobile assembly plant
28	Scripps Research Institute	$545,000,000	2003	FL	Nonprofit research institution
29	Forest City Covington	$500,000,000	2007	NM	Mesa del Sol land development
30	Hemlock Semiconductor (controlled by Dow Corning)	$479,400,000	2008	TN	Polycrystalline silicon plant

Source: Mattera and Tarczynska 2014.

to a "moral obligation" bond issue, which carried an implicit, if not binding, commitment to pay bondholders if the company defaulted.[4] Subsequently, 38 Studios did default after missing a scheduled $1 million loan payment and laid off its entire workforce, leaving the state government on the hook for an estimated $112 million in principal and accrued interest (Krakoff 2012).

It is important to note that news reports tend to inflate the headline value of some of these deals. The Alcoa incentives package reserves 478 megawatts of cheap hydroelectric power for the company's three aluminum smelters in Massena, in an economically depressed area of upstate New York, with a subsidy (the difference between the price charged to Alcoa and the price at which the electricity could be sold on the open market) valued at $186.7 million annually over thirty years. However, this figure is an estimate based on expected usage patterns and does not reflect, for example, Alcoa's decline in usage as world aluminum demand slumped after the 2008 financial crisis. Nevertheless, taking $186.7 million as a roughly accurate figure, if we discount it at the current prime lending rate of 3.25 percent, we arrive at a present value of $3.54 billion—a huge sum, to be sure, but substantially less than the more widely publicized undiscounted amount of $5.6 billion.

FISCAL INCENTIVES VERSUS FINANCIAL INCENTIVES

It is generally easier for governments to provide tax credits and similar fiscal incentives because they involve foregone future revenues rather than present cash outlays and future expenditures or losses may, in any case, be incurred by—and attributed to—a subsequent state administration. Nevertheless, many incentives packages are partially or entirely cash-based. They may include loan guarantees, which can result in substantial expenditures if the beneficiary defaults, as occurred in the 38 Studios example, as well as direct cash payments.

One example of this is Benteler International, an Austrian company, which in 2012 negotiated an $81.75 million incentives package with Louisiana Economic Development, a state agency, and Caddo Parish for its planned $975 million investment in a steel tube manufacturing plant in northwest Louisiana. The Louisiana Economic Development package included $12.75 million in grants to develop a new training facility and to reimburse certain associated relocation and internal training expenses and $57.4 million in additional performance-based grants to reimburse site development, infrastructure, and equipment costs incurred by the company. The Red Waterway Commission provided $6 million in infrastructure assistance, and the Port of Caddo-Bossier and the Caddo Parish government contributed additional sums of $3 million and $2.6 million, respectively.

Benteler, which broke ground on the project in 2013 and started production in September 2015, also qualified for other state incentives programs, including

- the Quality Jobs Program, which provides a 5 or 6 percent cash rebate of annual gross payroll for new, direct jobs for up to ten years and a 4 percent sales/use tax rebate on capital expenditures or a 1.5 percent investment tax credit for qualified expenses, and
- the Industrial Tax Exemption Program, offering a ten-year exemption from state and local property taxes.

Taking into account these additional benefits, the total estimated value of state, parish (county), and municipal incentives package rose to more than $228 million, raising the per-job value of incentives from $121,000 to more than $337,000 (Louisiana Economic Development 2013).

RISKY BUSINESS

The risks inherent in incentives packages often go unappreciated until it is too late to mitigate them. With respect to loan guarantees and cash grants, the risks may be more readily apparent, even if the responsible officials ignore them. In the 38 Studios case, the one question

Rhode Island Governor Donald Carcieri and the senior staff of the Rhode Island Economic Development Corporation should have asked, but didn't, is why Schilling's company couldn't raise the money it needed from venture capitalists. It wasn't for lack of trying. Before turning to the Rhode Island state government, Schilling had approached several Boston venture capitalists, who turned him down flat. As the *Boston Globe* reported, this was largely because, though a video-game enthusiast, Schilling had no experience developing one and no relevant business experience. There was a widespread impression among venture capitalists that an investment in Schilling's company "would require a lot of babysitting" (Wallack, Bray, and Arsenault 2012). Also, Schilling was asking for $48 million, a huge amount for first-round financing for a start-up with no revenue, and was unwilling to give up much stock in exchange. The venture capitalists, moreover, realized that $48 million would not be enough. The cost to develop a massive, multiplayer game is huge, and Schilling himself estimated that he might need an additional $100 million to finish development of *Copernicus*, his company's flagship product.

The Carcieri administration appears to have been dazzled by Schilling's celebrity and saw in his request the chance to develop a new, high-tech sector to replace Rhode Island's declining jewelry manufacturing industry. But the deal very nearly blew the state's entire $125 million allocation for business loan guarantees and in so doing violated one of the most fundamental precepts of venture investing: you don't put all your money into one company. By most estimates, 20 to 30 percent of venture-backed companies will fail outright, and another 50 or 60 percent will underperform, merely repaying the investment or providing a small return. What saves the venture capitalists from ruin is the one massive success—maybe one in ten investments for a successful firm—that pays for the failures many times over (Krakoff 2012).

If people whose sole business is to pick winning companies to invest in aren't terribly good at it, it should come as no surprise that public officials are even worse. Of course, there may be some cases in which a guarantee may be economically worthwhile: if the project has substantial positive externalities or if some inputs are mispriced in the market so that the economic benefits of the project are greater than those captured by investors. Public officials may want to make a bold commitment in order to help an investment get publicity and attract other investors to the area. The question is whether public officials are properly equipped to identify such potential externalities and then to measure their size and the accompanying risk.

Other incentives' risks are more insidious, as too often such incentives are no guarantee of permanence for a prized investment project. In 1991, General Motors (GM) shut down a plant in Ypsilanti, Michigan, after receiving tax breaks on $250 million in investments, saving 50 percent on its local tax bill. The city promptly sued and won, but the lower court judgment was overturned by the state appeals court on the grounds that soliciting tax breaks using the prospect of job creation or preservation does not constitute a binding promise (Zaretsky 1994). Even after closing this plant, GM continued to receive similar benefits for another plant in Ypsilanti, which remained open until 2010, with the combined tax savings estimated at $200 million (Lavery 2014). Many of the plants GM closed as part of its federally supervised bankruptcy had received generous tax incentives. These included $17 million in cash training grants in 2008 for its Spring Hill, Tennessee, assembly plant—GM subsequently shifted production of the Chevy Traverse from Spring Hill to its Lansing, Michigan, plant, putting 4,000 employees out of work ("GM Collected $17 Million" 2011)—and about $125 million in state training grants and property tax abatements for the plant in its previous incarnation as the main Saturn assembly operation from 1990 to 2007 ("GM Invests 167M" 2013; Bartik et al. 1987).

In spite of this dismal record, GM continues to receive incentives. In 2001, its Lake Orion assembly plant had received a twenty-year, $59 million tax abatement from the state to prevent the company from relocating its production ("State Encourages General Motors to Stay" 2001). In 2010, after its emergence from bankruptcy, it concluded a deal with the United Auto Workers and Michigan state authorities to spend $2 billion to retool the same Lake Orion plant and convert it into a "tier-two" facility, paying all workers $14 an hour instead of the customary $28. The deal included a twenty-year, $779 million package of state tax incentives and job training credits as the price for the company to relocate production of its Aveo subcompact car from South Korea (UAW 2010; Haglund 2009). In addition to the $779 million in state incentives, the Lake Orion plant, which by 2014 employed 1,470 workers, was given a further state grant of $130 million in federal funds for job training, while Oakland County, where the plant is situated, pledged $2 million for job training and the Orion Township offered $100 million in personal property tax exemptions, bringing the total to well over $1 billion (Haglund 2009). In November 2014, however, citing rising demand for sport utility vehicles over subcompacts as a consequence of falling gasoline prices, GM announced phased layoffs of 160 workers at the Lake Orion plant in addition to 350 layoffs at the Lansing Grand River plant (Shepardson, Burden, and Wayland 2014). Meanwhile, in March 2014, the company announced plans to build a $162 million stamping plant in Lansing, Michigan, creating sixty-five jobs, for which the city and the Lansing Economic Area Partnership offered a fourteen-year, 50 percent reduction in property taxes (VanHulle 2014).

This is not meant to single out GM: other car companies, including Ford and Chrysler, as well as companies in many other industries, have similarly closed factories after receiving substantial incentives from state and local governments. The city of Detroit, in cooperation with Michigan state agencies, continued to lavish investment subsidies almost up to the moment it declared bankruptcy in December 2013. In June 2013, the Detroit Downtown Development Authority, together with the Michigan Strategic Fund, agreed to raise $284.5 million in funds from a state public bond offering for partial financing of a $600 million "catalyst development" project anchored by a new arena for the Detroit Red Wings hockey team (Downtown Development Authority 2013).

In 1990, United Airlines, after launching a bidding war among ninety-three different locations across the United States, built a new, state-of-the-art aircraft maintenance facility in Indianapolis, promising to invest $500 million of its own funds alongside $320 million that the city and its airport authority raised through bond issues. The expectation was that United would ultimately employ 5,000 skilled mechanics at the facility, earning an average of $25 an hour, and that the income, sales, and property taxes paid by these employees and received through multiplier effects would easily offset the cost of the subsidy. In the end, United invested only $229 million and employed a maximum of 2,500 mechanics (most of them transferred from the airline's maintenance operations in California) before it walked away from the facility in early 2003 as part of a drastic cost-cutting campaign that saw it turn to cheaper private contractors in southern states (Uchitelle 2003).

The risks from incentives of this kind go far beyond the immediate revenues foregone or the debt obligations incurred, which may have to be repaid long after the revenues from the projects have evaporated. More fundamentally, they increase communities' dependence on single companies and projects, which makes them even more vulnerable to subsequent requests for subsidies by the same sets of investors. Ypsilanti, Michigan, and Spring Hill, Tennessee, are just two examples of communities that have acceded to GM's successive requests for tax credits, training grants, and other public expenditures in exchange for promises of new investments and the preservation of existing jobs otherwise at risk. When a company like GM employs 8,000 people in a community the size of Spring Hill, population 31,000 (it had only 1,500 residents before the Saturn plant came to town), the loss of a substantial number of those jobs can be ruinous to the extent that many laid-off workers have no choice but to accept new jobs at wages 50 percent lower than what they were formerly paid.

Ypsilanti, whose population fell more than 20 percent, from nearly 25,000 in 1990 to less than 20,000 in 2010 (City of Ypsilanti 2011), found itself in a similar bind. After suing GM twice, in 1991 and 2010, for shutting its Willow Run plants, the township sold most of the property in 2013 to a consortium that planned to demolish the factory and set up an advanced vehicle R&D and testing center ("Willow Run Bomber Plant to Be Demolished" 2013). This venture, which was greeted with enthusiasm by Ypsilanti Township officials, would be eligible for a number of state, county, and municipal investment incentives.

In Massena, New York, population 11,000, Alcoa has used the threat of cutting the 1,300 jobs in its three aluminum smelters as a lever to pry additional incentives from the state power authority. Although threats to move the plants to another state or country were hardly credible—it would have cost billions to replace their existing capacity—officials were clearly concerned by the prospect of cutbacks in production and jobs. The most recent incentives grant was conditioned not on creating new jobs or preserving all existing ones but rather on not letting total employment losses exceed 400.

Companies have learned to expect and negotiate hard for incentives, both internationally and domestically. Intel, for example, became adept at exploiting the willingness of various countries and U.S. states to offer incentives. When it was considering locations for two new facilities in the early 1990s, it issued formal requests for proposals to several western U.S. states. When Oregon said it could not provide any significant tax incentives, Intel chose to build its plant in Rancho Mirage, New Mexico, which offered to waive all property taxes, an estimated value of $1 billion (Spar 1998). As Intel CEO Paul Otellini put it, "We're building factories in Ireland, Israel, China, or Malaysia, and you get an incentive package that [includes] a . . . tax holiday or equipment credits or something like that worth several hundreds of millions of dollars because people want companies like ours to invest there and to hire their folks. What's different about Mississippi versus Malaysia?" (Atkinson and Ezell 2012, 113).

EVALUATING THE EFFECTIVENESS OF INCENTIVES

The evidence on the utility and effectiveness of subnational investment incentives in the United States is decidedly mixed. Most of the research on the topic has focused on fiscal incentives and has evaluated them in terms of net fiscal effect, as have most of those state governments that evaluate their incentives programs. Florida's state government uses as its metric incentives' return on investment and says, "Return-on-Investment (ROI) is synonymous with economic benefit, and is used in lieu of the statutory term. This measure does not address issues of overall effectiveness or societal benefit; instead, it focuses on tangible financial gains or losses to state revenues, and is ultimately conditioned by the state's tax policy" (Florida EDR 2014, 1). Florida defines its ROI from incentives as (increase in state revenue – state investment) / state investment, but it is difficult to establish any significant correlation between its magnitude and the benefits in terms of jobs or investment.[5] Advocates of such deals and programs often stress their less tangible benefits, as statements below illustrate.

Ireland's approach to investment incentives is relevant to the United States, not least because so many of the investments it has attracted have come from American corporations. Irish officials, for example, have robustly defended the billions of euros[6] in incentives awarded to Intel since it first invested in Ireland in 1989. Ireland's approach, especially in the electronics sector, "was to attract some key investments into Ireland and then leveraging further MNEs to locate on the basis that these key enterprises had chosen Ireland as a base in Europe. . . . With the location of Intel and Microsoft, and subsequently Hewlett Packard in the printing sector, Ireland effectively had an electronics hub and the spokes were quickly populated by dozens of smaller electronics and software enterprises, all of which wanted to interconnect with these key industrial leaders" (Ruane and Buckley 2006, 10).

Ireland's approach to incentives was highly discretionary: "A key industrial project, such as Intel, might expect to receive a higher rate of grant than a routine project in the electronics sector" (Ruane and Görg 1999, 8). Irish officials justified this approach as establishing the basis for development of competitive investment clusters as well as producing a demonstration effect, with prominent international investors providing confidence for others to invest. As Ireland's former minister for industry and commerce put it, "The fact that Intel came to Ireland and did so successfully attracted many others to come here that mightn't otherwise have done so" (O'Malley 2009).

We can contrast Ireland's discretionary approach to Intel's investment with that of Costa Rica, where Intel in November 1996 announced plans to build a $300 million semiconductor assembly and test plant.

> Costa Rican officials seem not to have offered any dramatic giveaways or extra-legal arrangements—and Intel explicitly never asked for any. The Costa Ricans definitely went out of their way to accommodate Intel and were willing to work with the legislature and government agencies to modify laws, policies, or procedures that would have been unfavorable to the company's pending investment. This was especially true in the areas of taxation, education, infrastructure and permitting. Deals were struck and laws creatively altered whenever possible. But all of the provisions Costa Rica made were designed to apply to all foreign investors in the country, and never just to Intel (Spar 1998, 17–18).

Although Intel in 2014 closed its assembly and testing operation in Costa Rica in the face of a shrinking market for personal computers, eliminating 1,500 jobs, it has increased employment in engineering and design center and global services center operations from 1,200 to 1,400 ("Business in Costa Rica" 2014). Intel's initial investment is also credited with spurring development of a high-tech cluster in Costa Rica, which includes companies such as Infosys, IBM, and HP and which has expanded to include a wide range of investments in engineering and design, automotive components, pharmaceuticals, and medical devices (CINDE 2015).

In response to a critical review of New York State's electricity subsidies by the nonpartisan Citizens' Budget Committee (CBC), Richard Kessel, the head of the New York Power Authority, said that removing or reducing Alcoa's subsidy would be a grave error and vowed to protect it as long as he remained in charge. "Alcoa is one of the most critical companies in our state," he said. "I think there's a lot we can do to reform our programs, but taking away the power from Alcoa is not on the table." Citing the dependence of the Massena area on Alcoa, he further stated that the value of the subsidy "cannot be measured by simple jobs-to-megawatts ratios" (Bomyea 2009).

Relying on those ratios alone would certainly call into question the wisdom of the subsidy. In return for the electricity subsidy, Alcoa pledged to invest $600 million to upgrade its Massena East plant and to preserve at least 900 of the 1,300 jobs in its three Massena plants. Using the discounted $3.54 billion as its total value, the subsidy will cost nearly six dollars for every dollar invested by Alcoa and nearly $4 million for each job preserved. By contrast, the CBC report estimated that if the subsidized electricity were sold at prevailing market rates, it would generate between $99 million and $131 million in incremental annual revenues, with a present value of between $1.9 billion and $2.5 billion. Investing even a small fraction of that amount in infrastructure and education in the area of the plants could potentially produce greater and more lasting benefits than protecting an industry whose long-term outlook is doubtful.

Many of the other megadeals are equally questionable. The Sasol incentive package in Louisiana amounts to nearly $1.6 million per job created; Iowa's package for the Orascom fertilizer plant could end up costing $1.45 million per job; and Shell's ethane cracker investment in Pennsylvania, granted an incentives package worth up to $1.65 billion over the next twenty-five years (Staub 2014), would cost $4.125 million for each of the 400 jobs created, well over double the expected lifetime earnings of each of those new employees, whereas the present value of the tax credits, at more than $1.1 billion, represents about 45 percent of Shell's planned capital expenditure (ICA 2014).[7]

It is exceptionally hard to prove a counterfactual. Would Ireland have succeeded in developing its technology sector had it not given those initial tax breaks to Intel, or were those incentives even essential to attracting Intel itself? We can't be sure, but Ireland's corporate tax rates (the lowest in Europe at the time), access to the European market, a well-educated workforce, an English-speaking environment, and even the affinity for Ireland felt by many Americans (nearly 40 million of whom claim some Irish ancestry according to U.S. Census data) may arguably have been more decisive.

As figure 6.1 illustrates, based on incentives data from Investment Consulting Associates (ICA) and data on levels of capital expenditure by state from the U.S. Census Bureau, there is no apparent correlation between investment incentives and capital investment in manufacturing, which accounts for about three-quarters of all state-level investment incentives nationwide.[8] For example, Alaska, by far the most generous state with investment incentives, at $991 per capita, ranks only forty-sixth in per capita capital expenditure in manufacturing. Delaware, which gave out only $48 per capita in incentives, ranked third in manufacturing capital expenditure, with $789 per capita.

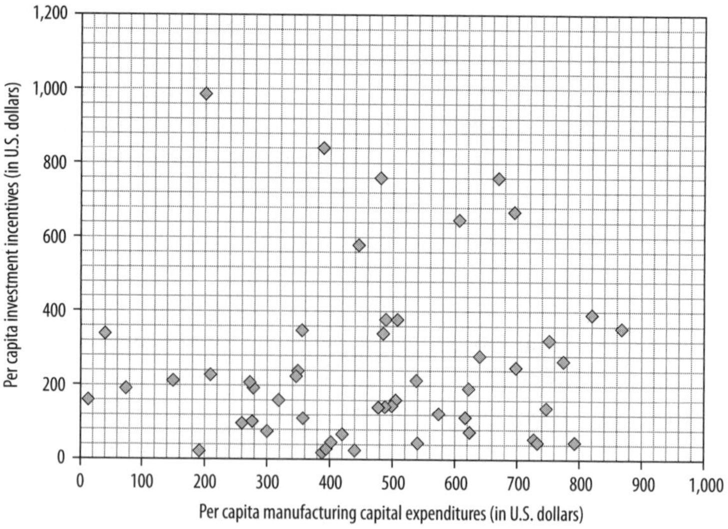

Figure 6.1 Manufacturing capital expenditures and state investment incentives, 2011 (per capita).

Sources: U.S. Census Bureau; Annual Survey of Manufactures: Geographic Area Statistics: Supplemental Statistics for the U.S. and States: 2011 http://factfinder.census.gov/faces/tableservices/jsf/pages/productview.xhtml?pid=ASM_2011_31AS202&prodType=table; U.S. Census Bureau Population Estimates: http://www.census.gov/popest/data/state/totals/2011/tables/NST-EST2011-01.xls; IncentivesMonitor.com; "United States of Subsidies" 2012.

Interestingly, as tables 6.3 and 6.4 illustrate, there is almost an inverse correlation between the generosity of state incentives and a state's position on the left-right political continuum. One might expect conservative or Republican states to adopt a parsimonious stance in keeping with their antispending, small-government views and liberal or Democratic states

Table 6.3 10 top states by per capita incentives

State	Per capita incentives	Party
AK	$991	Republican
WV	$845	Republican
NE	$763	Republican
TX	$759	Republican
MI	$672	Democratic
VT	$650	Democratic
OK	$584	Republican
LA	$394	Republican
PA	$381	Democratic
ME	$379	Democratic

Sources: IncentivesMonitor.com, politicalmaps.org.

Table 6.4 10 lowest states by per capita incentives

State	Per capita incentives	Party
NV	$12	Democratic
MO	$16	Republican
NH	$30	Democratic
SD	$34	Republican
IA	$43	Democratic
MN	$35	Democratic
DE	$48	Democratic
ND	$49	Republican
AL	$58	Republican
NC	$69	Republican

Sources: IncentivesMonitor.com, politicalmaps.org.

to be far more generous with incentives, but the opposite is very nearly true. Four of the top five states and six of the top ten states in terms of per capita incentives are conservative states, whereas three of the five least generous states and five of the ten least generous states are liberal states. Conservative suspicion of government market intervention, it appears, applies far more to Washington than to state capitals.

The connection between incentives and investment—or the benefits from investment—is tenuous at best. As figure 6.2 shows, there is no observable correlation between a state's per capita incentives and the percentage of its private-sector workers employed by foreign-controlled firms. To be sure, not all incentives go to foreign-owned companies, but "perhaps the most extensive use of incentives has come in those deals involving foreign investment" (ICMA 2012). And although there is often

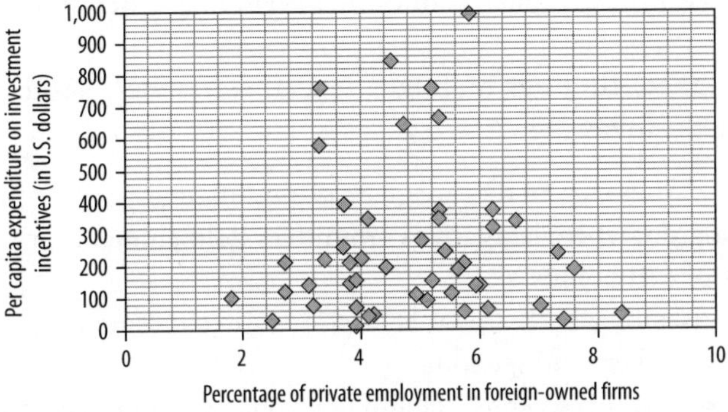

Figure 6.2 State investment incentives and employment in foreign firms.

Source: "United States of Subsidies" 2012; ITA 2014.

no direct correlation between dollars invested and jobs created, the number of jobs created is certainly one of the more important indicators of the economic and social value of these investments and, often, the main political justification for the incentives offered to attract them.

ICA has developed the Incentive Transparency Index, which assesses U.S. states on their openness in communicating the economic and social impacts of incentive programs. It also recently cross-referenced these findings against research from the Pew Charitable Trusts (2014) on the evaluation of the effectiveness of such incentives. Findings show that evaluation of incentives and transparency in their application appear to go hand in hand; states that score high on evaluation also score high on openness, and vice versa. This correlation seems to contribute substantially to the overall effectiveness and quality of tax incentives programs, as states that perform well on openness and on evaluation of effectiveness tend to offer more high-quality incentives programs.

According to Chris Steele, president of ICA North America, "There is a positive correlation between transparency and effectiveness. This strongly suggests that effectiveness is also correlated with a clear establishment of goals on behalf of the public sector. We suspect that this is another reason why so many states are looking to enhance the transparency of their programs" (Steele 2014).

As the Pew (2014) report observes, "Unlike direct state spending, which must be renewed with each budget, tax incentives frequently continue indefinitely without policy makers revisiting their cost or effectiveness. By integrating the evaluation of tax incentives into the policy-making process, states can ensure that incentives are reconsidered regularly and that elected officials make economic development decisions based on evidence."

Pew's (2014) findings highlight several states with good practices, including the following:

- Oregon, where tax credits are given expiration dates
- Washington, where legislative committees hold annual hearings on the results of evaluations
- Rhode Island, where a new law ensures that incentives are reviewed alongside other state spending
- Minnesota, which seeks to establish how much economic activity is directly attributable to incentives and how much would have happened anyway

- Louisiana, which looks at the wider effects of incentives, including the extent to which incentives may cause some companies to benefit at the expense of others
- Massachusetts, which evaluates the extent to which incentives require cuts to other state programs and the potential job losses that may result
- Maryland, Washington, and Vermont, which have enacted legislation that requires proposals for tax incentives to include a statement of purpose and a mechanism for evaluating whether that purpose has been achieved

Louisiana, in evaluating the state enterprise zone program, found that in certain sectors 90 percent of new jobs at companies participating in the program were displacing jobs with other employers and concluded that the program had created only 3,000 net new jobs instead of the 9,000 that participating companies had reported. In 2013, Massachusetts evaluated its film production tax credit, which from 2006 through 2011 had cost $326 million and created 5,900 jobs, a cost of $55,000 per job. But the program's cost had to be offset by cuts elsewhere in the state budget, which resulted in a loss of 3,700 jobs, leaving a net gain of only 2,200 jobs, at a cost per job nearly three times the initial estimate.

Sadly, these practices have yet to become widespread. The ICA and Pew findings show some fourteen states that can be considered strong or very strong performers, whereas twenty-four states are weak or very weak performers (see table 6.5).

Table 6.5 State ranking of incentives transparency and effectiveness evaluation

Very weak performance Score 2		Weak performance Score 3	Modest performance Score 4		Strong performance Score 5	Very strong performance Score 6
AL	OK	AK	NE	IL	KY	CT
DE	RI	CA	TX	IN	MA	LA
HI	SC	MD	VA	KS	MI	IA
ID	SD	MN	AR	WA	NC	MO
ME	TN	MS	AZ	GA	NY	NJ
MT	VT	NM	CO		OH	WI
NH	WV	UT	FL		OR	
NV	WY				PA	
ND						

Source: IncentivesMonitor.com.

ARE INCENTIVES WORTHWHILE? SELECT EXAMPLES

The absence of a meaningful correlation between per capita state incentives in the United States and either per capita direct investment or the percentage of the workforce employed by foreign-owned firms indicates that, even in states that have successfully attracted major investments by offering generous incentives, their overall incentive programs may not stand up to scrutiny. The experiences of towns like Ypsilanti, Michigan, represent the triumph of hope over experience as corporations, having received generous incentives packages, nevertheless close their factories when economic conditions so dictate. They also illustrate the danger that incentives may render a locality more vulnerable over time as a single company comes to dominate the economy. It is almost certain that in some of these cases the towns or states so affected would have been better off had the money spent on incentives been used differently—to improve infrastructure and education, strengthen the social safety net, and/or diversify away from declining industries.

The lack in most states of sufficient transparency with respect to incentives programs and of the kind of rigorous analysis of outcomes that could lead to better policy choices makes it difficult to determine whether incentives are worthwhile. We can't know, for example, whether Ypsilanti would have been better off had it forsworn further incentives for the automotive industry after GM shut its Willow Run plant for the first time in 1991. But the experiences of quite a few towns and cities in the United States indicate that it might have been.

A recently prepared economic development strategy for the long-declining paper mill town of Millinocket, Maine, pointed to other declining mill and mining towns across the United States that had successfully reinvented themselves as recreation, tourism, and innovation centers—not by lavishing subsidies on declining legacy industries but by investing in their own redevelopment (CZB Associates 2015). Similarly, Detroit, long a byword for declining economic fortunes, has embarked on a redevelopment strategy that relies far more on joint public-private initiatives than on fiscal incentives or subsidies and on new ventures in innovative and sustainable technologies rather than on hopes that the car industry will regain its former prominence. An estimated 10 percent of Detroit's metropolitan workforce is now employed in R&D in advanced industries. Similarly, Chattanooga, Tennessee, with a population of 160,000, has used its capital budget to build the fastest Internet in the United States in an effort to attract companies relying on big-data computing (Brown 2014).

Even in those instances in which a state or municipal incentive can be judged effective, one location's gain may be another's loss. When viewed from a national level, state or municipal incentives may contribute little to—or may even detract from—national welfare because for the most part they divert investment from one U.S. jurisdiction to another and divert resources from more productive uses. There is no evidence that state or municipal incentives have spurred companies to invest when they otherwise would not have invested at all, and there is very little evidence that such incentives have attracted investments that would otherwise have gone to another country.

Seeking to end bidding wars among states and provinces, many countries have tried to rein in these subsidies. Canada's federal and provincial governments in 1994 signed the Agreement on Internal Trade, which prohibits incentives intended to lure businesses from one location in Canada to another. Five of the six Australian states and the two major territories signed a similar agreement in 2003 (only Queensland refused to join), and the West German Länder in 1982 agreed to broad subsidy regulations in 1982 and 1983 (Thomas 2011, 343–57). (See chapter 11 in this volume for more on these agreements.)

A number of U.S. states have tried to do the same. In the 1980s, the Council of Great Lakes Governors agreed to an antipoaching pact, but it collapsed even before it went into effect, and efforts to revive the agreement in 1996 were unsuccessful. Also in 1996, the Ohio State Senate unanimously passed a resolution asking Congress to curb interstate incentives competition (Thomas 2000, 171).

The governors of New York, New Jersey, and Connecticut agreed in 1991 to stop running ads aimed at luring businesses from one other, but within months, New Jersey violated the terms, and the deal collapsed (Alden and Strauss 2014, 2). (See chapter 11 in this volume for more on national and subnational efforts to regulate competition for investment through the use of incentives.)

Not all of these attempts have failed. Some counties in metropolitan areas—including Dayton, Ohio, and Denver, Colorado—have agreed to limit subsidy competition, and Kansas and Missouri are considering similar measures with respect to Kansas City, which straddles their border. But these examples fail to amount to a trend. Only the

U.S. Congress could put an end to the subsidy war, but "historically Congress has been reluctant to interfere in what are seen as state-level prerogatives" (Alden and Strauss 2014, 2).

CONCLUSION

The evidence reviewed here leads to several tentative conclusions. First, a company's state or local tax burden typically constitutes a very small proportion of its overall operating costs, so tax reductions offered as fiscal incentives are probably rarely the decisive factor in investment location decisions. Nonfiscal incentives such as free or subsidized inputs (land, energy), capital grants and reimbursements, or loan guarantees are likely to be more effective than tax breaks in attracting investment. This is unsurprising, given that such incentives are often worth more than most tax incentives, their full value accrues to the beneficiary much earlier and is less dependent on future contingencies, and they more directly reduce investment risk.

Second, a large proportion of the investment attracted by incentives is diverted from other locations and therefore represents no net gain to the country as a whole and may constitute a net loss (for example, if relocation results in fewer total jobs or a lower total wage bill). There are very few cases that are unambiguous instances of new investment diverted to the United States from a foreign country—GM's decision to relocate production of the Aveo from South Korea to the United States is one example, but GM may have exaggerated the degree to which this was based on incentives rather than on a wider strategy to move some production back to the United States.

Third, the debate over the relative benefits and costs of negotiated incentives versus automatic incentives often centers on the purported wastefulness of automatic incentives, a significant portion of which go to companies that would have made a given investment in any case. But the evidence indicates that a significant proportion of negotiated incentives also go to companies that would have made the same investment even without the incentives.

Finally, evaluation of incentives' net fiscal effect may be an imperfect tool with which to assess their effectiveness, but it may be the only reasonably consistent and reliable indicator available to governments that seek sound policy guidance. Most other evaluation criteria require proof of counterfactual arguments or highly sophisticated sampling and analysis.

As a practical matter, measurements of the net fiscal effect of incentives often address the paramount concerns of officials who must provide an account of their use of public funds.[9]

Absent a federal prohibition, which would be of questionable constitutionality, incentives-based competition for investment among state and local governments will not disappear, especially as long as corporations deliberately encourage such competition by playing off one jurisdiction against another. What seems to matter most to states (or, by extension, to county or municipal governments) wishing to maximize benefits and minimize wasteful expenditure is not how much is spent on incentives or what sectors and industries those incentives target but rather how those incentives are conceived, structured, administered, and evaluated.

Incentives should ideally be limited in duration and renewable only by deliberate political decision rather than by default. Every incentive granted should have an explicit goal or goals and associated performance indicators for which data can readily be obtained. Incentives, finally, should be subject to regular evaluation, and the results of those evaluations should be made public. To the extent possible, evaluations should try to take into account the wider economic effects of an incentive, though in practice this may be very hard to do.

Adoption of these practices would not eliminate the risk to governments of negative outcomes from incentives. It would, however, allow governments to structure incentives more effectively, to target specific activities or companies, and to evaluate performance in a way that could inform future policy decisions. Finally, adoption of these practices might hold politicians more accountable for their incentives decisions and thus reduce or eliminate some of the wasteful incentives awards that have become all too prevalent.

NOTES

1. Net fiscal effects are not the only possible measure of the effectiveness or efficiency of investment incentives. Skills development, demonstration and clustering effects (one or more high-profile investments helping to attract other investments), community preservation, and many other spillover effects can be used to justify investment incentives, but it is much harder to quantify these indicators or attribute causality to a given investment or incentive. In addition, "calculating the benefits of any incremental foreign investment attracted by incentives requires an assessment of shadow prices and externalities. . . . It is doubtful, however, that calculations for any of today's relatively open economies would justify very high subsidy equivalents" (Wells

et al. 2001, 59). Because net fiscal effects tend to be easier to calculate than most other possible indicators, they tend to be the measure for most assessments of investment incentive effectiveness.

2. Carried interest, or the share of profits paid to general partners in hedge funds or private equity funds, is treated as a capital gain and taxed at the 15 percent rate applied to capital gains rather than the 35 percent most fund managers would pay on ordinary earned income. This practice has become highly controversial.

3. Shell has purchased and cleared a 991-acre site and secured a state air quality permit but has not yet confirmed whether it will go ahead with the project. It is nearly certain, however, that if it does, it will build the plant in Pennsylvania.

4. A moral obligation is a type of revenue bond, usually issued by a municipal or state authority, that gives investors the same tax exemptions as a municipal bond but that is also backed by a moral pledge or commitment against default, typically by the state or municipal government. Though the moral obligation is not legally binding, the issuing government will typically suffer negative credit rating effects if it fails to honor the pledge.

5. This calculation appears to be based on the assumption that the investment would not have taken place without state incentives. This may be the case in some instances, but it is not universally true. One of the persistent challenges in evaluating the effectiveness of incentives is precisely this: it is rarely possible to prove conclusively that a given investment would not have occurred (or would have been made elsewhere) if incentives had not been awarded. It can be even harder to establish the amount of incentives needed to secure a given investment without giving away more than necessary.

6. The exact value of fiscal incentives and grants awarded to Intel in Ireland has never been made public, in keeping with the highly discretionary character of Ireland's incentives programs. However, based on its capital investments of $12.5 billion since 1989 (ITA 2014), Intel is likely to have received at least $2 billion in capital grants, R&D grants, and fiscal incentives, and possibly double that amount, based on a historical average capital grant of 22.7 percent and a maximum grant of 60 percent (Yuill et al. 1997).

7. IncentivesMonitor is a global incentive deal database that tracks information on all major fiscal and financial incentives and subsidies awarded to foreign and domestic corporate investors in all industries and that monitors associated incentive programs. As of November 2014, it included more than 11,000 awarded incentive deals; covered more than sixty-three countries, including emerging markets such as Brazil, China, India, Mexico, South Africa, and Turkey; and traced more than 500 active incentive programs.

8. The data include only capital expenditures in manufacturing (NAICS classifications 31–33) and therefore do not capture investments in agriculture, financial services, retail and wholesale trade, or filmmaking, which are significant incentive beneficiaries in some states: many of California's incentives programs, for example, target agriculture and film, whereas Alaska's incentives go mainly to oil, gas, and mining

9. Of course, these measurements do not account for the use of public funds to promote investments with positive externalities or to correct for mispriced inputs.

REFERENCES

Akhtar, S. 2015. "Export-Import Bank: Overview and Reauthorization Issues." Congressional Research Service, March 25.

Alden, E., and R. Strauss. 2014. "Curtailing the Subsidy War Within the United States." Policy Innovation Memorandum No. 45, Council on Foreign Relations, New York.

Atkinson, R., and S. Ezell. 2012. *Innovation Economics.* New Haven, CT: Yale University Press.

Bartik, T., C. Becker, S. Lake, and J. Bush. 1987. "Saturn and State Economic Development." *Forum for Applied Research and Public Policy* 2 (1) (Spring): 29–40.

Bomyea, L. 2009. "NYPA Chief Backs Alcoa." *Watertown Daily Times*, September 27. Accessed November 26, 2014, http://www.watertowndailytimes.com/article/20090927/NEWS05/309279942.

Brown, J. 2014. "What British Cities Can Learn from Detroit: Motor City's Turnaround Should Be a Model for Regeneration." *Independent*, June 18.

"Business in Costa Rica: Intel Outside." 2014. *Economist*, April 19.

CINDE. 2015. Costa Rican Investment Promotion Agency, accessed September 15, 2015, http://www.cinde.org/en.

City of Ypsilanti. 2011. "South of Michigan Avenue: Community Needs Assessment." November 30. Accessed December 23, 2015. http://www.ewashtenaw.org/government/departments/community-and-economic-development/plans-reports-data/human-services/2012/city-of-ypsilanti-south-of-michigan-avenue-community-needs-assessment. p. 9.

CZB Associates. 2015. "An Open Letter to the Citizens of the Town of Millinocket, Maine," January 11. Accessed May 1, 2015. https://drive.google.com/file/d/0BwX4t-nQWwo5b3E5Y1JpZ3FIVlU/view?ref=inline.

Davis, C. 2013. "Tax Incentives: Costly for States, Drag on the Nation." Institute on Taxation and Economic Policy, Washington, DC, August 12.

De Rugy, V. 2015. "The Biggest Beneficiaries of the Ex-Im Bank." Mercatus Center, George Mason University, April 29. Accessed December 23, 2015. http://mercatus.org/publication/biggest-beneficiaries-ex-im-bank.

Detrow, S. 2012. "Corbett Administration Sells Ethane Cracker Tax Break; Secretary Says Shell Asked for It." *State Impact/NPR.* Accessed December 18, 2015, https://stateimpact.npr.org/pennsylvania/2012/06/14/corbett-administration-sells-ethane-cracker-tax-break-secretary-says-shell-asked-for-it/.

DOE. 2014. "Energy.gov. Loan Programs Office." U.S. Department of Energy, accessed May 30, 2015, http://energy.gov/lpo/projects.

Downtown Development Authority. 2013. "Authorization to Enter Into Memorandum of Understanding Relating to Catalyst Development Project," June 19. Accessed May 30, 2015, http://www.degc.org/data/uploads/MOU%20Memo%20Reso%20with%20Exhibits%206–19–13.pdf.

EWG. 2013. "Farm Subsidy Database, 2013." Environmental Working Group, accessed November 26, 2014, http://farm.ewg.org/index.php.

Fisher, P. 2004. "The Fiscal Consequences of Competition for Capital." Conference Paper, Humphrey Institute of Public Affairs, University of Minnesota, Minneapolis, February.

Florida Office of Economic and Demographic Research. 2014. "Return on Investment for Select State Economic Development Incentive Programs," January 1, accessed May 1, 2015, http://edr.state.fl.us/Content/returnoninvestment/EDR_ROI.pdf.

FRA. 2014. "Federal Railroad Administration," accessed November 26, 2014, http://www.fra.dot.gov/Page/P0021.

"GM Collected $17 Million from TN for Jobs, Then Left." 2011. *Tennessean*, July 31. Accessed May 1, 2015, http://archive.tennessean.com/article/20110731/NEWS0201/307310092/GM-collected-17-million-from-TN-jobs-then-left.

"GM Invests $167M at Spring Hill, Tenn., Factory, Will Add 2 New Models." 2013. *Detroit Free Press*, August 6. Accessed November 26, 2014, http://archive.freep.com/article/20130806/BUSINESS0101/308060079/general-motors-spring-hilll.

GSA. 2014. "Catalog of Federal Domestic Assistance," accessed May 1, 2015, https://www.cfda.gov/.

Haglund, R. 2009. "Tax Incentives, Job Training Funds Won Orion Township, Michigan GM's New Small Car Work," June 26, accessed November 26, 2014, http://www.mlive.com/auto/index.ssf/2009/06/tax_incentives_job_training_fu.html.

HUD. 2014. "Department of Housing and Urban Development," accessed November 26, 2014, http://portal.hud.gov/hudportal/HUD?src=/program_offices/comm_planning/economicdevelopment/programs/rc/businesses.

ICA and WavTeq. 2014. "Incentives Database," accessed November 26, 2014, www.incentivesmonitor.com.

ICMA. 2012. "Incentives for Business Attraction and Retention." ICMA, June 13, accessed November 26, 2014, http://icma.org/en/Article/102200/Incentives_for_Business_Attraction_and_Retention.

ITA. 2014. "Exports, Jobs, and Foreign Investment." U.S. Department of Commerce, International Trade Administration, March 3, accessed November 26, 2014, http://www.trade.gov/mas/ian/statereports/.

Joint Committee on Taxation. 2013. "Estimates of Federal Tax Expenditures for Fiscal Years 2012–2017." Prepared for the House Committee on Ways & Means and the Senate Finance Committee by the Staff of the Joint Committee on Taxation, Washington, DC, February 1.

Kenyon, D., A. Langley, and B. Paquin. 2013. "The Effective Use of Property Tax Incentives for Economic Development." *Communities and Banking* (Federal Reserve Bank of Boston), Fall.

Krakoff, C. 2012. "Good Money After Bad: Why Government Should Not Fund Private Businesses." *Emerging Markets Outlook* (blog), May 20. Accessed May 30, 2015, http://www.emergingmarketsoutlook.com/?p=1854.

Lavery, K. 2014. "Ypsilanti Offers Cautionary Tale on GM Tax Breaks." WKAR, Michigan State University, East Lansing, July 28.

Louisiana Economic Development. 2013. "SEDC Economic Development Incentives Discussion." Accessed December 22, 2015, http://c.ymcdn.com/sites/www.sedc.org/resource/resmgr/imported/D.%20Pierson.pdf. pp. 3–10.

Mattera, P., and K. Tarczynska. 2013. "Megadeals: The Largest Economic Development Subsidy Packages Ever Awarded by State and Local Governments in the United States." Washington, DC: Good Jobs First.

——. 2014. "Updated List of Megadeals in Spreadsheet Form." Good Jobs First, September, accessed November 26, 2014, http://www.goodjobsfirst.org/megadeals.

Morisset, J., and N. Pirnia. 1999. "How Tax Policy and Incentives Affect Foreign Direct Investment: A Review." Policy Research Working Paper, Foreign Investment Advisory Service. Washington, DC: World Bank Group.

NOAA. 2014. "National Oceanic and Atmospheric Administration," accessed November 26, 2014, http://www.nmfs.noaa.gov/mb/financial_services/ffp.htm.

O'Malley, D. 2009. Videotaped interview in "Intel—20 years in Ireland," Intel Case Study, IDA Ireland. Accessed November 26, 2014, http://www.idaireland.com/how-we-help/case-studies/intel/.

Peters, A., and P. Fischer. 2004. "The Failures of Economic Development Incentives." *Journal of the American Planning Association* 70 (1) (Winter): 27–37.

Pew Charitable Trust. 2014. "Strategies for Evaluating Tax Incentives." Fact Sheet, Pew Charitable Trust, Washington, DC, June 13.

Ruane, F., and P. Buckley. 2006. "Foreign Direct Investment in Ireland: Policy Implications for Emerging Economies." IIS Discussion Paper No. 113, Trinity College, Dublin, January.

Ruane, F., and H. Görg. 1999. "Some Reflections on Foreign Direct Investment Policy for the Manufacturing Sector in Ireland." Scott Policy Seminar, Economic Research Institute of Northern Ireland, Belfast, May.

Sheehan, A. 2015. "Many Still Concerned as Progress Continues at Site of Proposed Cracker Plant." KDKA/CBS Local TV, June 28. Accessed December 15, 2015, http://pittsburgh.cbslocal.com/2015/07/28/many-still-concerned-as-progress-continues-at-site-of-proposed-cracker-plant/.

Shepardson, D., M. Burden, and M. Wayland. 2014. "GM laying off 510 at 2 Michigan plants." *Detroit Free Press,* November 12. Accessed December 19, 2015, http://www.detroitnews.com/story/business/autos/general-motors/2014/11/11/gm-laying-orion-assembly/18853065/.

Spar, D. 1998. "Attracting High Technology Investment: Intel's Costa Rican Plant." Foreign Investment Advisory Service Occasional Paper No. 11. Washington, DC: World Bank.

"State Encourages General Motors to Stay in Lake Orion: Michigan Competing for More Than 2,200 Jobs." 2001. Michigan's Former Governors, November 13, accessed November 26, 2014, http://www.michigan.gov/formergovernors/0,4584,7–212–31303_31306–4946—,00.html.

Staub, A. 2014. "Corbett-Supported Ethane Cracker Plant Shuffles Ahead." *Pennsylvania Independent*, November 21, 2014. Accessed November 26, 2014, http://paindependent.com/2014/11/week-in-review-corbett-supported-ethane-cracker-plant-shuffles-ahead/.

Steele, C. 2014. "Six U.S. States Exemplify 'Best Practices' in Transparency and Evaluation of the Economic Impacts of Incentive Programs." ICA Press Release, May 27.

Thomas, K. 2000. *Competing for Capital: Europe and North America in a Global Era.* Washington, DC: Georgetown University Press.

——. 2011. "Regulating Investment Attraction: Canada's Code of Conduct on Incentives in a Comparative Context." *Canadian Public Policy* 37 (3): 343–57.

UAW. 2010. "UAW and GM Bring Small, Energy-Efficient Car to U.S. from South Korea," October 8, accessed November 26, 2014, http://www.uaw.org/taxonomy/term/222/all?page=3.

Uchitelle, L. 2003. "States Pay for Jobs, but It Doesn't Always Pay Off." *The New York Times,* November 10. Accessed May 1, 2015, http://www.nytimes.com/2003/11/10/business/states-pay-for-jobs-but-it-doesn-t-always-pay-off.html?pagewanted=all.

UNCTAD. 2004. "Incentives." UNCTAD Series on Issues in International Investment Agreements. Geneva: United Nations Conference on Trade and Development.

"United States of Subsidies: A Series Examining Business Incentives and Their Impact on Jobs and Local Economies." 2012. *New York Times*, December 21. Accessed November 26, 2014, http://www.nytimes.com/interactive/2012/12/01/us/government-incentives.html#home.

VanHulle, L. 2014. "GM to Build $162M Stamping Plant at Lansing Grand River, Add 65 Jobs." *Lansing State Journal*, May 6. Accessed May 1, 2015, http://archive.lansingstatejournal.com/article/20140306/BUSINESS/303060025/GM-build-162M-stamping-plant-Lansing-Grand-River-add-65-jobs.

Wallack, T., H. Bray, and M. Arsenault. 2012. "Curt Schilling's 38 Studios Lays Off All Staff." *Boston Globe*, May 24. Accessed May 1, 2015, https://www.bostonglobe.com/business/2012/05/24/curt-schilling-studios-lays-off-all-staff/G3eE1ygyIWl7JUL-NX045aO/story.html.

Wells, L. Jr., N. Allen, J. Morisset, and N. Pirnia. 2001. "Using Tax Incentives to Compete for Foreign Investment: Are They Worth the Cost?" FIAS Occasional Paper No. 15, International Finance Corporation and the World Bank, Washington, DC.

Whyte, R. 2012. "Do Incentives Influence FDI? Can Fiscal Incentives Compensate for a Poor Investment Climate?" Global Investment Promotion Best Practices 2012, Investment Climate Department. Washington, DC: World Bank Group.

"Willow Run Bomber Plant to Be Demolished; Vehicle Research Center Planned." 2013. *Detroit Free Press*, September 5. Accessed November 26, 2014, http://www.freep.com/article/20130905/BUSINESS0101/309050106/willow-run-bomber-plant-ypsilanti.

Woods, K. 2015. "Shell takes more steps for ethane cracker plant location in Monaca, Pennsylvania." *Shale Gas Reporter,* October 12. Accessed December 19, 2015, http://shalegasreporter.com/news/shell-takes-steps-ethane-cracker-plant-location-monaca-pennsylvania/57828.html.

Yuill, D., K. Allen, J. Bachtler, K. Clement, and F. Wishlade, eds. 1995. *European Regional Incentives, 1995–96.* 15th ed. London: Bowker-Saur, cited in S. Roper and A. Frenkel. 2000. "Different Paths to Success—The Growth of the Electronics Sector in Ireland and Israel." *Environment and Planning C: Government and Policy* 18 (6): 651–65.

Zaretsky, A. M. 1994. "Are States Giving Away the Store? Attracting Jobs Can Be A Costly Adventure." *Regional Economist* (Federal Reserve Bank of St. Louis), January.

CHAPTER 7

Tax Incentives Around the World

Sebastian James

In 2013, Jamaica, under severe fiscal pressure, agreed to undertake comprehensive tax reform and eliminated many of its generous and discretionary tax incentives for investment (Collister 2013). On the passing of the legislation, the minister of justice, Senator Mark Golding, said, "The Jamaican economy has not been well served by the existing regime of sector-based incentives. The consensus is that such incentives may have been partly responsible for Jamaica's lackluster record of growth by encouraging the misallocation of limited economic resources in our country." He also explained that the reform would ensure that an equitable rules-based system is created for all players within the industry and not just those who have "access to ministerial decision-makers" (Linton 2013). Uganda ("Uganda Budget" 2014) and Pakistan (Anthony and Mangi 2014) carried out similar tax incentives reforms in 2014 as a result of losses to their treasury.

On the other hand, in the not too distant past, the finance minister of Grenada announced that, in order to encourage the resort group Sandals to invest in Grenada, the government had agreed to waive the company's payment of corporate taxes for twenty-five years, place a cap on Sandals' property taxes for twenty-five years, waive all import duties for twenty-five years, and waive the value-added tax on consumer goods for fifteen years. He further announced that the benefits to the economy were an injection of US$100 million and the creation of 425 jobs ("Sandals Investing US$100 Million" 2012). In 2013, Malaysia announced new tax incentives for its Refinery and Petrochemical Integrated Development (RAPID) Complex, which included tax exemptions for capital expenditure, and in 2014, Italy passed legislation providing a tax credit for investments in plant and equipment.

These instances highlight the very justifiable confusion on the use of tax incentives around the world today. While some countries are scaling them down, others are providing new ones. Even within countries, one sees gyrations in the policy across time. Indonesia, for example, went from providing tax holidays to eliminating them for investments made after 1983, only to reverse its policy in 1994. It now offers tax holidays for certain "pioneer" industries. Wells et al. (2001) show that the elimination of tax holidays in 1983 had no impact on the foreign direct investment (FDI) into Indonesia, but the government felt pressured by a temporary dip in FDI in 1994 to reintroduce them.

Attracting FDI, as well as encouraging domestic investments, is an important goal for countries that aim to create jobs, bring in new technology and skills, and improve their competitiveness and access to international markets. Investment incentives—be they tax incentives that exempt companies from taxation either partially or fully, nontax financial incentives such as cash grants and loan guarantees, or regulatory incentives—are commonly used to encourage investments and/or influence the activities of investors/investments. In trying to use investment incentives, governments face the difficult task of managing the budgetary implications that those measures entail. Hence, there is a constant tension faced by governments when setting the appropriate tax and other policies so that they neither discourage investment nor hurt the government budget. It is not surprising that this results in policy dilemmas and reversals in policies related to incentives.

As demonstrated by the examples above, governments try to fine-tune their tax policy by offering incentives to encourage investments into certain sectors, specific kinds of investments (as in the cases of Malaysia and Italy above), or investments into certain regions that otherwise might not happen due to market failures—and even compete with their neighbors for investment (as in the case of Grenada); at least, that is the theory. In practice, however, tax incentives are driven not only by economics but also by politics. In many cases, politicians find it easy to announce new tax incentives so that they are seen to be proactive in dealing with an economic downturn or unemployment. Further, the costs of these decisions are nontransparent, as they relate to foregone tax revenues sometime in the future. In other cases, they are the result of the government acquiescing to pressure by large businesses as a condition to invest (James 2009).

The tax incentives provided around the world that this chapter surveys reflect these varied situations and pressures faced by the government.

They are provided by nearly all the governments in the world, they are numerous, and they are provided for not just in the tax laws but also in various other laws. As a result, they are complex in both their design and their administration.

Tax incentives are further complicated by the fact that they change quite often, as demonstrated by the case of Indonesia. As a result, providing a summary of the investment incentives schemes within a country is itself quite challenging, and doing so for the whole world is even more difficult. This chapter attempts to summarize the different kinds of tax incentives provided around the world and the manner in which they are administered. It is intended to give the reader a sense of their use by different countries as a tool for attracting investments and how they have changed over time.

Most investment incentives schemes involve exemption from or reduction in various taxes, especially the income tax, the value-added tax (VAT), and customs duties. These schemes may also include exemptions from property tax and from smaller taxes and fees such as stamp duties and registration fees. Some countries may also provide cash incentives and in-kind incentives such as free land (sometimes even free electricity). Loan guarantees are also given to ensure that investors can get the funding required to get started. These nontax incentives are highly complex and particularly challenging to identify and summarize. That being said, nontax incentives, especially cash incentives, are much less common than tax incentives (see also chapter 2 in this volume).[1] As a result, this chapter focuses on tax incentives involving income tax, customs duties, and the VAT.

This chapter does not analyze incentives that flow through international tax treaties that provide special tax treatment for certain kinds of income that accrues to nonresidents. These incentives have been increasingly in the news these days because of the spotlight on the low taxes that multinationals such as Apple, Google, and Microsoft pay in jurisdictions such as Ireland, Luxembourg, and the Netherlands.[2] These special provisions are basically tax incentives because they accord special tax treatment to certain kinds of income for nonresidents of certain countries. Another mechanism that has come under scrutiny recently is the use of lax transfer pricing rules[3] and advance pricing agreements (APAs) as tax incentives. An APA is an agreement between a multinational and the tax administration of a country that governs how price (and hence income) is determined on transactions between agencies of the same multinational but across different tax jurisdictions. When an agreement allows a disproportionate amount of income to accrue to a tax haven and hence lower the tax liability, such an agreement is seen as providing a special tax treatment to that multinational. The European Commission is investigating whether one such special treatment that the government of Ireland allegedly provided to Apple Operations International is prohibited under its State aid rules ("State Aid SA.38373" 2014). It is also launching a similar investigation of APAs allegedly used by the government of Luxembourg to provide special tax treatment to Amazon ("State Aid: Commission Investigates" 2014). In October 2015 the European Commission ruled that the Netherlands provided illegal State Aid to Starbucks and that Luxembourg did the same for Fiat ("Commission decides selective tax advantages" 2015). These special tax arrangements, although important, are beyond the scope of this chapter.

The chapter is organized as follows: First, it summarizes the income tax incentives offered around the world. It then describes VAT incentives and their use in some parts of the world. Next, it briefly describes countries' use of customs duty exemptions and their increasing use of duty relief in special economic zones as tools for attracting investment. Lastly, it describes the different ways in which investment incentives are administered and their implications for application and governance of the incentives.

INCOME TAX INCENTIVES AROUND THE WORLD

Table 7.1 shows the prevalence of the different tax incentives among the 153 countries surveyed.[4] Despite the differences in opinion on their effectiveness, the fact remains that income tax incentives in one form or another are used by nearly all countries in the world.

Among the different regions around the world, except for the OECD countries, tax holidays, which exempt investors from 100 percent of the taxes on income for one or more years, are the most common tax incentive. Tax holidays are offered by all of the countries in South Asia. In some countries in the Caribbean, tax holidays could extend as long as twenty-five years ("Sandals Investing US$100 Million" 2012). In contrast, in the OECD countries, investment allowances are the most common. Among the countries of Sub-Saharan Africa, tax holidays and investment allowances are equally prevalent, whereas among the Latin American countries, investment allowances are the second most popular tax incentive (after tax holidays).

Table 7.1 Prevalence of income tax incentives around the world

	Number of countries surveyed	Tax holiday/tax exemption	Reduced tax rate	Investment allowance/ tax credit	R&D tax incentive*	Super-deductions
East Asia and Pacific	12	92%	75%	67%	83%	33%
Eastern Europe and Central Asia	17	82%	35%	24%	29%	0%
Latin America and the Caribbean	24	92%	33%	50%	8%	4%
Middle East and North Africa	15	80%	40%	13%	0%	0%
OECD	34	12%	32%	65%	76%	21%
South Asia	8	100%	38%	75%	25%	63%
Sub-Saharan Africa	44	80%	64%	77%	11%	18%

Source: James 2014.

* R&D tax incentives are included as a separate category although the instruments used are either tax holidays or investment allowances or super-deductions (i.e., costs that could be deducted in excess of 100 percent).

Tax holidays are frequently abused, as companies commonly extend their tax holidays by reorganizing their business under a different name. Further, tax holidays have a disadvantage, as compared to investment-linked incentives such as investment allowances and accelerated depreciation, in that the incentive is not aligned with the growth of the business's capital expenditures. The benefits provided by investment-linked incentives increase as the business expands, and, hence, there is an incentive to grow.

Governments continue to offer tax holidays despite their disadvantages. One reason for this might be the popularity of tax holidays with businesses. In addition to having the potential to extend their tax holidays through corporate reorganization, businesses might also favor tax holidays because, as compared with investment-linked incentives, there is a reduced requirement (or even no requirement in some countries) to deal with the tax authorities (in some countries, taxpayers are not even required to file tax returns). It becomes even more difficult for governments to prevent abuse of tax holidays through corporate reorganization or to administer their tax policies once the holidays expire.

Table 7.2 shows how the use of tax holidays has changed over time. In 2000, UNCTAD surveyed fifty countries around the world on their use

Table 7.2 Prevalence of tax holidays in 2000 v. 2014

	Number of countries surveyed (UNCTAD 2000)	Number of countries with tax holidays	
		In 2000	In 2014
East Asia and Pacific	7	7	6
Eastern Europe and Central Asia	3	3	2
Latin America and the Caribbean	10	10	8
Middle East and North Africa	4	4	4
OECD	8	6	3
South Asia	2	2	2
Sub-Saharan Africa	See table 7.3		

Sources: UNCTAD 2000; James 2014.

of tax incentives (UNCTAD 2000). This survey covered the main types of tax incentives, including tax holidays. When comparing these results with the incentives being offered in 2014, 94 percent of the countries surveyed in 2000 offered tax holidays, whereas 74 percent of them did in 2014. Hence, despite their extensive use today, fewer among the surveyed countries offer tax holidays today than in 2000. This reduction is most marked among the OECD countries, which have mostly moved to using investment-linked incentives, reflecting a shift to more targeted and precise use of investment incentives.

When one looks only at the non-OECD countries surveyed, the prevalence of tax holidays has come down slightly from 100 percent in 2000 to 85 percent in 2014. Their use has remained unchanged in the Middle East and North Africa (MENA) and in South Asia.

An extensive survey of incentives in over forty countries conducted by Keen and Mansour (2009) illustrates their use in Sub-Saharan Africa. Table 7.3 shows that the number of the particular tax incentives, including tax holidays, offered by these countries has actually gone up between 2005 and 2014 (the investment codes show a higher number because they typically include a number of different tax incentives). What is most marked is the increase in the number of countries offering tax incentives in free zones—from seventeen out of forty in 2005 to twenty-seven out of forty in 2014. In fact, when one looks at the countries (Cameroon, Mozambique, Namibia, Senegal, and Zambia) that did not provide tax holidays in 2005 but did so in 2014, they did so only for investments within the free zones. Limiting tax holidays to free zones is growing in popularity not just in sub-Saharan Africa as countries seek to limit the

Table 7.3 Tax incentives in Sub-Saharan Africa, 2005 v. 2014

	Countries providing investment incentives out of 40 surveyed	
	2005 (Keen and Mansour 2009)	2014
Tax holidays	27	31
Reduced CIT rates	20	26
Investment allowances	22	31
Free zones	17	27
Tax incentives provided through investment codes	31	23

Sources: Keen and Mansour 2009; James 2014.

"damage" that a tax holiday may cause by confining it to a geographically contiguous area (the free zone). Its use may reflect the need by countries to "target" these tax holidays to certain businesses (such as exporters) and for certain sectors. This issue is dealt with further later in this chapter when discussing free zones. Another interesting fact is that fewer countries in Sub-Saharan Africa offered tax incentives through investment codes or other sectoral laws in 2014, with more of the incentives being provided through the tax laws (research on this phenomenon in other regions of the world is pending).

Tables 7.2 and 7.3 indicate that the popularity of tax incentives worldwide has not significantly diminished over the last decade and, in Sub-Saharan Africa, has even increased.

The OECD countries, while limiting the use of tax holidays, increasingly use carryforward of losses as an incentive. The treatment of tax losses can be very valuable to businesses because the income tax is applied to income earned during the previous year. When a business suffers a loss in one year, no tax is owed, but when it earns a profit, tax is due. However, when one looks at the business not on a year-to-year basis but rather on a multiyear basis, losses in one year could be absorbed by profits in other years, resulting in reduced tax overall. Carrying losses forward allows businesses to benefit from such a multiyear approach to taxing their income. A limitation on carrying losses forward may disincentivize businesses that take many years to become profitable, consequently discouraging projects with long gestation periods.

Table 7.4 shows the divergence in the treatment of tax losses between East Asian countries and some OECD countries. Although three countries in East Asia allow tax losses to be carried forward indefinitely, the others do

Table 7.4 Carryforward/carryback of tax losses in a selection of countries

	Number of years of carryforward, carryback of losses		Number of years of carryforward, carryback of losses
East Asian countries		OECD countries	
Brunei	6, -1	Australia	∞, 0
Cambodia	5, 0	Austria	∞, 0
China	5, 0	Canada	20, -3
Hong Kong	∞, 0	Denmark	∞, 0
Indonesia	5, 0	France	∞, -3
Laos	3, 0	Germany	∞, -1
Malaysia	∞, 0	Ireland	∞, -1
Myanmar	3, 0	Italy	5, 0
Philippines		Japan	9, 0
Singapore	∞, -1		
Thailand	5, 0	Mexico	10, 0
Vietnam	5, 0	Netherlands	9, -1
		New Zealand	∞, 0
		South Korea	10, 0
		Spain	15, 0
		Sweden	∞, 0
		Switzerland	7, 0
		United Kingdom	∞, -1
		United States	20, -2

Sources: James 2014; OECD 2011; KPMG 2013.

not allow tax losses to be carried forward for more than six years, with the most common limit being five years. Indefinite carryforward of losses is much more common among the OECD countries, and the United States and Canada allow losses to be carried forward for up to twenty years. Similarly, in the case of carryback of losses (which allows a loss in the current year to be set off against income of the previous year), seven of the OECD countries allow this, whereas only Singapore and Brunei allow it among the East Asian countries. The difference in approach between the East Asian countries and the OECD countries reflects the use of tax incentives by the former as signaling devices (tax holidays sound more investor friendly than a more generous loss carryforward, though the impact may be similar[5]).

Apart from using tax holidays to exempt 100 percent of income, some countries provide reduced tax rates distinct from tax holidays that exempt only a part of the income from taxation. In many cases, these are granted along with tax holidays, with 100 percent of the income exempt for a few years and only a part of it exempt for the rest of the period (when this is the case, the country is included with those providing tax holidays in table 7.1). Brazil, for example, does not provide tax holidays but reduces the tax rate on income. Such reduced tax rates are most common among the East Asian and Pacific countries, followed by those of Sub-Saharan Africa, with their use having increased in the latter group of countries in 2014, as compared to 2005 (see table 7.3).

After tax holidays and reduced tax rates, investment-linked incentives such as investment allowances, accelerated depreciation, initial allowances, and tax credits are the most prevalent. By design, these incentives are arguably superior to tax holidays because they are linked to the size of the investment. As the benefits accruing to the investment are, in general, proportional to the size of the investment, the motivations of the government, to encourage businesses to invest more in their business, and of the businesses, to garner more tax benefits by investing more in their business, are aligned.[6] As mentioned above, most OECD countries have moved away from tax holidays and toward such investment-linked incentives. Countries in Sub-Saharan Africa, which use tax holidays extensively, also use investment-linked incentives, with many countries using both kinds of incentives. Investment-linked incentives are least common among MENA countries.

Despite their advantages over tax holidays, investment-linked incentives are not without their problems, as unscrupulous investors could artificially inflate the value of their investments in order to increase their tax benefits (Modi 2004).[7] For this reason, the benefits of the investment allowance are sometimes capped. Malaysia, for example, uses generous investment allowances to encourage investments in its manufacturing, tourism, and agriculture sectors. The benefit accorded by those investment allowances is, however, capped at 60 percent of the taxable income, and any unabsorbed allowance can be carried forward and set off against income in other years. Furthermore, the investment allowances Malaysia grants in most cases are limited to five years.

This practice is not uncommon. In Burkina Faso, for example, the investment allowance cannot reduce the taxable income to less than 50 percent of the income taxable without counting the allowances. In India, the benefit of all incentives, including the investment allowance (15 percent of investment made above $4 million), is limited, as corporations are liable to pay a minimum alternate tax of 18.5 percent (20 percent with the surcharge and education tax) of the book profit (calculated without providing for any tax benefits).[8]

Super-deductions, deductions allowed for more than the actual cost of certain expenses, are most prevalent in South Asia and are used mainly to subsidize the cost of investments when starting a business. For example, in Thailand, businesses are allowed to deduct 150 percent of their actual expenditure on training for their employees, whereas the usual accounting treatment would allow them to deduct only the actual amount spent. Such additional deductions are common for research and development (R&D) expenditures. South Africa and China allow businesses a super-deduction of up to 150 percent of the actual R&D expenses, and India and Malaysia allow 200 percent of qualifying R&D expenditures to encourage more of such activity.

With the exception of countries in the MENA region, which do not use tax incentives to explicitly target R&D, there is now much greater use of tax incentives by countries worldwide to encourage R&D expenditures (see chapter 4 in this volume). These types of incentives are especially common in the OECD countries and countries in East Asia and the Pacific. China offers reduced corporate tax rates for companies that are granted High and New Technology Enterprise (HNTE) status (Deloitte 2014). Many countries are increasingly using a tax incentive or Patent Box that reduces the tax rate for income attributable to intellectual property. In the United Kingdom, this incentive allows a lower corporate tax rate of 10 percent (the main corporate tax rate is 21 percent) on profits earned from patented inventions and certain other inventions.

The use of incentives for businesses located in special economic zones /free trade zones/export processing zones (collectively referred to as SEZs) is quite popular across all the regions. These zones are generally contiguous areas that are outside the customs territory of the country and hence allow free movement of goods without duties and the VAT. In many cases, income tax incentives are also included. For example, in the case of South Korea's Incheon Free Economic Zone, large investments benefit from a tax holiday of up to five years over and above customs duty exemptions (Investment Incentives—Foreign Investment Business Support 2014). Indeed, in some countries, the tax holiday is limited to investments inside SEZs (table 7.1 includes tax holidays if offered inside or outside these zones). Kenya and Tanzania, for example, offer a ten-year tax holiday for investments inside their export processing zones, but investments outside the zones are not eligible for it. In fact, Tanzania replaced the tax holidays outside the zones with enhanced capital allowances.

Other SEZs do not provide income tax incentives. France's Verdon Free Zone/Port is an example, limiting the benefits to exemptions from customs duties, the VAT, and excise taxes for imports as long as they remain within the free zone. If they are released outside the free zone, these taxes have to be paid (Suspensive Arrangements and Free Zones 2011).

Most SEZs are designed in a manner that attracts export-oriented investment because they greatly reduce the procedural burden on imports that are primarily used for the purposes of exports. This makes them more attractive to exporters of those goods that have a significant proportion of imported inputs. The exemptions provided on border taxes (customs duties and the VAT on imports) are discussed later in the chapter.

EXEMPTIONS AND ZERO-RATING UNDER THE VALUE-ADDED TAX

Governments around the world offer incentives under the VAT, which may be exemptions or the zero-rating of supplies of goods or services (henceforth referred to simply as *supplies*). For those who are not very familiar with the VAT, a brief summary of this tax is useful for understanding the role of incentives provided under it.

Only businesses registered for the VAT are allowed to charge the VAT (which is the sales price times the VAT rate) and collect it from the buyer /purchaser. However, the amount collected is not entirely owed to the government. This is because the business is allowed to deduct the taxes it pays on its purchases from the tax it collects on its supplies/sales (input credit method[9]). As a result, the VAT is a tax collected on the difference between a business's sales and its purchases (which is the value added). Because the VAT-registered business is allowed to deduct all the taxes on inputs, including tax paid on investments made into the business, in theory it is an investment-friendly tax.

When a supply is exempt, it means that no tax can be charged on its sale by the supplier. However, the supplier will continue to pay tax on the inputs into the production process that are not exempt. If a supply is zero-rated, then not only are sales of that supply not taxed, but also all of the taxes paid on inputs to produce that supply are reimbursed to the supplier.

Not all exemptions are investment incentives: some are not provided with the aim of encouraging investment. Some exemptions are part of the design of the VAT, which needs to compromise between wide coverage of the tax and administrative feasibility of collecting it. This will be discussed in detail later in this chapter.

The costs to businesses of complying with the VAT are nontrivial. Businesses have to keep track of sales that are exempt and those that are not. Furthermore, the taxes they paid on purchases are calculated based on the invoices that they were issued for those purchases; hence, businesses have to keep track of all the invoices paid on the inputs into the production process, or they cannot deduct the taxes paid on these inputs (from the taxes due to be paid to the government on sales).[10] VAT returns have to be filed with the necessary information on exempt sales and regular sales and the correct tax rate applied when a business supplies both kinds of supplies (exempt supplies and the inputs that go into them are treated differently from regular supplies, which are taxable). Because of the high cost of compliance with the VAT, most governments do not allow businesses with sales below a certain threshold to register for the VAT and collect taxes on sales (though some countries do allow these "small" businesses to register for the VAT on an optional basis).[11]

Complications also arise in the operation of a VAT for reasons related to the peculiarity of the sector, the difficulties in administering the VAT, or public policy. Exceptions to the charging of the regular VAT may be classified as exceptions for "out-of-scope" supplies, which are supplies that are not consumed locally (e.g., zero-rating of exports and international transport); merit or concessional exemptions (e.g., education, health care, and charitable services); and technical exemptions (e.g., the financial sector, real estate, and gambling). In the case of financial services, the technical exemption is given because it is difficult to correctly assign the value added. In the case of durable goods such as real estate, which is consumed over a long period of time, computing the value added is difficult and not practical. Policy makers further try to reduce the burden of the VAT on goods consumed by the poor, such as bread and grains, by allowing businesses to sell them free of the VAT and to claim refunds on the taxes paid on inputs (zero-rating).

When certain supplies or businesses are exempt from the VAT, the advantage is both the lower cost of compliance[12] and the benefit that they are not charged tax on the value added.[13] Producers of zero-rated supplies benefit even more, as taxes on inputs are refunded. Producers of supplies that have inputs that are exempt also benefit from lower input costs.

A comprehensive analysis of VAT systems around the world is very complex, as there can be dozens of exemptions under a given VAT.

Table 7.5 Prevalence of VAT exemptions and zero-ratings, Africa versus OECD countries

	% of countries in the region providing exemptions		% of countries in the region providing zero-rating	
	Africa	OECD	Africa	OECD
Agricultural inputs	50%	9%	32%	15%
Agricultural produce	71%	6%	50%	27%
Transport	68%	24%	39%	30%
Real estate	71%	100%	7%	3%
Education	93%	12%	18%	0%
Health/pharmaceuticals	79%	94%	29%	27%
Capital goods	11%	0%	4%	9%
Fuel	7%	0%	0%	3%
Cultural	64%	97%	4%	27%
Finance (does not include insurance)	82%	100%	7%	6%
Mining/petroleum	36%	0%	11%	0%
Charitable	7%	97%	4%	6%
Construction	7%	12%	0%	6%
Tourism inputs/services	18%	6%	4%	9%

Sources: PwC 2014; OECD 2012; James 2014.

Nevertheless, drawing from surveys done by Pricewaterhouse Coopers on the VAT in Africa and by the OECD on the VAT in the OECD countries, table 7.5 summarizes the principal exemptions and zero-ratings in Africa and the OECD for various kinds of supplies or sectors.

All of the VAT exemptions with the exception of finance and real estate could be classified as incentives. As shown in table 7.5, nearly all of the countries surveyed provide exemptions to the finance and real estate sectors. The exemptions given to the cultural sector include supplies such as books, newspapers, films, and art. VAT exemptions given to the agriculture sector are specifically for agricultural inputs such as fertilizers, agricultural implements, and seeds. The main purpose of these exemptions is to reduce the costs of inputs to the agricultural process. Exemptions for agricultural produce are for sales of agricultural commodities, which are driven by the desire of governments to keep the agriculture sector out of the VAT.

In Africa, the most common VAT-related incentives are given to the education, health, transport, culture, and agriculture sectors. Among most OECD countries, supplies related to the cultural, health, and charitable sectors benefit from exemptions. Although there are therefore similar patterns, in Africa the governments provide more support to the agriculture, education, transport, and mining sectors through VAT exemptions than do the OECD countries. These differences—especially in education, transport, and agriculture—may reflect differences in the level of development of these sectors between these two groups of countries. Interestingly, the treatment of the health sector is quite similar.

VAT zero-rating is less common than exemptions and mainly targets the agriculture sector. This is done with the aim of reducing the incidence of the tax on the poor, especially for food items, and hence lowering prices on basic agricultural produce. The zero-rating for transport shown in table 7.5 refers to the tax treatment of international transportation, which is essentially treated as consumption abroad on which the VAT is not levied. As in the case of exemptions, the treatment on average is similar between the two groups of countries for health care but divergent in the case of the education sector.

The tax incentives for the VAT provide at least two advantages for businesses. First, they allow businesses to lower the prices they charge to consumers, and, second, they eliminate the need to comply with the administrative requirements of the VAT. However, tax exemptions and zero-rating (except in the case of technical exemptions) increase reporting requirements for businesses that provide a combination of standard supplies and exempt supplies. Further, when these exemptions are part of a VAT chain, they cause breaks in the reporting along the chain (as those exempt are not required to collect tax and file returns). As a result, it makes the enforcement of the VAT more difficult for tax administrators. An even bigger issue is that when exempt supplies are used in the production chain, the un-reimbursed taxes on inputs (or a part of those) remain in the sale price, which is then taxed again down the supply chain—sometimes multiple times (cascading of taxes).

CUSTOMS DUTY RELIEF AND EXEMPTION REGIMES

Duty exemptions and duty relief can be important tools to increase the attractiveness of a country as an investment destination.

Customs duty relief refers to customs regimes under which goods are imported but their duty payments are suspended pending their reexportation. The common forms of duty relief include manufacturing under bond, customs warehousing and duty-drawback regimes, and temporary admissions for reexportation in the same state. Duty relief is used to reduce the cost of exports by eliminating all of the duties that go into the cost of production, thereby helping exporters become more competitive.

Table 7.6 Use of special regimes for duty relief

	Number of countries surveyed	SEZ/free zone/EPZ/ free port
East Asia and Pacific	12	92%
Eastern Europe and Central Asia	16	94%
Latin America and the Caribbean	25	71%
Middle East and North Africa	15	80%
OECD	33	68%
South Asia	7	63%
Sub-Saharan Africa	45	66%

Source: James 2014.

Customs duty exemptions are full or partial exemptions from duties unrelated to exportation (Goorman 2005). Hence, they are exceptions made to the application of the ordinary customs tariff.[14] These exemptions may be stipulated under international agreements.

Duty relief is generally used inside SEZs. These enclaves have special schemes whereby inputs for the production of goods (destined for export) can enter duty-free. If the final goods are sold in the domestic market, they typically attract all of the taxes that have been suspended. As this incentive regime is compatible with the World Trade Organization (WTO) rules regarding prohibited subsidies on exports (because the suspension of duties on imported goods that are used in the production of products that are destined for export is not treated as an export subsidy prohibited under WTO rules[15]), they have become increasingly popular around the world. Table 7.6 shows the prevalence of the use of these regimes. They are most common in the regions of Eastern Europe, Central Asia, and East Asia and the Pacific and are least common in the OECD countries, although still used by two-thirds of them.

This chapter does not provide a summary of duty exemptions provided in the countries around the world, as it is very difficult to capture the various complex exemption regimes that are employed. Nevertheless, table 7.7 provides examples from several countries to illustrate some practices and provide a glimpse of the challenges to presenting a broader picture of these exemptions.

This survey provides the reader with a glimpse of the kinds of incentives involving reduction of or relief from customs duties. A more detailed assessment is beyond the scope of the chapter. Nevertheless, these types of incentives are important because duty relief schemes are widely used and duty exemptions sometimes apply to 30 percent or even half of all imports (Goorman 2005).

Table 7.7 Duty exemption regimes—Some examples

Ethiopia	Exemption of customs duty on import of all investment capital goods such as plant, machinery, and equipment; construction materials; and spare parts worth up to 15 percent of the value of the imported investment capital goods
Turkey	Exemption of customs duty on imported machinery and equipment for approved projects
Malaysia	Import duty exemption on machinery and equipment excluding spare parts and consumables
Zimbabwe	Rebate of duty on specified goods for the mining industry; materials used in preparation and packaging of produce for exports; goods imported for tourist zones; parts and materials imported for aircraft assembly; motor vehicle assembly; registered electrical manufacturer; pharmaceutical manufacturer; etc.

Source: James 2014.

This chapter has to this point discussed certain common investment incentives offered in the different regions around the world. These incentives are exceptions to the general tax treatment, and there are procedures for their applicability as well as their reporting. This chapter will now discuss the manner in which these incentives regimes are implemented in practice.

PROCEDURES FOR GRANTING INVESTMENT INCENTIVES

The manner in which tax incentives are provided and administered varies greatly across the world. However, one practice that is apparent across all regions is the use of discretionary procedures to provide tax incentives. Through such discretionary procedures, investors can apply for a new tax incentive or duty exemption, typically to an agency outside the tax administration, provided they satisfy certain broad criteria. This allows the government to customize the tax incentive to each investor. In theory, such customized solutions allow for fine-tuning of the incentives; in practice, such a system is susceptible to corrupt practices, delays the investment process, and vitiates the business environment by introducing uncertainty, as investors cannot predict what "deal" they will get or whether it will be similar to what their competitors receive. Despite these disadvantages, many countries adopt such practices.

The discretion mentioned above refers to the provision of the tax incentive; that is, the incentive is not granted automatically, by law or regulation, to anyone meeting particular criteria but is provided on a case-by-case basis to investors who ask for it. Discretion can also refer to the application of a tax incentive that is already specified in the law; that is,

Table 7.8 Discretion in the provision and application of tax incentives

	Number of countries surveyed	% of countries following a discretionary process for investment incentives
East Asia and Pacific	12	83%
Eastern Europe and Central Asia	16	38%
Latin America and the Caribbean	25	40%
Middle East and North Africa	15	40%
OECD	33	33%
South Asia	7	43%
Sub-Saharan Africa	45	82%

Source: James 2014.

the tax incentive that the investor may qualify for is specified in the tax law or investment code but is generally given broad interpretation, which requires an approval process. This type of discretion also raises opportunities for corruption, as the approval is valuable for investors and officials administering the process have the ability to refuse it. In many cases, the approval by an agency outside the tax administration is not final because the latter has to comply with its own procedures to ensure that the tax incentive or duty exemption is correctly claimed. The approval process thus becomes an additional burden on investors because it is duplicated by the outside agency and the tax administration.

The automatic process, on the other hand, is one in which tax incentives are provided for in the tax legislation and there is no requirement to apply for them separate from the tax procedures. Taxpayers in this case directly claim their tax incentives during tax filing or during importation.

Table 7.8 indicates the use of discretionary procedures in the qualification for as well as the application of the tax incentives. Among all the regions in the world, countries in East Asia and the Pacific use discretionary procedures the most, followed by the Sub-Saharan African region, while the OECD countries use them the least. The heavy use of discretionary practices mostly reflects the use of investment codes, under which investors typically need to apply for tax incentives before investment promotion agencies. One would expect that the OECD countries would completely do away with discretion and prefer a rule-based system applicable to all investors in a transparent manner, but at least a third of these countries have some kind of discretion.

In the Czech Republic, for example, a business seeking to benefit from tax incentives submits an investment incentives application to the Ministry of Industry and Trade, which could take up to six months to approve or reject the request. In India, on the other hand, no such pre-approval is required (i.e., the grant of the incentive is automatic), and taxpayers apply for their income tax incentives when they file their tax returns. In the case of duty exemptions in India, however, the business needs to apply to the director general of foreign trade to benefit from the various government schemes. In Bangladesh, tax exemptions are provided on application to the National Board of Revenue, whereas in Senegal, all tax incentives outside the tax code require the approval of the minister of finance. In Bangladesh and Senegal, there is discretion in the provision and application of the tax incentive even though it is the tax collecting agency or the ministry that is approving the applications. That being said, investors in many countries have the opportunity to seek an advance ruling with the tax authorities on their eligibility for a particular tax incentive. The advance ruling is a procedure laid out in the tax law by which investors may seek a clarification from the tax administration on the application of certain tax provisions: for example, whether they qualify for a certain tax incentive based on the tax administration's interpretation of the tax law. As this is a clarification of the law, it is not treated as a use of discretion by the tax administration.

A big driver of discretion regarding tax incentives is the granting of these incentives through laws outside the tax and customs laws. In many countries, incentives are offered through the investment code or investment law. This in most cases provides the handle for agencies outside those administering taxes to become involved with the approval process. As shown in table 7.9, of the forty-nine countries in Sub-Saharan Africa that were surveyed, thirty provided tax incentives outside the tax laws, and in 93 percent of those thirty, there was discretion in the granting of the tax incentive. However, among the countries that provided tax incentives only through the tax laws, only 47 percent of them provided discretionary tax incentives.

Some countries have moved away from providing tax incentives through investment codes. Tanzania, for example, transferred all of the tax incentives provided through the Tanzania Investment Act to the Income Tax, Customs, and VAT Acts. Recently, Senegal and Guinea did the same, though they retain some elements of discretion in their administration.

The need to move tax incentives from other laws into the tax laws is a critical first step in better managing the use of tax incentives. Providing tax incentives outside the tax laws by agencies not involved in the collection of taxes presents a moral hazard problem because those agencies

Table 7.9 Tax incentives through investment codes and discretion in Sub-Saharan Africa

	Incentives in investment code	Discretionary incentives
Angola	x	x
Benin	x	x
Burkina Faso	x	x
Burundi	x	x
Cameroon	x	x
Cape Verde	x	x
Central African Republic	x	x
Chad	x	x
Comoros	x	x
Congo	x	x
DRC	x	x
Equatorial Guinea	x	x
Eritrea	x	
Ethiopia	x	
Gabon	x	x
Gambia	x	x
Guinea-Bissau	x	x
Ivory Coast	x	x
Madagascar	x	x
Mali	x	x
Mauritania	x	x
Niger	x	x
Rwanda	x	x
Sao Tome and Principe	x	x
Senegal	x	x
Sierra Leone	x	x
Southern Sudan	x	x
Sudan	x	x
Togo	x	x
Zambia	x	x
% of countries with discretionary incentives for countries with investment code		**93%**
Botswana		x
Djibouti		
Ghana		x
Guinea		x
Kenya		
Lesotho		x
Liberia		x
Malawi		x
Mauritius		
Mozambique		
Namibia		x
Nigeria		
Seychelles		x
Somalia		

(*Continued*)

Table 7.9 *(Continued)*

South Africa	
Swaziland	x
Tanzania	
Uganda	
Zimbabwe	
% of countries with discretionary incentives for countries without investment code	**47%**

Source: James 2014.

are evaluated on how much investment is generated and how many tax incentives are granted, but they do not bear any responsibility for losses of revenue that may result. Despite this potential conflict of interest, many countries have taken the power to administer tax incentives from the tax authorities and given it to investment promotion agencies on the ground that tax authorities are too conservative in granting tax incentives and not sufficiently investor friendly. Yet, as table 7.10 indicates, the impact on investor friendliness may be the opposite of what was intended: when an investment promotion agency provides tax incentives, the time it takes for investors to start their businesses is actually increased.

CONCLUSION

Tax incentives are widely prevalent and reflect the desire of governments to support economic growth and provide value for the local economy through jobs, new skills, and technology. Governments also provide tax incentives in

Table 7.10 Discretion in granting tax incentives and delay in starting a business

Countries surveyed	Average delay in days for granting of incentives*	Tax incentive provided by investment promotion agency?
Serbia	6	No
Rwanda	10	No
Tanzania	15	No
Uganda	18	No
Jordan	21	Yes
Nicaragua	42	No
Burundi	47	Yes
Kenya	63	Yes
Guinea	80	Yes
Tunisia	95	Yes

Source: James 2014.

* Data from Investor's Motivation Surveys conducted by the World Bank Group in response to this question: "Approximately how many days/weeks/months were required to obtain the incentives over and above the time needed for standard registration and start-up procedures?"

order to diversify their economies and support activities they hope will lead to new sources of growth that use the untapped potential of the country. The widespread use of investment incentives indicates that governments continue to feel that these instruments are useful and effective tools. However, there are indications that tax incentives are increasingly being limited in various ways. For one, countries are confining them to free zones to better target them and to limit their revenue impacts. Similarly, governments have attempted to target tax incentives by providing them on a case-by-case basis and only to those investments that provide the intended benefits. However, this has had unintended consequences, resulting in increasing opportunities for rent seeking, as discretionary power can be misused.

Overall, the true impact of these incentives on investment is much harder to gauge. There is evidence that some tax incentives are not effective in meeting the intended goals that governments seek to achieve, and their continued use, despite the evidence on their ineffectiveness, reflects the political economic realities. Further, there is weighty evidence to show that policies that go beyond tax incentives are more effective in encouraging investments than policies that focus narrowly on tax incentives (James 2009). The goal is to have greater transparency on the costs as well as the benefits of the tax incentives so that taxpayers are able to question their effectiveness and governments can, in turn, design better policies to encourage investment (see chapter 10 in this volume).

NOTES

1. Other incentives such as guaranteed pricing mechanisms and subsidies are quite common in developing countries but are beyond the scope of this chapter.

2. The Dutch sandwich is an example of a tax avoidance mechanism provided through the Ireland tax treaty, which exempts certain receipts from EU Member States, including the Netherlands, from tax withholding. This enables multinationals with specially designed structures to book tax that accrues to an Irish company to flow through the Netherlands to a low-tax jurisdiction such as Bermuda or the Cayman Islands without paying any tax in Ireland.

3. The double Irish is a tax arrangement that allows tax avoidance by multinationals through the use of Ireland's lax transfer pricing rules.

4. Mining incentives have not been included in this survey, as the tax regime for the mining sector can be quite distinct from those of the others. Some countries do have a mining code that in many cases also governs the taxation of the mining sector, but the fiscal terms of most large mining projects are negotiated.

5. It is sometimes more beneficial for businesses to have an indefinite or long-term loss carryforward than a tax holiday, given the fact that tax holidays often cover a

period where the company is in a no-tax position. Tax holidays also pose the risks for governments explained above. Thus, instead of a strategy giving tax holidays and limiting the loss carryforward, both governments and companies may prefer one that avoids tax holidays and instead provides long-term or indefinite loss carryforward.

6. Critics have argued that such incentives distort the decision to make capital-intensive investments, which may not be optimal in some cases.

7. Some types of investment-linked incentives may not necessarily advance the government's aims. A government focused on increasing the number of jobs, for example, may not want to provide incentives for increased investments in labor-saving equipment. However, governments can address those issues by tying their investments-linked incentives to particular types of investments such as investments in employee training and R&D.

8. The corporate tax rate for India in 2014 was 30 percent, and when the surcharge and education tax are included, it was 34 percent.

9. The subtraction method is the other way to calculate the VAT, but this is rarely used.

10. The cost of compliance is generally higher in the case of the VAT than the corporate income tax, as the reporting requirements are much more onerous. This is because the businesses are only collecting agents, depositing the VAT they collect from consumers in the government treasury, typically on a monthly basis.

11. As a result, such "small" businesses end up bearing the tax on inputs, as they are treated as final consumers and not allowed to claim any deduction of the taxes paid on inputs.

12. Say a producer uses inputs in the production process that cost $100 and bear a VAT of 20 percent; the total cost of these inputs is thus $120. She then adds value of $30. Say the market price of the good with tax is $150 (and the producer cannot affect this price). This is equivalent to a tax-free price of $125, as $125 + tax of 20 percent of this amount (which is $25) makes the total price $150. Under the regular VAT, the producer/seller charges the buyer a tax of $25. The producer/seller is then allowed to deduct the $20 of tax paid on inputs; thus, she pays a net tax of $5 and keeps the difference of $125 – $100 – $5 = $20. If the producer is exempt, she does not charge any tax on the sale but also cannot credit any tax paid on the inputs; hence, the producer gets to keep $150 – $120 = $30. In such a scenario, having an exemption is better than being taxed.

13. This assumes the sellers of those inputs have passed on the lower tax in the price of the product.

14. The special treatment of imports such as duty exemptions and duty reliefs is governed by the International Convention on the Simplification and Harmonization of Customs Procedures (which was adopted in Kyoto on May 18, 1973, and which entered into force on September 25, 1974), as amended by the 1999 Protocol of Amendment, also known as the Revised Kyoto Convention.

15. The suspension of duties on goods imported for the purpose of reexport or on goods used as inputs into manufacturing for the purpose of export is not a prohibited subsidy by the WTO because it has not been found to be a barrier to international trade. However, such treatment could be seen as an incentive, given that the default position is that all businesses pay duty on goods that are imported.

REFERENCES

Anthony, A., and F. Mangi. 2014. "Pakistan Cuts Power Subsidies, Corporate Taxes to Woo IMF." Bloomberg, accessed June 4, 2014, http://www.bloomberg.com/news/2014–06–03/pakistan-cuts-power-subsidies-overhauls-tax-rules-in-imf-push.html.

Collister, K. 2013. "Jamaica Tables Most Dramatic Tax Reform Bills Since the 1980s." *Jamaica Observer*, November 15. Accessed October 9, 2014, http://www.jamaicaobserver.com/business/Jamaica-tables-most-dramatic-tax-reform-bills-since-the-1980s_15444640.

Deloitte. 2014. "2014 Global Survey of R&D Tax Incentives," accessed October 8, 2014, http://www2.deloitte.com/content/dam/Deloitte/global/Documents/Tax/dttl-tax-global-rd-survey-aug-2014.pdf.

European Commission. 2015. "Commission decides selective tax advantages for Fiat in Luxembourg and Starbucks in the Netherlands are illegal under EU state aid rules." European Commission Press Release database, October 21. http://europa.eu/rapid/press-release_IP-15-5880_en.htm

Goorman, A. 2005. "Duty Relief and Exemption Control." In *Customs Modernization Handbook*. Washington, DC: World Bank Group.

"Investment Incentives—Foreign Investment Business Support." 2014. Incheon Free Economic Zone, accessed September 12, 2014, http://ifez.go.kr/jsp/eng/invest/invest3.jsp.

James, S. 2009. "Effectiveness of Tax and Non-tax Incentives and Investments: Evidence and Policy Implications." Investment Climate Advisory Services of the World Bank Group Policy Working Paper, Washington, DC. https://www.wbginvestmentclimate.org/uploads/IncentivesandInvestments.pdf.

——. 2014. "Tax and Non-Tax Incentives and Investments: Evidence and Policy Implications." Investment Climate Advisory Services of the World Bank Group, Washington, DC.

Keen, M., and M. Mansour. 2009. "Revenue Mobilization in Sub-Saharan Africa: Challenges from Globalization." Working Paper No. 09/157, International Monetary Fund, Washington, DC.

KPMG. 2013. "ASEAN Tax Guide." KPMG Asia Pacific Tax Centre, Page 10, November.

Linton, L. 2013. "Senate Passes Omnibus Tax Legislation." Jamaica Information Service, December 7, accessed October 9, 2014, http://jis.gov.jm/senate-passes-omnibus-tax-legislation/.

Modi, A. 2004. "A Cautionary Tale from India." In *Effectiveness and Economic Impact of Tax Incentives in the SADC Region* by B. Bolnick. Arlington, VA: Nathan Associates.

OECD. 2011. "Corporate Loss Utilisation through Aggressive Tax Planning," OECD Publishing. (Page 36) http://dx.doi.org/10.1787/9789264119222-en.

——. 2012. "Consumption Tax Trends 2012: VAT/GST and Excise Rates, Trends and Administration Issues," OECD Publishing. (Chapter 3) http://dx.doi.org/10.1787/ctt-2012-en.

PWC. 2014. "Helping you navigate Africa's VAT landscape." Overview of VAT in Africa—2014.

"Sandals Investing US$100 Million in New Grenada Resort." 2012. Caribbean 36.com, November 15, accessed October 9, 2014, http://www.caribbean360.com/business/sandals-investing-us-100-million-in-new-grenada-resort.

"State Aid: Commission Investigates Transfer Pricing Arrangements on Corporate Taxation of Amazon in Luxembourg," 2014. European Commission Press Release database, October 7. http://europa.eu/rapid/press-release_IP-14–1105_en.htm.

"State Aid SA.38373 (2014/C) (ex 2014/NN) (ex 2014/CP)—Ireland, Alleged Aid to Apple." European Commission, June 11. http://ec.europa.eu/competition/state_aid/cases/253200/253200_1582634_87_2.pdf.

"Suspensive Arrangements and Free Zones." 2011. Trade—Export Helpdesk—VAT Overview of France, European Commission, January 11. http://exporthelp.europa.eu/thdapp/taxes/show2Files.htm?dir=/taxes/notes&reporterId2=FR&file2=ehit_fr11_06v001/fr/main/ovr_vat_fr_0612.htm&reporterLabel2=France&languageId=en&status=PROD.

"Uganda Budget—'Tighten Your Belts.'" 2014. East African Business Week, June 15, accessed October 8, 2014, http://www.busiweek.com/index1.php?Ctp=2&pI=1323&pLv=3&srI=68&spI=107&cI=10.

UNCTAD. 2000. *Tax Incentives and Foreign Direct Investment: A Global Survey.* ASIT Advisory Studies No. 16. New York: United Nations Conference on Trade and Development.

Wells, L. Jr., N. Allen, J. Morisset, and N. Pirnia. 2001. "Using Tax Incentives to Compete for Foreign Investment: Are They Worth the Costs?" FIAS Occasional Paper 15. Washington, DC: Foreign Investment Advisory Service.

PART III

Designing Incentives Programs to Get Value for Money and Achieve Intended Goals

CHAPTER 8

A Holistic Approach to Investment Incentives

Louis Brennan and Frances Ruane

As the process of globalization took off in the 1990s, countries on every continent began to look to foreign direct investment (FDI) as a means to propel growth. For some countries, such as Singapore, the Netherlands, and Ireland, this belief in the growth-enhancing potential of FDI represented a further intensification of existing strategies; for others, such as Poland, Hungary, and Vietnam, it marked a completely new approach to development. Many countries have begun to view inward investment positively as a source of new capital, ideas, and access to networks and markets—reflecting a change from an earlier stance that was suspicious of FDI as an exploiter of national resources and domestic markets. The move toward welcoming FDI has brought increased competition among countries, as they have begun actively to market their advantages to global enterprises. This competition has primarily taken the form of offering financial, fiscal, and regulatory incentives at the country, region (within a country), or city level.

The changed attitude toward FDI has led to a highly competitive environment for inward investment by global enterprises in key sectors. Locations (countries, regions, or cities) offer incentives packages to these enterprises, often taking account of what they see competitor locations offering. Locations differ in their offerings, depending on their stage of economic development, the extent of their existing engagement with global enterprises, their sectoral focus, and what specifically they seek to gain from the presence of these enterprises—such as access to technology, global value chains, and scarce skills. As locations progress in terms of their development, their strategies regarding FDI tend to evolve. For example, locations at a relatively early stage of development, such as Morocco and Indonesia, may seek FDI that will help them to exploit their natural resources, as they do not have the capacity (skill/technology/capital) without FDI. At a later stage, these locations may seek FDI that will move them up the global value chains that can be key conduits for accessing skills, technologies, and markets. In this, they are following the recent patterns of more developed locations, such as European Union (EU) countries.

In the highly competitive global market for FDI, there are dynamic elements on both sides. On the one side, we have locations moving through their development cycles, with consequences for their motives and interests in potential FDI. At the same time, their political and economic relationships with their neighbors and other countries competing for similar investments are continuously changing. On the other side, the FDI enterprises themselves are always evolving as well, so the value of what an individual location actually offers to a mobile investor is not static. A consequence of this is that the time frame of the FDI investor will likely be very short relative to the development needs of the location that is competing for investment from it. A further complication in this market is the very significant asymmetry of information and sophistication between most locations seeking FDI and the majority of the FDI investors, usually multinational enterprises (MNEs), that they are seeking to attract. For example, unless highly specialized in terms of the sectors it is seeking to promote, the location is likely to have much less information available to it about the potential value or risk of the investment. This feeds into the challenges locations face in defining a suitable framework for designing investment incentives.

Our focus in this chapter is the host location's perspective on FDI, though we also keep an eye on the potential investor's perspective. Our interest is how locations approach the issue of giving incentives to encourage the increased flow of inward investment and what types of incentives they might use. Our argument is that locations should adopt a holistic approach—and specifically that they should see their FDI policy as part of their overall economic development policy and not build the policy in a stand-alone manner. This means that their rationale for promoting, or not promoting, FDI should be fully embedded in their broad development strategy and implemented by government officials responsible for fiscal policy, infrastructure development, education policy, investment promotion, and the like.

Although the chapter focuses on the use of incentives to attract FDI and describes elements of FDI that typically present unique challenges and opportunities for firms and locations, much of the discussion is also relevant for the use of incentives to attract investment from domestic firms, a phenomenon that (as detailed in chapter 6 in this volume) is particularly important in large economies. However, as can be observed in the United States, for example, where subnational entities often provide incentives to domestic firms, such incentives can simply divert investment from one jurisdiction to another.

We start in the next section by setting out the context in which locations should consider their options in relation to inward FDI. Following that, we identify four steps that locations should take before considering whether to provide incentives and, if so, what types. Against the background of those two sections, we then set out the principles that locations should adopt regarding incentives design in order to ensure that any incentives offered are grounded in an overall development framework. We then outline how locations should evaluate the approach being adopted to ensure that it is holistic.

THE CONTEXT FOR FDI

The process of globalization has seen increasing numbers of locations in all regions of the world adopting measures that affect FDI. The majority of these measures positively affect inward FDI by liberalizing inward investment regulations and by promoting/facilitating FDI; much smaller numbers are setting regulations/restrictions on FDI (UNCTAD 2013, chap. 3, sec. A). However, before considering introducing any such measures, locations should ensure that conditions in their domestic markets are conducive to growth. Specific incentives will not be effective if these market conditions are not in place: incentives may compensate for some minor market or institutional failures (e.g., bureaucratic delays), but if the location does not have well-functioning markets and institutions, the availability of specific incentives will not compensate, and either the investor will not locate its FDI project there, or if it does so, the investment project may fail.

Furthermore, in a world of increasingly mobile capital, the attractiveness of one location depends on a comparison with similar potential host locations. For example, a developing country in Asia seeking FDI in manufacturing for export markets is, for the most part, in competition with other developing countries in Asia. Similarly, for EU countries, their competitors for such investment are predominately other EU countries, as the market for outputs is the regional market (the EU). Where the sector involves natural resources, the reference locations are the other locations where the same resources are available and can be extracted at a similar cost.

This section now looks at four key elements in the dynamic context facing locations considering promoting FDI: evolving enterprise motives, changing patterns of trade, emerging FDI players, and emerging integrated regions.

EVOLVING ENTERPRISE MOTIVES

Locations need to be cognizant of the motives and strategies of enterprises engaging in FDI. These enterprises tend to evolve their strategies over time. Whereas American and European investors were traditionally dominated by resource-seeking and market-seeking objectives, a variety of factors has led enterprises to engage in FDI for efficiency-seeking and asset-seeking objectives. As trade barriers have been lowered and regional integration has taken hold, enterprises have moved from investing on a country-by-country basis to serve each national market to investing in a few locations (and sometimes one location) to serve regional and in some cases global markets. This development has coincided with and also contributed to increased opportunities for the fragmentation of production and the development of global and regional value chains, which have enabled enterprises to invest in locations that offer efficiency advantages such as lower labor costs. MNE strategies based on arbitrage have extended beyond labor arbitrage to encompass regulatory and tax arbitrage. Increasingly over the past decade, enterprises are also investing with asset seeking as their motive as they look to access and capture talent and gain innovation opportunities and capabilities wherever they are to be found (for more on the motivations of MNEs, see chapter 3 in this volume).

These changes in enterprises' motives and strategies have been reflected in the manner in which they seek to organize and structure their operations. This extends to the design and configuration of their assets and capabilities, the roles and mandates of their overseas operation, and the approach they take to the development and diffusion of knowledge (Bartlett and Beamish 2014).

For example, the typical multinational structure of the European MNE (Bartlett and Ghoshal 1989) consisted of a number of largely self-sufficient units, each of which focused on its local market. By contrast, the classic international structure of the American MNE implied that core competencies were retained in the home country and knowledge was transferred, as needed, from the home country to its subsidiary units. These units adopted and leveraged the parent's competencies in the markets in which they were located. As Japanese enterprises appeared on the global landscape through the 1970s and particularly in the 1980s, they adopted the classic global structure, emphasizing global scale and centralization, with knowledge retained at the center and with subsidiaries implementing their parent's strategy (Bartlett and Ghoshal 1989).

Those approaches to subsidiary roles and operations reflected the varying approaches adopted by enterprises to the exigencies of the external environment. However, recent decades have seen considerable changes in the external environment, with trade barriers lowered and regions integrated. These developments, coupled with other changes in technology, competition, transportation, and industry structures, have tended to alter the approach taken by enterprises investing internationally. The fragmentation of production via regional and global value chains has seen enterprises adapt their approaches to one in which operations tend to be more dispersed, interdependent, and specialized and in which knowledge is now increasingly likely to be developed jointly across the different units of the organization and shared on a worldwide basis.

Thus, the transnational model of the enterprise that has emerged pursues simultaneously global efficiency, flexibility, and worldwide learning capability (Bartlett and Ghoshal 1989). The geographic coverage of the subsidiary can be regional rather than national, and in some cases, enterprises establish regional headquarters sites to oversee the different regions of the world. Product divisions are more likely to be organized globally, and functional activities are likewise increasingly organized globally and not necessarily in the home country. Many of these functional activities may be located in shared services sites that serve operations across all units and are often located outside the home country. At the same time, knowledge and innovation seeking has emerged to form part of an enterprise's chief motivation when investing overseas (as mentioned in chapter 3 in this volume in explaining the strategic asset–seeking motivation for FDI).

The more dispersed yet specialized operating form of the transnational enterprise today raises both challenges and opportunities for locations seeking FDI. On the one hand, there are opportunities to capture slices of the value chain and upgrade the existing activities of overseas firms (OECD 2013). On the other hand, the reconfiguration of the corporation, the slicing and reslicing of value chain tasks, and the more knowledge-intensive needs of the investing firms[1] create challenges for locations seeking to secure and retain FDI.[2]

CHANGING PATTERNS OF TRADE

The fragmentation of production and the global propagation of supply chains have had a transformative impact on the global economy in recent decades. An inward FDI strategy needs to take into account the resultant changing patterns of trade and FDI and, in particular, the increasingly significant role of global value chains (Baldwin 2013). Before the development of these global chains as a key part of the process of globalization, it was possible to view FDI as having a single focus (e.g., market seeking, efficiency seeking, resource seeking), with impacts on the location, coming from upstream and downstream activities, being readily identifiable. However, the complexity and dynamic nature of global value chains today have widened the set of possible motivations for FDI and make its likely contribution much harder to ascertain ex ante without a very detailed understanding of how the relevant value chain operates and is likely to evolve.

Although access to global value chains is a natural objective for many locations to seek in promoting FDI, reaping the anticipated benefits of these value chains is not inevitable. Furthermore, whereas seeking FDI as a means to position the location in global value chains may be an initial consideration, the investment environment will require ongoing monitoring and possible recalibration to ensure that the location maintains its global value chain positioning. Ensuring cost competitiveness, improving connectivity with international markets, and responding to the business and investment climates are essential to securing the location's positioning in global value chains (Cattaneo et al. 2013). Maintaining the location's positioning will likely require the fostering of innovation and the building of capacity, thus also contributing to the upgrading of the region's global value chain positioning. Indeed, given the changing nature of global value chains, such upgrading may be a prerequisite to sustaining the region's positioning beyond the short term. Locations that are advanced in terms of their knowledge and innovation capacities and the sophistication of their markets may be attractive sites to enterprises whose objective is to attain a competitive advantage precisely by disrupting existing global value chains or developing completely new ones.

EMERGING FDI PLAYERS

A new issue for locations considering adopting a more effective pro-FDI stance is the increasing presence of small and medium-sized enterprises (SMEs) in the globalization process. The growth in born-global enterprises, which engage not only in exporting but also in FDI activities from their early stages of inception, makes them increasingly worthy of consideration for investment-seeking locations. Born-global enterprises are particularly common in information and communications technology (ICT)–related manufacturing and service sectors.

From the location's perspective, these new types of entities represent very different combinations of attributes, compared with the traditional large-scale, long-established multinational. The dynamic process of enterprise creation and evolution means that early movers often have significant advantages over late entrants. This, in turn, means that locations are faced with new opportunities to adopt policies focused on less-certain but higher-potential SMEs rather than on more-established FDI enterprises. A location's strategy in relation to high-potential start-ups in the form of FDI through SMEs will need to reflect that location's strength in terms of its entrepreneurial talent and its receptivity to externally sourced entrepreneurial talent. Locations at similar stages of development may differ significantly in relation to the availability of local entrepreneurial talent as well as to the likelihood that an FDI project may crowd out domestic activity that is potentially viable in the long term. Thus, locations with a vibrant local entrepreneurial talent pool will not have the same need to have policies in place designed to attract entrepreneurial talent as those with a dearth of such talent. For example, tax packages may be designed specifically to promote inward entrepreneurship, giving preferential tax rates in the early years for new arrivals. Because these enterprises tend to be knowledge intensive in nature, the knowledge and innovation capacities of the location will have an important bearing on its attractiveness to such enterprises in the medium term.

EMERGING INTEGRATED REGIONS

A final issue for locations seeking FDI to consider is the development of integrated economic regions in different parts of the world, with the EU being the most developed. These regions have a significant impact on the flow of FDI, with large enterprises strategizing in regional rather than single market terms. Here the size of the domestic market can be much less of an issue, with the focus being the size of the regional market to which a location has access. A consequence of the growth of integrated regions is the creation of greater market scale for the enterprise through the creation of (1) export platforms to serve many locations within a region and (2) regional headquarters functions, which give it significant strategic corporate power. In this regard, the more integrated the region in which the location is based, the more attractive it is to investing enterprises. Hence, the reduction of tariffs and administrative burdens associated with rules of origin (in the case of free-trade areas), the harmonization or mutual recognition of standards, and the embrace of trade facilitation measures within the region (Cattaneo et al. 2013) are important factors to be addressed by the locations within the region.

After addressing in this section many of the diverse issues that locations face in seeking to attract FDI, the next section introduces a holistic approach that represents the basis on which the design of incentives should be undertaken.

DEVELOPING A HOLISTIC APPROACH

Before a location considers a strategy of promoting FDI, it should clarify the role that it envisions for this strategy as part of its economy-wide growth policy. This is central to ensuring that the approach is holistic and takes account not only of the needs of MNEs and the sectors being targeted but also, more importantly, of considerations that include the location's strengths and weaknesses and its stage of development. A broad-based or sector-specific strategy for FDI needs to reflect what benefits the location is seeking from the FDI and how the FDI will support economic development. In the absence of this strategic approach, locations are more likely to be captured by interest groups for whom the promotion of inward FDI is of direct benefit without necessarily being of wider economic benefit. If this happens, the potential virtuous circle involving economic development and FDI is unlikely to be realized. So, in very practical terms, there is a set of crucial steps to be taken before considering incentives and their design in the context of a pro-FDI strategy. These steps are evaluating the location's stage of economic development, assessing its current stage of globalization, identifying the potential supply of FDI it faces, and analyzing what it can expect to get from inward FDI.

STAGE OF ECONOMIC DEVELOPMENT

The location needs to conceptualize its FDI strategy in the context of the stage of economic development it has reached. The diversity across countries (e.g., in terms of population size, income, and resources) and within countries (e.g., in terms of skill levels, resource concentration, availability of technology, and economic dispersion) means that locations differ widely in their capacities for successfully attracting and absorbing the benefits of FDI. Thus, an economy such as India is in the market for some of the world's most high-tech activities and yet has levels of development that are most akin to the least developed economies. Ideally, incentives, where they are given, should compensate for structural deficits and factor market conditions that cannot be more effectively addressed by broader policies and should contribute to the location's development while improving its attractiveness to investors. In this way, the design of incentives can play a role in ensuring that the FDI regime is supportive of the location's development.

A good first step for locations is to benchmark their position relative to competitors using metrics such as those available in the World Bank's Development Indicators[3] or its Ease of Doing Business rankings[4] and in other global indicators of institutional quality, infrastructure, and technological readiness. Where locations are seeking to access knowledge-intensive FDI, metrics from innovation scoreboards, such as the European Commission Innovation Scoreboard[5] and the Global Entrepreneurship Monitor,[6] can be usefully deployed for benchmarking purposes. Where locations observe deficits or underperformance in comparison to competitor locations, they should consider how to address these in their overall development policies before considering specific investment incentives.

STAGE OF GLOBALIZATION

Locations need to evaluate the extent to which they are already globalized and the nature of that globalization. Strong globalization will be reflected in significant capital flows (inward and outward); trade of goods, services, technology, and ideas (inward and outward); labor migration (inward and outward migration); and cultural integration. Truly globalized locations will also have policies that foster strong and stable globalization patterns, making it easy for externally based enterprises to engage with local enterprises, and vice versa. Weaker levels of globalization will likely be reflected in much lower engagement across some or all of these measures. Measures of globalization (e.g., the EY Globalization Index[7]) indicate wide differences among countries in terms of their level of globalization, with countries that are relatively small and that have developed export platforms for FDI, often with a regional focus, being the most globalized. Although higher levels of globalization will generally make locations more attractive to FDI, these locations may provide a lower potential benefit to FDI enterprises if there is little additional value to be reaped from servicing the local (or regional) market or if the real income gains from globalization are reflected in higher unit labor costs. In such circumstances, policies to promote clusters can drive the attractiveness of these locations.

POTENTIAL SUPPLY OF FDI

A location's policy stance vis-à-vis FDI needs to reflect the potential supply of FDI it faces. For example, a resource-rich location will be attractive to enterprises in the extractive industry sectors, and the extent of its bargaining power in relation to inward FDI will depend particularly on two factors: the number of alternative locations with similar resources that are open to FDI investment and the policies those locations are pursuing in regard to the exploitation rate of these assets.[8] To be strategic in its approach, a location needs to determine the terms of extraction that are best aligned with its overall economic development strategy; in particular, this should not be seen merely as an issue for the extractive industry in question. Two locations with similar resource endowments might rationally pursue totally different strategies because of differences in other parameters (e.g., income per capita, age of population, skilled labor and technology, and administrative capacity). Likewise, in the services sector, a location faces variation in the potential FDI supply in terms of its value positioning. Thus, in the case of call centers, locations at an early stage of development face a potential FDI supply that encompasses activities that are routine and low value in nature. Those locations at more advanced stages of development face a potential FDI supply that involves more complex and high-value activity. Thus, human capital needs to be developed so as to ensure that an adequate supply of the requisite skill sets is available to match the needs of the activity.

EXPECTED BENEFITS FROM FDI

Against a backdrop of the extent of its development, the state of its globalization, and the specific supply of FDI that it faces, the location must analyze what it expects to get from promoting FDI. This analysis is essential if the location is to ensure that its FDI strategy is fully aligned with economy-wide policies.

We identify eight potential benefits of FDI that may prompt a location to seek to attract it through use of incentives or other tools:

1. *Output growth*: FDI that is market seeking (in terms of the domestic or the regional market) opens up the potential for more output to be produced locally while servicing the market at the same or lower prices. As long as this does not reduce tax revenue (say if there is a loss of existing tariff revenues or quota incomes) or crowd out existing production that could be sustainable in the medium to longer run, there is an unambiguous gain to the location from the FDI. Similarly, if the location has natural resources that it is not in a position to extract at what it sees as the optimal rate or cost, then FDI can enable the extraction rate or efficiency of production to be increased.

2. *Employment growth*: If there is a supply of competitively priced labor (in terms of unit labor costs) that would otherwise be underutilized (unemployed or underemployed), then FDI brings the opportunity of further employment and tax revenue without any reduction in the competitiveness of other local enterprises, assuming that there is no impact on local wage rates. In most developed locations where there is no underutilized labor, the positive impact of the FDI will be reflected more in higher incomes than in additional new employment.

3. *New technology*: If FDI brings in new capital that embeds technology that is not available locally, the location can develop its ability to host entirely new economic activities or become more competitive in existing sectors. Un-embedded technology may also come in the form of patents and propriety software to which those working for the FDI enterprise may have access.

4. *New sectors*: FDI enterprises may contribute to the development of entirely new sectors (e.g., medical devices) and be a catalyst for further growth in those sectors from local sources or from other FDI entrants (wishing to engage with the FDI either upstream or downstream). Hence, the location may become a center for a whole range of economic activities

that follow and are related to that initial FDI. Particularly in the case of developing countries, this can help to diversify the sectoral portfolio and hence reduce the risk associated with too much sectoral concentration, especially in primary production.

5. *New networks and clusters*: Where the location becomes a hub for new activities, there is the additional potential of securing investments from a range of enterprises in a given industry. This gives rise to the potential for an FDI enterprise to become the keystone for creating spillovers through the emergence of networks and clusters. Thus, over a period of time, an initial investment can lead to a major alteration in the composition of economic activities.

6. *New skills and practices*: FDI may augment local skills through the impact of higher-level technological, specialist, and managerial skills within FDI enterprises. This skill augmentation can be accessed directly by locals working in FDI enterprises and also through the business dealings of FDI enterprises with local enterprises. Thus, FDI can be the channel through which new and improved practices and systems are disseminated within the location, thereby contributing to productivity gains within the wider economy. These intangible effects are known to be highly significant in certain industries, such as software (O'Malley and O'Gorman 2001), but the extent of their importance will vary by location, depending on the receptivity of local businesses and people to adopting practices and engaging in training.

7. *Spatial balance*: FDI can assist a location in reaching its desired spatial pattern of economic activities. For example, if greater spatial concentration is desirable, then locating FDI in already concentrated areas can increase the potential for scale and scope externalities in those areas. If greater spatial diversification is desirable, then a location may be able to achieve that if the FDI projects are mobile within the location. This outcome is not inevitable, however; if spatial diversification is desirable but FDI can operate profitably only in areas where activity is already highly concentrated, then FDI may work against this other policy objective. For example, if the Harris-Todaro type of rural-urban migration (Harris and Todaro 1970) is an issue, then there may be significant costs to offset against the other benefits of FDI, as further agglomeration in urban areas promotes the growth of urban unemployment while at the same time reducing the level of rural underemployment.[9]

8. *External market access*: A key attraction of FDI for many locations is that MNEs can provide access to foreign markets for products and services.

This is more likely to occur when the FDI enterprise uses the location as an export platform and when it has immediate access to global value chains. This engagement in trade provides the location with an increased volume of trading activities and hence improves its viability as a trading location and encourages the growth of its logistics capability. This positive effect from FDI is all the more pronounced for economies where domestic enterprises are not integrated into global value chains.

Based on its economic development, its level of globalization, its potential supply of FDI, and the benefits it can expect to gain from FDI, each location should develop its FDI strategy. If it is clear that there are significant potential benefits from FDI, then the location needs to design its incentives package to make sure that these potential benefits are realized. For example, if sustainable development is a key issue for the location (see chapter 9 in this volume), then the incentives need to clearly reflect that objective.[10] This approach is holistic in that it embeds the FDI strategy into the economic development strategy. More specifically, this approach is preferred to one that merely copies what other locations are offering, thereby avoiding the risks of inappropriate policy emulation. Some locations, such as Ireland and Singapore, have pursued a more holistic approach to incentives design for decades—and arguably with considerable success, as evident in the extent to which they have high levels of FDI and economic growth. More recently, China could be seen as adopting a relatively holistic approach and consequently experiencing significant developmental benefits from FDI. In the next section, we explore the principles that should be built into the design of the incentives.

PRINCIPLES OF INCENTIVES DESIGN

Many locations that perceive benefits from FDI see merits in using incentives policies to enhance their success in winning desirable FDI projects. Accordingly, we consider in this section the types of incentives that locations might use to foster inward investment.[11]

We distinguish three broad types of incentives that can be used to help realize the eight potential benefits from FDI listed in the preceding section: cost-reducing incentives, profitability-enhancing incentives, and incentives designed specifically to deepen the engagement of FDI enterprises in the location. We then look at three related implementation issues: implementation mechanisms, time frames, and accountability.

The key point underlying these issues is that incentives design should take into account the perspectives of both the granting location and the potential investing enterprise so that the incentives system delivers a win-win outcome for both parties.

COST-REDUCING INCENTIVES

Locations can offer various incentives to reduce the initial costs of the FDI enterprise (e.g., investment grants) or contribute to cost reduction in its early years (e.g., subsidized interest rates, electricity tariffs, local labor training). The provision of land at deeply discounted prices, as in the case of inland locations in China, is an example of one such incentive that can be used to help reduce initial costs. These incentives directly affect the location's ability to realize the benefits of output growth, employment growth, and new technology where it is embedded in capital because they can positively impact the cost-benefit calculus for the investor.

Up-front investment grants are attractive to the locating enterprise, as they carry certainty and reduce setup costs in a clearly defined way. In relation to mineral extraction, for example, incentives that lower the costs of exploration can provide very significant encouragement to FDI investors.

Continuous subsidies can be attractive, as they may scale with the level of activity; however, they can carry greater risk, such as that the government might renege on commitments or terminate a subsidy program. In the case of continuous incentives, it is highly desirable to have a broad political consensus in favor of these within the location and to make these commitments legally enforceable. This serves two purposes: it increases the degree of certainty in the eyes of potential investors about the durability of the incentives being offered, and it mitigates the risk of claims being made by investors against the location in the event that such incentives are arbitrarily withdrawn. It also serves to reduce any risk that there will be high costs of exiting where the investment is unsuccessful.

Up-front grants are administratively attractive from the location's point of view but carry risk if the project fails. That risk can be mitigated somewhat if the grants are repayable (as is the case in Ireland) or if the linked investments have alternative uses (e.g., buildings that can house other productive activities). Continuous subsidies also have possible risks such as government exposure to large subsidies if the project is really successful. Other actions that can reduce costs generally, such as lower regulatory and administrative burdens, can provide important incentives to FDI enterprises, as they may be more likely than local investors to be affected by such rules.

However, there is a need to exercise caution in relation to the lowering of such burdens, as they may result in negative externalities and associated costs for the location in the future. For example, a relaxation of environmental controls may lead to damage, which the location bears the long-term cost of addressing.

PROFITABILITY-ENHANCING INCENTIVES

These are incentives that directly enhance and reward the profitability of FDI enterprises. The most obvious of these is a reduced rate of corporate taxation, which might apply widely to all FDI or to FDI in specific sectors or locations (e.g., export processing zones). Where locations compete to attract stages of the global value chain, the location offering a reduced rate of corporate taxation may be more attractive to the investor. This operates as a gain-sharing/pain-sharing incentive for both the location and the enterprise. In addition to generating potential government revenue streams, these incentives can help realize benefits from FDI through higher output growth and associated employment growth. Countries such as Ireland, the Netherlands, the United Kingdom, and many of the EU accession countries have implemented lower rates of corporate taxation as part of their pro-FDI strategies. To the extent the corporate tax rate is generally applicable to all companies, it is not considered an incentive within the meaning of this book. Nevertheless, it can have an effect on investment decisions.

Another recent example of profitability-enhancing incentives is related to the case of China, which provides preferential taxation rates on imports of equipment, technologies, and materials by foreigners investing in the central and western areas of the country (UNCTAD 2014). Although taxation-related incentives can be very effective in attracting investors (see the concise review of empirical studies on tax-related incentives in chapter 2 in this volume), locations should be conscious of the danger of incurring reputational damage if their tax regime is overly lax. Similarly, locations should ensure that they do not give away too much and that the benefits of the incentives align with their costs (as discussed in chapter 10 in this volume).

ENGAGEMENT-DEEPENING INCENTIVES

Engagement-deepening incentives encourage enterprises to change their behavior by stimulating them to become more embedded in the location than they would otherwise. These incentives typically apply only to particular enterprises in selected sectors that have been identified as strategically significant to the location's development. They can take several forms. For example, an FDI enterprise in the primary (food) sector might receive a financial incentive to participate in networks and clusters that support the creation of linkages with and spillovers to local businesses. In certain cases, that incentive could take the form of a financial payment or a mandatory requirement to engage in such networks as a condition for establishing the enterprise in the location.[12]

In relation to building human capital, a location could encourage enterprises to bring in scarce talent if this would help ensure that local scarce talent is not bid away excessively from existing (local) enterprises or if the location does not want to invest in all of the skills required for a particular enterprise to prosper. For example, the introduction of lower personal tax rates related to duration of stay could make the location attractive to senior management and people with technical skills.[13]

In the same vein, locations might want to introduce incentives in order to encourage existing FDI enterprises to engage in continuous innovation. This could take the form of research and development (R&D)[14] or product development grants or allowances (e.g., Bulgaria recently adopted legislation that grants reimbursement of up to 50 percent of spending on educational and R&D activities [UNCTAD 2014]) or of inducements for the enterprises to become regional headquarters (where strategic decision making would be centered). MNEs widely avail themselves of the favorable treatment of R&D for tax purposes within the EU (see chapter 4 in this volume). These types of incentives are easily run on a competitive basis if the location establishes a clear set of criteria to determine the level of incentive to be given.

IMPLEMENTATION MECHANISMS

Turning to implementation, the first set of issues relates to the mechanisms through which incentives should be administered. For example, should the incentives be universal (applying to all FDI) or highly targeted (applying only to particular types of FDI and/or domestic investments that are being encouraged actively)? In practice, locations may offer a combination of both for legal and administrative reasons.

Another question (and one that is also discussed in chapter 7 in this volume) is whether the incentives should be operated in a rule-based or discretionary form. The former has the advantage of administrative simplicity and reduced opportunities for corruption. The latter provides the location with flexibility to negotiate with particular enterprises, which is not possible in a rules-based system. Negotiated incentives can enhance the effective marketability of the incentives and allow the characteristics and track record of the potential investor to be considered. Although the discretionary form does mean that the investor cannot predict at the outset what incentives it might get, the process of their determination can mean that the eventual agreed-upon outcome better fits the needs of both the location and the investor.

However, a discretionary approach[15] requires safeguards to mitigate the risk of corruption and rent seeking. This suggests that it must be accompanied by its own rules and analysis and that it should be subject to several stages of approval before actual implementation and to ongoing monitoring.

Table 8.1 offers a simple classification of incentives to demonstrate how these administrative elements interact at the polar extremes. Where the scope of application is all-embracing (general), there is a strong argument for a rules-based incentive form.[16] This simplifies both the approval and the monitoring processes. On the other hand, where the scope of application is targeted, a discretionary approach is likely to be more appropriate. This can ensure that the incentives offered are more tailored to the targets and that they also reflect the strategic considerations of the location. The application of a completely rules-based form where incentives are targeted is likely to be ineffective. Likewise, the application of a discretionary form where incentives are generally applied is likely to be administratively cumbersome from an evaluation and monitoring perspective and hence inefficient. Most systems will tend to be blended to accommodate the mixture of targeted and general incentives.

Table 8.1 Classification of incentives

	Scope of application	
Incentive form	General	Targeted
Rule-based	Effective	Ineffective
Discretionary	Inefficient	Effective

TIME FRAMES

The next element relating to implementation is the time frame during which incentives are offered and the time frame over which results are measured. First, over what specific time frame should the incentives package operate for an individual enterprise—for the next five years, ten years, or fifteen years? Second, if incentives operate on an ongoing basis, over how many years should the location continue to market them as a set of incentives? In relation to both sets of interrelated decisions, the location needs to manage the balance between creating certainty, which is very attractive to potential FDI enterprises, and allowing for flexibility, which may be needed in the context of a dynamic global market. For example, as new industries and value chains emerge, locations may find that existing ties to a specific incentives regime may reduce the availability of resources that could be applied with greater impact in other ways to take advantage of those emerging and growing opportunities. Incentives that encourage MNEs to have a longer-term time frame can offer the advantage that they are more likely to contribute to the long-term sustainability of the location when compared to incentives resulting in short time frames. This logic applies to the EU Member States' tax incentives that encourage investment in R&D.

ACCOUNTABILITY

Another aspect of the time-frame element relates to the period over which the impact of the incentives should be measured. This, in turn, links to the final implementation element: the degree of accountability required in meeting the incentives conditions. Just how far are the authorities willing to go to ensure full compliance and to penalize enterprises that do not meet the agreed-upon terms/targets? Locations need to be mindful of the reputation- and corruption-related risks that can arise as a result of both overly demanding monitoring and inadequate monitoring. This, in turn, affects the views of the population about the perceived benefits of having incentives to encourage FDI. Appropriate monitoring can help to ensure that MNEs deliver on the commitments they make in the negotiation process, whether in relation to job creation, technology and skill transfer, or minimum investment and export requirements.

Having considered incentives design in terms of three broad types of incentives and related implementation issues, we next introduce a framework for evaluating the incentives design.

PRINCIPLES OF EVALUATION

Central to taking a holistic approach to inward FDI is linking the design of any incentives regime to an objective evaluation process that evaluates the design itself. This type of evaluation comes before any attempt to evaluate the costs and benefits of using incentives to promote individual FDI projects. Although standard ex ante cost-benefit analyses are desirable, they can be extremely difficult and, hence, may not always prove fruitful in practice. Where they can be done, the standard approaches, such as those proposed by the World Bank,[17] should be adopted and adapted accordingly.

In this section, we address the initial evaluation process: that used to evaluate the appropriateness of the set of incentives designed to be used by a location to promote FDI investment. We suggest this be done by adopting a structured approach to evaluating the incentives package that is grounded in clarity around exactly what is being sought from FDI by the location and the extent to which the incentives regime is designed to ensure that those benefits are attained in a cost-efficient manner. This approach is akin to the logic model approach used for program evaluation (McLaughlin and Jordan 1999). Figure 8.1 provides a simple framework that allows us to enunciate a number of principles against which the design of any incentives regime needs to be evaluated.

The starting point in the framework for evaluating a location's set of FDI incentives is the requirement that there must be an alignment between these incentives and the location's development priorities (see the

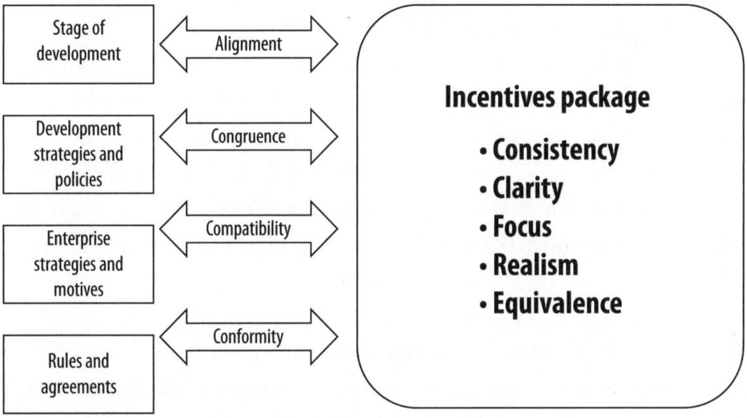

Figure 8.1 Framework for evaluating the incentives package.

section on "Developing a Holistic Approach" in this chapter). Thus, for example, certain locations may benefit more from an incentives regime that is tied to quantitative targets (e.g., number of jobs), whereas others may seek qualitative targets (e.g., quality of jobs) to better align the investment with their policy aims.

Furthermore, there must be congruence between the outcomes sought by the incentives and the overall development strategies and policies of the location; that is, the incentives must recognize the existing institutions and policies in place. The need for such congruence reflects the inappropriateness of putting in place incentives to drive a particular behavior on the part of enterprises if other policy conditions within the location serve to obstruct or discourage such behaviors. This would be the case, for example, if the incentives were designed to encourage enterprises to engage in R&D but the laws in place did not appropriately support the protection of intellectual property.

To be successful, the incentives regime must demonstrate compatibility with the strategies and motives of the enterprises on which they are focused. There is little point in having incentives that are tailored to the needs of the location if they are not sufficiently attractive to MNEs or not sufficiently realistic about the environmental and competitive considerations that need to be compensated for through incentives. In addition, locations can benefit from seeking to understand the accounting considerations that will apply to MNEs that receive incentives, thus helping to ensure greater compatibility. However, it must be borne in mind that although incentives that can be reflected positively in the bottom line of investors' accounts are attractive to investors (i.e., the incentives are compatible with investors' strategies), bottom line impacts of large magnitude can carry reputational risk for the location.[18]

Furthermore, it is essential that there be conformity between the incentives and the prevailing legal frameworks in place in relation to FDI. Failure to ensure that the incentives regime conforms to international rules and practices and does not violate any local laws or regulations or agreements undermines the credibility and reputation of the location.

Turning to the incentives regime itself, it needs to be evaluated against five key principles:

1. *Consistency*: One risk that can arise, especially in the case of a complex incentives regime, is that the separate elements of the regime may not be internally consistent and mutually reinforcing. The incentives are likely

to be much more effective if they act to reinforce rather than oppose one another. Thus, in the case of a location whose goal is to attract labor-intensive investment, the provision of both labor- and capital-related incentives might undermine the location's strategy.

2. *Clarity*: To realize the potential benefits of FDI to the location, potential investors should be able to see clearly the thrust of the design so that there is no risk of confused signals. This clarity must extend to the time frame in which the incentives regime is operative so that potential investors have greater certainty and the incentives design can be revisited in a manner appropriate to changing circumstances. This might, for example, involve the inclusion of all tax incentives in tax laws so that there is clarity for the investor.

3. *Focus*: To be successful, an incentives regime must adopt a disciplined and focused approach. Whereas embracing a scattergun approach to incentives may have the effect of securing some early wins, it is unlikely to contribute to the location's development in any meaningful way. By contrast, a focused approach (that does not necessarily exclude an opportunistic strategy that is open to emerging and growing opportunities) is more likely to benefit the location in the medium to longer term. An example of a focused incentives regime would be one that prioritizes one or a few sectors as target areas of investment while not necessarily ruling out investments in other sectors.

4. *Realism*: The incentives design needs to be realistic with respect to the location's capacity to deliver on the design and also in terms of what the competitive environment suggests. There is little value to the location in offering an incentives regime that is overly generous, in the context of the FDI supply and the positioning of competitor locations. Equally, overpromising and then failing to deliver will have the effect of tarnishing the location's credibility and denting investors' confidence in the location.

5. *Equivalence*: The level and composition of incentives should demonstrate an appropriate equivalence to the level of commitment that the MNE is prepared to make in terms of employment numbers, investment levels, tenure, and the like. When designing what they are prepared to offer, locations should therefore have a clear view of what they expect from the MNE for different levels of incentives. Without this, their negotiation position will be unclear, and their strategy may be ineffective or unduly costly.

Evaluating the incentives design against the above principles can serve to ensure that the location's incentives regime is both holistic and effective. On an ongoing basis, the incentives regime and its measures need to be assessed for their effectiveness in terms of what actually works (e.g., elasticity of response of FDI to incentives). In addition, the direct costs of the different measures within the incentives regime need to be considered in terms of public expenditures, government revenues foregone, and any possible displacement effects (e.g., destruction of potentially profitable emerging local enterprises). More generally, the complex range of benefits, such as the demonstration effects on the sector and the location that may accrue, needs to be assessed in terms of the extent to which the incentives regime contributes to their capture by the location (Wells et al. 2001).

CONCLUSION

A holistic approach to investment incentives—one that incorporates a series of design principles and a structured evaluation process—is needed. This approach offers a number of compelling benefits. It provides a systematic point of departure for locations in starting the design process. By taking account of the circumstances of both the location and the investing enterprises, as well as changes in those circumstances over time, it offers a greater prospect of win-win outcomes for both parties. It is also consistent with the sustainability approach that is addressed in chapter 9 in this volume. In addition, the holistic approach helps to ensure that the incentives design contributes to the overall economic development of the location and that the benefits gained from FDI justify the incentives offered.

The holistic approach further has the benefit of mitigating risk for the host location. By aligning the design with the location's characteristics and its overall development strategy, the location reduces the risk of becoming overly dependent on the FDI sector as an engine of growth. The principles of design and the structured evaluation process encompassed within our holistic approach to investment incentives serve to mitigate that risk. Furthermore, the approach proposed here can bring greater clarity to the incentives strategy as the location considers whether the goal in its pursuit of FDI is the realization of its comparative advantage or the development of its competitive advantage.

A holistic approach is essential for low-income or less developed locations, but it also has value for more developed locations, reinforcing the impact of marketing and promotion efforts aimed at potential inward investors.

This is true notwithstanding the strong centripetal forces that operate to attract FDI to more developed locations.

Whereas the approach as presented here is a high-level one, it does not preclude its application at a disaggregated level. Such disaggregation could extend to the level of the individual MNE, where the evaluation process can provide important input into the development of a business case aimed at the potential investing MNE. At the enterprise level, an important source of learning and insight for the location can relate to those investment opportunities that were sought by the location but that ultimately went elsewhere. An evaluation of those lost opportunities can form the basis for improved incentives design.

Throughout this chapter, we have used the generic term *location* to refer to the geographic area that is promoting inward FDI. We chose this term quite consciously to take account of the fact that the competitors in the global market for FDI are not necessarily countries but may be regions within countries or indeed cities. This distinction is important for several reasons. It takes account of the potential political/fiscal autonomy of certain subnational regions, so that regions within countries (U.S. states, for example) may be competing with each other as well as with specific regions in other countries that may have the same resource attractions.

This terminology also allows the approach to be used in the context of the increasing competition between cities for investments that require the scale of large cities to operate successfully and from which agglomeration economies are expected. Thus, the competition for investment might be among London and Berlin and Paris but not among England and Germany and France. Similarly, competition for FDI might be between Guangdong and Bangalore rather than between China and India. A fully holistic approach should see the relationships between regions within countries as aligned with national economic development policies.

Even though a holistic approach toward inward investment incentives is crucial, implementing it can be complex. Locations need to develop the capacity to adopt such an approach, especially if they lack the necessary financial and administrative resources and if certain government or private interests may dominate at the expense of the location's overall development. Global rules covering the types of incentives that may be allowed can help in this regard but will not be sufficient. Development organizations, such as the World Bank, can contribute to crucial capacity building and support in this area. Only by adopting a more holistic approach to investment incentives will locations be able to maximize the potential development benefits that such measures might produce.

NOTES

1. See OECD 2013, chap. 7, on the role of knowledge-based capital in global value chains.

2. This is also highlighted in chapter 3 in this volume.

3. See http://data.worldbank.org/data-catalog/world-development-indicators.

4. See http://www.doingbusiness.org/rankings.

5. See http://ec.europa.eu/enterprise/policies/innovation/policy/innovation-scoreboard/index_en.htm.

6. See http://www.gemconsortium.org/.

7. See http://www.amcham.ro/UserFiles/articleFiles/Globalization%20report_01211008.pdf. The EY Globalization Index is based on standard IMF/UNCTAD measures as well as scoring done by the Economist Intelligence Unit.

8. It will also depend on other factors, such as the value and scale of the deposit, internal transportation systems, and other relevant infrastructure.

9. This model was developed to analyze the phenomenon of very high levels of urban unemployment experienced in many developing countries as they began to industrialize. Urban unemployment is the result of internal migration from rural to urban areas, where the concentration of higher-paid jobs induces migration driven by the expectation of getting a job rather than the certainty of getting employment. The equilibrium level of migration results in urban unemployment. See Harris and Todaro 1970.

10. Even where the location is particularly attractive for investors, as in the case of a large mining deposit, incentives may still be necessary to align the time horizons of the location and investor.

11. The extent to which they can use such incentives may depend on international, national, or subnational rules on the provision of state assistance to inward investment projects. For example, the European Commission controls the use of financial and fiscal incentives and restricts incentives to certain cases—for example, in order to attract investment in relatively low-income areas or in order to increase investments in R&D, which are seen as enhancing the innovative capacity of the EU (in this volume, see chapters 5 and 12 for more on the EU's regulatory framework for State aid and chapter 4 for incentives related specifically to investments in R&D).

12. There may, however, be a concern that such incentives violate trade or investment rules. Exploring these issues, however, is outside the scope of this chapter.

13. Ireland is one of many countries that offer lower income tax rates to immigrants with scarce skills coming to work in the Irish ICT sector, which is dominated by MNEs.

14. R&D-related incentives are considered at length in chapter 4 in this volume.

15. The degree of discretion could apply to both the level and the composition of the incentives provided.

16. An automatic system can mean that unnecessary incentives are given.

17. See http://ieg.worldbank.org/methodology.

18. This issue became the subject of discussion in the OECD in 2014 when major U.S. MNEs, such as Google and Starbucks, were seen to be taking such advantage of the complexities of different EU countries' tax regimes that they were paying virtually no corporation tax.

REFERENCES

Baldwin, R. 2013. "Global Supply Chains: Why They Emerged, Why They Matter, and Where They Are Going." In *Global Value Chains in a Changing World*, ed. D. K. Elms and P. Low, 13–59. Geneva: World Trade Organization.

Bartlett, C. A., and P. W. Beamish. 2014. *Transnational Management*. New York: McGraw-Hill.

Bartlett, C. A., and S. Ghoshal. 1989. *Managing Across Borders: The Transnational Solution*. Cambridge, MA: Harvard Business School Press.

Cattaneo, O., G. Gerrefi, S. Miroudet, and D. Taglioni. 2013. "Joining, Upgrading and Being Competitive in Global Value Chains: A Strategic Framework." World Bank Policy Research Working Paper, WPS 6406, Washington, DC.

Harris, J. R., and M. P. Todaro. 1970. "Migration, Unemployment and Development: A Two-Sector Analysis." *American Economic Review* 60 (1): 126–42.

McLaughlin, J. A., and G. B. Jordan. 1999. "Logic Models: A Tool for Telling Your Program's Performance Story." Evaluation and Planning 22: 65–72.

OECD. 2013. *Interconnected Economies: Benefiting from Global Value Chains*. Paris: Organisation for Economic Cooperation and Development. http://dx.doi.org/10.1787/9789264189560-en.

O'Malley, E., and C. O'Gorman. 2001. "Competitive Advantage in the Irish Indigenous Software Industry and the Role of Inward Foreign Direct Investment." European Planning Studies 9 (3): 303–21.

UNCTAD. 2013. *World Investment Report 2013: Global Value Chains: Investment and Trade for Development*. New York: United Nations Conference on Trade and Development.

——. 2014. *World Investment Report 2014: Investing in the SDGs*. New York: United Nations Conference on Trade and Development.

Wells, L. Jr., N. Allen, J. Morisset, and N. Pirnia. 2001. "Using Tax Incentives to Compete for Foreign Investment: Are They Worth the Costs?" FIAS Occasional Paper No. 15. Washington, DC: Foreign Investment Advisory Service. Accessed August 15, 2014, http://documents.worldbank.org/curated/en/2001/01/1614958/using-tax-incentives-compete-foreign-investment-worth-costs.

CHAPTER 9

Investment Incentives for Sustainable Development

James Zhan and Joachim Karl

Governments widely use investment incentives, including fiscal, financial, and regulatory incentives, to further certain policy objectives—above all, job creation, technology and skills transfer, and research and development (R&D). According to UNCTAD's Investment Policy Monitor Database, between 2009 and 2013 investment incentives measures comprised 39 percent of all investment promotion and facilitation measures adopted during this period.[1] A recent UNCTAD survey of investment promotion agencies (IPAs) found that fiscal incentives are the most frequently used type of incentives for attracting and benefiting from foreign investment, whereas financial and regulatory incentives are less commonly used for these purposes.[2]

Despite their popularity, location-based investment incentives have been criticized for often not achieving their objectives and for being economically inefficient and potentially harmful to sustainable development (SD)—that is, "development that meets the needs of the present without compromising the ability of future generations to meet their own needs" (WCED 1987). Furthermore, the point has been made that international as well as subnational competition for investment can result in a financially detrimental "race to the top" with regard to the amount or degree of investment incentives or a "race to the bottom" with regard to SD-related regulatory incentives (UNCTAD 2014; Oman 2000).

Against this background, this chapter explores ways and means to make investment incentives a policy tool for promoting SD. To this end, it advocates the redesign of investment incentives schemes, reorienting them from a location-based to an SD contribution–based system to attract investment in SD-relevant sectors and to achieve SD outcomes. Whereas chapter 8 in this volume proposes a holistic approach

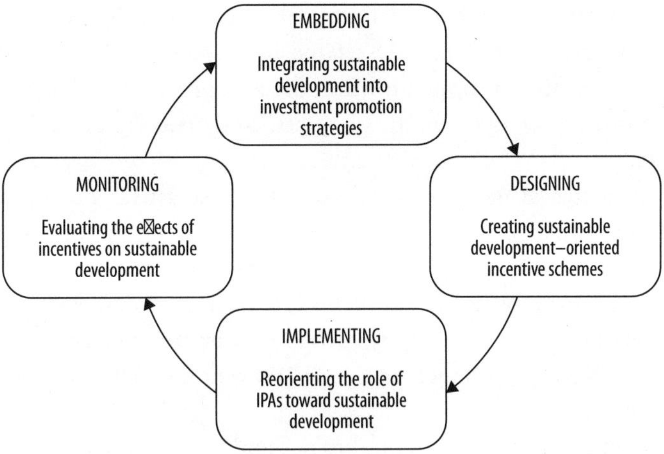

Figure 9.1 Core elements of a promotion strategy for investment for sustainable development.

Source: UNCTAD.

to incentives, including embedding investment incentives schemes into a broader economic development strategy, this chapter suggests more specifically that incentives schemes can be designed and implemented to promote SD goals. Using incentives in a more focused and targeted manner can improve the risk-return profile for investors and influence investor behavior, thereby helping to attract investment into the most-needed sectors for SD. This requires, inter alia, identifying industries and activities eligible for SD-related investment incentives, selecting the "right" type of incentive for the "right" sectors and activities, and giving more weight to SD considerations in the work of IPAs (figure 9.1). Accordingly, investment incentives could be granted to specific industries identified as SD friendly or in a more general manner to investor activities (independent of a specific industry) that promote SD. This chapter proposes a strong and comprehensive mechanism to monitor the SD impact of incentives so as to shift the approach to incentives granting from ex ante to ex post.[3]

EMBEDDING SD INTO INVESTMENT PROMOTION STRATEGIES

Investment incentives are only *one* element of a comprehensive policy strategy to promote investment for SD. Such a strategy needs to address the major constraints that investment in SD-related industries or activities may face. These include entry barriers for investment, inadequate risk-return ratios for SD-related investments, a lack of information about investment opportunities, the absence of effective packaging and promotion of investment projects, and insufficient investment expertise.

When addressing these investment constraints, policy makers should be guided by some core principles. They must balance investment liberalization and promotion, on the one hand, with adequate regulation, on the other hand. Second, they must balance the need for attractive risk-return rates for the investor with the need for accessible and affordable services (such as electricity, water, education, and health services) for all.

To encourage investment in industries and activities that will promote or contribute to SD, it is important to review existing investment barriers. Investment incentives cannot make up for major deficiencies in the investment climate, such as unfavorable entry conditions, an unstable regulatory framework, or a lack of capable institutions, so strengthening the investment climate should be a first priority.

Policy options to facilitate investment are manifold and reach from full or partial liberalization and privatization to concession agreements and public-private partnerships (PPPs). Liberalizing investment in sectors closely linked to SD such as infrastructure development, energy, education, and health care must not come at the price of compromising legitimate public interests. This calls for a vigorous, comprehensive regulatory framework, covering a broad range of policy areas, such as environmental protection, core labor standards, social protection, safety standards, and competition policies, among others. Also important are initiatives concerning corporate social responsibility at the firm level.[4]

Promoting investment for SD is also an important issue when negotiating international investment agreements (IIAs). These agreements should thus not exclusively focus on the protection of foreign investment but should also aim to mobilize and channel investment into SD-related activities—for instance, through a preamble to the IIA that highlights the importance of SD and a commitment for the parties (especially the capital-exporting state) to encourage and facilitate investment for SD. At the same time, IIAs need to preserve appropriate regulatory space—for instance, through the confirmation of governments' right to regulate, exception clauses for SD purposes, reference to investor responsibilities, and reforming investor-state dispute settlement (UNCTAD 2012, 2014).

Host countries can also opt for additional measures that promote and facilitate investment in priority sectors for SD, such as fast-track approval procedures. In recent years, there have also been numerous examples of investment contracts between the host country and foreign investors in which the former has granted specific advantages under the condition that the investor make a specific contribution to SD. For instance, foreign investors have received the right to exploit natural resources or certain tax benefits in exchange for a commitment to build certain infrastructure or social institutions, such as hospitals or schools.

The overall investment policy framework needs to be coherent, and its elements should be mutually reinforcing (table 9.1).

How to translate these general policy challenges related to investment for SD into concrete action plans depends on country-specific circumstances. There is no "one size fits all" solution. Countries may have diverging views regarding their national priorities for SD, their target industries, and their concrete investment-related policy instruments. Their strategies may also vary between piecemeal approaches and more comprehensive SD-oriented strategies (table 9.2).

DESIGNING SD-ORIENTED INVESTMENT INCENTIVES SCHEMES

The above-mentioned UNCTAD IPA survey (2014) revealed that job creation, transfer of technology, and export promotion are the top three policy objectives of existing investment incentives schemes. Thus, these schemes focus primarily on *economic* goals. Environmental and social SD considerations are not top priorities, although responding agencies confirmed that they have recently gained importance in investment promotion policies. About 40 percent of IPAs consider SD to have been only somewhat or not at all important five years ago, compared to only 5 percent today.

When asked about the importance of foreign investment for each of over a dozen industries and activities related to SD, the UNCTAD IPA survey (2014) revealed that IPAs consider foreign investment to be most important for R&D, renewable energy, and infrastructure development. Foreign investment appears least important for protection of oceans and

Table 9.1 Pursuing SD through investment regulation and facilitation—key elements

Economic sustainability (*General and industry specific*)	Environmental sustainability	Social sustainability
Industrial policies	Pollution emission rules (e.g., emission limits or carbon taxes)	Labor laws and regulations
Intellectual property policies	Environmental protection zones	Human rights
Competition policies	Environmental impact assessments of investment	Land tenure rights
Sector-specific entry restrictions for foreign direct investment	Import restrictions for environmentally harmful goods	Migration policies
Sector-specific operational rules and monitoring (e.g., contract farming, financial supervision)	Corporate social responsibility requirements	Safety regulations
	Regional cooperation and regulation on cross-border environmental harm	Prohibition of discrimination based on class, gender, ethnic origin, religion, or race
	Nonlowering of standards clause in IIAs	Right to education, basic health services, and basic infrastructure (e.g., water, sanitation)
	Other international treaties and principles (e.g., UN Global Compact, IPFSD)	Price caps on services to the poor
		Social impact assessments of investment
		Import restrictions for goods produced in a socially harmful manner
		Corporate social responsibility requirements
		Nonlowering of standards clause in IIAs
		Other international treaties and principles (e.g., ILO Tripartite Declaration, UN Guiding Principles on Business and Human Rights, PRAI, IPFSD)
Project-specific promotion and facilitation		
Preparing bankable projects		
Providing for investment contracts, including PPPs		
Investor targeting, matchmaking, and after-care		
Institutional setup of IPAs		
Subsidized insurance against political risks		

Table 9.2 Country examples of investment-related action plans for SD

Republic of Korea

Green growth			Social progress		
Program/act	**Policies and regulation for investment**	**Incentives to promote investment**	**Program/act**	**Policies and regulation for investment**	**Incentives to promote investment**
National Vision "Low Carbon/ Green Growth" (2008)	Framework Act on Low Carbon, Green Growth (2010)	Greenhouse gas emissions trading systems (2015)	2020 National Employment Strategy (2010)	Act on Employment Promotion and Vocational Rehabilitation for Disabled Persons (1993)	Giving preference to employers who employ disabled persons when they bid for public contracts and apply for preferential interest rate loans (2013)
National Strategy for Green Growth (2009)	Enforcement Decree on the Framework Act on Low Carbon, Green Growth (2010)	Feed-in tariff (FIT) system 2002		Social Enterprise Promotion Act (2007)	Financial aid (subsidy of 1.2 million won per month for three months), tax incentive (50% income reduction) for social enterprises (2007)
	Special Taxation Act (1965)	10-year plan for Green Technology-Related R&D (2009)		Special Taxation Act (2007)	10% tax credit for investment related to employment creation (2010)
	Average Fuel Economy regulation (AFE) (2006)	Public credit for green technology and industry through public financial institutions such as the Korea Development Bank, the Industrial Bank of Korea, and the Korea Credit Guarantee Fund (2009)		Balanced Regional Development and Support of Local SMEs Act (2009)	Incentives for private capital inducement projects for regional development (2009)

Table 9.2 *(Continued)*

	Korea Certified Emissions Reductions (KCERs) (2005)	Public Procurement System for Minimum Green Standard Products (2009)			Financial subsidies and tax incentives for enterprises that move their head offices from metropolitan areas to certain locations in other provinces (2001)
	Act on the Encouragement of Purchasing Environmental-Friendly Products (2013)	Tax credit of 20% (30% for SMEs) for various R&D activities including in environmental areas (2010)			

Brazil

	Green growth			Social progress	
Program/act	**Policies and regulation for investment**	**Incentives to promote investment**	**Program/act**	**Policies and regulation for investment**	**Incentives to promote investment**
National program (2012)	National Environmental Policy, Law No. 6938 (1981)	Credit lines for developers of renewable energy projects (2009)	National Educational Plan (2014)	Government's Brasil Maior Plan (2011)	
National policy (2011)	Regulation of the National Policy on Waste Management Established by Decree No. 7404/10 (2010)	Preferential credit to support ethanol storage (2009) National Ethanol Program (low-interest loans for agro-industrial ethanol firms) (1975)		Fund for the Development of Basic Education and Appreciation of the Teaching Profession	Allocation and distribution of 20% of resources from state and federal taxes among all state municipalities in proportion to the number of students enrolled in school (2006)

Profile of the Southern Zone (2006)	National Climate Change Plan (2010)	Developers of electricity projects to receive long-term credit from Brazilian National Economic Development through a financing programme (1952)		Bolsa Familia (2004)	Financial aid to poor Brazilian families that ensure their children attend school and are vaccinated (2004)
	12 sector-based policies developed and implemented in 2011 to achieve emission reduction targets on an economy-wide scale	INOVAR-AUTO programme encourages automakers to, inter alia, produce more efficient vehicles (2012)		Amazon/Manaus Free Trade Zone (1967)	Income relief from 37.5 to 75% for investors in free-trade zones (1967)
		Deduction of total amount of expenditure related to R&D for income tax purposes and additional deduction equal to 60% of total R&D expenditures (2005, R&D does not need to be specific to SD)		Investment Fund (FINAM, FINOR, FUNRES) (1974)	Investors contributing to these funds can claim a 30% deduction of income tax (1974)

Source: UNCTAD based on information from government websites.

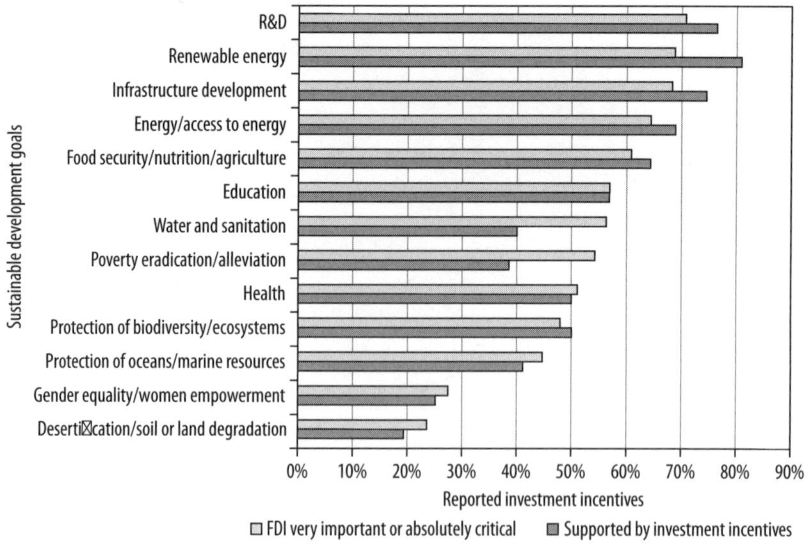

Figure 9.2 Importance of FDI for SD areas and reported investment incentives.

Source: UNCTAD IPA survey (2014).

marine resources, gender equality and women empowerment, and prevention of desertification or degradation of soil or land (figure 9.2).

The findings presented in figure 9.2 show that despite some attention to SD in incentives policies, this has so far not translated into comprehensive strategies that would make SD an integral part of investment promotion through incentives, as a number of industries and activities important for SD are not supported by investment incentives and IPAs do not consider investment to be very important for them. Indicated priority objectives and industries for investment incentives suggest that there is considerable room for improvement when it comes to connecting investment incentives strategies with SD. However, one also needs to take into account that countries may consider some SD-related industries, such as water and sanitation, to be politically sensitive and restrict foreign direct investment in those industries.

FACTORING SD INTO INVESTMENT INCENTIVES SCHEMES

Designing SD-conducive incentives schemes implies putting more emphasis on the quality of investments in terms of their social and environmental effects rather than looking only at the short-term impact on job creation and economic growth.

Used wisely, policies for incentivizing investment for SD can be an effective tool to remedy market failures related to SD and a response to the criticism raised against the way investment incentives have traditionally been used. Because these kinds of incentives pursue the universally recognized goals of environmental and social sustainability, in addition to economic sustainability, there is a lower risk that they distort international competition for investment and result in a harmful race to the bottom. Rather, investment incentives for SD can be considered an important tool to improve the risk-return ratio for investors—an essential precondition for making an investment in SD-related industries. Also, the "picking the winner" strategy in industrial policies, with all its uncertainties about making the "right" choice, may pose fewer problems in a scenario where the granting of investment incentives depends primarily on specific and well-defined social or environmental behaviors of the investor.

On the other hand, using investment incentives for SD purposes has its limitations. First, there may be limited room for private investment in sectors that relate to core public responsibilities, such as the provision of education and basic health care and that must remain affordable to the poor. Second, even investments in an apparently SD-conducive industry (e.g., renewables) can have significant negative social or environmental consequences (e.g., the construction of a hydropower plant resulting in the dislocation of the local population). Third, to avoid investment incentives becoming permanent, the supported industries must have the potential to become self-sustaining over time—something that may be difficult to achieve (e.g., in the case of solar energy[5]). Finally, although investment incentives in SD can help to improve the overall return ratio for investors, they can be expensive and remain limited in their ability to turn an economically unviable investment project into a viable one. All this shows the importance of monitoring the actual effects of investment incentives on SD, including a robust cost-benefit analysis ex ante (see chapter 10 in this volume) and the possibility of their withdrawal if the SD impact proves to be unsatisfactory (see below).

IDENTIFYING SD-RELATED INDUSTRIES OR ACTIVITIES ELIGIBLE FOR INVESTMENT INCENTIVES

Governments can promote SD through their industrial policies by identifying specific priority industries in which they want to attract investment. Although there is hardly any sector or industry that would a priori qualify

Table 9.3 Examples of incentives related to R&D, education, training, and skills development

Country	Examples
Argentina	Financing for development of renewable energy projects and science and technology institutions engaged in related R&D Promotion of biotechnology industry projects resulting in a social and economic impact
Brazil	Export processing zone supports technology dissemination Renewable energy R&D center and companies are partnering with universities and municipalities to create technical courses on solar and wind energy
Canada	Automotive Innovation Fund supports automotive firms' strategic, large-scale R&D Ontario offers support for building, renovating, and equipping research facilities for college-industry partnerships with potential benefits to Ontario, including visibility in the scientific community
France	Expenditure in connection with R&D operations contracted out to public-sector agencies is double-counted Staff expenses related to final-year doctoral and postdoctoral research personnel are counted in the research tax credit base at 400% of their value for the first two years of employment Seventy-one innovation clusters provide additional tax benefits
Germany	High-tech strategy and a Central Innovation Program for SMEs Grants for eligible R&D projects (but not tax incentives), R&D loans can be an alternative to R&D grants
India	200 percent super-deduction in biotechnology R&D
Italy	Tax credit for hiring researchers
Mexico	Cash for percent of R&D expenses and fund for S&T research on energy sustainability Incentive to strengthen research networks and foment the knowledge flow among universities, research centers, and the private sector
Republic of Korea	Tax credit for human resources development
Saudi Arabia	Loans for technology transfer
Turkey	Financial support for new technology adaptation and environmental modification projects achieved via university partnerships

Source: UNCTAD based on information from government websites.

or not qualify for SD-related investment incentives, some industries seem more likely than others to have a positive impact on SD. Examples include the renewable energy industry, infrastructure development, and education or health services as well as agribusiness, which constitutes the backbone of the economy of most developing countries. Many existing incentives schemes focus on green industries (UNCTAD 2014).

Another frequently used eligibility criterion for investment incentives is the requirement that investors undertake certain activities that the host country considers conducive to SD. In particular, investment incentives related to R&D, education, training, and skills development can help to increase the SD impact of the investment. Numerous countries provide incentives in one or several of these areas (table 9.3). (See also chapter 4 in this volume.)

Table 9.4 Pursuing SD through investment incentives

Economic sustainability (*General and industry specific*)	Environmental sustainability	Social sustainability
General incentives schemes (e.g., for creating linkages and spillovers, R&D, start-ups)	Incentives for renewables (e.g., subsidies, market creation policies)	Investment incentives linked to employment and training requirements
Industrial parks	Feed-in tariffs	Public procurement of goods produced in a socially favorable manner
Export processing zones	Public procurement of green products	Subsidies to impoverished households to afford social services and access to electricity, water, and sanitation
Sector-specific incentives		
Financial support for smallholders		

Source: UNCTAD.

SELECTING THE "RIGHT" TYPE OF INCENTIVE

Pursuing SD through investment incentives may have implications for the choice among different types of incentives. A first distinction can be made concerning the specific sustainability aim pursued through investment incentives—that is, whether the investment focuses on economic, environmental, or social sustainability (table 9.4).

For instance, regulatory incentives may be important to help developing industries where as yet there is no sufficiently large market (e.g., the market for renewables in numerous countries) or where there is a "first mover" problem because of the risks attached to innovations (UNCTAD 2011). Public procurement policies favoring green products can play an important role. At the local level, cities increasingly have programs relating to the purchase of hybrid fleets or renewable power, the upgrading of mass transportation systems, green city buildings, or recycling systems.

The choice among different types of investment incentives also depends on a number of other policy considerations, such as the likely implications of a specific form of incentives for the state budget or the kinds of incentives that provide the best means to effectively control their proper use. Performance-based incentives may be preferable to industry-specific incentives that are given automatically at the time the investment is made, although the latter are still preferable to general, non-performance-based incentives. Likewise, fiscal incentives provided after an ex post facto assessment of the SD impact of the investment may be better

Table 9.5 Responding to SD challenges through different types of investment incentives

SD-related policy challenge			
Avoid strain on state budget	*Control proper use and effectiveness of incentives*	*Provide tailor-made incentives*	*Create market for new SD-related industries—first mover issue*
Policy response through incentives			
Consider fiscal incentives instead of up-front financial incentives	Grant incentives ex post instead of ex ante	Condition incentives on specific investor performance	Provide regulatory incentives (e.g., feed-in tariffs for energy providers)
Introduce an incentive ceiling or a time limit	Establish public procurement policies	Link incentives specific contractual commitments of investors	
Coordinate internationally to avoid a race to the top	Coordinate internationally to avoid a race to the bottom	Reserve incentives for specific SD-related industries	
Check whether cost-neutral regulatory incentives could be an alternative			

Source: UNCTAD.

than financial incentives that are granted ex ante. Another important consideration relates to the duration of incentives—including the fiscal sustainability of tax incentives over time and the related tax/debt ratios—and potential incentive ceilings (table 9.5).

CREATING SYNERGIES AND DEALING WITH TRADE-OFFS

Ideally, investment incentives granted for SD purposes should seek synergies among the three pillars of economic, environmental, and social sustainability. As indicated in table 9.6, there are numerous examples where one kind of investment incentive can have multiple impacts. For instance, incentives for infrastructure development in remote areas can have a positive effect on both economic and social development. Government support for green technologies may not only contribute to a better environment but also help to generate green economic growth poles. Incentives relating to the better integration of minorities into the workforce not only increase social well-being but also may trigger more economic growth.

Promoting SD through investment-related policies may result in trade-offs between potentially conflicting policy objectives. For example, fiscal or financial investment incentives for the development of one sustainability

Table 9.6 Examples of SD-related synergy effects of investment incentives

Main policy area		
Economic sustainability	*Social sustainability*	*Environmental sustainability*
Synergies in other SD-related policy areas		
Incentives for infrastructure development in remote areas	Incentives for safe production processes, leading to efficiency gains and preventing harm to human health and the environment	Incentives for green technology as an economic growth pole
R&D incentives for environmental purposes	Incentives to employ local workforce and minorities, leading to more economic growth	Incentives for cross-border green investment projects bringing economic benefits to a whole region
Education incentives to bring people out of poverty and to achieve social upgrading		
Investment incentives focusing on environmentally and socially friendly investment		

Source: UNCTAD.

pillar can reduce the budget available for the promotion of the other pillars. Also, within regions or among social groups, choices may have to be made when it comes to prioritizing incentives for individual investment projects.

Synergies and trade-offs of investment incentives are best considered among all relevant government agencies to ensure a coordinated approach. Integrating budgets and allocating resources to the achievement of specific SD goals rather than to individual ministries can enhance coherence across different government entities. Integrated decision making is also important at the subnational level (Clark 2012). Stakeholders from civil society, business, trade unions, and nongovernmental organizations should be given a voice in the process.

IMPLEMENTING SD-ORIENTED INVESTMENT INCENTIVES SCHEMES

A stronger focus on SD in connection with investment incentives is likely to have implications for the work and mandate of IPAs. Their goals should be to target investors in industries or activities that are particularly conducive to SD and to help bring to the market a pipeline of prepackaged bankable projects. In this process, IPAs are likely to face a number of challenges beyond those experienced in the promotion of conventional foreign investment.

IPA networks need to expand to include public-sector institutions, nonprofit organizations, and other development stakeholders dealing with SD-related industries, such as infrastructure, health, education, energy, or rural development. IPAs also need to broaden contacts with wider groups of targets and potential investors, including sovereign wealth funds, pension funds, and asset managers. Also, more in-house expertise on SD-related investment projects, new sectors, and possible support measures has to be developed.

IPAs would also be well advised to develop a pipeline of bankable SD-related investment projects that are attractive to foreign investors. IPAs' key roles are prioritization, preparation, and packaging. Political prioritization involves the identification of priority projects and the determination of priority sectors, based on national development objectives and strategies. Regulatory preparation involves the preclearing of regulatory aspects and the facilitation of administrative procedures that might otherwise deter investors. Packaging relates to the preparation of concrete project proposals that show viability from the standpoint of all relevant stakeholders—including, for example, technical feasibility studies for investors, financial feasibility assessments for banks, and environmental impact studies for wider stakeholders (UNCTAD 2014). To enhance their capacity and increase the credibility of their products and services, IPAs need to acquire business expertise and seek partnerships with specialized international agencies, business associations, and outward IPAs of home countries.

MONITORING THE EFFECTS OF SD-ORIENTED INVESTMENT INCENTIVES SCHEMES

As is the case with all other incentives, investment incentives for SD need to be closely monitored to determine the extent to which they actually fulfill their purpose. Effective monitoring can also protect against the abuse of incentive programs and opportunities for corruption. Furthermore, governments would be well advised to address the risk of a race to the top in terms of the amount of investment incentives or a race to the bottom in terms of regulatory incentives.

ASSESSING THE EFFECTIVENESS OF SD-RELATED INVESTMENT INCENTIVES

Evaluating the effectiveness of investment incentives requires clear rules on the eligibility criteria for these incentives and a set of indicators against which to evaluate what these investments have contributed to SD. The incentives scheme would also benefit from a deeper assessment of whether the incentives themselves were effective at changing the behavior of the firms and whether the SD outcomes would have occurred absent the incentives.

Through the 2015 version of its Investment Policy Framework for Sustainable Development (Policy Framework), UNCTAD has suggested a number of guiding principles that are relevant in this context. Investment incentives should be based on a set of explicitly formulated policy objectives related to SD and ideally include a number of quantifiable SD goals for both the attraction of investment and the impact of investment on SD (table 9.7). The objectives should set clear priorities, a time frame for achieving them, and the principal measures intended to support the objectives. A review process should be put in place to ensure that investment incentives schemes are correctly implemented.

In addition, corporate sustainability reporting can play an important role in enabling governments to monitor the effective use of investment incentives. This involves generating internal company data on sustainability-related activities and control systems, facilitating proactive management, setting targets, and benchmarking.

If the expected SD impact does not materialize, rules should be in place allowing for a withdrawal of the investment incentive. Depending on the concrete circumstances, there may also be a case for the phasing out of entire incentives schemes considered to be potentially harmful for SD. Incentives for investment in highly polluting industries could be a prime target. Other examples include incentives for export-oriented industries that produce in a manner that is dangerous for human life or health or that disregards other core labor standards. Under performance-based incentives, some of these considerations could be factored up-front, with the provision of incentives contingent on meeting environmental and other requirements.

Reducing existing investment incentives schemes may infringe on the rights of investors who already receive incentives. In such cases, disgruntled foreign investors have invoked the "fair and equitable treatment" (FET) standard in IIAs to claim that their "legitimate expectations" have

Table 9.7 Possible indicators for the creation of investment impact objectives and the measurement of policy effectiveness

Area	Indicator	Details and examples
Economic value added	→ Total value added	→ Gross output (GDP contribution) of the new/additional economic activity resulting from the investment (direct and induced)
	→ Value of capital formation	→ Contribution to gross fixed capital formation → Reinvestment of earnings into the host country
	→ Total and net export generation	→ Total export generation; net export generation (net of imports) is also captured by the value-added indicator
	→ Number of formal business entities	→ Number of businesses in the value chain supported by the investment; this is a proxy for entrepreneurial development and expansion of the formal (tax-paying) economy
	→ Total fiscal revenues	→ Total fiscal take from the economic activity resulting from the investment, through all forms of taxation and royalties
Job creation	→ Employment (number)	→ Total number of jobs generated by the investment, both direct and induced (value chain view), dependent and self-employed, temporary and permanent
	→ Wages	→ Total household income generated (direct and induced)
	→ Typologies of employee skill levels	→ Number of jobs generated, by ILO job type as a proxy for job quality and technology levels (including technology dissemination)
Sustainable development	→ Labor impact indicators	→ Employment of women (and comparable pay) and of disadvantaged groups → Skills upgrading, training provided
	→ Social impact indicators	→ Health and safety effects, occupational injuries → Number of families lifted out of poverty, wages above subsistence level → Expansion of goods and services offered, access to and affordability of basic goods and services

Table 9.7 *(Continued)*

	→ Environmental impact indicators	→ Contributions to proximity of public transport → Greenhouse gas emissions, carbon offsets/credits, carbon credit revenues → Energy and water consumption/ efficiency, reduction and mitigation of adverse impacts of hazardous materials → Enterprise development in eco-sectors
	→ Development impact indicators	→ Development of local resources → Knowledge and technology dissemination

Sources: UNCTAD 2014; Thomas 2009; OPIC 2013a, 2013b.

been violated and that they are therefore entitled to compensation (e.g. *Bogdanov v. Moldova,* SCC Case No. V (114/2009)). Also, investors may invoke so-called respect clauses (or umbrella clauses) in IIAs to challenge the withdrawal of investment incentives (e.g., *Veolia v. Egypt,* ICSID Case No. ARB/12/15). Recent developments show that such claims can be successful (box 9.1). (See also chapter 12 in this volume.) These cases show the importance of carefully drafting the content of the FET clause and the respect clause in IIAs. UNCTAD's Policy Framework offers guidance in this regard.

Effective monitoring of the effects of investment incentives on SD calls for transparency with regard to their granting. Promoting transparency and access to information on the SD impacts of investment (e.g., through performance evaluations and ratings programs) can generate social pressure to minimize negative impacts. In addition, offering incentives in a transparent manner can reduce the risk of corruption. Granting incentives based on performance can facilitate meeting desired targets, and awarding them after the sought results have been achieved and verified rather than ex ante can avoid the need to enforce clawback provisions. Complex issues of risk distribution may arise in the case of contract-based incentives. One challenge is to sufficiently specify the kind of performance expected from the investors and the SD goal to be achieved (e.g., a certain reduction in CO_2 emissions or a specific technology transfer). Second, there is the issue of which contracting party should carry the risk

Box 9.1 Challenging the Withdrawal of Investment Incentives Through IIAs

In a series of recent investor-state dispute settlement (ISDS) cases, or threats thereof, foreign investors claimed that the unilateral withdrawal of incentives by host countries constitutes a violation of the IIA obligation to grant FET.

In *Micula et al. v. Romania*, the claimants alleged that Romania violated the Sweden-Romania bilateral investment treaty (BIT) when it altered or terminated various incentives that had been extended earlier to encourage investments in an economically disadvantaged part of Romania. Romania, in turn, argued that changes to its incentives program were warranted as part of its accession to the European Union. The arbitral tribunal ruled that the unilateral withdrawal of incentives by Romania breached the BIT's FET obligation and awarded damages of US$250 million, including interest (Ioan Micula et al. v. Romania 2013).

In 2013, seven investors in photovoltaic energy production argued that the Czech Republic's rollback of incentives, previously put in place to attract investment in the renewable energy sector, violated several of the country's BITs. In one of the cases the claimants are seeking damages in the range of 50–70 million euros ("Solar Investors File Arbitration" 2013).

During 2012–2015, foreign investors in the renewable energy sector filed more than 23 ISDS cases against Spain. At stake are the country's subsidies to attract investments in renewables, which were withdrawn in a time of financial crisis and economic austerity.

During 2014-2015, Italy was also confronted with three IIA claims arising out of similar circumstances.

Sources: UNCTAD, Investment Dispute Settlement Navigator database available at: http://investmentpolicyhub.unctad.org/ISDS.

that the agreed-upon SD goal cannot be achieved. Contractual options range from an absolute obligation of the investor to force majeure clauses and the taking into account of other circumstances beyond the investors' control (e.g., the R&D undertaken does not produce the expected SD-relevant results).

AVOIDING HARMFUL INTERNATIONAL COMPETITION INVOLVING INVESTMENT INCENTIVES

Monitoring the effects of investment incentives also calls for an examination of the implications of international competition among host countries for foreign investment. More international cooperation with regard to investment incentives could help to avoid a detrimental race to the top among countries. Up to now, such coordination has been relatively rare and mainly limited to the regional level (box 9.2). At the global level, there exists the WTO Agreement on Subsidies and Countervailing Measures; however, this is mainly limited to trade. An attempt to discipline the use of investment incentives at the plurilateral level was made in

Box 9.2 Examples of International Coordination in the Use of Investment Incentives

At the international level, several treaties restrict the use of trade-distorting incentives practices (for more on this, see chapter 12 in this volume). For instance, the Treaty on the European Union restricts the ability of Member States to provide investment incentives, and the European Commission oversees compliance with these rules. Disputes can be submitted to the European Court of Justice, which has the authority to issue legally binding interpretations of the rules on State aid, including investment incentives (see chapter 5 in this volume).

In Africa, the East Africa Community has made progress toward a code of conduct to harmonize the incentive regimes of Member States. It is also undertaking studies to guide the harmonization of incentives packages offered to investors within and among Member States. The members of the West African Economic and Monetary Union have agreed to harmonize aspects of their tariff and tax regimes, including rules on income taxation. However, officials are exploiting institutional weaknesses and gaps in relevant rules to give investment deals that deviate from standard tax regimes. This has increased the opacity and complexity of tax systems and contributed to a culture of tax negotiation.

Source: CCSI 2015.

the 1990s during the unsuccessful OECD negotiations on a Multilateral Agreement on Investment. In the context of the current negotiations between the European Union and the United States on a Transatlantic Trade and Investment Partnership (TTIP), the EU has suggested to provide for the possibility of consultations between the Contracting Parties when a Member considers that a subsidy adversely affects or may adversely affect its interests (EU proposal published on 7 January 2015).

More international cooperation could also address the risk that investment incentives might result in a harmful race to the bottom with regard to regulatory standards. This can be achieved by agreeing on certain international principles or guidelines that investors and states have to respect. Examples are the ILO Tripartite Declaration of Principles Concerning Multinational Enterprises and Social Policy (ILO 1977), the UN Global Compact (UN 2000, the UN Guiding Principles on Business and Human Rights (UN 2011), the FAO/World Bank/UNCTAD/IFAD Principles for Responsible Agricultural Investment (PRAI; FAO 2010), and the OECD Guidelines for Multinational Enterprises (OECD 2011). Another approach, adopted in numerous IIAs, is to agree on not lowering environmental or social regulatory standards as a means to attract foreign investment.

CONCLUSION

Investment incentives are likely to remain an important policy instrument in the global competition to attract investment—not least because they are easier to implement than complex and often painful structural reforms of the domestic economy. Although some policy objectives pursued through investment incentives already have a specific SD angle (e.g., R&D, technology and skills transfer, local development, and renewable energy), current incentives schemes often lack a systematic and consistent approach.

This chapter advocates a reorientation and redesign of investment incentives programs. SD should become the overarching reason for granting these incentives and the main guideline when monitoring their effect. SD considerations should be put at the core when attracting investment rather than the prospect of short-term economic gains. Such rethinking is prone to create win-win situations, as incentives may improve the risk-return profile for investors in politically and economically sensitive SD sectors while at the same time helping the poor to access infrastructure and health and education services at affordable rates.

Due to space limitations, this chapter deals only with the investment policy aspects of this challenge. However, mobilizing investment for SD and channeling it into SD-related industries and activities has a broader dimension and calls for action far beyond investment policies *sensu stricto*. First, SD requires host countries to build up their domestic capacities and better integrate their domestic economies into the global economy. Second, there is a need for innovative financing mechanisms and a reorientation of financial markets toward SD. Third, it is important to change the business mindset to give more weight to the social and environmental impacts of investment decisions. UNCTAD's *World Investment Report 2014* explores these manifold challenges and suggests a variety of policy responses.

NOTES

The views expressed by the authors are not necessarily those of UNCTAD. The authors thank Thomas van Giffen, Ventzislav Kotetzov and Jason Munyan of UNCTAD for their contributions.

1. Policy measures are identified through a systematic review of government and business intelligence sources. Individual measures are verified, to the fullest extent possible, by referencing government sources. The compilation of different measures is not exhaustive and does not provide information on their monetary value. Investment promotion and facilitation measures other than incentives include, for instance, the establishment of free economic zones or "one-stop shops" for business registration. Visit the Investment Policy Monitor Database at http://investmentpolicyhub.unctad.org.

2. UNCTAD conducted a global survey of investment promotion agencies (IPAs) in early 2014. Of the 257 IPAs contacted, 75 completed the questionnaire, representing an overall response rate of 29 percent. Respondents included 62 national and 13 subnational agencies. A geographical breakdown of the responses shows a relatively high response rate from agencies from economies in transition (South-East Europe and the Commonwealth of Independent States), Africa, and Latin America and the Caribbean.

3. The present chapter does not address questions related to the impact of investment incentives on investor location decisions or whether investment incentives justify their cost. These issues are highly specific and depend on a variety of factors, including the sectors, status of the economy, and type of investment incentive. For more information, see Blomström and Kokko 2003; full access to the document is available at: http://earthmind.net/fdi/misc/eijs-fdi-incentives.pdf. See also James 2009.

4. Corporate social responsibility standards exist at several levels: (1) intergovernmental organization standards derived from universal principles as recognized in international declarations and agreements, (2) multistakeholder initiative standards, (3) industry association codes, and (4) individual company codes.

5. In some cases, a government could decide that the public benefits of a certain investment justify continued incentives, although given the costs of a long-term incentive, such a decision should proceed only after a robust cost-benefit analysis.

REFERENCES

Blomström, M., and A. Kokko. 2003. "The Economics of Foreign Direct Investment Incentives." NBER Working Paper No. 9489. Washington, DC: National Bureau of Economic Research. http://www.nber.org/papers/w9489.pdf.

CCSI. 2015. "Investment Incentives: The Good, the Bad and the Ugly." *2013 Columbia International Investment Conference Report.* New York: Columbia Center on Sustainable Investment.

Clark, H. 2012. "The Importance of Governance for Sustainable Development." Remarks at "The Importance of Governance for Sustainable Development," Singapore Lecture Series of the Institute of Southeast Asian Studies, Singapore, March 13. http://www.undp.org/content/undp/en/home/presscenter/speeches/2012/03/13/the-importance-of-governance-for-sustainable-development.html.

Dunning, J. H., and S. M. Lundan. 2008. *Multinational Enterprises and the Global Economy.* Cheltenham, UK: Edward Elgar.

FAO, World Bank, UNCTAD, and IFAD. 2010. "Principles for Responsible Agricultural Investment that Respects Rights, Livelihoods and Resources (PRAI)."

ILO. 1977. *Tripartite Declaration of Principles Concerning Multinational Enterprises and Social Policy.* http://www.ilo.org/empent/Publications/WCMS_094386/lang--en/index.htm.

Ioan Micula, Viorel Micula, S.C. European Food S.A, S.C. Starmill S.R.L., and S.C. Multipack S.R.L. v. Romania. 2013. ICSID Case No. ARB/05/20, Final Award of December 11.

James, S. 2009. "Incentives and Investments: Evidence and Policy Implications." World Bank Group, Washington, DC. https://www.wbginvestmentclimate.org/uploads/IncentivesandInvestments.pdf.

OECD. 2011. *OECD Guidelines for Multinational Enterprises.* Paris: Organisation for Economic Cooperation and Development.

Oman, C. 2000. *Policy Competition for Foreign Direct Investment—A Study of Competition Among Governments to Attract FDI.* Paris: Organisation for Economic Cooperation and Development. http://www.oecd.org/mena/investment/35275189.pdf.

OPIC. 2013a. "Office of Investment Policy Questionnaire." Washington, DC: Overseas Private Investment Corporation.

——. 2013b. "Self-Monitoring Questionnaire for Finance, Insurance, Reinsurance, and Investment Funds Projects." Washington, DC: Overseas Private Investment Corporation.

"Solar Investors File Arbitration Against Czech Republic; Intra-EU BITs and Energy Charter Treaty at Center of Dispute." 2013. *Investment Arbitration Reporter* 6 (10), May 15. http://www.iareporter.com/articles/20130515_1.

Thomas, K. P. 2009. "Assessing Sustainable Development Impacts of Investment Incentives: A Checklist." Winnipeg: International Institute for Sustainable Development. http://www.iisd.org/tkn/pdf/assessing_sd_investment.pdf.

UN. 2011. *Guiding Principles on Business and Human Rights.* http://www.ohchr.org/Documents/Publications/GuidingPrinciplesBusinessHR_EN.pdf.

——. 2000. "United Nations Global Compact." https://www.unglobalcompact.org/.

UNCTAD. 2004. *Pink Series on Issues in International Investment Agreements Incentives.* New York: United Nations Conference on Trade and Development.

——. 2011. "Investment for Development: Current Policy Challenges." TD/B/C.II/MEM.3/11. Geneva: United Nations Conference on Trade and Development.

——. 2012. *World Investment Report 2012: Towards a New Generation of Investment Policies.* New York: United Nations Conference on Trade and Development.

——. 2014. *World Investment Report 2014: Investing in the SDGs: An Action Plan.* New York: United Nations Conference on Trade and Development.

——.2015. Investment Policy Framework for Sustainable Development. UNCTAD/DIAE/PCB/2015/5.

WCED. 1987. "Our Common Future." World Commission on Environment and Development, http://www.un-documents.net/our-common-future.pdf.

Zhan, J. 2011. "Making Industrial Policy Work." Project Syndicate, March 10, https://www.project-syndicate.org/commentary/making-industrial-policy-work.

CHAPTER 10

Cost-Benefit Analysis of Investment Incentives

Ellen Harpel

Global competition for investment and the desire to increase the quantity and quality of jobs within their jurisdictions have led governments to expand their use of economic development incentives. These incentives are intended to influence where private companies invest and set up operations in order to generate net benefits for the jurisdiction hosting those operations and financing the incentives. This chapter addresses steps governments can take to assess both costs and benefits in order to make sound decisions when providing incentives to investors.

WHY COST-BENEFIT ANALYSIS IS IMPORTANT

Governments providing incentives are increasingly concerned that the benefits they expect to receive after offering incentives packages might not come to fruition. They also frequently feel at a disadvantage during the site selection process and during incentives negotiations because they have relatively little insight into the company's intentions. Politically, the stakes can be high to "win," or at least not "lose," promising investment opportunities. Due diligence and cost-benefit analyses can improve the confidence levels associated with incentives decisions and help shift the focus away from making a deal to where it should be: determining whether any given opportunity will create net benefits for the community, defined here as the residents of the jurisdiction offering the incentives.

A good cost-benefit analysis can help mitigate several potential problems associated with incentives. First, by quantifying expected costs, a government can avoid overcommitting its resources to investors. Second, the process of comparing costs with benefits over time gives the government the opportunity to understand more specifically whether and how an investment is likely to improve economic prospects in a community.

Third, the analysis can be used to build support for high-quality projects and to steer the government's interest away from lower-quality opportunities. Fourth, the expectations set as a result of the cost-benefit analysis can be used after the fact to monitor and evaluate the actual outcomes of the investment to determine whether net benefits were achieved.

This chapter is organized as follows. The second section describes three elements of cost-benefit analyses—project attributes, fiscal impact, and economic impact—and addresses key issues for implementation. The third section provides examples of the incorporation of cost-benefit analyses into U.S. state and local economic development programs as well as descriptions of several cost-benefit analysis tools. The fourth section briefly addresses compliance and program evaluation. The final section provides concluding remarks on the value of conducting quality analysis up-front during the incentives process.

A THREE-STEP APPROACH TO COST-BENEFIT ANALYSIS

Incentives are not just about winning a deal or completing a transaction with an investor. As explained in chapter 8 in this volume, effective incentives use must be part of a holistic economic development strategy. Incentives are one economic development tool among many that can be used to achieve a community's goals. Cost-benefit analyses help determine whether or not an incentives deal and the investment it supports can contribute to those goals.

To this end, cost-benefit analyses for incentives should address three questions:

1. Is this a gainful opportunity for the location offering incentives?
2. What is the fiscal (budgetary) impact of the proposed incentives package?
3. What is the potential economic impact of the investment?

These three questions are designed to assess whether a given investment *can* generate net benefits for a community, not whether it *will*. The latter depends on multiple factors that will drive operational success, many of which (such as economic cycles or market trends) are beyond the control of either the company making the investment or the individual government. Further, the question of whether an investment *did* generate net benefits is another matter that will be addressed briefly in the fourth section.

This approach, for two reasons, purposely steers the discussion away from the question of whether an investment would have been made without the incentive. First, this determination is extremely difficult to make for many proposed investments, which means it is not a helpful decision-making criterion. The value of incentives to the investor is blended with many other location- and company-specific factors, and as a result, there is no practical way to say definitively that an incentive or set of incentives makes the ultimate difference in an investment decision. Further, the relative value of location attributes and incentives offered by other jurisdictions to the investor is generally unknown, making it impossible to compare total costs and therefore determine the optimal incentive amount.

Second, trying to determine whether the company "needs" the incentive before making the investment can inadvertently focus too much attention on the company and the deal rather than on creating the community, economic, and fiscal benefits that should be the driving force behind all decisions to provide investment incentives. Governments can certainly consider whether an incentive is "necessary," but the approach outlined in this chapter enables them to make good decisions without being paralyzed by the need to resolve definitively whether an investment would have occurred but for the incentive.

PROJECT ATTRIBUTES: IS THIS A GAINFUL OPPORTUNITY FOR THE LOCATION OFFERING INCENTIVES?

The first step in the cost-benefit analysis is simply summarizing in layman's terms the benefits a deal could bring to a community. Project proponents should, without falling back on modeling results or jargon, be able to explain to citizens and elected officials why it is a worthwhile "investment." If it requires a tremendous stretch of the imagination to understand the upside potential, this should give deal makers pause. The two main categories of benefits are (1) basic project characteristics (jobs, job quality, investment, location) and (2) fit with the community's broader economic development strategy. Timing and project risk are two additional factors that should be considered.

Economic development organizations (EDOs) or investment promotion agencies (IPAs) are typically the lead entities in terms of interacting with private companies that might be seeking incentives. EDOs may be government, private, or hybrid groups operating at the local, regional, state, or national level to "improve the economic well-being and quality of life for a community, by creating and/or retaining jobs that facilitate growth and provide a stable tax base" (IEDC 2014). IPAs tend to be more narrowly focused, with a mandate to "facilitate and promote investment at the regional, national and sub-national levels" through image building and sector branding, investment targeting, and facilitation, among other services (UNCTAD 2014). In short, EDOs and IPAs exist in order to increase jobs and/or investment in their communities or countries. Therefore, reporting on expected job creation and investment value is a fundamental part of their mission.

An important aspect of the first factor, a project's basic characteristics, is job quality, often determined by pay levels, benefits, educational or skill requirements, or industry sector associated with the proposed investment. Defining the location where the project will take place and where benefits will accrue is also important. Many EDOs are tasked with increasing economic opportunities in distressed areas, and determining the geographic distribution of benefits (and costs) is a necessary step for reporting and assessment.

Chapters 8 and 9 in this volume both stress the importance of embedding incentives in a broader economic development framework. Therefore, any project for which incentives are offered should also be evaluated in the context of those economic goals and strategies, the second factor to consider when analyzing benefit. Many communities have some sort of economic development strategy in place, though perhaps of varying quality, and making sure that an incentivized project aligns with the broad statements and values within that strategy is a good initial step. In the United States, both state and local policy makers are also increasingly ensuring that individual incentives programs have well-defined goals, although many statutes authorizing these programs remain unclear, making both administration and evaluation difficult. Clearly defining the purpose of an incentive policy or program helps ensure it will be used as intended. Otherwise, it runs the risk of being offered to all comers regardless of their capacity to connect to community goals.

Governments often have specific objectives related to supporting certain target industries or developing certain individual sectors of the economy. Economic developers may be urged to support small businesses or businesses meeting certain demographic criteria (such as women- or minority-owned companies). Individual communities, EDOs, and IPAs may be members of broader regional or national organizations and need to align their efforts with these wider strategies. At the same time, they may wish to avoid investments that hurt neighboring communities or work against regional or national objectives. Sustainable development may be a priority. These are all additional strategic factors that should be considered when assessing the basic project benefits that an investment might generate.

A third factor that is frequently overlooked is project timing. Too often, projects are presented to the public as if all benefits will start flowing on day 1, which is rarely the case. It is important to be clear about when the project is expected to begin, when the investment and hiring are anticipated to occur, and what the lifespan of the project is. Further, the timing of the project and its anticipated benefits should be connected to the flow of funds for the incentives offering. Incentives frequently have a long time frame. Ten years is not an unusual time frame for an incentive, with the fiscal payback kicking in after that time, but it may not be realistic to assume a steady-state operation for a decade or longer.

A fourth and related factor is risk assessment. EDOs and IPAs should consider the likelihood of success for the investment as proposed. Different communities have different appetites for risk, and no investment is risk-free, but it is important to have a rough sense of the potential for success or failure. Some basic factors to consider are the investor's track record, other partners and financial backers involved in the project, and whether the investment involves a new or unproven technology.

Set standards do not exist for any of these items. They all depend on the community, what it is striving to achieve, and the nature of the proposed investment. Good economic development organizations know their communities well and should be able to assess whether a proposed investment aligns with community values on these factors, singly or in combination, and to develop a rough sense of timing and project risk. The objective is not to be "right" every time but to be able to explain the decision to provide incentives and to be in a better negotiating position by understanding some of the basic pros and cons of a given opportunity from a community perspective.

FISCAL IMPLICATIONS: WHAT IS THE FISCAL (BUDGETARY) IMPACT OF THE PROPOSED INCENTIVES PACKAGE?

The second step in the cost-benefit analysis is assessing the tax and budgetary implications of the incentive decision. The purpose is to understand how the taxes expected to be generated by an investment compare to the cost of the incentives and any additional services that must be provided by the government. Governments often choose to offer incentives even when they are a net cost to the treasury because they accomplish other economic development objectives. However, it is still important to understand what the fiscal impact is likely to be.

There are three major elements to a fiscal impact analysis. The first is calculating the cost of the incentives themselves. Second, new taxes likely to be generated should be estimated. Third, additional government expenditures that will be required because of the investment need to be taken into consideration.

COST OF THE INCENTIVES

The cost of the incentives package should be the easiest element to calculate because its value is determined by the government. This may in fact be true for some grants and local incentives, but the actual cost of incentives can be surprisingly difficult to determine. Some factors complicating the calculation are estimating the total value of the incentives over time (especially for certain types of tax breaks) and incorporating the time value of money. Anticipating the timing of disbursements for different elements of the incentives package can also be complex, especially when in-kind, cash, and tax-based incentives are combined. Incentives packages also often involve several different state, local, or national jurisdictions, which may experience the impact of those incentives at different levels and different times.

Estimating the costs of tax credits poses specific challenges. The inability to know how many companies will be eligible and/or when companies will use tax credits they have been granted has created tremendous headaches for state budget officials and revenue forecasting offices in the United States. Tax incentives are often created with no limit on their cost. "As a result, the financial impact of tax incentives can grow quickly and unexpectedly without any explicit choices by state lawmakers to expand them" (The Pew Center on the States 2012a, 3). The tax burden can be significant, especially when tax credit agreements may extend for years or even decades. This has led to efforts in some states, such as Michigan, to reduce their reliance on major tax credit programs altogether, whereas other states, such as California, have placed caps or other limits on tax credit use. In *Avoiding Blank Checks*, the Pew Center on the States (2012a, 4) advises creating reliable cost estimates for tax incentives and setting annual cost controls while also noting that quality "cost estimates for tax incentives are difficult to do."

NEW TAXES

Estimating new taxes likely to be generated by a project requires a strong understanding of the tax structure and several assumptions about who will pay what and when. Company and individual tax estimates should be calculated. Major tax categories typically include business and personal income, sales and excise, and property taxes. Tax rates and the tax structure can vary widely, depending on the jurisdiction. There may be other, lesser taxes and fees that will also be affected. Multiple taxing jurisdictions may be involved.

A new project that will bring new jobs may also bring new people to the area. These individuals will pay taxes, and most communities can make a good estimate of the likely amount of taxes to be generated per capita or per household based on past revenue data. New jobs that do not bring new residents may have a less meaningful impact on tax revenue.

Companies that are new to the community will also pay taxes, minus any that have been abated. Estimating taxes to be paid by any one company can be challenging. Rough estimates of new taxes can be made from basic information provided by the company regarding assets and operations. However, in many jurisdictions, a variety of factors influences taxable income, which makes that element difficult to model or estimate, though rules of thumb are often used to make calculations. The future value of real and personal property, sales subject to taxation, local purchases, utility usage, and other taxable items or transactions should also be estimated but are difficult to predict accurately.

COST OF NEW SERVICES

New people and new businesses require additional levels of service. Education and public safety tend to be the biggest categories requiring increases in expenditures (based on household size and number of children), but additional investments in transportation or utility infrastructure may also be needed to provide service for major new operations, which may, in turn, affect debt levels and capital budgets.

Experts suggest considering average cost versus marginal cost when calculating the impact of expanding government services. Average costs are calculated using current data on what public services cost on a per unit (household, individual, or land unit) basis and then applied to the project. However, in communities experiencing rapid growth or decline, a major investment could require significant capital improvements, and existing ratios or standards might not capture the full range of impact. Marginal costs consider the infrastructure and capital capacity of the community to determine the incremental cost of serving one more unit (Morgan 2010).

MODELS AND MODELING ISSUES

Because of the complexity of the calculations, many communities use a fiscal impact model to estimate the budgetary implications of incentives packages. The models range from simple spreadsheets based on a few inputs and rules of thumb to sophisticated software packages and online models requiring detailed inputs and some technical expertise. Some models have geographic information system (GIS) integration that can show impacts by site or neighborhood.

Whichever type of model a community uses, it is important to have a basic understanding of the assumptions and mechanics built into the system. The analytics should not be a mystery, and the output should be explainable. As with all models, it is important to keep in mind the trope that all models are wrong but some are useful. Modeled output is built on assumptions because full data are not available, and the estimates they generate are based on expectations of future actions. Even the most sophisticated fiscal impact models must be used thoughtfully and their findings interpreted carefully. Given the wide range of assumptions going into an incentives evaluation, these models are most helpful for providing a sense of the order of magnitude of the impact and a rough calculation of positive or negative returns in order to support decision making.

Some models take into consideration not only direct new jobs or investment associated with the incentivized project but also indirect and induced employment, calculated using economic impact analyses (see below). This approach should be used cautiously, as it requires assumptions built on assumptions that may exaggerate the actual likely budgetary flows associated with the project at hand.

Timing, again, is an issue, especially with phased investments in which year 1 revenues and expenditures may not be representative of future years and with a project whose true lifespan may not be clear. Revenues and expenditures will likely occur at different times in the project's life cycle, with many of the benefits not expected to accrue until after the incentive period ends, so the time value of money must also be considered.

ECONOMIC CONTRIBUTION: WHAT IS THE POTENTIAL ECONOMIC IMPACT OF THE INVESTMENT?

Economic impact analyses trace the flow through an economy of activity stemming from an initial investment. They attempt to estimate the total contribution of different types of economic activities to a regional or state economy. An infusion of spending in one sector spurs additional economic activity in other sectors as the money is respent, generating a multiplier effect. Multipliers quantify direct industry impacts but also recognize interindustry linkages and the successive rounds of spending that occur within an economy. The total economic contribution of this added spending is estimated by tracing the flow of money between industries and households until all of the initial investment eventually leaves a region through foreign or domestic trade or is collected as a tax.

Economic impact models should be tailored to the expenditure patterns and industry mix of the jurisdiction in order to estimate the direct, indirect, and induced effects from various economic activities.

- Direct effects refer to the gross expenditures and employment of the studied industry and project.
- Indirect effects are the spending and employment of suppliers and contractors to produce inputs for the industry and project.
- Induced effects include household spending on goods and services by both industry employees and the employees of contractors and suppliers (both direct and indirect employees).

Total economic impact is the sum of direct, indirect, and induced effects.

In contrast to fiscal impact analyses, generating the inputs for economic impact analyses is straightforward. Models generally require inputs on annual operational expenditures, jobs and payroll, and construction spending (where relevant). Selecting the industry classification for the initial investment is an important choice that can significantly affect the total value of estimated impacts. Geographic definitions also matter; economic impact will increase along with the size of the jurisdiction.

Although the initial inputs are easier to define, running the model and correctly interpreting the results are more difficult. Economic impact modeling typically requires some up-front cost for data and model purchases. (Few U.S. locations devote the resources to creating their own, though it can be done.) Translating the basic project data into appropriate model inputs requires a good understanding of the project, the economy, and the model. The results are often presented in a tidy, simple format summarizing total jobs, income, and output impacts, but the implications are not so clear.

For example, many economic impact models are static rather than dynamic, so they do not take into account structural change in the economy. That is, they assume that the economy basically stays the same while absorbing a new investment (Morgan 2010). A related point is that many modelers do not consider risk and variability over time. In other words, they assume that the impact every year will be similar to that in the year for which the initial inputs were generated. Another weakness is that models generally do not take into account replacement spending; they assume all spending is completely new to the economy, which may not be the case, especially for induced effects. Some projects—in retail, for example—can have high displacement effects if the new business gains at the expense of an existing business (Morgan 2010).

When the total impact findings are presented as stand-alone figures, it can be easy to confuse the direct impact of the initial investment being incentivized with the overall impact, including indirect and induced effects. This can unduly raise expectations about how one investment can "transform" economies. With the exception of the largest investments, many of the indirect and induced effects will be difficult to count or even see in something as big and diverse as a regional economy. Finally, the models make assumptions about how money will be spent in the region based on the industrial structure—but that does not mean money related to a specific project *will* be spent in the region in that way.

Economic impact analyses are valuable tools because they generate insights into the value a new investment can bring to a region, but too often their findings are oversimplified and overstated. Economic impact analyses are good inputs for decision makers, but they should not be the only tool used for incentive investments or cost-benefit analysis.

IMPLICATIONS

These three cost-benefit analysis elements are based on assumptions and preinvestment inputs about the nature of the project under consideration for incentives. They provide insight into the potential community, fiscal, and economic impacts of the proposed investment and are therefore valuable decision-making tools for policy makers. They may not always yield the "right" answer, but they should provide sufficient insight for decision makers to be confident that benefits for the community will likely outweigh costs and to have a rough sense of the order of magnitude of those costs and benefits.

"Systematic cost-benefit or fiscal impact analyses are complex, demanding tasks requiring substantial time and expertise" (Ha and Feiock 2012, 482). But given the high dollar value and substantial commitment in increasing numbers of incentives packages, it is important for decision makers to devote some up-front time and resources to establishing a process for estimating the costs and benefits of incentives.

HOW COST-BENEFIT ANALYSIS IS PUT INTO PRACTICE—EXAMPLES AND RESOURCES

State and local governments prepare cost-benefit analyses for incentives decisions more often than in the past, but the practice is not yet ubiquitous. The Pew Center on the States (2012a) reported that states develop cost estimates for tax incentives policies inconsistently. Other researchers found that 75 percent of cities require cost-benefit analysis prior to awarding incentives (Sharp and Mullinix 2012), up from 50 percent only five years earlier (Weber and Santacroce 2007), whereas another study reported that 10 percent of local governments never conduct such an analysis (Ha and Feiock 2012).

Work conducted by Smart Incentives, a firm founded by the author that advises communities throughout the economic development incentives process, indicates that state and local governments increasingly conduct some type of cost-benefit or return-on-investment (ROI) analysis when granting discretionary incentives. However, the quality and type of analysis vary considerably across jurisdictions and individual incentives programs. Further, many are loath to share their analyses or make their decision-making process public. The first two states described below have been open about their process and offer very different examples—one focused exclusively on fiscal impact and the second emphasizing economic impact and strategic value. A third state describes its up-front review process for a specific major incentives package. Local governments are also improving their analytical capabilities and offer some of the most sophisticated approaches to cost-benefit analysis. A set of local examples is also provided below.

Different places have different economic development strategies and reasons for offering incentives. The key point here is that it is important to conduct the cost-benefit analysis in such a way that it determines how well a given investment supports those strategies and helps a community achieve its economic development goals. Accordingly, there is not one "right" way to conduct such an analysis, as the examples below indicate; multiple variations are possible within the framework outlined in this chapter.

STATE GOVERNMENTS

VIRGINIA

Virginia's economic development group uses an ROI model to compare the costs of proposed incentives to expected returns. The model is specific to the state and was developed with the help of economists from several state universities and the state Department of Planning and Budget. The model considers the expected number of new jobs, their average salary, and the total capital investment in order to estimate taxes paid by direct workers and indirect workers (the latter figure is determined by the industry multiplier for the initial investment) and on taxable equipment and personal property, construction materials (when applicable), and direct and indirect construction employment. The model does not include corporate income taxes, nor does it address any additional costs for government services. The main objective is to consider the fiscal impact for the state, but the model would also indicate economic impact. Incentives packages are adjusted to balance costs with anticipated benefits. The model is primarily used for upfront decision making but has also been used to evaluate program effectiveness (Virginia Senate Finance Committee 2010; JLARC 2012).

CALIFORNIA

The California Competes tax credit is offered through a competitive process that requires an application, a two-stage review, and approval by a committee comprising the state treasurer, the director of the Department of Finance, the director of the Governor's Office of Economic Development (GO-Biz), and one appointee each by the Speaker of the Assembly and Senate Committee on Rules. The credit is available for firms originating in California or moving to California, and it is designed to support attraction and retention of high-value companies.

The two-phase review process works as follows. Phase I "is an automated phase in which the applicant's amount of tax credit requested, aggregate employee compensation, and aggregate investment" are evaluated to determine the rate of return. The credit requested is divided by the sum of compensation and investment to generate a ratio. Applicants with the lowest ratios are most likely to pass on to phase II, though there is a special track for companies that certify the project *will* occur in another state if they do not receive the tax credit.[1]

During phase II, the committee evaluates several factors, including unemployment or poverty in the area where the proposed project will be located; other incentives available to the applicant from other jurisdictions or within California; economic impact in the state; strategic importance of the project to the state, region, or locality; number of existing employees expected to be retained; opportunity for growth and expansion in the state; salary and benefits provided to employees; and financial statements and other relevant business documents related to the project.

The final value of the credit is determined by negotiations between GO-Biz and the business. Agreements set a specific dollar value for the credit and the time frame in which it may be taken. Each application round involves a cap on the total amount of tax credits that may be offered so the total fiscal impact is known up-front (GO-Biz 2014).

WASHINGTON STATE—BOEING

The offer Washington State made to Boeing to keep 777X assembly and wing fabrication in the state is reportedly the largest incentive deal ever. The $8.7 billion package includes tax reductions and tax credits—many extending until 2040—as well as workforce, training, and regulatory elements.

The process by which Washington arrived at this package makes it an interesting case study. Ensuring that the 777X would be built in Washington was one of the state's highest economic development priorities, according to the Washington Aerospace Industry Strategy released by the Governor's Office of Aerospace. The incentives package is one element of a larger strategy built around growing and diversifying the aerospace cluster, cultivating a deep and talented aerospace workforce, fostering a culture of aerospace innovation, and linking the aerospace support chain to allow the industry to prosper in the state.

The package itself was crafted with the oversight of a legislative task force that included participants from four major caucuses plus six nonlegislative members (three labor representatives and three business/industry representatives). The state completed a fiscal impact analysis that indicated the fiscal gain would be $21.3 billion over the incentives period, compared to the $8.7 billion estimated to be foregone due to the incentives (Harpel 2013).

LOCAL GOVERNMENTS

Local governments are also deploying different types of analytical tools to understand the fiscal and economic impacts of incentive decisions, as described below.

ERIE COUNTY, NEW YORK

The Erie County Industrial Development Agency (ECIDA) uses a cost-benefit model developed by the Center for Governmental Research in Rochester, New York. This model was created so that economic development professionals could analyze the impact of proposed projects quickly and consistently. It models costs, especially local incentives, against project benefits, such as jobs, labor income, and sales, property, and income taxes (informAnalytics 2014).

ECIDA uses the model for many projects. One example involved Welded Tube USA, a company that produces tubular steel for the oil and gas industries and constructed a new facility in the Buffalo region. Using the model, ECIDA estimated that the total state and regional benefits based on tax revenues alone exceeded the costs of the proposed project incentives (Table 10.1).

ECIDA also uses a process it calls *incentive layering*, in which the total value of incentives starts with a baseline and is increased based on cost-benefit analysis, physical site issues, industry cluster, and compliance with regional goals. In other words, the granting of incentives packages is connected to how well individual projects align with the local economic development strategy and community goals.

MONTGOMERY COUNTY, MARYLAND

The Montgomery County Department of Economic Development (DED) uses an internally developed fiscal impact model for its incentives programs. Inputs are the planned investment, number of jobs created or

Table 10.1 Cost-benefit analysis for the ECIDA using informAnalytics

Estimated state and regional benefits/estimated project incentives analysis	
Total state and regional benefits	$23,808,362
Total project incentives	$7,022,139
Total employment	830
Direct	121
Indirect	332
Induced	228
Temporary construction (Direct and indirect)	149
Estimated state and regional benefits (Discounted present value)	
Total state and regional benefits	$23,808,362
Income tax revenue	$14,564,505
Property tax/PILOT revenue	$208,173
Sales tax revenue	$9,035,684

Source: "Building a Smart Incentives Package: Using a Community Impact Model." 2013. Presented by John Cappellino, executive vice president, Erie County Industrial Development Agency, at an International Economic Development Council webinar, May 22.

retained, and average salaries. The model then estimates the increase in county revenue in several tax categories (including property and income taxes plus other taxes, fees, and charges) and the expected increases in service costs, especially those related to local government, school, and community college activities. In addition to these fiscal impacts, the model estimates secondary investment and new job creation. A built-in assumption is that 60 percent of newly created jobs will be filled by new residents.

DED reports that it favors projects in which the fiscal impact exceeds the public investment within three years. It also considers whether the project has strategic significance to the county, supports a target industry or geographic location, or benefits a specific sector of the workforce (Howard and Carrizosa 2013).

AUSTIN, TEXAS

The Austin Economic Development Policy and Program uses a firm-based incentive matrix, first adopted by the City Council in 2004, to evaluate companies under consideration for incentives.[2] At a minimum, companies are required to be located in the Desired Development Zone, comply with environmental regulations, and meet certain other wage and benefit requirements (though exceptions are available for some criteria). Companies meeting these criteria are then scored based on the project's overall economic and fiscal impact, linkages to the local economy, infrastructure impact, character of jobs and labor force practices, and quality of life and cultural vitality aspects. The score determines the company's eligibility for varying levels of incentives (EGRSO 2013).

Governments do not always have the capacity to develop robust models internally. Box 10.1 describes several cost-benefit analysis tools that are available to help governments make economic and fiscal impact calculations to support decision making.

COMPLIANCE AND EVALUATION

Conducting a cost-benefit analysis before providing incentives helps governments make better decisions based on estimates of the strategic, fiscal, and economic gains a community can expect to achieve.

Box 10.1 Cost-Benefit Tools

There are many different tools available from private companies, not-for-profit groups, universities, and government organizations that can be used to conduct a cost-benefit analysis. Most of the examples provided here are customizable to each community and offer a combination of economic and fiscal impact analyses primarily designed for U.S. state and local governments.

informAnalytics (http://informanalytics.org) was developed by the Center for Governmental Research to help local governments analyze the impacts of proposed projects. It includes both economic and fiscal impact components and generates reports summarizing costs and benefits for key stakeholder groups.

Impact DataSource (http://impactdatasource.com) specializes in economic and fiscal impact reports for economic development projects and in analysis to help communities understand the ROI and the expected payback period for incentivized investments.

REMI (http://www.remi.com) offers advanced economic and fiscal impact tools. The REMI model is a dynamic forecasting and analysis tool that allows users to develop sophisticated economic development scenarios.

The Triple Bottom Line tool (http://tbltool.org) combines cost-benefit and sustainability concepts. It was commissioned by the U.S. Economic Development Administration for use by public, private, nonprofit, and philanthropic organizations that approve, fund, or engage in economic development.

Economic development groups should also implement procedures to monitor project activity to determine whether those benefits were actually realized.

Whereas up-front cost-benefit analysis is not easy, post-award evaluation poses daunting technical, management, and political challenges. Most states still do not provide evidence of whether or not incentive tools work as intended (Pew Center on the States 2012b). Many governments and EDOs are improving tracking and reporting on incentives use, but quality data on the incentive deals and programs that perform well and help communities reach their economic development goals remain sorely lacking (Mattera et al. 2011).

Incentive program assessments should examine both project compliance with deal terms and overall program effectiveness. This section outlines some basic topics EDOs and IPAs should consider for post-award assessments.

The first step is to determine whether the company receiving an incentives package generated the direct benefits that were expected when the agreement was concluded. Incentives negotiations generally conclude with a performance agreement. Following are some essential questions to keep in mind when drafting the agreement: Are the performance requirements clearly defined? Is the company required to report on its progress in meeting those requirements? Who within the government is reviewing those reports? Are policies in place to protect the community in case of nonperformance?

EDOs and IPAs should receive resources to manage and monitor incentives as well as to enforce contract provisions when necessary. When agreements and up-front analyses are not followed up by a commitment to monitor compliance, the value of those analyses is undermined (Weber and Santacroce 2007). Many organizations are finding it best to create separate compliance departments or use third-party entities (either within or outside of government) instead of asking their deal makers to monitor their own projects.

The second step is to assess program effectiveness. Beyond individual project compliance, EDOs, IPAs, elected leaders, and the community wish to understand which incentive programs and policies are most effective in achieving economic development objectives, including whether incentives programs have created benefits that would not have occurred in their absence. Assessing program effectiveness is a different evaluation process than determining basic project compliance. It requires monitoring over the long term, addressing data quality and validation issues, and enabling comparisons across disparate incentives programs, to name just a few challenges.

In addition to these technical issues, effective evaluation requires thoughtful management and strong political leadership. The better program evaluations come from organizations that have

- considered the entire portfolio of incentive offerings;
- defined the goals of each incentives program clearly (a surprisingly common gap that makes both compliance monitoring and evaluation extremely difficult);
- used real, validated data—not modeled or imputed figures;
- created a multidisciplinary evaluation team with strong economic development knowledge, experience working with businesses, political awareness, analytical skills, and information system expertise;
- collaborated with other agencies to collect data and share analytics expertise; and
- provided a supportive environment and training to the evaluation team. Leadership is critical to creating an atmosphere of accountability and transparency in incentives use. Leadership should also focus the effort on improving future decisions, not punishing past decisions.

A variety of economic development, good government, fiscal policy, and elected official organizations are focusing on this issue, and some are taking on the challenge of improving methodologies for evaluating incentives. For example, The Pew Charitable Trusts is working with the Center for Regional Economic Competitiveness (CREC) on the Business Incentives Initiative. This initiative is built on the premise that "accurate data on the performance of economic development programs could greatly improve decision-makers' ability to craft policies that deliver the strongest results at the lowest possible cost" (Pew Charitable Trusts 2014). Pew and CREC are working to improve the quality of data around incentives program use by (1) identifying effective ways to manage and assess economic development incentives policies and practices, (2) improving data collection and reporting on incentive investments, and (3) sharing best practices that states can use to successfully gather and report data on economic development incentives (Pew Charitable Trusts 2014).

The guidelines provided here are useful but broad. We can continue to make progress in developing concrete guidance for EDOs and IPAs on how best to conduct quality incentives program evaluations. The next few years should see significant improvements in the way we evaluate and report on economic development incentives, but we are still in the early phases of these efforts.

CONCLUSION

Cost-benefit analysis of investment incentives can help economic development and government leaders make better decisions when using incentives to attract investment. Assessing project benefits and strategic value, estimating fiscal impact, and modeling the economic impact of a proposed investment will direct resources to the most promising opportunities while limiting exposure to weak projects that are unlikely to generate net benefits.

Employing cost-benefit analysis and other data and analytical tools can also shift the focus of incentives use from a transaction orientation, in which completing the deal is the prime objective, to an economic development orientation, in which helping a community prosper is the primary goal. It can also help to rebalance the interaction with the potential investor and eliminate some of the risks posed by information asymmetry by emphasizing the need for the investment to meet some baseline criteria in order to be worthwhile for a government or community to participate in via incentives. These criteria can then become the foundation for post-award compliance assessment and program evaluation.

Cost-benefit analysis is not necessarily easy, but it does not have to be overly complicated either. It is worth some time and resources to develop internal analytical tools or procure existing models to allow a government to answer basic questions about the expected costs and benefits of a proposed incentives package relative to an investment. Government agencies, economic development agencies with similar fiscal structures, and regional or national organizations serving EDOs or IPAs can band together to share costs and expertise in order to maximize internal investment in these models.

Incentives are one tool in the business attraction toolbox, and business attraction is one element of a good economic development strategy. Thoughtful cost-benefit analysis and quality evaluations can help ensure that incentives programs take their rightful place within economic development efforts and do not obscure their broader objectives.

NOTES

1. This certification requirement is stronger than asking the investor merely to certify that it "might locate" or "is considering locating" the investment in another jurisdiction.

2. The matrix is available at http://www.austintexas.gov/edims/document.cfm?id=205680 (accessed July 27, 2015).

REFERENCES

EGRSO. 2013. "2013 Report and Recommendations on the City of Austin Economic Development Policy." Economic Growth and Redevelopment Services Office, Austin, TX.

GO-Biz. 2014. "California Competes Tax Credit" and "California Competes Tax Credit Regulations, Adopted August 18, 2014 as Emergency Regulations." Governor's Office of Business and Economic Development, accessed September 25, 2014, http://www.business.ca.gov/Programs/CaliforniaCompetesTaxCredit.aspx.

Ha, H., and R. C. Feiock. 2012. "Bargaining, Networks, and Management of Municipal Development Subsidies." *American Review of Public Administration* 42 (4): 481–97.

Harpel, E. 2013. "A Closer Look at the Boeing Incentive Deal." Smart Incentives, November 27, accessed September 25, 2014, http://www.smartincentives.org/blogs/blog/10447101-a-closer-look-at-the-boeing-incentive-deal.

Howard, C., and N. Carrizosa. 2013. "Review of Montgomery County's Economic Development Incentive Programs." Office of Legislative Oversight Report No. 2013–2, Rockville, MD.

IEDC. 2014. "IEDC at a Glance," International Economic Development Council, accessed October 24, 2014, http://www.iedconline.org/web-pages/inside-iedc/iedc-at-a-glance/.

informAnalytics. 2014. "FAQ," accessed September 25, 2014, http://informanalytics.org/faq.

Joint Legislative Audit and Review Commission. 2012. "Review of State Economic Development Incentive Grants. Report to the Governor and General Assembly of Virginia," Senate Document No. 8, Richmond.

Mattera, P., T. Cafcas, L. McIlvaine, A. Seifter, and K. Tarczynska. 2011. *Money for Something: Job Creation and Job Quality Standards in State Economic Development Subsidy Programs*. Washington, DC: Good Jobs First.

Morgan, J. Q. 2010. "Analyzing the Benefits and Costs of Economic Development Projects." UNC School of Government Community and Economic Development Bulletin No. 7, April, Chapel Hill.

Pew Center on the States. 2012a. "Avoiding Blank Checks: Creating Fiscally Sound State Tax Incentives."

——. 2012b. "Evidence Counts: Evaluating State Tax Incentives for Jobs and Growth."

The Pew Charitable Trusts. 2014. "The Business Incentives Initiative," April 8, accessed September 26, 2014, http://www.pewtrusts.org/en/about/news-room/news/2014/04/08/the-business-incentives-initiative.

Sharp, E. B., and K. Mullinix. 2012. "Holding Their Feet to the Fire: Explaining Variation in City Governments' Use of Controls on Economic Development Subsidies." *Economic Development Quarterly* 26 (2): 138–50.

UNCTAD. 2014. "Skills and Foreign Direct Investment Promotion." IPA Observer No. 3, United Nations Conference on Trade and Development, New York.

Virginia Senate Finance Committee. 2010. "Economic Development Incentives." November 18–19, Staunton, VA. http://sfc.virginia.gov/pdf/retreat/2010_Retreat/8_Econ_Develop.pdf.

Weber, R., and D. Santacroce. 2007. *The Ideal Deal: How Local Governments Can Get More for Their Economic Development Dollar*. Washington, DC: Good Jobs First and Center for Urban Economic Development, University of Illinois at Chicago.

PART IV

Reducing Incentives Competition: Regulatory Efforts to Limit "Races to the Bottom"

CHAPTER 11

Regulation of Investment Incentives

NATIONAL AND SUBNATIONAL EFFORTS TO REGULATE COMPETITION FOR INVESTMENT THROUGH THE USE OF INCENTIVES

Kenneth P. Thomas

Investment incentives have substantial potential drawbacks, particularly in terms of reduced economic efficiency; increased post-tax, post-transfer inequality; and sometimes even contributions to environmentally harmful projects (Thomas 2011a). Yet, as we know, government use of incentives is pervasive and increasing, as documented in chapter 7 in this volume. Interestingly, this is recognized by the governments themselves, a good example being that of the National Governors Association (NGA; Kayne and Shonka 1994) in the United States. In a report on state development policies and programs, the NGA argued that state governments should reduce their use of such incentives because it was bad policy to offer them, but it opposed federal control of state incentives. Unfortunately, this exhortation to state governments fell on deaf ears, and the volume of state and local incentives increased from about $26.4 billion in 1995 to approximately $49 billion in 2005 (Thomas 2011a).

Why the disjuncture between statements and action? The answer is that the NGA report does not recognize the strategic situation in which states find themselves when competing for investment. Simply put, ending the competition for investment is a Prisoners' Dilemma for governments. They would be collectively better off if none offered incentives and they each received what might be called their "nondistorted" level of investment. But, individually, each has the opportunity to increase the investment it receives by offering incentives and will lose investment if it does *not* offer incentives while other governments do. Thus, outside the European Union (EU), we see an equilibrium where virtually all governments offer incentives and wind up with essentially the same nondistorted level of investment they would have received in the cooperative scenario, as the various governments' incentives merely offset each other (for a full discussion, see Thomas 2000, chap. 2 and app. 1).[1] This chapter, then, addresses efforts by national and subnational governments to solve their Prisoners' Dilemma.

At a practical level, governments have two further problems. The first is the possibility of overbidding for an investment project, eliminating much or all of the value for the jurisdiction of the investment being made. The 2013 decision by the state of Washington to award Boeing Corporation $8.7 billion in tax breaks over fifteen years is a good candidate for this category, especially because it was combined with substantial concessions by the workforce over pensions and other benefits. The huge supply of workers trained specifically for aerospace jobs in Washington made it implausible for Boeing to relocate much of the work out of state. Recognizing this, the workers' union, the International Association of Machinists, rejected the company's first contract offer, although, as noted above, it eventually agreed to a contract that had significant concessions (Thomas 2013).

Second, national governments face the difficulty that subnational governments' use of subsidies may directly or indirectly move existing jobs from one jurisdiction to another, with no benefits for the country as a whole and significant loss of tax revenue for subnational jurisdictions. Note, however, that this doesn't necessarily hold true in the case of competition between jurisdictions with different levels of development. Incentives could help rebalance the economic disequilibrium in favor of the disadvantaged jurisdiction.[2]

As an example of the direct relocation of jobs via subsidies, in 1991 the Canadian province of Saskatchewan induced Crown Life Insurance to move its headquarters, and 1,200 jobs, from Toronto, Ontario, to Regina, Saskatchewan, in return for a C$250 million loan guarantee (Thomas 2000). Indirect displacement of existing jobs is much more common because if you add new capacity to an industry, it is likely that there will be some job loss at existing firms due to increased production not caused by an increase in demand. Two cases are very well documented. Rubenstein (1992) shows that for every automobile and truck assembly plant that opened between 1979 and 1990 (all of which received subsidies) in the United States and Canada, one closed. Similarly, the St. Louis, Missouri, metropolitan planning agency has documented that between 1990 and 2007, local governments in the region gave $2 billion in subsidies to shopping malls and other retail projects, yet total employment of retail workers increased by only 5,400, resulting in a nominal cost of $380,380 per job. The study shows that the subsidies had merely relocated retail activity around the area, with the job growth accounted for by the area's income growth, not subsidies (East-West Gateway Council of Governments 2011).

This chapter looks at examples of attempted solutions to the second problem—that is, how subnational governments can reduce their competition through voluntary agreements or binding national legal instruments. Because the EU case is analyzed in chapters 5 and 12 of this volume, this chapter focuses on agreements in Australia, Canada, and the United States. Overall, there is one binding agreement, in Canada, along with six voluntary no-raiding agreements, one among Australian states, three among U.S. states, and two in U.S. metropolitan areas.

AUSTRALIA: THE RISE AND FALL OF THE INTERSTATE INVESTMENT COOPERATION AGREEMENT

In Australia, the issue of incentives and bidding wars was crystallized by a A$100 million incentives package given to Fox News to build a A$430 million studio in Sydney (Markusen and Nesse 2007). The federal government's Industry Commission had criticized state incentives in 1996, and its successor, the Productivity Commission, published estimates of the incentives given by each state in 2002 (Productivity Commission 2004).

The Interstate Investment Cooperation Agreement (IICA) was championed by the state of Victoria's treasurer, John Brumby, though it had originally been proposed by economist Wolfgang Kasper in the 1990s (Novak 2011). Prior to the agreement itself, Victoria had begun to exchange information with the state of New South Wales (NSW). According to Brumby, "Victoria has already exchanged information with NSW on 30 projects, and companies have been caught out overstating the incentives offered by the potential 'rival' location. It's estimated that this action alone has already saved taxpayers around A$20 million" (State of Victoria 2003, 1). Motivated by the significant sums lost to incentives, Brumby's office drafted the agreement.

The IICA provided (State of Victoria 2003, 2):

> During the period of this agreement, the States and Territories will
>
> (a) Co-operate in any case involving a potentially footloose investment where there is no national economic benefit (such as relocating a business from one State to another) with a view to declining to offer any financial incentive.
>
> (b) Co-operate whenever possible to minimise incentives when it is clear that new projects and events are committed to Australia.

Table 11.1 Australian state/territory governing party, 2003, 2006, 2011

State/territory	2003	2006	2011
Australian Capital Territory	Labor	Labor	Labor
New South Wales	Labor	Labor	Liberal
Northern Territory	Labor	Labor	Labor
Queensland	Labor	Labor	Labor
South Australia	Labor	Labor	Labor
Tasmania	Labor	Labor	Labor
Victoria	Labor	Labor	Liberal
Western Australia	Labor	Labor	Labor

The original 2003 agreement was signed by five of Australia's six states (New South Wales, South Australia, Tasmania, Victoria, and Western Australia) plus the Australian Capital Territory. However, Queensland refused to sign on to the agreement because, according to Markusen and Nesse (2007, 5), it "was successfully bidding corporate headquarters and facilities away from Victoria and New South Wales with undisclosed deals."

In 2006, the IICA was renewed for five years. In addition to the original signatories, the Northern Territory signed the agreement. Queensland again refused to join. Interestingly, this divergence between Queensland and the signees was not due to any grand ideological issue: the Labor Party was in control of all of the country's six state governments, as well as the Australian Capital Territory and Northern Territory, in both 2003 and 2006. See table 11.1.

Keeping in mind the difficulty of attaining agreements in competitive situations (Thomas 2000, 2011a), it appears that for the five states and two territories that were part of the IICA, there was genuine normative agreement that poaching investment from other states was bad policy. Of course, this view was promoted by the federal government through the Industry Commission/Productivity Commission. Only Queensland took the view that it would do anything, including job poaching, to improve its economic fortunes.

When the agreement came up for renewal in 2006, Victoria Treasurer Brumby said it "would continue to save participating States and Territories tens of millions of dollars." Moreover, he claimed, "Some jurisdictions have noticed a decrease in the number of companies seeking incentives to relocate from one State or Territory to another" (State of Victoria 2006, 1).

Meanwhile, however, over the period 1998–2010, the Queensland government paid out A$180 million in subsidies to attract 133 companies. In 2010, the federal government sponsored a study of the IICA ahead of a planned meeting of state treasurers in 2011 to decide on renewing the agreement (Dunckley 2011). When I interviewed a member of the Victoria Treasury's staff in 2010, there was every indication the agreement would be renewed in 2011.

When Liberal Party–led administrations took office in Victoria in 2010 and New South Wales in 2011, however, both state governments turned against the IICA. This shift occurred most decisively in New South Wales, coming even before the state elections that brought the Liberals to power; Victoria then followed suit. Indeed, the Liberals hammered on Victoria's governing Labor Party during the 2010 election (by which time Brumby had risen to the office of premier of Victoria), blaming the state's involvement in the IICA for a decline in its share of the country's investment from 25 percent to less than 22 percent under the two previous Labor governments (Novak 2011, 8). Novak disputes this view, saying "After all, Western Australia, Tasmania and the two territories, which are signatories to the anti-poaching pact, have increased their national investment share over the past 10 years." She blames Victoria's decline on intense foreign competition with Victoria's large manufacturing sector. Regardless, the die was cast, and New South Wales and Victoria pulled out of the agreement. According to Tomazin (2011), with the three largest states (i.e., including Queensland) outside the agreement, it was "unviable" for the remaining parties to maintain the pact. Thus ended what was, as we shall see, the most successful attempt at regulation of incentives at the state or provincial level.

We should note one drawback of the agreement from the point of view of taxpayers: although the states were required to report the incentives they gave, these reports were not available to or accessible by the public. This was a missed opportunity to increase the transparency of, and hence government accountability for, the use of investment incentives.

CANADA: THE CODE OF CONDUCT ON INCENTIVES

Like Australia, in Canada the impetus to control provincial incentives came in part from a dramatically large incentives package. In 1991, the Toronto-based insurance company Crown Life moved its headquarters, along with 1,200 jobs, to Regina, Saskatchewan, with the help of a C$250 million loan guarantee from the provincial government (Motherwell 1991). In eastern Canada, New Brunswick Premier Frank McKenna made the attraction of call centers a centerpiece of his economic development strategy, and he targeted existing facilities as well as enticing new ones (DeMont 1994). By 1995, he had brought 2,500 call center jobs to the province ("Utopia in the Boardroom" 1995).

During the negotiations of Canada's Agreement on Internal Trade (AIT), British Columbia was the main proponent of its Code of Conduct on Incentives. Doern and Macdonald (1999, 70), who conducted numerous interviews with provincial officials across the country in connection with their book on the AIT, write, "As a major location for inward investment, B.C. was concerned, like Ontario, that other provinces would entice investment that would otherwise 'naturally' have come to it." They further imply that British Columbia would not have signed the overall agreement without the inclusion of the code.

The AIT came into effect on July 1, 1994. Its Code of Conduct, which comprised Annex 608.3 of the investment chapter, included two major provisions of interest here. Under Prohibited Incentives, point 4: "No Party shall provide an incentive that is contingent, in law or in fact, and would directly result in an enterprise, located in the territory of any Party, relocating an existing operation into its territory" (Internal Trade Secretariat 2007, 79). Under Avoidance of Certain Incentives, point 8, the signatories further committed themselves to engage in best efforts to refrain from getting into bidding wars for new investments. Finally, the code required each signatory to notify the Internal Trade Secretariat of its incentives, but, as in Australia, these notifications are not public documents (Thomas 2011b).

Unlike Australia, however, the first of these provisions, the no-poaching clause, was legally binding on all the provinces and territories. (When the agreement was signed, the territory of Nunavut did not yet exist; it has observer status for the AIT.) It quickly became clear, however, that the agreement's enforcement mechanism was quite ineffective.

In 1995, New Brunswick provided C$11 million in incentives in the form of forgivable loans to United Parcel Service (UPS). These supported the company's consolidation of its call centers to the province and caused the termination of 870 existing jobs in British Columbia, Manitoba, and Ontario (Anderssen 1995). British Columbia cried foul and filed a complaint under the Code of Conduct the following year. Although the two parties flung charges and countercharges at each other (Thomas 2000), British Columbia did not press its complaint further, which, according to Brown (2006), caused discouragement among subsidy critics. The lack of an enforcement mechanism in the AIT (until 2008, as discussed below) explains the failure of the Code of Conduct, given that clearly there was no normative agreement as there had been in Australia until 2010.

Not only did the UPS case in 1996 end without a real decision, but also it is unclear what penalties could have been given at that time. In 2008, however, the Council of the Confederation brokered an agreement to institute fines for violating provision of the AIT as determined through the dispute resolution process. Specifically, it created the possibility of fines on a sliding scale from C$250,000 to C$5 million, depending on the size of the province (Committee on Internal Trade 2008). With these new, specific penalties in place, a subsidized relocation on the scale of UPS or Crown Life Insurance could result in a complaint under the code, although there have been no disputes filed over the small relocation subsidies that have been used.

Thomas (2011b) showed that poaching was not eliminated in Canada despite the binding nature of Article 3 of the Code. He found that Nova Scotia has given three relocation subsidies, whereas Prince Edward Island had done so three times, Ontario once, and Quebec an undetermined number of times (Thomas 2011b). Since that article was published, there appears to have been one further poaching case, which harkens back to UPS and overturns a change by New Brunswick in the post-McKenna era (Thomas 2011b). In 2011, the province gave $3.15 million to ING Direct to expand its Canadian bilingual call center and relocate from Ottawa to Moncton (Government of New Brunswick 2011; Pilieci 2011). According to the government, the company would create "up to 300" jobs, of which 130 would be transferred from the Ottawa call center. Thus, the largest of these subsidized relocations involved 130 jobs, far fewer than in the cases of UPS and Crown Life Insurance. As a result, it is possible to argue that the code has had some small impact, even if it has not lived up to its promise.

UNITED STATES: VOLUNTARY STATE NO-RAIDING AGREEMENTS FAIL, BUT TWO LOCAL AGREEMENTS HAVE WORKED

As the introduction pointed out, state and local governments in the United States are certainly aware of the problems stemming from bidding wars for investments. At the same time, they have resisted federal intervention along the lines of the EU's State aid rules, preferring that states refrain from subsidy battles because it is "good policy" (Kayne and Shonka 1994, 25–26). In fact, though, these state and local governments do not act as if refraining from subsidy wars is good policy. They do not, in practice, share the normative agreement that existed among all Australian states but Queensland prior to 2010, regardless of the pronouncements of the National Governors Association. Rather, as with Queensland, these states and localities want to see nothing that restricts them in their economic development "powers." This was most evidently on display in the reaction to the lawsuit *Cuno v. Daimler-Chrysler*, which went to the U.S. Supreme Court in 2006 (Johnston 2006). In that case, taxpayers in Toledo, Ohio, sued the city and state over tax breaks given for a Jeep plant there. Although the state court and U.S. District Court ruled against the plaintiffs, the U.S. Court of Appeals ruled that the state tax credits were a violation of the Commerce Clause of the U.S. Constitution, which prevents state governments from levying tariffs or otherwise interfering with trade among the states. While waiting for the Supreme Court to rule on Ohio's appeal from the Appeals Court, a bipartisan group of senators led by George Voinovich (formerly Ohio's governor) introduced a bill that would have explicitly allowed states to offer investment incentives, thereby overturning the Supreme Court's decision if it were to rule in favor of the plaintiffs (Koff 2006).[3] In the end, the Supreme Court vacated the Appeals Court decision because the plaintiffs did not have standing to sue, but it was clear that Voinovich's bill would have passed easily had the Supreme Court ruled in their favor.

Cuno v. Daimler-Chrysler was the best opportunity to bring about a federal solution to interstate bidding wars for investment. The only federal restrictions on state and local government incentives are provisions in various federal programs (Small Business Administration, Community Development Block Grants, etc.) that ban the use of these subsidies to induce the relocation of an existing facility and limit the amount of tax-free Industrial Revenue Bonds local governments can issue (Thomas 2000). What we have seen in terms of other control efforts are proposals by several groups of neighboring states to refrain from offering relocation subsidies to companies in the other participating states as well as similar cooperative efforts in two metropolitan areas. Of these, the state efforts have been complete failures, although one may soon be revived; the local agreements have proved more durable.

The first such "no-raiding zone" was created by an agreement sponsored by the Council of Great Lakes Governors in the 1980s that banned relocation subsidies among the group's members. One state offered incentives to a company to move from another signatory state before the nonbinding agreement came into force, and, unsurprisingly, the agreement collapsed immediately (Gauf 1992; Schweke, Rist, and Dabson 1994). In 1991, an agreement among Connecticut, New Jersey, and New York similarly collapsed within days of coming into effect, as both Connecticut and New Jersey approved new subsidies targeting New York City (Thomas 2000).

The third agreement was between Kansas and Missouri in the mid-1990s; job piracy is rampant in the Kansas City metropolitan area (LeRoy et al. 2013; Mansur 2010). One study funded by the Hall Family Foundation found that, since 2009, the two states had given a combined $217 million in tax incentives to companies moving across the state line within the Kansas City area (Lieb 2014). A number of large businesses in the region tried to persuade leaders of the two states to end the raiding, and their efforts were given a boost when the *New York Times* highlighted this negative-sum game as part of a ten-month investigation into what it called "The United States of Subsidies" (Story and Bishop 2012). Although Missouri Governor Jay Nixon, a Democrat, and Kansas Governor Sam Brownback, a Republican, both told *New York Times* reporter Louise Story that there was no chance their state would stop raiding the other, in 2014 the Missouri legislature (with a Republican majority in both houses, it should be noted) passed a bill to end the use of state subsidy programs for relocations from Kansas if Kansas passed a complementary law within two years (Missouri General Assembly 2014; Stafford 2014). At the time of this writing, however, that has not yet happened.

In contrast, at the local level, there have been two significant cases where metropolitan areas having numerous local governments—Dayton, Ohio, and Denver, Colorado—have succeeded in avoiding ruinous bidding wars and job piracy. A 2014 study by Good Jobs First (McIlvaine 2014) recounts success stories lasting over twenty years in these two regions.

In Dayton/Montgomery County, municipalities share a $5 million per year incentive fund for "regionally significant projects" (McIlvaine 2014, 13). Recommendations on which projects should be funded are made to the County Commission by a twenty-seven-member Advisory Committee drawn from the area jurisdictions participating in the Economic Development/Government Equity program. Founded in 1991, this program also directs the increased tax revenues from fast-growing parts of the county to slower-growing areas. A second program—Business First!—creates a no-raiding zone that extends beyond Montgomery County to neighboring counties. It provides for information exchange among jurisdictions that may find a company trying to move from one to another and even for transitional tax sharing if a company does move.

In the Denver metropolitan area, virtually all the local economic development agencies are members of the Metro Denver Economic

Development Corporation (EDC), which markets the region as a single entity and has a Code of Ethics that prohibits job piracy. Even though this code has no force of law, it does provide for a dispute resolution process, one that has been used only three times in twenty-six years. In addition, no member of the EDC has had to be expelled, the most serious sanction available under the code (McIlvaine 2014, 12).

The Good Jobs First analysis of these successes in Dayton and Denver emphasizes the importance of transparency and information exchange regarding local economic development issues (McIlvaine 2014, 18). It also highlights the necessity of involving economic development officials—not only because they carry out the policies but also because they represent each municipality's institutional memory, helping to ensure that agreements can be carried into the future.

CONCLUSION

This examination of national and subnational incentives controls mostly finds failure to control even the most egregious abuse of subsidies, granting them to relocate an existing facility. Even Canada's legally binding Code of Conduct on Incentives has been unable to stop such job piracy. Simply establishing a law isn't enough if there is no effective way to enforce it. This is what distinguishes the Code of Conduct from the EU's State aid rules. The latter are backed up by a professional staff that can act on its own initiative (unlike with the complaint-driven Code of Conduct), decades of case law and administrative experience, and a court system that has backed up the European Commission's enforcement efforts. The Code of Conduct system, in contrast, resembles GATT-era (as opposed to WTO-era) dispute resolution characterized by dependence on complaints and weak central enforcement mechanisms.

The local successes in Dayton, Ohio, and Denver, Colorado, along with the eight-year run of Australia's IICA, show that there are limited circumstances in which voluntary no-raiding agreements can work: that is, when there is genuine normative agreement that job piracy is bad policy for a region or country. In Australia's case, that view was shared by all the state- and territorial-level Labor Parties except Queensland's. As we saw in 2010–2011, however, it was not shared by the Liberal Party, so when Liberal governments came to power in the two largest members of the IICA, the agreement collapsed. In Dayton and Denver, it appears that the systems there depoliticize economic development to a significant degree and depend on buy-in from economic development officials who are committed to avoiding subsidized relocations.

Two recommendations follow from this analysis: First, governments need to ensure the transparency of the subsidy process because no democratic accountability is possible without information. Transparency is an essential underpinning for either informal or formal controls on incentives.

Second, national governments should impose mandatory no-raiding agreements on subnational units, as the case studies highlight the weakness of voluntary agreements. As noted, Dayton, Denver, and Australia show that the situation in which informal job piracy bans can succeed is very circumscribed, and Australia shows that normative agreement can be vulnerable to shifts in the political winds. Thus, it is better to have a mandatory agreement with effective enforcement mechanisms.

Because the use of incentives is pervasive and growing, finding ways to control them should be a high priority. The EU's State aid rules are the most effective solution currently existing in the world (see chapter 5 in this volume), but for the many places where the EU approach is politically infeasible, the ideas discussed here represent the first steps toward incentive control.

NOTES

1. This is not to say that the ideal is necessarily a complete ban on investment incentives. Considerations of economic backwardness may justify allowing them in some instances. A system that bans the use of incentives in rich regions makes it possible for poorer regions to use smaller incentives to attract investment than would be the case in an unregulated environment, such as that of the United States. Precisely such a system of differentiated maximum incentives is used in the EU (see chapter 5 in this volume). Thomas (2012) shows on a company-by-company basis how this allows EU Member States to give smaller incentives than do U.S. states for similar projects.

2. Other than the EU, no country or supranational area has a mechanism in place to control and enable this differentiation. In the United States, for instance, as explained below, the U.S. Supreme Court short-circuited the possibility of national-level rules that would enable differentiation; moreover, Congress was poised to pass legislation nullifying a Supreme Court ruling in favor of such central control.

3. Disclosure: The author was a signatory to a friend-of-the-court brief arguing for the plaintiffs when the case was before the U.S. Supreme Court.

REFERENCES

Anderssen, E. 1995. "New Brunswick Playing with Fire, Critics Say." *Calgary Herald*, February 8.

Brown, D. M. 2006. "Still in the Game: Efforts to Govern Economic Development Competition in Canada." In *Racing to the Bottom? Provincial Interdependence in the Canadian Federation*, ed. K. Harrison. Vancouver: UBC Press.

Committee on Internal Trade. 2008. "Advancing Trade and Prosperity Among Provinces/Territories." Press Release, June 10, accessed August 10, 2008, http://www.ait-aci.ca/index_en/news.htm.

DeMont, J. 1994. "Fast Frank: How New Brunswick's Premier Turned His Province Into Canada's Social Laboratory." *Maclean's*, April 11, 22–29.

Doern, G. B., and Macdonald, M. 1999. *Free Trade Federalism: Negotiating the Canadian Agreement on Internal Trade.* Toronto: University of Toronto Press.

Dunckley, M. 2011. "Business Wins in Poaching Wars; States to Dump Truce—Incentives up for Grabs—Industry Welcomes Competition." *Australian Financial Review*, January 19, 1.

East-West Gateway Council of Governments. 2011. "An Assessment of the Effectiveness and Fiscal Impacts of the Use of Development Incentives in the St. Louis Region." Final Report, St. Louis.

Gauf, M. 1992. "In the Midwest, It's Every State for Itself." *St. Louis Post-Dispatch*, December 2, 3C.

Government of New Brunswick. 2011. "ING DIRECT Investing in 300 Jobs in Moncton." Press Release, July 5, accessed July 9, 2014, http://www2.gnb.ca/content/gnb/en/news/news_release.2011.07.0749.html.

Internal Trade Secretariat. 2007. "Agreement on Internal Trade, 2007 Consolidated Version," accessed September 13, 2014, https://www.ic.gc.ca/eic/site/ait-aci.nsf/vwapj/AIT_agreement_2007–05_en.pdf/$FILE/AIT_agreement_2007–05_en.pdf.

Johnston, D. C. 2006. "Legalities of Corporate Tax Incentives Before Court." *New York Times*, March 1, C1.

Kayne, J., and M. Shonka. 1994. *Rethinking State Development Policies and Programs.* Washington, DC: National Governors Association.

Koff, S. 2006. "Court Sides with Ohio on Tax Breaks: Taxpayers Lack Standing to Sue, Justices Say." *Cleveland Plain Dealer*, May 6, C1.

LeRoy, G., K. Tarczynska, L. McIlvaine, T. Cafcas, and P. Mattera. 2013. *The Job-Creation Shell Game: Ending the Wasteful Practice of Subsidizing Companies That Move Jobs from One State to Another*. Washington, DC: Good Jobs First.

Lieb, D. A. 2014. "Mo. Lawmakers Hear Plans to End Kan. Tax Break War." Associated Press, February 5.

Mansur, M. 2010. "Loss of Jobs to Kansas Irks Kansas City's Mayor." *Kansas City Star*, November 25, A1.

Markusen, A., and K. Nesse. 2007. "Institutional and Political Determinants of Incentive Competition." In *Reining in the Competition for Capital*, ed. Ann Markusen, 1–41. Kalamazoo, MI: W. E. Upjohn Institute.

McIlvaine, L., with G. LeRoy. 2014. *Ending Job Piracy, Building Regional Prosperity*. Washington, DC: Good Jobs First.

Missouri General Assembly. 2014. "Bill Summary of SB 635," accessed July 3, 2014, http://www.moga.mo.gov/.

Motherwell, C. 1991. "Provincial Loan Will Help Crown Life Move to Regina: Toronto Mayor Outraged at 'Raid' by Saskatchewan." *Globe and Mail*, September 10.

Novak, J. 2011. "Dropping the Lure." *The Age* (Melbourne), February 11, 8.

Pilieci, V. 2011. "ING Direct to Close Ottawa Centre; Call Operations Will Be Moved to Moncton, N.B., Next Year." *Ottawa Citizen*, June 30, D1.

Productivity Commission. 2004. *Annual Report 2002–03*. Canberra: Productivity Commission. Accessed September 21, 2007, www.pc.gov.au/research/annrpt/annualreport0203/annualreport0203.pdf.

Rubenstein, J. 1992. *The Changing U.S. Auto Industry: A Geographic Analysis*. London: Routledge.

Schweke, W., C. Rist, and B. Dabson. 1994. *Bidding for Business: Are Cities and States Selling Themselves Short?* Washington, DC: Corporation for Enterprise Development.

Stafford, M. 2014. "Missouri Offers Truce in Kansas Business Battle." Associated Press, July 1.

State of Victoria. 2003. "States Agree to End Investment Bidding Wars." Press Release, Office of the Treasurer, September 5, accessed July 2, 2007, http://www.dpc.vic.gov.au/domino/Web_Notes/newsmedia.nsf/b0222c68d27626e2ca256c8c001a3d2d/fb21eee7f27c4044ca256d9a0080fb0b!OpenDocument.

——. 2006. "Historic Anti-Bidding War Agreement Renewed." Press Release, Office of the Treasurer, March 30, accessed July 2, 2007, http://www.dpc.vic.gov.au/domino/Web_Notes/newsmedia.nsf/798c8b072d117a01ca256c8c0019bb01/5214506f6c9c5543ca2571410007fee72!OpenDocument.

Story, L., and M. W. Bishop. 2012. "Border War." *New York Times* video, accessed December 1, 2012, http://www.nytimes.com/video/business/100000001832941/border-war.html.

Thomas, K. P. 2000. *Competing for Capital: Europe and North America in a Global Era*. Washington, DC: Georgetown University Press.

——. 2011a. *Investment Incentives and the Global Competition for Capital*. Houndmills, Basingstoke, UK: Palgrave.

——. 2011b. "Regulating Investment Attraction: Canada's Code of Conduct on Incentives in a Comparative Context." *Canadian Public Policy* 37 (3): 343–57.

——. 2012. "EU Control of State Aid to Mobile Investment in Comparative Perspective." *Journal of European Integration* 34 (6): 567–84.

——. 2013. "America's Most Wanted: Boeing," blog post, December 11, http://www.middleclasspoliticaleconomist.com/2013/12/americas-most-wanted-boeing.html.

Tomazin, F. 2011. "Victoria Spurns No-Poach Pact Between States." *Sunday Age* (Melbourne), November 20, 5.

"Utopia in the Boardroom." 1995. *Globe and Mail*, January 12.

CHAPTER 12

Regulation of Investment Incentives

INSTRUMENTS AT AN INTERNATIONAL/SUPRANATIONAL LEVEL

Lise Johnson

Over the past several decades, as countries have increasingly opened their markets, cross-border flows of foreign direct investment (FDI) have grown rapidly, albeit sometimes erratically. With that overall rise in FDI flows, we have also seen a growth in competition for capital. Nations and subnational jurisdictions are adopting a range of strategies to court new investors and encourage existing ones to stay and even expand their operations. As detailed elsewhere in this volume, those strategies often entail offering investors a range of potentially costly incentives.

To date, as described in chapter 11 in this volume, national regulatory regimes seeking to prevent subnational jurisdictions from engaging in a "race to the bottom" in their competition for capital are largely lacking. The international arena, with certain exceptions, is similarly devoid of comprehensive legal controls restricting the use of incentives by countries to pull investment from one location to another. The challenges of achieving coordinated and collective action keep solutions elusive, so effective systems for equitably reining in the use of incentives remain undeveloped. This largely unchecked competition is welfare-reducing and past due for discipline.

And just as time is ripe for restricting wasteful location incentives, it is also ripe for thinking more strategically about whether and in what circumstances countries should be able to and should use investment incentives to achieve sustainable development objectives. If properly designed and implemented,[1] incentives can be an efficient and effective way to leverage public resources to catalyze private-sector investment in regions and activities currently receiving suboptimal levels of interest and capital. Thus, it is crucial that international rules enable incentives to play that catalyzing role.

With the rapid changes in governance of international investment that have been occurring over the past several decades, as well as pressing challenges of sustainable development, the roles of interstate agreements in this area need to be (re)examined. As one step toward meeting that need, this chapter outlines the development and current form of the core international legal frameworks that govern use of incentives by or within countries. The first section provides a brief overview of what various international trade treaties within the World Trade Organization (WTO) system do and do not do in terms of incentives regulation. The second section builds on chapter 5 in this volume by elaborating on the State aid regime developed by the European Union (EU) to restrict competition for capital among and use of wasteful incentives by Member States. Although other regional groups, including the Southern African Development Community and East African Community, have taken some steps to restrict incentives competition among their Member States (CCSI 2015), the EU's State aid regime is by far the most developed and rigorous. The third section describes more recent developments that have appeared in international investment agreements (IIAs) and regional free-trade agreements (FTAs), highlighting how those instruments can potentially serve as tools that may both limit the use of incentives and increase and entrench the use of incentives. The final section provides suggestions for ways forward that can be taken by states as well as other actors, such as tribunals interpreting IIAs.

This chapter focuses on rules regarding investment incentives given to services and industry generally but not to the agricultural sector. There are supranational legal regimes governing incentives given to agricultural investments. These include, most notably, the WTO's Agreement on Agriculture and specific EU State aid rules on agricultural investments. Those regimes have important implications for the themes of investment and sustainable development addressed in this book and merit a deeper discussion, but that discussion is outside the scope of this chapter. Also not addressed are the rules in industry-specific agreements, such as the WTO's plurilateral Agreement on Trade in Civil Aircraft, even though such agreements might provide a feasible way of achieving interjurisdictional consensus on incentives policies.

REGULATION OF INVESTMENT INCENTIVES IN THE WTO

The WTO's agreements do not aim specifically to tackle wasteful incentives competition; nevertheless, through their rules on trade in goods and services, they do impose a patchwork of restrictions on the use of various investment incentives. The relevant agreements are the Subsidies and Countervailing Measures (SCM) Agreement, the Agreement on Trade Related Investment Measures (TRIMs Agreement), and the General Agreement on Trade in Services (GATS). These treaties, and the ways in which they govern use of incentives, are described briefly below.

THE SCM AGREEMENT

The SCM Agreement imposes some restrictions on the use of various investment incentives granted by governments but only when they constitute "subsidies"—a specifically defined term—that (1) are tied to export performance or the use of domestic over foreign goods or (2) are "specific" and have an "adverse effect" on a WTO Member.

DEFINITION OF A SUBSIDY

The SCM Agreement defines a *subsidy* as (1) a "financial contribution" or "any form of income or price support" (2) granted or directed by "a government or any public body" (3) that confers a "benefit" on its recipient. The SCM Agreement and WTO case law interpreting it elaborate further on each of these elements. With respect to the first part of the definition, the SCM Agreement (Article 1.1) explains that a financial contribution may be a direct transfer of funds (e.g., a grant, loan, equity infusion, interest rate reduction, interest deferral, or debt forgiveness[2]), a potential direct transfer of funds (e.g., a loan guarantee[3]), revenue "otherwise due" that is foregone or not collected (e.g., a tax holiday, tax credit, or reduced tax rate[4]), the provision of goods or services (e.g., the construction of infrastructure for an investment other than general infrastructure or the grant of a mining lease[5]), or the purchase of goods (e.g., a feed-in-tariff program for the purchase of energy[6]). That definition of a financial contribution can therefore sweep within its coverage a wide range of fiscal and financial incentives granted by government entities to investors.

The SCM Agreement indicates that, in addition to financial contributions, a subsidy can be income or a price support. Some commentators have suggested that the concept may have particularly broad application and restrict any measure that directly or indirectly impacts the market (Luengo Hernandez de Madrid 2006; Coppens 2014). Such restrictions could include export restrictions that depress the price for raw materials or other inputs and reduce the cost of higher value–added manufacturing using those inputs; they could also include restrictions on imports that support domestic producers, thereby increasing the domestic price for their goods.[7] WTO decisions, however, have declined to interpret the phrase "income or price support" so broadly. Rather than restricting measures that merely affect domestic prices, it covers those that are "designed to fix the price of a good at a particular level" (Coppens 2014, 59).

REQUIREMENT OF A BENEFIT

As noted above, to constitute a subsidy, an incentive must provide a benefit to the recipient. According to WTO jurisprudence, there is a benefit if the incentive provides advantages to the recipient on terms that are better or more favorable than a comparator benchmark, which is generally considered to be a market benchmark.[8] As the WTO's Appellate Body has clarified, the cost to the government—that is, the return, if any, the government receives as a result of the incentive—is irrelevant. This test illustrates that the aim of the SCM Agreement is not protecting governments against their own potentially wasteful uses of subsidies; rather, its aim is preventing WTO Members from using subsidies that put their goods producers in a better competitive position than goods producers of other WTO Members.[9] Absent any of those trade-related benefits, the SCM Agreement leaves incentives unregulated irrespective of how costly they are to the governments granting them.

REQUIREMENT OF SPECIFICITY

Covered incentives are prohibited under the SCM Agreement only if they meet the definition of a subsidy, discussed above, and are specific. This includes incentives that are de jure specific (i.e., the express terms of the incentive make it specific) as well as those that are de facto specific (i.e., the incentive is in fact specific when it is applied) (Article 2.1).

There are four main types of specific subsidies:

- *enterprise-specific subsidies*: subsidies that are available or given only to an enterprise or group of enterprises
- *industry-specific subsidies*: subsidies that are available or given only to an industry or group of industries
- *region-specific subsidies*: subsidies that are available or given only to enterprises or industries located within a designated geographical region or

identified tract of land within the jurisdiction of the authority granting the subsidy

- *export performance and local content subsidies*: subsidies that are automatically deemed specific irrespective of whether and how they are limited to certain enterprises or industries

With the exception of the fourth category (export performance and local content subsidies, which are deemed to be specific and are therefore prohibited under the SCM Agreement), the general rule is that the broader the subsidy's reach and the more objective the criteria for awarding it, the less likely it is that it will be deemed specific. As Article 2.1(b) explains, if

> the granting authority, or the legislation pursuant to which the granting authority operates, establishes objective criteria or conditions governing the eligibility for, and the amount of, a subsidy, specificity shall not exist, provided that the eligibility is automatic and that such criteria and conditions are strictly adhered to. The criteria or conditions must be clearly spelled out in law, regulation, or other official document, so as to be capable of verification.[10]

Measures that grant incentives to all industries based on objective criteria (e.g., number of employees or size of the enterprise) and that do not expressly or effectively favor certain enterprises over others are also not likely to be considered specific. With respect to region-specific subsidies, those can be specific even if they are granted to all enterprises within a particular region. Nevertheless, if those subsidies are granted through a generally applicable tax rate, they will not be deemed specific. A low corporate income tax adopted by a city or state for its taxpayers is therefore not likely to be prohibited by the SCM Agreement, so nations and subnational jurisdictions have latitude to use such tax strategies to compete for new investments and support existing ones.

Relevant to the issues discussed in chapter 7 in this volume, the SCM Agreement's rules on specificity give heightened importance to the processes through which investment incentives are actually granted and used. If a law establishes an incentives scheme that is widely available but the authorities administering that scheme exercise their power and discretion in such a way that they grant incentives only to particular enterprises or industries, the grant of those incentives may constitute a specific subsidy even if the generally applicable law would not. Similarly, a subsidy can be specific if only certain enterprises or industries actually use it or if they receive a disproportionate amount of the subsidy.

In this context, investor-state contracts may be particularly likely to satisfy the test of specificity. These contracts create a specific legal regime applicable to the private party to the contract under which that private party may receive various contributions from the government or public body. Even when the contract calls for the private party to give something to the government in return, the government's contribution can still be determined to be a subsidy under the SCM Agreement.

PROHIBITED SUBSIDIES

If an incentive meets the definition of a subsidy, it will be categorized as either a prohibited or an actionable subsidy. Each of those categories has its own set of rules regarding whether the incentive can be used, when it can be used, and what measures or remedies are available to other WTO Member States for a breach of the SCM Agreement.

Prohibited subsidies are those that are de jure or de facto contingent on (1) export performance or (2) the use of domestic over imported goods. These subsidies are considered to be "the most pernicious of subsidies because they directly aim to distort the pattern of trade" (Bhala et al. 2013, 409). Consequently, they are deemed to be specific and illegal and are prohibited irrespective of whether they result in any adverse effects on other Member States.

Determining whether subsidies are prohibited because they are contingent either on export performance or on the use of domestic over imported goods is not always clear, with much of that uncertainty relating to the question of what constitutes de facto contingency.

De facto export contingency, for instance, is not established merely because the recipient of the subsidy exports its products; nor is it enough for the domestic market to be unable to absorb the products produced by the enterprises or industries receiving the subsidies. Furthermore, as the WTO Appellate Body clarified in the *EC—Aircraft* dispute, de facto export contingency is not established simply by showing that the government was motivated to grant the subsidy based on its intent to promote exports or due to its expectation or anticipation of export earnings. Rather, according to the Appellate Body, in order to determine whether a subsidy is de facto export contingent, the inquiry is objective and fact specific, looking into whether "the granting of the subsidy provides an incentive to skew anticipated sales towards exports, in comparison with the historical performance of the recipient or the hypothetical performance of a profit maximizing firm in the absence of the subsidy."[11]

Satisfying that test, however, is difficult: in the *EC—Aircraft* case, the Appellate Body ultimately decided that, despite the voluminous factual submissions in the lengthy litigation, it did not have enough evidence to decide whether the subsidy was de facto contingent on exports. The challenges of establishing de facto contingency make it easier for investment incentives to fall out of the prohibited category; as a result, and as discussed further below, they will qualify only as actionable subsidies, which are permitted unless there is evidence that they result in adverse effects on other Member States.

With respect to import substitution subsidies, although the text of the SCM Agreement does not expressly cover or restrict those subsidies that are only de facto (as opposed to de jure) contingent on use of domestic products, WTO decisions have made it clear that the prohibition on such supports extends to de facto contingency. Nevertheless, it remains uncertain how far the prohibition on these de facto contingent measures reaches. Decisions have indicated that the SCM Agreement classifies as prohibited subsidies those measures that effectively require or incentivize use of domestic products in order to obtain the subsidy (Horlick 2010). Yet the relatively few disputes examining the issue leave many questions unanswered. An incentive that is contingent on manufacturing taking place within a certain territory but that is not expressly contingent on use of an amount or percentage of domestic goods could, for example, arguably be considered a prohibited import substitution subsidy if it has the effect of favoring the use of local physical inputs. But WTO jurisprudence to date has not clarified whether and when the restriction on the domestic content contingency can reach that far.

In sum, by covering measures that are either de facto or de jure tied to export performance or the use of local goods, the SCM Agreement has a potentially expansive reach, enabling it to cover what could be a broad range of investment incentives that have the *effect* of incentivizing exports or the greater purchase of domestic inputs. As noted above, these subsidies are deemed specific and are illegal under the SCM Agreement even if no adverse effect on other Member States is shown. Yet, whereas establishing de jure contingency may be relatively straightforward, establishing de facto contingency is much less so, with the result that identifying ex ante (when the measure is adopted) or ex post (when a trade dispute arises) whether a subsidy is prohibited under the SCM Agreement entails application of a complex test that may allow many de facto export or local content subsidies to avoid being deemed prohibited (Horlick 2010).

ACTIONABLE SUBSIDIES

The second category consists of domestic or industrial subsidies. These subsidies are not prohibited under the SCM Agreement but are actionable by WTO Member States if the subsidies cause them adverse effects. According to Article 5, an adverse effect is shown if a subsidy of one Member causes (1) "injury to the domestic industry of another Member," (2) nullification or impairment of benefits accruing "directly or indirectly" under the GATT, or (3) "serious prejudice" (which is defined in Article 6) to the interests of another Member.

Because a Member must prove an adverse effect in order to successfully challenge an actionable subsidy, it is more difficult to prevail in actions against actionable subsidies under the SCM Agreement than in actions against prohibited subsidies, potentially leaving various incentives unregulated by that treaty. Again, this highlights that the focus of the SCM Agreement is not to control the use of investment incentives. Indeed, the test for determining whether actionable subsidies will be prohibited further reveals the disconnect between the purposes of the SCM Agreement and policies seeking more directly to limit wasteful or costly incentives.

The panel and Appellate Body decisions in *United States—Large Civil Aircraft* illustrate. In that dispute, the panel assessed whether certain incentives for research and development (R&D) provided by the U.S. National Aeronautics and Space Administration (NASA) and Department of Defense (DOD)—measures deemed to be specific actionable subsidies within the meaning of the SCM Agreement—caused adverse effects on other WTO Members. According to the panel, those incentives were provided as part of "strategically-focused R&D programmes" undertaken by the government "in collaboration with U.S. industry to provide competitive advantages to U.S. industry by funding research into high risk, high pay-off research of the sort that individual companies are unlikely to fund on their own."[12] The panel stated that the government's R&D incentives aimed at and were effective in overcoming the "large disincentives for private sector investment in long term, high risk aeronautical R&D (stemming from the inability of individual firms to fully capture the benefits from the research efforts)."[13] Rather than simply lowering the operating costs and increasing the profits of the firm, the R&D subsidies actually shaped the company's R&D activities and resulted in the development of technologies for governmental and commercial use. The value of the technological advances achieved as a result of the R&D incentives, the panel further explained, could not "be reduced to their cash value."[14] Rather, their benefits were "multiplied."[15]

The panel report's description of the R&D incentives paints them as a success if judged in terms of effectiveness. Yet it was precisely such effectiveness that led the panel to conclude that the incentives were inconsistent with the SCM Agreement. According to the panel, the R&D incentives made a "genuine and substantial contribution" to technological development and innovation that, among other effects, enabled Boeing to build better and cheaper airplanes and to do so more quickly than it otherwise would have, thereby conferring on the U.S. company a competitive advantage. These findings, in turn, led to the panel's subsequent findings of "adverse effects" and were subsequently upheld by the Appellate Body.[16]

In contrast, the panel determined that there was inadequate evidence that certain other specific subsidies caused adverse effects, resulting in these subsidies withstanding the challenge under the SCM Agreement. The subsidies that were deemed permissible included roughly $11 million in relocation incentives provided by the U.S. state of Illinois and municipalities therein in order to induce Boeing to move its headquarters to Illinois from Washington State. They also included $476 million in property and sales tax abatements provided through bond programs that officials in the U.S. state of Kansas gave in order to incentivize Boeing to expand and maintain its manufacturing facilities in the state.[17] Notably, in January 2012, after the WTO Appellate Body's decision was issued, Boeing announced it would close a plant in Wichita, Kansas, that had benefited from the subsidies at issue in the WTO dispute (Bhala et al. 2013, 417–18).

The *U.S.—Large Civil Aircraft* dispute highlights the SCM Agreement's limitations as an instrument regulating investment incentives. Although the types of location and relocation incentives provided by authorities in Kansas and Illinois may be among the most pernicious in terms of their welfare effects on the jurisdictions granting them, as well as the jurisdictions competing for investment, those incentives remained outside of the SCM Agreement's reach. In comparison, incentives provided by NASA and the DOD—incentives that appeared to effectively target and overcome market failures discouraging investment in R&D for governmental and commercial purposes—did not fare as well under the WTO's rules.

DISCLOSURE, REVIEW, AND ENFORCEMENT

As the WTO (2006) recognizes, "transparency is essential for operation of the [SCM] Agreement" and for ensuring compliance with its provisions. To that end, Article 25 of the SCM Agreement requires WTO Members to disclose the salient characteristics of each of their specific subsidies. It also explains that these notifications are to be "sufficiently specific to enable other Members to evaluate the trade effects and to understand the operation of notified subsidy programmes." Member States are to provide new and full notifications of their specific subsidies every two years (SCM Committee 2003).

To help enforce that requirement and ensure that disclosures are meaningful, Article 25.6 provides that any Member State may ask another for more-specific information about its subsidies and that, if the requested party does not comply, the requestor may bring the matter to the attention of the SCM Committee, a body established by the Subsidies Code to help monitor and support compliance with the subsidies rules. Pursuant to Article 27, the SCM Committee is required to examine states' notifications every third year.

But although transparency is meant to be an integral part of the SCM Agreement's controls on subsidies, partial compliance and noncompliance with the transparency requirements have prevented those disclosure obligations from serving their potential and intended purposes. States lack motivation to improve reporting because consequences for failing to disclose a subsidy are slight and states may fear that compliance with notification requirements can expose them to claims (Steenblik and Simón 2011). Consequently, as of October 21, 2013, eighty-four states had still not submitted their subsidy notifications that had been due on June 30, 2013; sixty-two had still not submitted their subsidy notifications that had been due in 2011; sixty-two had still not submitted their subsidy notifications that had been due in 2009; and seventy had still not submitted their subsidy notifications that had been due in 2007 (SCM Committee 2013). Moreover, when submitted, the reports are often of poor quality, limiting their utility (Steenblik and Simón 2011).

Apart from the soft regulation of incentives possible through the disclosure of subsidies, review in the SCM Committee, and evaluation through the WTO's Trade Policy Review Mechanism,[18] the WTO provides its Member States with two avenues for formally challenging and seeking relief from illegal subsidies.

The first is through use of the WTO's dispute settlement system. As described in Article 4 of the SCM Agreement, states can bring these issues before WTO panels and can appeal panel rulings to the WTO's Appellate Body. If a WTO panel or Appellate Body finds that a state has granted a prohibited subsidy, the WTO's Dispute Settlement Body (DSB) will recommend that the subsidy be withdrawn. If the subsidy is found to be an actionable subsidy causing adverse effects, the DSB may recommend that the subsidy be withdrawn or that appropriate steps be taken to remove its adverse effects. Retaliation through the imposition of countermeasures is available only when the offending state refuses to alter its WTO-inconsistent policy[19] (Brewster 2011).

The second route is through unilateral action. The SCM Agreement permits its Member States to impose countervailing duties on foreign products that have been illegally subsidized. The countervailing duties are meant to enable one WTO Member State to offset the negative impacts another Member State's subsidy has on its domestic industry.[20]

Through these mechanisms, WTO Members are able to challenge certain incentives programs. With a mandatory agreement and strong complaint-based system, the SCM Agreement satisfies the institutional criteria identified in chapter 11 of this volume as being crucial for effectively reining in welfare-reducing incentives competition. Yet, as noted above, the substantive rules of the SCM Agreement are not designed for or appropriately suited to that task.

EXCEPTIONS OR CARVE-OUTS FOR SUBSIDIES SERVING CERTAIN POLICY OBJECTIVES

As profiled in other chapters of this book, governments often offer investment incentives to encourage a range of public policy objectives such as increased use of renewable energy, development of small and medium-sized enterprises (SMEs), and investment in R&D. The SCM Agreement, however, does not contain any express exceptions for subsidies based on these or other policy aims. This stands in notable contrast to similar schemes in the EU (described further below and in chapter 5 in this volume), which include carve-outs for investment incentives in order to advance certain EU policy objectives.

When the SCM Agreement was concluded, the negotiators included in Article 8 a provision stating that subsidies would be nonactionable subsidies if they met certain criteria for supports used to promote R&D, to provide assistance to disadvantaged regions, or to enable compliance with environmental regulations. That protective cover, however, lapsed on December 31, 1999[21] (Horlick 2010).

Subsequent to that lapse, various scholars have advocated for WTO Members to revive (and potentially broaden or otherwise modify) the "green light" category (Aguayo Ayala and Gallagher 2005; Green 2006; Howse 2010). Yet states have not appeared willing to adopt those proposals. Consequently, the restrictions on investment incentives under the SCM Agreement apply irrespective of the purpose of or public need for the measure.

Some have argued that the exceptions that are contained in Article XX of the GATT can and should apply to subsidies under the SCM Agreement (Howse 2010; Rubini 2012). These include the exceptions in GATT Article XX(b) for measures "necessary to protect human, animal or plant life or health" and in GATT Article XX(g) for measures "relating to the conservation of exhaustible natural resources." To date, however, no WTO decision has addressed the question of whether the GATT's exceptions can apply to shield measures that are otherwise inconsistent with the SCM Agreement (Whitsett 2013; Wu and Salzman 2014).

This leaves open significant questions about the latitude governments have under the SCM Agreement to use investment incentives to advance environmental and other public interest aims, and the need to answer those questions is increasingly pressing, as industrial policy has been regaining favor among academics and government leaders (Wu and Salzman 2014). Green industrial policies, for instance, have grown in popularity as officials seek to advance environmental aims while achieving other objectives, such as enhancing energy security, creating jobs, and promoting domestic competiveness and economic growth. Yet these green industrial policies (discussed further in chapter 9 in this volume), which often include a mix of sector-specific subsidies, supports contingent on local content, and export restraints, can run afoul of WTO rules, including the SCM Agreement. The result has been a rise in WTO disputes challenging these types of strategies, with green industrial policies alone giving rise to twelve significant trade and environment conflicts between 2008 and 2014 (Wu and Salzman 2014).

PROVISIONS FOR DEVELOPING COUNTRIES

The SCM Agreement specifically recognizes that "subsidies may play an important role in economic development programmes of developing country members" (Article 27.1). Consistent with that principle, it provides special and differential treatment to developing countries with regard to certain of their obligations under the SCM Agreement.

In particular, the SCM Agreement exempts two categories of developing countries from the prohibition on export subsidies: (1) least developed countries (LDCs) and (2) developing countries with a GNP per capita of less than US$1,000 per year, which are listed in Annex VII to the SCM Agreement. In accordance with the Doha Ministerial Declaration on Implementation-Related Issues and Concerns, a developing country falling into that second category will be removed from the Annex VII list and lose the benefit of the exemption if its GNP per capita reaches US$1,000 in constant 1990 dollars for three consecutive years.[22]

Developing country Members not falling into either of those categories were given an eight-year period to phase out their export subsidies (and were prohibited from increasing the amount of export subsidies during that time) (Article 27.4). Although that transition period would have expired in 2003, Article 27.4 permitted countries to seek extensions. In accordance with that provision, decisions taken at the Doha Ministerial Conference, and decisions adopted by the General Council and the SCM Committee, nineteen countries were permitted to maintain their export subsidies through 2013 but then entered into a two-year phase-out requiring all export subsidies to be terminated by December 31, 2015 (General Council Decision WT/L/691; WTO 2014).

CONCLUSION AND KEY MESSAGES

The SCM Agreement restricts the use of some investment incentives but leaves many gaps. Various measures, such as incentives that are not de jure or de facto contingent on exports or the use of domestic products and that do not cause adverse effects or that relate only to trade in services can escape discipline by the SCM Agreement.

Further limiting the effectiveness of the SCM Agreement in controlling the use of subsidies is the lack of transparency that persists, notwithstanding the SCM Agreement's notification requirements. This opacity allows many investment incentives and other subsidies to remain in place and unchallenged.

Fundamentally, as the *U.S.—Large Civil Aircraft* dispute highlights, the SCM Agreement is simply not designed to combat the problems associated with investment incentives that have been highlighted throughout this volume, which relate to the costliness, wastefulness, and ineffectiveness of various incentives and the mounting pressure to engage in a race to the bottom in the global competition for capital. Moreover, although the SCM Agreement thus leaves large areas un- or underregulated, thereby permitting WTO Members to continue to engage in costly and inefficient competitions for capital, it lacks exceptions important for protecting governments' abilities to use investment incentives that are tailored to overcome market failures and meet public policy objectives such as encouraging investment in developing and deploying new green technologies.

From the perspective of optimal incentives regulation (see discussion later in this chapter), other WTO agreements similarly have the advantage of providing supranational controls and mechanisms for enforcement but are likewise ill-suited to the role of appropriately controlling investment incentives, lacking a real mandate or rules through which to serve that purpose.

TRIMS AGREEMENT AND THE GATS

Two other WTO instruments that are relevant to the use of investment incentives are the TRIMs Agreement and the GATS.

THE TRIMS AGREEMENT

The TRIMs Agreement prohibits WTO Member States from imposing (or making incentives contingent on compliance with) certain performance requirements that discriminate against products produced by other Member States.

In essence, the TRIMs Agreement merely codifies and clarifies pre-WTO case law declaring that a country may not use investment measures to undermine certain obligations under the GATT. Pursuant to Article 2 of the TRIMs Agreement, WTO Member States are not to impose investment measures that breach Article III of the GATT by treating foreign products less favorably than domestic products (e.g., through requirements to use local goods) or that breach Article XI's prohibitions on quantitative restrictions on exports or imports (e.g., through export restraints).

The TRIMs Agreement also contains an illustrative list of measures that it bars. Importantly, the TRIMs Agreement applies only to measures relating to trade in goods, not services.

Although the TRIMs Agreement does impose some restraints on the use of investment incentives, its impact in this area is relatively limited, leaving many types of investment incentives unregulated. Nevertheless, by preventing WTO Member States from providing incentives that are contingent on use of domestic rather than imported goods, it does place notable limits on governments' freedom to use investment incentives to advance certain policies such as supporting domestic industries or encouraging development in disadvantaged regions or communities.

As illustrated by recent WTO disputes involving local-content-contingent investment incentives that were given to firms in the renewable energy industry, measures that are barred by the TRIMs Agreement can include the types of policies adopted and used by national and subnational governments around the world to develop domestic renewable energy industries (Wu and Salzman 2014).[23] Wu and Salzman (2014, 423–24) report on the first such program to give rise to a TRIMs challenge, a feed-in-tariff (FIT) program implemented in the Canadian province of Ontario, which aimed to encourage producers of renewable energy by guaranteeing purchase of that energy at set prices:

> Having campaigned on a platform of a "Greener Ontario," the ruling Liberal Party implemented a FIT to spur renewable energy investment. However, the program came with a catch. To qualify for the FIT, after 2011, a solar energy producer [had to] source at least 60 percent of its components from Ontario, while for large-scale wind energy producers, the threshold [was] 50 percent. The Liberals sought to spur job creation through pro-environmental policies designed to catapult Ontario to the forefront of clean technology manufacturing in North America. By that measure, the local content requirements [were] successful. In the first year alone, ten solar energy manufacturers and several wind energy and solar inverter companies "committed to [set] up solar module assembly plants in Ontario to meet" the requirement. The most visible of these [was] a multibillion-dollar deal with Korean manufacturer Samsung to build wind and solar energy plants in the province. (Wu and Salzman 2014, 423–24).

Although the exceptions in the GATT also apply to the TRIMs Agreement and can potentially shield measures appropriately targeted at certain environmental or other specified policy aims, the exceptions do not afford protective cover to measures based on their effectiveness at achieving industrial policy or other development aims. Reflecting that reality, when a WTO panel was constituted to review Ontario's FIT scheme, it determined that the scheme violated the TRIMs Agreement by making the FIT program's benefits contingent on the use of local goods.[24] The panel's findings on those issues were undisturbed on appeal to the Appellate Body.[25]

GATS

The General Agreement on Trade in Services (GATS) includes provisions that can restrict the use of investment incentives. It covers trade in services that occurs through different modes, one of which is through "commercial presence" (mode 3).[26] Commercial presence/mode 3 is the supply of services through foreign investment. As a result, the GATS can be relevant to and regulate how countries treat foreign and domestic service suppliers established within their borders.

Article XV of the GATS requires WTO Members to enter into negotiations regarding the possible development of controls on the use of service-sector subsidies. It states:

> 1. Members recognize that, in certain circumstances, subsidies may have distortive effects on trade in services. Members shall enter into negotiations with a view to developing the necessary multilateral disciplines to avoid such trade-distortive effects. The negotiations shall also address the appropriateness of countervailing procedures. Such negotiations shall recognize the role of subsidies in relation to the development programmes of developing countries and take into account the needs of Members, particularly developing country Members, for flexibility in this area. For the purpose of such negotiations, Members shall exchange information concerning all subsidies related to trade in services that they provide to their domestic service suppliers.
>
> 2. Any Member which considers that it is adversely affected by a subsidy of another Member may request consultations with that Member on such matters. Such requests shall be accorded sympathetic consideration.

Although work on that mandate has begun, there have been no agreed-upon outcomes yet.

Apart from that article on subsidies, the GATS contains other articles that are relevant to the use of investment incentives. Article II contains the most-favored-nation (MFN) treatment obligation, which prevents a Member State from treating services and service suppliers from one Member State less favorably than "like" services and service suppliers from another Member State. The MFN treatment obligation applies on a default basis[27] to foreign investors in all service sectors and prevents governments from discriminating between different foreign-owned service providers by, among other measures, giving investment incentives to service suppliers from one Member State and not giving the same incentives to "like" service suppliers from another Member State.[28]

Also relevant is Article XVII, which contains the national treatment requirement. This article prevents states from treating foreign services or service suppliers less favorably than "like" domestic services or service suppliers. In contrast to the MFN obligation, the national treatment commitment applies only to those service sectors that a government has specifically "scheduled" and then only to the extent that the government has not included exceptions narrowing the scope of its GATS commitments in the scheduled sector. When it applies, the national treatment provision can, among other things, restrict governments' use of investment incentives that are provided to service suppliers located in or owned by investors of the granting jurisdiction but not provided or not provided on the same terms to service suppliers located in or owned by nationals of other Member States.[29]

If, for instance, the government of a WTO Member granted investment incentives to services firms owned by minority or economically disadvantaged citizens in order to address and overcome consequences of historical discrimination but did not similarly provide those incentives to competitor firms owned by investors of other Member States, the government granting the incentives could find itself in breach of the GATS' national treatment obligation (if and to the extent the government had made commitments in the relevant sector). The nondiscrimination obligation in the GATS could thus restrict the use of measures aimed at advancing inclusive growth and development.

One possible consequence of these nondiscrimination provisions is that they could expand the use of investment incentives but dilute their policy efficacy. If, in the example above, a government established narrow eligibility criteria in order to ensure that its incentives policies actually benefited the intended communities, the risk increases that application of those criteria would discriminate against foreign-owned firms and violate the GATS. In order to avoid a challenge that its policies are WTO-inconsistent, a government might make its investment incentives more widely available and easier to access. Yet, although potentially helping the country avoid any trade disputes, that response could also dilute the power of these incentives to serve their policy aims.

Another notable effect of the national and MFN treatment provisions is that they can limit Member States' abilities to provide incentives to service suppliers located *in their territories* when those incentives negatively affect the competitive position of service suppliers *located in other countries*. The *Canada—Autos* case illustrates this issue. Among the measures challenged in that case was a requirement that manufacturers achieve a minimum of "Canadian value-added" (CVA) in order to receive an import duty exemption. They could meet the CVA requirements for services through "(i) the cost of maintenance and repair work executed in Canada on buildings, machinery and equipment used for production purposes; (ii) the cost of engineering services, experimental work and product development work executed in Canada; [and] (iii) administrative and general expenses incurred in Canada."[30] The complaining WTO Members argued "that the CVA requirements provide an incentive for the beneficiaries of the import duty exemption to use services supplied within the Canadian territory rather than like services supplied in or from the territory of other Members, thus modifying the conditions of competition among them."[31]

The WTO panel agreed with the complainants. After determining that Canada had scheduled the relevant service sectors and had not taken any applicable exceptions, the panel concluded that the CVA requirements were inconsistent with Canada's national treatment obligations under the GATS:

> 10.307. We note that the CVA requirements ... do not discriminate between domestic and foreign services and service suppliers operating in Canada under [mode 3—commercial presence of the service supplier through foreign investment]. This observation, however, does not suffice to conclude that the requirements of Article XVII are met. In our view, it is reasonable to consider for the purposes of this case that services supplied in Canada through Mode 3 . . . and those supplied from the territory of other Members through Modes 1 and 2,[32] are "like" services. In turn, this leads to the conclusion that the CVA requirements provide an incentive for the beneficiaries of the import duty exemption to use services supplied within the Canadian territory over "like" services supplied in or from the territory of other Members . . . , thus modifying the conditions of competition in favour of services supplied within Canada. Although this requirement does not distinguish between services supplied by service suppliers

> of Canada and those supplied by service suppliers of other Members present in Canada, it is bound to have a discriminatory effect against services supplied through Modes 1 and 2, which are services of other Members.
>
> 10.308. In light of the foregoing, we find that the CVA requirements on manufacturer beneficiaries accord less favourable treatment to services of other Members supplied though modes 1 and 2 and are therefore inconsistent with Canada's obligations under Article XVII of the GATS.

Importantly, the panel's decision depended on its conclusion that foreign-based service suppliers can be "like" locally established service suppliers for the purposes of the GATS' nondiscrimination obligation.[33] But from the perspective of a government seeking to encourage investment and the benefits that can accompany it, the two types of service suppliers—those based in the territory of the granting jurisdiction and those based outside of it—are fundamentally different.

This decision suggests limits on the use of direct and indirect tools to attract and keep investments by service suppliers and to encourage linkages among service suppliers and between service suppliers and firms in the manufacturing and primary sectors. A government seeking to encourage investment in high-tech manufacturing, for example, may also seek to leverage that investment to increase investment in highly skilled and competitively priced domestic service providers. Yet if the government grants manufacturers incentives that are contingent on the use of locally established service providers (whether foreign- or domestic-owned) and those incentives place foreign-based service suppliers at a competitive disadvantage, the incentives could be inconsistent with the GATS.

There are several important ways in which the GATS' power to broadly restrict use of de facto or de jure discriminatory incentives is weakened. For one, as noted above, the national treatment requirement applies only to service sectors that WTO Member States have specifically listed or "scheduled," and when formulating their schedules, Member States have the opportunity to further limit the scope of their commitments by negotiating exceptions. Similarly, Member States can include exemptions to their MFN obligations. Depending on the commitments made and limits asserted, the GATS can leave Member States a certain degree of latitude to use incentives to attract and sustain investments from service suppliers.

In addition to those country-specific exemptions and exceptions, the GATS specifies in Article XIII that its national treatment obligation does not apply to government procurement and adds in Article 1.3(b) that it does not apply to "services supplied in the exercise of government authority."[34] Moreover, in Article XIV, the GATS, like the GATT, contains various general exceptions that can safeguard measures otherwise inconsistent with the agreement, including exceptions for measures "necessary to protect public morals or to maintain public order" (Article XIV[a]) and "necessary to protect human, animal or plant life or health" (Article XIV[b]).[35]

Although numerous questions can arise about the precise meaning of each of these exceptions, they can, to some extent, help shield governments' powers to use investment incentives and other measures to achieve economic and other policy goals, such as ensuring low cost and wide availability of public services. Yet there are no broad exceptions for overcoming market failures, encouraging investment in R&D, furthering environmental aims, or promoting local development similar to what is found in the EU rules on State aid (discussed below). Depending on the commitments a WTO Member has made and the exceptions it has scheduled, the national treatment and MFN rules can limit that government's use of investment incentives that discriminate—whether in fact or in law—against foreign-owned or foreign-based service suppliers.

CONCLUDING REMARKS ON WTO RULES ON INVESTMENT INCENTIVES

Focused as they are on removing obstacles to international trade in goods and services, the WTO agreements are not designed for governing investment incentives. Although instruments such as the GATS, TRIMs Agreement, and SCM Agreement do impose some rules and restraints on the use of investment incentives, the agreements result in those measures being both under- and overregulated by WTO controls.

In terms of underregulation, WTO rules have been unable to adequately prevent the use of costly and wasteful investment incentives or to stop races to the bottom in terms of competition for capital. For one thing, the potential of the WTO system's rules in this area is left unfulfilled due to weak compliance with transparency requirements. Additionally, unless they are contingent on the use of domestic inputs or export performance or have adverse effects on other WTO Members, domestic production subsidies (e.g., incentives provided directly to local manufacturers) can remain undisciplined.

With respect to investments in services, there are no express rules on subsidies. In addition, although the GATS' nondiscrimination provisions can restrict discriminatory use of incentives, application of those rules may simply result in governments shifting toward use of investment incentives with broad, nonspecific eligibility criteria, even though those may not be as optimally tailored to meet their policy goals.

In terms of overregulation, the SCM Agreement notably includes no exceptions allowing Member States flexibility to use SCM-inconsistent investment incentives targeted at correcting market failures and achieving important policy objectives, such as encouraging investment in low-carbon technologies. Moreover, as the *U.S.—Large Civil Aircraft* dispute shows, the more successful some R&D subsidies are in shaping investors' conduct, the more likely they are to run afoul of the WTO's rules—imposing a penalty on governments for effectively advancing policy aims. The test of whether a subsidy violates the SCM Agreement narrowly focuses on whether and how the support impacts the ability of other WTO Members to engage in international trade in goods. The fact that a measure may be aimed at an environmental, social, or other development objective will not save it.

The WTO's rules on services place additional restraints on incentives that may similarly have beneficial policy outcomes. In particular, WTO panel decisions interpreting "likeness" suggest that the GATS' nondiscrimination provisions can prevent governments from granting incentives that aim to encourage manufacturing or other firms to establish and deepen linkages with locally established services firms. For countries seeking to maximize the potential—but not inevitable—benefits of FDI through fostering and nurturing those types of linkages, such restrictions remove a potentially important tool from their toolbox of policy options.

The resulting legal framework regulating investment incentives is thus simultaneously inadequate and overly restrictive, raising important questions about whether WTO agreements adequately advance, and do not restrain, incentives strategies for achieving sustainable development objectives.

REGIONAL REGULATION OF INVESTMENT INCENTIVES IN THE EU

In comparison to the WTO, whose rules largely regulate investment incentives incidental to their controls on subsidies affecting cross-border trade in goods, the EU has established a State aid regime more specifically designed to govern the use of investment incentives. As is described below, this regime potentially provides a model that can be drawn on for incentives regulations by other groups of countries or on a broad multilateral basis.

BASIC LEGAL FRAMEWORK

European regulation of state subsidies—including investment incentives—dates back many decades. In 1951, six states—Belgium, France, West Germany, Italy, Luxembourg, and the Netherlands—entered into the Paris Treaty to govern the coal and steel industries and, through that agreement, prohibited individual Member States from granting subsidies or aids to those industries (Treaty Establishing the European Coal and Steel Community 1951). Several years later, those states entered into the Treaty Establishing the European Economic Community, which set forth additional rules on State aid applicable to a broader range of industries and laid the foundation for current regulation of state supports.

As noted in chapter 5 in this volume, the overarching rules on State aid are currently set forth in Articles 107 through 109 of the Treaty on the Functioning of the European Union (TFEU). Due to the limited nature of the guidance provided by those treaty provisions, a host of guidelines, communications, and decisions by the European Commission (EC) and judgments of the European Court of Justice (ECJ)[36] plays a crucial and ongoing role in elaborating the substantive content of those TFEU provisions and the standards and procedures used for promoting and verifying compliance. There is now a relatively robust body of rules and guidelines governing the use of State aid, providing guidance regarding when and under what circumstances it will be allowed to support inward and outward investment.

Through application of that legal framework, the granting of State aid by European countries has been in decline. Constituting roughly 2 percent of GDP in the 1980s, non-crisis-related State aid constituted 0.49 percent of GDP in 2013 (European Commission 2014i). Moreover, the aid that is granted appears to be more tailored to meeting specific policy aims, such as increased use of renewable energy, development of disadvantaged regions, and promotion of R&D. The sections below describe some of the core features of the EU State aid regulatory regime that are relevant for governing the use of investment incentives, focusing in particular on implementation of that regime through requirements for transparency, enforcement, and evaluation.

STATE AID—HOW IT IS DEFINED AND WHEN IT IS PERMITTED

According to Article 107 of the TFEU, State aid is any advantage to an undertaking constituting a charge on the public account that is provided by an EU

Member State on a selective basis and that distorts or threatens to distort competition in a manner that affects trade in goods or services between EU Member States.

The elements of that definition leave at least two important gaps that cause various measures to fall outside the scope of EU State aid regulations. First, because an incentive must be selective in order for it to constitute State aid, laws of general applicability fall outside its scope, leaving Member States significant freedom under State aid rules to engage in tax competition. Second, an incentive counts as State aid only if it distorts or threatens to distort trade in goods or services among EU Member States. If it distorts or threatens to distort trade in goods or services only outside of the EU, the rules on State aid become irrelevant.[37]

The forms that State aid can take are broad and varied and include a range of measures such as grants; low-interest loans or interest rebates; state guarantees; capital injections; exemptions from or reductions in taxes, social security, or other compulsory charges; and the supply of land, infrastructure, goods, or services at favorable prices. Any of those measures meeting the definition of State aid is generally considered to be incompatible with the common market and not allowed unless it is aimed at one of several European Community objectives or corrects particular market failures.

There are three categories of State aid that are always permitted in order to achieve certain policy goals of the European Community (Article 107[2] of the TFEU):

- aid with a "social character" granted directly to individual consumers, as long as it is granted without discrimination relating to the origin of relevant products (e.g., tax deductions for low-income or disabled persons or tax benefits for the purchase of low-carbon products)
- aid to repair damage caused by natural disasters or other exceptional occurrences
- aid granted to certain parts of Germany to compensate for economic consequences of the former division of the country

There are also are several objectives that *might* justify use of State aid:

- furthering economic development of areas where the standard of living is abnormally low or where there is serious underemployment, as compared to EU averages (Article 107[3][a])

- promoting important projects of common European interest (e.g., construction of a power plant to provide energy to other EU members, construction of infrastructure linking EU states, formulation of industrial standards and environmental protection) or projects intended to remedy a serious disturbance in the economy of a Member State that affects the country as a whole (as opposed to just certain regions or sectors) (Article 107[3][b])
- facilitating the development of certain economic activities or certain economic areas (regions that are economically disadvantaged relative to the state in which they are located), provided that such aid does not adversely affect trading conditions to an extent contrary to the common market (Article 107[3][c])
- promoting conservation of culture and heritage (Article 107[3][d])
- achieving other goals specified by decision of the European Council acting on a proposal by the EC (Article 107[3][e])

In contrast to the first three objectives specified in Article 107(2), objectives for which State aid is always allowed, the EC has discretion regarding whether to authorize State aid targeting any one of the policy goals specified in Article 107(3). Through various guidelines, communications, and decisions, the EC and the ECJ have developed detailed rules and guidance regarding the circumstances in which State aid will be permitted under those Article 107(3) categories.

The guidelines for regional aid—the type of aid referred to in Article 107(3)(a) and (c), which is designed to promote economic development of disadvantaged areas within Europe—merit special attention (European Commission 2014e). The regional aid framework grants certain designated disadvantaged areas special flexibilities to use incentives in order to attract investment. Permissible levels of aid increase with the severity of the economic problems affecting the jurisdiction, giving those areas plagued by the worst socioeconomic conditions the greatest flexibility to use incentives to compensate for their weaknesses as an investment destination.

Yet, although regional aid thus allows these jurisdictions an extra margin of policy space, there remain important limits. The Regional Aid Guidelines caution that incentives will be permitted only if their positive effects outweigh their negative effects. Moreover, the negative effects that are to be contained in that equation include effects on other jurisdictions. Particularly notable in this context, the Regional Aid Guidelines state that the negative effects of aid "manifestly outweigh any positive effects" and cannot be permitted if the aid diverts new investments away from other regions in the EU that are equally or more disadvantaged or if it causes investors to relocate existing investments from one area of the EU to the area granting the incentives (European Commission 2014e, 21). Through these rules, the EU seeks to prevent poaching and bidding wars, especially wasteful uses of investment incentives.

Overall, the exceptions and the limits to those exceptions in the EU State aid regime stand in notable contrast to the WTO's regulation of investment incentives through the SCM Agreement. Whereas in the EU there is a general prohibition on the use of State aid, incentives may still be used to advance one or more predefined EU goals if the incentives are consistent with relevant guidelines. As explained above, the WTO's SCM Agreement does not contain similar carve-outs for investment incentives appropriately aimed at achieving specified government objectives.

NOTIFICATION, TRANSPARENCY, MONITORING, AND EVALUATION

In principle, under Article 107(1) of the TFEU, all grants of State aid are subject to requirements for prior notification to and approval from the EC. Elements that must appear in the notification include the authority granting the subsidy; the intended beneficiaries and their locations and sectors; and the amount, form, source, and objectives of the aid. This feature of advance notification and approval is another notable way in which the design of the EU system regulating the use of incentives differs from that of the WTO: whereas the former seems to rely on ex ante controls, the latter relies more heavily on ex post enforcement.

In practice, however, a large and growing share of State aid has been exempted from the EU's notice and approval rules.[38] There are three main types of exemptions:

- exemptions for de minimis aid, which is defined as aid to a single undertaking that does not exceed the value of 200,000 euros by a given Member State over a three-year fiscal term (European Commission 2013a)
- exemptions for aid granted pursuant to an aid scheme[39] that had already been notified to and authorized by the EC
- exemptions for State aid covered by the General Block Exemption Regulation (GBER)

As discussed in chapter 5 in this volume, the GBER that came into force on July 1, 2014, amended the 2008–2013 version of that regulation by, inter alia, adding new categories of State aid that are covered by the block exemption and setting higher notification thresholds and aid intensities for types of State aid that were covered by the previous block exemption. The types of State aid now covered by the 2014 GBER include aid for SMEs, R&D, environmental protection, employment and training, innovation clusters, broadband infrastructure, local infrastructure, sport infrastructure, regional development, and culture and heritage conservation.

However, projects falling within these broad categories of "good aid" must still satisfy various conditions in order to be covered by the GBER. Article 13 of the GBER, for instance, sets out conditions that are designed to prevent one Member State from using regional development aid to poach investment from another Member State. Where regional State aid does not meet those criteria, it is not covered by the GBER.

With the expansion of the GBER's reach, the number of aid measures covered is expected to rise from 60 percent under the previous version to between 75 and 90 percent under the new version, and the amount of State aid covered is anticipated to increase from 30 percent to roughly 66 percent (European Commission 2014f, 2014g).

As signaled by these amendments, the EU has shifted away from using ex ante controls to ensure that State aid rules are complied with and meet European Community objectives. Instead, it is placing a greater emphasis on three other strategies: (1) ensuring greater overall transparency of State aid, (2) strengthening ex post controls on compliance, and (3) evaluating existing programs to help in the design of "smarter" investment schemes (European Commission 2014g).

First, on the issue of transparency, by July 1, 2016, all EU Member States are expected to have established national or regional websites on which they will publicly disclose summary information regarding all awards of State aid over 500,000 euros, including State aid covered by the GBER (European Commission 2014a, 2014c). Such information will include the identity of the beneficiary, the sector in which it is active, the form and amount of aid granted, and the legal basis for granting the aid.[40] Prior to the adoption of these new transparency requirements in May 2014, all Member States were already required to provide annual reports to the EC on their existing aid schemes, but there were no obligations for public disclosure of this range of State aid measures or at this level of detail. With these amendments, therefore, the public and the private sector will have greater ability to scrutinize and to help enforce compliance with State aid rules.

Second, on the issue of enforcement, the EC explains that by having to spend fewer resources on ex ante review of notified aid schemes, it can dedicate more time to monitoring existing grants of State aid and ensuring that they were authorized and maintained in compliance with EU rules.

Third, on the issue of evaluation, the EC introduced new requirements aiming to enhance understanding of the positive and negative impacts that grants of State aid have had on their policy aims and on competition. Such understanding, it explained, was lacking, as there had been no systematic requirements for or practices regarding evaluation of existing State aid measures. The new measures require Member States to develop comprehensive, "objective, rigorous, impartial and transparent" evaluation plans covering certain large State aid schemes, including those covered by the GBER (European Commission 2014b). Pursuant to these evaluation plans, which must be approved by the EC, Member States are to collect and analyze data enabling them to, to the extent possible, identify the direct and indirect costs and benefits of their aid schemes and assess the proportionality and appropriateness of those aid schemes relative to their intended goals (European Commission 2014b). After the evaluation reports are submitted, they will be used at the micro-level to determine whether to renew each scheme and, if so, whether and how that scheme should be modified as well as at the macro-level to determine whether the results suggest there should be any changes in State aid policies or practices.

A study of twenty-eight investment projects receiving regional aid illustrates the information and lessons that can be gleaned from such evaluations (Ramboll and Matrix 2012). This study, which was conducted in order to inform the EC's review of its Regional Aid Guidelines,[41] covered projects in six industries and seven Member States that were carried out between 2002 and 2010. The case studies included (1) seven investment projects in the pharmaceutical industry in Ireland, (2) three investment projects in the solar industry in Germany, (3) three investment projects in the car industry in Slovakia and Hungary, (4) eight investment projects in internal business services in Poland, (5) two investment projects in the cement industry in Hungary, and (6) five investment projects in the pulp and paper industry in Spain and Portugal.

Among its findings, the study determined that certain Member State agencies are more diligent about conducting cost-benefit analyses of projects and incentives than others but that in no case was there actually a careful review of the incentive effect—that is, whether the incentive would impact investors' investment or locational decisions. It also found that although some jurisdictions controlled the discretion of the granting authority to negotiate and renegotiate incentives packages, others took a more flexible approach, loosening controls over efforts to ensure that the incentives provide value for money and are used to meet intended objectives. A summary of the key findings is contained in box 12.1.

Box 12.1 Lessons from the Eu Regulation of State Aid, 2007–2013: Findings from the Ex Post Evaluation of the Regional Aid Guidelines and Their Implementation in Twenty-Eight Investment Projects in Seven Member States

What are the general procedures and criteria for granting aid?

Regional aid schemes are designed in accordance with predefined development strategies identifying priority sectors, types of projects, and regions. Individual aid projects are generally evaluated against these schemes.

Granting authorities offer a variety of aid schemes, differing, for example, in terms of the types of eligible expenditures to be covered and the forms of aid to be provided.

Who decides whether to grant the aid, and what policy implications does that have?

Different authorities at different levels of government have authority to grant aid.

Where decisions are made at the subnational level, as opposed to national level, there appears to be an increased risk of a "race to the bottom."

What is the ex ante process prior to an incentives decision?

In no case is there evidence that ex ante project evaluation carefully considered the effect the incentive would have on an investment or location decision.

In terms of deciding on the amount of aid to be provided, practices differ significantly from one granting authority to another, with the most structured approach being in Poland and the least in Germany.

All granting authorities except for the Polish granting authority negotiate the level of the incentive provided. The bargaining power of the firm vis-à-vis the government is strengthened if (1) the potential value for the regional economy is high and (2) there is a high probability that, in the absence of the State aid, the investment will move to another country.

How much aid was given, and what were its terms?

The level of aid varied significantly from one case study to another, as did the extent to which awarded aid reached the maximum permitted level set by the EU's Regional Aid Guidelines.

In Ireland, Poland, and Slovakia, authorities made payment of aid conditional on the achievement of objectives relating to job creation. Ireland strictly applied the rules and refused to renegotiate when targets were not met, whereas Poland was more flexible and renegotiated at least one deal.

In Germany, Spain, and Portugal, there were examples of cases in which aid was fully paid even though the objectives were not completely achieved.

What is the connection between aid intensity[42] and incentive effect?

A low or nonexistent incentive effect translates into low or no value for money. High aid intensity is thus not be recommended for a project with a low incentive effect.

In all of the case studies examined except for the case of incentives given in Hungary for the cement industry, there was a link between the aid intensity and the incentive effect, with a low aid intensity for projects with low incentive effects.

Only one case study (the case of Hungarian incentives for investments in cement plants) clearly failed to provide value for money. There was a low incentive effect, and the projects promised little in the way of agglomeration effects or linkages. Nevertheless, authorities gave the projects a significant amount of aid.

Other aid was provided where there was little or no incentive effect (i.e., incentives for the development of business services in Poland and incentives for the pharmaceutical industry in Ireland), but the aid values were also low and tied to achievement of certain obligations, thus helping to link benefits (direct and indirect) to costs.

In two cases, there was a moderate incentive effect (i.e., incentives for the solar industry in Germany and incentives for the automobile industry in Hungary and Slovakia):

- The investment per job ranged from roughly 50,000 euros in the car industry in Slovakia and Hungary to 200,000 euros in the solar industry.
- In both cases, incentives reached the maximum amount of aid allowed under the relevant aid ceiling.

In Germany, there was an indication that there was a subsidy race within the country, though the aid ceilings likely prevented that from being a race to the bottom. If aid ceilings had been raised, the amount of the incentive might also have increased. If they had been lowered, however, the investment might have been lost to other potential locations in China and the United States.

What are the implications outside the jurisdiction of the granting authority?

The study reviewed the potential impacts of the incentives on the EU more broadly, noting that those effects are more challenging to gauge, particularly due to complexities in understanding whether jobs created in these areas using regional aid would result in job loss in other parts of Europe and/or strengthen the competitiveness of the relevant firms over time.

Source: Ramboll and Matrix 2012.

ENFORCEMENT

The EC has relatively significant powers to monitor compliance with its decisions and the State aid rules. It can conduct on-site monitoring relating to existing aid programs and review whether they continue to comply with relevant rules. In cases where a Member State has

1. Not notified the EC of the State aid and that aid is later determined to be incompatible with the common market or
2. Notified the EC of the State aid and obtained approval but implemented the aid in a manner contrary to the decision approving it,

the EC may order the Member to terminate the scheme and take all steps necessary to recover aid already granted.[43] It can also assess fines against Member States failing to recover incompatible aid.

To support the EC's ability to monitor and enforce compliance with State aid rules, EU law grants any "interested party" the right to inform the EC of any alleged unlawful aid and any alleged misuse of aid (European Council 1999). The definition of an *interested party* is broad, consisting of "any Member State and any person, undertaking or association of undertakings whose interests might be affected by the granting of aid, in particular the beneficiary of the aid, competing undertakings and trade associations" (European Council 1999). Through these provisions, the EC allows other government entities, companies, and stakeholders to instigate its investigative activities.

Decisions and orders by the EC, including decisions on whether to open an investigation after receiving a complaint from an interested party, decisions on whether aid is compatible with the common market, and orders to suspend or recover aid, can be appealed to the ECJ. The right to challenge the EC's decisions and orders to the ECJ belongs to any Member State as well as to any third party if the decision is of "direct and individual concern" to it (European Commission 2013a). This likely includes the beneficiary of the aid but can also be other individuals and entities such as competitors of the aid beneficiary (European Commission 2009, 2013a).

National courts do not have the authority to review compatibility of aid with the common market or hear appeals of the EC's decisions, but they do have the authority to order remedies (e.g., nonpayment or repayment of State aid) and to safeguard competitors and other third parties against unlawfully granted aid. National courts also are required under EU law to annul any act that the EC determines to be an unlawful grant of State aid and order recovery.[44]

This distribution of powers and obligations between national courts and the ECJ gives national courts an important role in enforcing EU law while also helping to ensure that EU law is not eroded de facto or de jure by national courts or officials that might be inclined to be more protective or forgiving of their domestic State aid measures.

CONCLUDING REMARKS ON EU STATE AID RULES ON INVESTMENT INCENTIVES

Although the EU is not the only regional international organization that has sought to regulate investment incentives (CCSI 2015), it has by far the most detailed rules relevant to the issue. It also has the most comprehensive system in place to monitor and enforce those rules, using the EC, "interested parties," and national and supranational courts to ensure compliance. Consequently, its laws and policies on State aid regulation seem to have been effective in reducing the amount of investment incentives given while also channeling those that are given toward predefined policy objectives of the European Community. Yet, as the EU shifts away from a system based on ex ante notification and approval and sweeps more types and greater volumes of aid within the GBER, it will become increasingly important for it to ensure there is robust ex post monitoring and enforcement of investment incentives to prevent abuse of the increased flexibilities.

Overall, there are gaps in the EU system's coverage, and policy flexibilities may be vulnerable to misuse. However, that system provides a useful model of how an international framework of incentives regulation among jurisdictions of different economic strengths and levels of development might work and highlights some of the ingredients—namely, the existence of overarching institutions that can enforce binding rules—that appear to be fundamental to its success.

BILATERAL AND MULTILATERAL INITIATIVES THROUGH IIAS AND NONINVESTMENT CHAPTERS IN FREE-TRADE AGREEMENTS: CURRENT PRACTICES

IIAS

OVERVIEW OF IIAS

International investment agreements (IIAs) are bilateral and multilateral treaties designed for the promotion and protection of international investment. Some IIAs are stand-alone treaties, dealing solely with international investment. Others are embedded as chapters within more comprehensive free-trade agreements. In those cases, the investment chapters are contained alongside chapters addressing issues such as trade in goods, trade in services, government procurement, and competition policy. Including both the stand-alone texts and the FTAs with investment chapters, states have signed over 3,000 IIAs to date and continue to conclude new ones.

IIAs commonly contain a core set of provisions. These are obligations on host states (1) to treat covered investors "fairly and equitably" (the FET obligation); (2) to treat foreign investors as favorably as similarly situated domestic investors (the national treatment obligation) and as favorably as similarly situated foreign investors from third states (the MFN obligation); (3) to abstain from direct or indirect expropriation except when done for a public purpose, in accordance with due process of law, and upon payment of compensation; and (4) to permit investors to freely transfer funds in and out of the host country. A small but growing share of investment treaties also contains a broader set of obligations, including (5) provisions on transparency that require governments to disclose actual and, in some agreements, proposed measures affecting investment and (6) restrictions on performance requirements that either incorporate or go beyond restrictions imposed under the TRIMs Agreement.

Whereas IIAs have traditionally offered protection only to foreign investment already within a state's borders, a growing number of them provide foreign investors rights to enter a foreign market and establish a commercial presence there. These types of provisions are included in the so-called mega-regional IIAs, such as the twelve-country Trans-Pacific Partnership (TPP) and the Trans-Atlantic Trade and Investment Partnership Agreement (TTIP) between the United States and EU, which, as of this writing, are being negotiated, and the agreement between Canada and the EU (Comprehensive Economic and Trade Agreement, or CETA) that was concluded in September 2014.

Another common feature of these treaties that distinguishes them from many other treaties relates to the issue of standing—that is, who has the right to enforce the treaty. Under WTO agreements like the TRIMs Agreement and the GATS, for example, only Member States are entitled to bring claims before WTO panels and the Appellate Body. In contrast, under IIAs, foreign investors can bring claims and seek damages before international tribunals based on alleged violations of IIA obligations. By giving foreign investors these powers to sue, host states open themselves to a greater number of complainants, and the obligations in IIAs gain important practical weight.

GENERAL CONNECTIONS BETWEEN IIAS AND INVESTMENT INCENTIVES

There are a number of connections between IIAs and investment incentives that make these instruments relevant and important to the issue of international governance of investment incentives. For one, both IIAs and investment incentives are instruments governments are using to attract investment and promote outward investment. As discussed in chapter 4 in this volume, investment treaties may even be seen as one form of investment incentive. Moreover, like investment incentives, IIAs trigger continuing policy debates as to whether they are effective in achieving their intended goals and, if effective, whether that result comes at too high a price. (In the case of IIAs, the price can consist of constrained domestic sovereignty, increased investor-state litigation, increased litigation costs, expanded liability, and negotiation costs.) IIAs also raise some of the same equity concerns as investment incentives, as the price paid by states as a result of IIAs can constitute a transfer of wealth from the public to the private interests protected by the treaties.

Another connection between IIAs and investment incentives is that, through their liberalization and free-transfer provisions, IIAs make it easier for companies not only to expand but also to move their existing investments across borders. This potentially exacerbates interjurisdictional competitions for capital, which, in turn, trigger increased offers of investment incentives.

Aside from those general commonalities and links, IIAs also have more direct—but arguably inconsistent—impacts on the use of incentives. As described further below, IIAs have provisions that can and, to a limited extent, already do regulate use of such supports and also have provisions that can effectively require and lock in the use of incentives.

One important caveat to the discussion below is that although issues and trends may be identified, little can be said about IIAs with absolute certainty. This is partly because, as noted above, there are roughly 3,000 IIAs that have been concluded and each instrument reflects a different negotiated outcome, contains different language, and may be understood differently by its state parties. The lack of certainty about the meaning and impact of IIAs is also due to the fact that different tribunals have been constituted in hundreds of different cases in order to decide the outcomes of particular investor-state disputes. In these disputes, the tribunals pronounce on the meaning of IIAs' core standards but are not required to follow any line of precedent and are not subject to any appellate mechanism. Consequently, decisions in investor-state arbitrations have taken notoriously divergent views of similar, if not identical, treaty provisions, making it challenging to say what the law under IIAs is. Nevertheless, one can at least identify how some have interpreted the law of IIAs and what those interpretations can mean for policy makers.

REGULATING INCENTIVES

Some IIA obligations can be used to restrict or regulate the use of investment incentives. These include (1) the national treatment and MFN obligations (together, the nondiscrimination obligations), (2) the nonlowering of standards provisions, (3) restrictions on performance requirements, and (4) transparency obligations.

NONDISCRIMINATION RESTRICTIONS IIAs' nondiscrimination obligations can restrict the use of selective incentives that favor one or more enterprises over others. Although some states and commentators have argued that discrimination must be intentional and on account of nationality in order to be prohibited, decisions like *Occidental v. Ecuador* and *Bayindir v. Pakistan* have taken the position that de facto and unintentional discrimination against an investor that "happens to be a foreigner" can also give rise to claims and liability.[45]

Notably, in contrast to similar restrictions imposed by the GATS, IIAs typically operate on a negative list rather than a positive list basis. As noted above, under the GATS, WTO Member States need to accord national treatment only to service sectors they have specifically scheduled. In IIAs, the national treatment obligation generally applies to all sectors unless a state has taken a reservation carving that sector out from the scope of its commitments.

Among their effects, the nondiscrimination obligations in IIAs may reduce the ability of governments to grant incentives through specifically negotiated investor-state contracts. One case addressing these issues is *Mesa v. Canada*. In that dispute, a U.S. investor alleged that Canada violated the IIA's nondiscrimination obligations when officials from the Canadian province of Ontario entered into a contract with a consortium of Korean companies, granting that consortium various preferences and advantages in exchange for the consortium's commitment to establish manufacturing and other facilities in the Canadian province. According to the U.S. investor, the contract with the Korean consortium established a "non-transparent and privileged legal and business micro-climate" from which the U.S. company was discriminatorily excluded (Johnson 2014). Canada, however, defended the investment incentives on the ground that they did not result in any discrimination between "like" investors. According to the government, the specific advantages given to the Korean consortium were due to the particular commitments those firms made to invest in the development of local industries. Other firms that are not bound to the same investment obligations are not entitled to receive the same benefits.

This case is notable because governments around the world similarly use specifically negotiated investment contracts in a range of sectors, granting fiscal, financial, and regulatory incentives ostensibly in exchange for investors' commitments to establish new manufacturing factories; invest in R&D; explore for, extract, and/or process natural resources; or undertake other activities. On the one hand, the specificity of these deals raises the risk that they may be deemed to improperly subject similar firms to different treatment and offer them different competitive opportunities. Yet, on the other hand, the specificity of the deals can be used to establish that a firm subject to one set of contractual obligations is not "like" and does not deserve the same treatment as a firm subject to different or no contractual obligations.

At the time of writing, *Mesa v. Canada* was still pending, so it is unknown how this tribunal and future tribunals will rule on such nondiscrimination claims. Nevertheless, the mere threat or launch of such claims may be enough to make governments hesitant to negotiate and provide incentives on a selective basis through individual investor-state contracts, particularly where it appears to result in similarly situated investors being accorded different treatment. This, in turn, may move investment incentives into a more law-based and less discretionary system, a development consistent with the recommendations of various commentators such as James in chapter 7 of this volume.

But there may be other troublesome effects. IIAs' nondiscrimination provisions can also potentially hinder governments' willingness and ability to provide incentives aiming to address and ameliorate issues of inequality by, for example, providing investment incentives only to minority-owned businesses or indigenous communities. To the extent that foreign investors are not able to access those incentives on the same terms, the use of those incentives may be challenged under the IIA's nondiscrimination obligations.

Overall, IIAs' nondiscrimination obligations have wide-ranging implications for incentives regulation. Their national treatment and MFN provisions may discourage the use of individually negotiated and selectively applied incentives, which could limit the use of excessive, unjustified, and discretionary contract-based incentive deals. But these provisions can also limit governments' abilities to use investment incentives as part of programs seeking to address policy objectives like combating the persisting effects of historical wrongs or inducing companies to make particular commitments to the development of the host economy.

RESTRICTIONS ON THE USE OF INVESTMENT INCENTIVES TIED TO PERFORMANCE REQUIREMENTS Similar to the restrictions imposed under WTO law, some IIAs contain provisions on performance requirements that prevent countries from conditioning investment incentives on compliance with certain requirements, including requirements to use or accord a preference to local goods, to achieve a particular level of domestic content, or to comply with trade-balancing requirements (CETA 2014). These restrictions are commonly phrased so that they apply to *all* investments, domestic or foreign, within the host state's territory, not just investments made by foreign investors from the treaty party.

Although these provisions are similar to the restrictions imposed under the TRIMs Agreement, GATT, and SCM Agreement, IIA provisions on investment incentives and performance requirements also differ in several significant ways. For one, as noted above, investors, and not just states, are entitled to bring claims for breach. There may be cases in which WTO Members would choose not to challenge another WTO Member's measure granting investment incentives contingent on compliance with local content requirements. If, however, an IIA with relevant restrictions on performance requirements is in place, an investor can bring a claim directly, whether to contest enforcement of the local content requirement or potentially to challenge the state's grant of a local-content-contingent investment incentive to a competitor firm. Through those expanded routes for enforcement actions, IIAs can strengthen controls on investment incentives.

Another difference is that IIAs' restrictions often go beyond those in the TRIMs Agreement. As explained above, the TRIMs Agreement prevents governments from requiring or conditioning incentives on compliance with measures that violate Articles III and XI of the GATT. Nevertheless, it leaves untouched a range of performance requirements—such as requirements to use or accord a preference to locally established service providers—along with the use of incentives in order to compensate for imposition of those requirements.[46]

Some IIAs add new restrictions, further limiting the types of performance requirements states can impose or can require as a prerequisite to obtaining government incentives. Article 6 of the IIA between Japan and Papua New Guinea, for example, prohibits each state party from making incentives contingent on requirements "to purchase, use or accord a preference to goods produced or services provided in its Area, or to purchase goods or services from natural or legal persons or any other entity in its Area."

Similarly, some IIAs prevent states from requiring or incentivizing compliance with domestic content requirements. When included in IIAs, the restrictions on domestic-content-contingent incentives are inserted in addition to restrictions on incentives contingent on the use of locally produced goods. This suggests that the term *domestic content* means something other than and additional to procurement or use of local goods and also bars incentives contingent on the use of domestic services, domestic labor, or other expenditures in the local economy. The precise meaning of the phrase is unclear, as IIAs restricting domestic content requirements generally do not define the term. Nevertheless, it appears likely that restrictions on requiring or incentivizing compliance with domestic content requirements bar more than just measures contingent on the use of local goods.

Some IIAs that contain restrictions on domestic content performance requirements do include exceptions clauses protecting the ability of governments to condition investment incentives on requirements to make certain domestic expenditures. These exceptions include commitments to invest in a particular location, carry out R&D in the government's territory, construct or expand facilities, and train or employ workers.

Overall, provisions on performance requirements in IIAs do not prevent governments from granting incentives, but they do limit governments' abilities to tie incentives to investor commitments to invest in the local economy. These restraints potentially make it difficult for states to follow policy recommendations, such as those proposed in chapters 8 and 9 in this volume, to better ensure that the incentives they grant result in sustainable development returns as opposed to wasteful giveaways.

RESTRICTIONS ON REGULATORY INCENTIVES Some IIAs restrict certain types of regulatory incentives in order to prevent races to the bottom in terms of environmental and social protections (Johnson and Sachs 2015). More specifically, a growing minority of IIAs include provisions stating that the contracting parties should not or must not reduce or fail to enforce environmental or labor standards in order to attract investment.

The 2012 U.S. Model Bilateral Investment Treaty (BIT), for instance, states in Article 12:

> The Parties recognize that it is inappropriate to encourage investment by weakening or reducing the protections afforded in domestic environmental laws. Accordingly, each Party shall ensure that it does not waive or otherwise derogate from or offer to waive or otherwise derogate from its environmental laws in a manner that weakens or reduces the protections afforded in those laws, or fail to effectively enforce those laws through a sustained or recurring course of action or inaction, as an encouragement for the establishment, acquisition, expansion, or retention of an investment in its territory.

In Article 13, the BIT includes similar language on labor:

> The Parties recognize that it is inappropriate to encourage investment by weakening or reducing the protections afforded in domestic labor laws. Accordingly, each Party shall ensure that it does not waive or otherwise derogate from or offer to waive or otherwise derogate from its labor laws where the waiver or derogation would be inconsistent with the labor rights referred to in subparagraphs (a) through (e) of paragraph 3, or fail to effectively enforce its labor laws through a sustained or recurring course of action or inaction, as an encouragement for the establishment, acquisition, expansion, or retention of an investment in its territory.

The treaties containing such provisions also typically include language ensuring that states' domestic environmental and labor laws do not fall below a set floor established by international standards and law.

These provisions could be important tools for ensuring that states do not, in their efforts to attract and retain capital, fail to enforce their environmental and labor laws or fail to maintain those laws at a level at or above international norms. But these obligations generally do not have the same force as other IIA provisions. In contrast to articles on standards of investment protection, which investors and investors' home states can enforce directly in investor-state arbitration or state-to-state arbitration, IIAs typically carve out these provisions from all or some of the investor-state and state-state dispute settlement mechanisms available under the treaty.[47]

Moreover, the types of races to the bottom targeted by these provisions are only a subset of the legal and regulatory races that can occur due to countries' efforts to attract and retain mobile capital. States may, for example, try to compete for investment by relaxing their rules on corporate governance or reducing transparency of financial transactions, moves that can have negative implications for corporate accountability and social welfare but that, to date, have not been directly addressed in IIAs.

REQUIREMENTS ON REGULATORY TRANSPARENCY A fourth way in which IIAs regulate the use of incentives is through provisions on regulatory transparency. Although these provisions are still absent from the majority of IIAs, they are increasingly being included and are increasingly detailed in their requirements.

Although they vary by IIA, these transparency provisions may require all levels and branches of government to disclose any actual or proposed laws, regulations, procedures, rulings, and decisions relating to investment (UNCTAD 2012b). These obligations thus can be used to mandate disclosure of certain programs and grants of investment incentives. As noted in chapter 11 of this volume, these types of provisions could do much to combat the problematic opacity surrounding the use of investment incentives. Yet, in addition to being found in only a minority of treaties, these transparency obligations are often carved out from all or some of the IIA's dispute settlement mechanisms. That narrows options for enforcement and reduces the strength of the transparency mandates.

EXCEPTIONS As noted briefly above, alongside the provisions that can control the use of various investment incentives, IIAs often contain various exceptions that narrow the impact of those restrictions. States, for example, have (1) specifically carved out subsidies and grants from the scope of their nondiscrimination obligations; (2) safeguarded measures in force at the time of the treaty's conclusion that might be inconsistent with the nondiscrimination obligations or restrictions on performance requirements; (3) inserted policy- or industry-related exceptions, such as exceptions for measures designed to accord preferences to socioeconomically disadvantaged groups, for measures targeted at achieving environmental aims, for government procurement, or for cultural industries; (4) carved out measures taken by local levels of government from the nondiscrimination requirements and restrictions on performance requirements; and (5) excluded or limited the IIAs' coverage of taxation measures.

Each of these exceptions can enable states to provide incentives otherwise barred or limited under the IIA and can be crucial for ensuring that states retain adequate policy space to achieve sustainable development outcomes.

Yet the scope and nature of these exceptions vary significantly from agreement to agreement and from country to country. In the IIA that entered into force between Canada and Ecuador in 1997, for example, Canada included an exception to the articles on national treatment, MFN treatment, and performance requirements, which states that those obligations do not apply to "any measure denying [Ecuadorean investors and their investments] any rights or preferences provided to aboriginal peoples of Canada."[48] Ecuador, however, did not include a similar carve-out for indigenous peoples in its territory.

Similarly, in a 2014 IIA concluded with Benin, Canada took several exceptions to its obligations under the national treatment, MFN treatment, and performance requirements provisions, including exceptions for measures relating to the "rights and preferences of aboriginal peoples" and the "rights and preferences of socially or economically disadvantaged minorities." Benin, in contrast, did not include exceptions to those obligations for similar policy aims.[49]

ENCOURAGING, REQUIRING, AND LOCKING IN HOST COUNTRY INCENTIVES

Alongside the provisions in IIAs that can limit the use of incentives, there are provisions that can lock in place incentives that governments do use. Moreover, in the treaties that contain restrictions on performance requirements, there are provisions that effectively require some type of incentive to be granted in order for certain performance requirements to be allowed.

LIABILITY FOR REMOVING OR REDUCING INCENTIVES Once incentives are provided, investment treaties may freeze them in effect, irrespective of their efficiency or effectiveness in meeting policy goals or shifts in the needs, priorities, and resources of governments. More specifically, after a government establishes an incentive program, it may wish to modify or eliminate that program if it runs into budget shortfalls, has to tackle new challenges and priorities, and/or determines that the incentives as designed or implemented are not efficient or effective. As tribunals have interpreted investment treaties, however, investment protection obligations including in particular, the FET obligation, may limit governments' abilities to amend or remove incentives programs once in place.

The reason IIAs may have this force is that tribunals have interpreted the FET obligation to protect investors' "legitimate expectations."

As various tribunals have declared, government interference with those legitimate expectations—whether that interference is through new court decisions; changes in relevant laws, regulations, or policies; or other measures—violates the FET obligation and subjects the government to claims and liability under its IIAs (UNCTAD 2012a; Dolzer 2014).

One factor that various tribunals have cited as influencing the existence and scope of legitimate expectations is whether the government took policy action or made implicit or explicit representations to the investor to induce its investment (Dolzer 2014). Because investment incentives by their design aim to have that incentive effect[50]—that is, to influence an investment decision—they will, by their very nature, arguably give rise to the types of legitimate expectations that are protected by IIAs from further government interference.

Notably, although an actual incentive effect is likely *sufficient* to give rise to a protected legitimate expectation, at least some tribunals' decisions indicate the incentive effect might not be strictly *necessary*. Some tribunals have stated that, in addition to the express or implied signals sent by the government to create the investor's legitimate expectations about a particular legal or business environment, the investor must establish that it acted in reliance on those signals. But notwithstanding those pronouncements, the decisions raise a host of questions regarding the exactness with which tribunals will actually enforce that reliance requirement. It is unclear, for instance, (1) whether tribunals will view reliance to be established upon a showing merely that the investment was ultimately made or upon proof that inducements or commitments were taken into account or were a factor in the investment decision or (2) whether tribunals will apply a stricter test, requiring proof that the investor would not have made the investment at issue (or would not have made it in the manner that it did) "but for" the inducement.

In the 2013 decision in *Micula v. Romania*, the tribunal took an approach that leans toward a relaxed requirement of reliance.[51] The tribunal stated that it was "evident from the record that [the claimants'] initial investments were not made in reliance" on the relevant incentives and that there were other factors influencing their decisions relating to operation and expansion of their investments.[52] Indeed, one of the claimants testified that the investment "made economic sense" even without the relevant incentives. The tribunal, however, ultimately concluded that the requirement of reliance was met, stating that "the Tribunal is satisfied that the existence of the incentives was one of the reasons for the scale and manner of those investments. It is evident from the record that the Claimants built a large and complex platform for the production of food and drink products, and that its profits depended largely on the reduction of their operating costs resulting from the Raw Materials Incentive." [53]

This decision suggests that there is a requirement that investment incentives be *a* factor in the investment decision but that they need not be *the* determinative factor. The decision also suggests that if an incentive increases profitability—an effect of incentives that is likely to be common—then that impact on profits weighs in support of finding reliance.

Each part of the tribunal's decision sets a low bar for establishing reliance and signals that investors can successfully sue states for revoking or reducing investment incentives even if those incentives were not crucial to or determinative of their investment decisions. Under this approach, governments may need to be concerned about breaching their IIA obligations even when seeking to narrow or remove superfluous or ineffective investment incentives.

Another notable and problematic aspect of the *Micula* decision for governments is the tribunal's determination that the claimants had enforceable "legitimate expectations" to benefit from the incentives over a ten-year period even though it was not clear that the claimants had such rights under domestic law. Romania had argued that, under its law, the investors did not have a "right" to receive the relevant incentives and that the government maintained power to modify or remove them. According to the tribunal, however, the question of whether the investors had vested rights to those incentives for a ten-year period under domestic law did not determine whether they had legitimate expectations under the IIA to receive them and likewise did not determine the government's liability under the treaty. Rather, the tribunal took the view that even if the government could legitimately remove or alter the incentives under the domestic legal framework pursuant to which the incentives were granted, a breach of the investment treaty could still be found. The tribunal proceeded to determine that Romania's removal of certain incentives did indeed violate the investor's legitimate expectations (though not necessarily its domestic legal rights) and consequently breached the FET obligation of the IIA.

These issues of whether the investors had legal rights to the incentives and whether Romania had the power to alter or modify them were especially important given Romania's accession to the EU, where such incentives could be, and were in fact, challenged as being inconsistent with

EU restrictions on State aid. Romania had contended that the investors could not have had legitimate expectations that Romania would maintain incentives the very legality of which was in dispute. The tribunal, however, did not agree that those questions of consistency with EU law defeated the legitimacy of the investor's expectations. Thus, in its decision dated December 11, 2013, the tribunal ordered Romania to pay the claimants roughly 82 million euros as compensation for the withdrawn incentives.

That decision triggered a prompt and adverse reaction by the EC. On January 31, 2014, it informed Romanian officials that any payment of money in accordance with the tribunal's award would constitute new State aid that would have to be notified to the EC. Weeks later, Romanian authorities notified the EC that the government had partially complied with the award by forgiving roughly 76 million euros in tax debt owed by the claimants to Romania (European Commission 2014h).

In March 2015, the EC announced it had finished its investigation of whether Romania's payment of the arbitration award was illegal State aid. It concluded that it was in fact illegal and declared that the investors would "have to pay back all amounts already received, which are equivalent to those granted by the abolished aid scheme" (European Commission 2015). With that EC decision, State aid rules and international investment law are at apparent odds, with no clear path for reconciling the legal regimes.

Because tribunals are not bound by precedent in investor-state arbitration, it is impossible to predict whether future cases will follow the *Micula* tribunal's reasoning and approach to liability for removal of (inefficient and illegal) investment incentives. Indeed, even the issue of whether legitimate expectations deserve protection under investment treaties is not a settled matter in investment law.

Nevertheless, it is clear that these issues will be examined in other cases, as a number of other investment treaty claims have already been filed to challenge government actions to withdraw or modify incentives. As of October 1, 2014, roughly twenty cases had been filed by investors against EU Member States alone relating to their decisions to reduce or eliminate incentives for the renewable energy industry (Peterson 2014). Similarly, other actions have been brought to challenge government efforts to collect back taxes and penalties as a result of investors misusing or abusing incentives programs through transfer pricing and other strategies.[54] Even if not ultimately successful, these cases can be costly for governments to defend and may have a chilling effect on governments, making them reluctant to change unwise or costly incentives programs. Consequently, if the *Micula* approach is followed, IIAs may hinder otherwise advisable review and reform of incentives schemes.

LIABILITY FOR INFORMATIONAL AND PROMOTIONAL INCENTIVES In addition to holding governments liable under IIAs for withdrawing or modifying fiscal and financial incentives, tribunals have determined that governments can be liable for acting inconsistently with commitments or signals generated by promotional activities.

In a 2015 award against Canada in *Bilcon v. Canada*, for instance, the majority of the tribunal reasoned that the actions taken by provincial officials to attract investment generally and to encourage investment by the claimants in that case in particular were factors that led to the government's ultimate liability under the relevant IIA. According to the majority's approach, the government's conduct—namely, its general policy and publications welcoming investment in mining and advertising the province as "open for business," its actions providing the relevant investors promotional materials regarding possible opportunities for investment in mining, its practices of holding meetings with the relevant investors on various occasions, and its taking of the investors' geological expert on a helicopter ride to explore potential mining sites—gave rise to legitimate expectations by the investors that, once breached, led to Canada's liability under the IIA.[55]

The majority decision, although not binding precedent, suggests a possible heightened standard of care for governments and consequent liabilities that can be generated by investment promotion activities, sending investment promotion agencies and other government officials a signal to exercise caution when adopting what might otherwise be considered sound and cost-effective investment attraction strategies.

INCENTIVES REQUIRED FOR SOME PERFORMANCE REQUIREMENTS As noted above, some IIAs prevent governments from (1) imposing mandatory performance requirements on foreign investors, such as requirements to procure or favor local providers of goods or services, and (2) making receipt of investment incentives or other advantages contingent on fulfillment of performance requirements. The types of performance requirements covered by the first category (mandatory performance requirements) are typically broader than those covered by the second category (those for which compliance is required in order to obtain an incentive or advantage). Consequently, some performance requirements are permitted under IIAs only if the government offers an incentive or other advantage in exchange for compliance.

As in the CETA (2014) and US-CAFTA-DR (2004),[56] performance requirements that IIAs appear to commonly put in this category of measures that may be imposed only if made contingent on incentives or advantages include requirements to transfer technology, a production process, or other proprietary knowledge to a legal or natural person in its territory.

By mandating that certain performance requirements can be imposed only if rewarded through an incentive or other advantage, IIAs potentially increase the cost of those requirements to governments as well as increasing the use of incentives. Although some jurisdictions may already be compensating investors for costs of complying with performance requirements by granting incentives, these types of provisions make doing so mandatory.

OTHER CHAPTERS OF FREE-TRADE AGREEMENTS

The section above discussed provisions in stand-alone investment treaties as well as in investment chapters in FTAs. But other chapters of FTAs also contain provisions relevant to the use and international regulation of investment incentives. Some of these provisions appear in chapters on trade in goods and trade in services that elaborate on and may also deepen commitments under the WTO. Other relevant chapters are those on transparency, environmental issues, and labor issues, which are similar to but tend to be more detailed and stronger than the transparency and the non-lowering-of-standards provisions in IIAs.

Beyond those chapters, some FTAs contain other relevant obligations. These include controls on competition or subsidies and commitments to cooperate on promoting sustainable investment.

PROVISIONS ON COMPETITION AND SUBSIDIES

Some FTAs—including, in particular, the FTAs concluded by the EU with third states—have provisions on subsidies that are contained in dedicated subsidies chapters or in chapters on competition.

In the FTA between the EU and Singapore, for example, negotiations on which were concluded in 2013, the parties included restrictions on subsidies in the agreement's competition chapter. That chapter notes that it adopts the definition of *subsidies* contained in the SCM Agreement but expands it to cover subsidies relating to trade in goods *and* services. In Article 12.7, it prohibits two types of subsidies (unless the government providing the subsidy can demonstrate that the subsidy does not affect trade of the other treaty party and is not likely to do so): (1) certain subsidies in which the government or public body commits to cover the debts or liabilities of undertakings and (2) certain subsidies provided to support insolvent or ailing undertakings.[57]

The parties to the EU-Singapore FTA also agreed in Article 12.8 to "use their best efforts to remedy or remove . . . distortions of competition caused by other specific subsidies related to trade in goods and services which are not covered by Article 12.7 (Prohibited Subsidies), insofar as they affect or are likely to affect trade of either Party, and to prevent the occurrence of such situations." In Annex 12-A, the parties explain that such subsidies should, in principle, not be granted. But, the annex continues, the subsidies may be provided if "necessary to achieve an objective of public interest, and when the amounts of the subsidies involved are limited to the minimum needed to achieve this objective and their effect on trade of the other Party is limited." Annex 12-A then sets out a list of objectives that can justify these subsidies. The list is similar to the categories of State aid that may be permitted under EU law, including subsidies to promote economic development of areas where standards of living are abnormally low or where there is serious underemployment and subsidies for environmental purposes, SMEs, and R&D.

With respect to compliance and enforcement, the agreement imposes disclosure requirements designed to encourage and ensure adherence to its subsidies controls but permits states to initiate dispute settlement under the treaty only to challenge the grant of subsidies prohibited under Article 12.7, not to allege breach of Article 12.8 or noncompliance with the disclosure obligations.

The EU's agreement with Canada (CETA 2014) likewise includes provisions on subsidies but is narrower and weaker. Its chapter on subsidies defines *subsidies* as measures relating to trade in goods (but not services) meeting the definition of a *subsidy* under the SCM Agreement. The chapter contains no specific categories of prohibited subsidies and no agreement to use "best efforts" to remove "other subsidies." Rather, the chapter focuses on using disclosure requirements and obligations to engage in "informal consultations" in order to address concerns that subsidies granted by one party adversely affect the interests of the other.[58]

These two agreements illustrate that, at least in some FTAs, chapters on competition and subsidies are being used to control the use of incentives beyond the multilateral restraints imposed under the WTO while also including protections not available under the WTO's SCM Agreement. Such bilateral, regional, or mega-regional solutions to the issue could be an important and feasible way forward. As these agreements further liberalize and encourage cross-border capital flows, it seems natural that government entities such as the EU that have internal restrictions on the use of investment incentives would seek to extend those rules to their treaty parties. The risk for the EU of not doing so is that its internal restrictions on the use of location and other incentives could put its Member States at a disadvantage when competing with treaty parties for investments, particularly when those treaty parties offer comparable possible locations. Moreover, countries entering into treaties with such rules could use those international commitments as a way to regulate subnational competition.

Yet one very real issue that arises through negotiation of these instruments is that of special and differential obligations. The WTO's rules contain certain flexibilities for developing and least developed countries. Similarly, the EU's State aid scheme takes into account and aims to combat disparities in income levels among and within EU Member States. In contrast, the rules that have developed in IIAs are much stricter and less responsive to developmental needs and differences. As noted above, many IIAs contain restrictions on performance requirements that go beyond the restrictions imposed under the WTO. The measures prohibited by these "WTO+" restrictions in IIAs could be used to encourage linkages between foreign investments and the domestic economy and to harness benefits from FDI; yet those WTO+ rules are often not accompanied by WTO+ or even WTO-equivalent flexibilities for countries based on their levels of development. Moreover, the author is not aware of any IIA that contains any provision like that which can be found in the EU regime that restricts the use of investment incentives offered by high-income countries or subnational jurisdictions while allowing lower-income areas additional policy space to use those tools.

CHAPTERS ON COOPERATION FOR SUSTAINABLE DEVELOPMENT

Some relatively modern FTAs contain chapters or articles on sustainable development that provide restraints on certain types of incentives and/or encouragement for others. Article 13.11 of the EU-Singapore FTA's trade and sustainable development chapter includes both of these elements—discouraging (albeit weakly) fossil fuel subsidies and encouraging investment to promote a shift to a low-carbon economy. It states:

> The Parties recognise the need to ensure that, when developing public support systems for fossils fuels, proper account is taken of the need to reduce greenhouse gas emissions and to limit distortions of trade as much as possible. While subparagraph (2)(b) of Article 12.7 (Prohibited Subsidies) does not apply to subsidies to the coal industry, the Parties share the goal of progressively reducing subsidies for fossil fuels. Such a reduction may be accompanied by measures to alleviate the social consequences associated with the transition to low carbon fuels. In addition, both Parties will actively promote the development of a sustainable and safe low-carbon economy, such as investment in renewable energies and energy efficient solutions.

Agreements the EU has concluded with developing countries in the African, Caribbean, and Pacific (ACP) regions, including the framework Cotonou Agreement (2010), similarly address the use of incentives as a policy tool for catalyzing and channeling investment. The agreements contemplate EU financial assistance (e.g., insurance and guarantees) as well as other forms of assistance (e.g., capacity building and technical support) to catalyze outward private investment by European companies in ACP territories and enterprises.

These types of provisions represent a new generation in FTAs, harnessing the rules on international economic governance to encourage investment that is consistent with sustainable development objectives while discouraging investment that is not.

CONCLUSION AND WAYS FORWARD

As shown above, there are various international economic treaties that govern, in some way, the use of investment incentives. However, this patchwork of international agreements is inadequate to send appropriate signals consistent with modern sustainable development objectives and to prevent the competition for capital that is occurring in an increasingly globalized world.

WTO agreements—which were crafted to govern international trade in goods and services—contain rules that are relevant for, but not designed to address, the needs for and challenges of sound policies for investment attraction. Consequently, a regional, not global, framework currently provides the most robust regime for governing investment incentives. This framework can be found in the EU, where a supranational institution sets the rules, possesses significant authority, and enlists other actors such as taxpayers, the private sector, and national courts to assist with monitoring and enforcement. Moreover, the system is designed to allow states to use incentives to accomplish specific EU-approved policy aims.

Expanding the EU framework or one similar to it on a global basis would be a daunting task. Nevertheless, with states worldwide engaged in negotiations to create comprehensive IIA regimes to govern international investment, it is a particularly appropriate time to think carefully about the scope of those regimes and how rules providing strong protections for foreign investors and increasing liberalization can and should interact with the use of incentives. As discussed above, the increased liberalization can increase competition for capital and, with it, the use of incentives, and the rules on investor protections can prevent states from reforming their costly, inefficient, outdated, or improper incentives. As a result, IIAs may exacerbate existing problems with investment incentives and undermine domestic attempts to rein in government giveaways.

At the same time, other provisions in IIAs already do regulate investment incentives to some extent, and there is work by negotiators of the TPP and other agreements to reduce government subsidies to state-owned enterprises and to fossil fuels. The task for IIA negotiators is therefore not to embark on rule making in an area tangential to IIAs' policy focus; rather, they merely need to ensure the consistency of IIAs' approach to and impacts on incentives policy and to strengthen IIAs' ability to regulate incentives effectively. Even modest steps such as antipoaching rules or strengthened transparency requirements in mega-regional IIAs such as the TPP and TTIP could have significant impacts, particularly if the agreements provide for monitoring and enforcement mechanisms and establish an independent supranational institution to ensure implementation.

Policy coherence requires governments to consider the investment-related issues of liberalization, incentives, and protection in a holistic manner and establish legal frameworks that ensure new international controls in one area do not undermine efforts in another. New international controls on investment incentives should also recognize and safeguard the ability of those tools to be used in certain circumstances to overcome market failures and help achieve sustainable development goals while, as is done in the EU regime, taking into account the varying needs and capabilities of different jurisdictions based on their level of development.

Other potential channels for modern regulation of investment incentives include the ongoing negotiation of the Trade in Services Agreement (TISA) and the negotiation of instruments on climate change. Although rules would likely not be as comprehensive as they could be under an IIA or an FTA with an investment chapter stretching across sectors and activities, provisions in the TISA or a climate change agreement could benefit from being more tailored and specific.

Of course, including investment incentives on the negotiating agenda for any of these agreements may not be easy. But growing recognition of the harmfulness of incentives competition and the need to be particularly strategic in the use of public funds in light of the sustainable development challenges facing the world today may finally provide the necessary impetus for action.

NOTES

1. As other chapters have illustrated, this can be a challenging task.

2. Grants, loans, and equity infusions are specifically mentioned in the SCM Agreement (Article 1.1[a][1][i]); other types of direct transfers have been identified in WTO decisions (see, e.g., Panel Report, Korea—Measures Affecting Trade in Commercial Vessels, paras. 7.411–7.413, 7.420, WT/DS273/R [March 7, 2005]; Panel Report, European Communities and Certain Member States—Measures Affecting Trade in Large Civil Aircraft, para. 7.1318, WT/DS316/R [June 30, 2010]).

3. Another item that might fit in this category is an economic equilibrium clause, a type of stabilization clause in which the government promises to compensate a company for changes in the legal framework that increase the company's cost of doing business.

4. In *U.S.—Large Civil Aircraft (2nd complaint)*, the Appellate Body upheld the panel's previous determination that by reducing the tax rate applicable to commercial aircraft and component manufacturers, a U.S. state forewent revenue otherwise due (Appellate Body Report, Measures Affecting Trade in Large Civil Aircraft (Second Complaint), paras. 801-31, WT/DS353/AB/R [March 12, 2012]).

5. In *U.S.—Carbon Steel (India)*, the WTO Appellate Body upheld the panel's finding that the grant of a mining lease by the government of India was "provision" of a good within the meaning of the SCM Agreement (Appellate Body Report, US—Countervailing Measures on Certain Hot-Rolled Carbon Steel Flat Products from India, paras. 4.60–4.75, WT/DS436/AB/R [December 8, 2014]).

6. A WTO panel made this finding in *Canada—Renewable Energy/Feed-in Tariff Program* (Panel Report, Canada—Renewable Energy/Feed-In Tariff Program, paras. 7.194–7.249, WT/DS412/R; WT/DS426/R [December 19, 2012]). The WTO's Appellate Body upheld that on appeal (Appellate Body Report, Canada—Measures Relating to the Feed-In Tariff Program, paras. 5.122–5.128, WT/DS412/AB/R; WT/DS426 /AB/R [May 6, 2013]).

7. The WTO Appellate Body addressed this issue in United States—Final Countervailing Duty Determination with Respect to Certain Softwood Lumber from Canada, WT/DS257/AB/R (adopted February 17, 2004).

8. In Canada—Certain Measures Affecting the Renewable Energy Generation Sector, WT/DS412/AB/R, WT/DS426/R (May 6, 2013), the Appellate Body elaborated on how to identify the relevant "market benchmark." Notably, it held that the relevant benchmark can be a government-created market and stated that "where a government creates a market, it cannot be said that the government intervention distorts the market." Id. at para. 5.188.

9. Appellate Body Report, European Communities and Certain Member States—Measures Affecting Trade in Large Civil Aircraft, paras. 969–83, WT/DS316/AB/R (May 18, 2011).

10. Consideration of the factors in Article 2.1(b), however, is not necessarily conclusive. Even if a subsidy has the appearance of nonspecificity based on the principles set forth in Article 2.1(b), Article 2.1(c) clarifies that it may nevertheless be found to be specific based on consideration of other factors.

11. Appellate Body Report, European Communities—Large Civil Aircraft, para. 140.

12. Panel Report, United States—Measures Affecting Trade in Large Civil Aircraft, para. 7.1764, WT/DS353/R (March 31, 2011).

13. Id.

14. Id. at para. 7.1760.

15. Id.

16. Appellate Body Report, United States—Measures Affecting Trade in Large Civil Aircraft, paras. 960–1012, WT/DS353/AB/R (March 12, 2012).

17. Panel Report, United States—Large Civil Aircraft, para. 7.1433.

18. The Trade Policy Review Mechanism was established during the Uruguay Round of negotiations that established the WTO (Trade Policy Review Mechanism, annex 3, April 15, 1994, 1869 U.N.T.S. 480).

19. For prohibited subsidies, the countermeasures must be "appropriate." For actionable subsidies, the countermeasures are to be "commensurate."

20. As some scholars have highlighted, the differences between the two options have important implications. In particular, whereas unilateral trade remedies may provide states and their domestic industries faster and more direct relief from injuries

caused by illegal subsidies, they also may be more vulnerable to political influence, can create inconsistencies and uncertainty in interpretation and application of trade law, and may increase the cost of socially and environmental beneficial goods (e.g., wind turbines and solar panels) produced by subsidized investments irrespective of the public purpose of the subsidy (Wu and Salzman 2014).

21. WTO Members (through the Committee on Subsidies and Countervailing Agreement established in the SCM Agreement) had the option to but did not renew these Article 8 protections.

22. At the end of 2013, non-LDC countries in this Annex VII category included Bolivia, Cameroon, Congo, Côte d'Ivoire, Ghana, Guyana, Honduras, India, Indonesia, Kenya, Nicaragua, Nigeria, Pakistan, Senegal, Sri Lanka, and Zimbabwe (WTO 2014).

23. Examples of such disputes include the case brought by the United States against China relating to production of wind power equipment (Request for Consultations by the United States, China—Measures Concerning Wind Power Equipment, WT /DS419/1 [January 6, 2011]) and the complaint brought by Japan and the EU against Canada referred to in the text, which relates to Ontario's FIT program (Request for Consultations by Japan, Canada—Certain Measures Affecting the Renewable Energy Generation Sector, WT/DS412/1 [September 16, 2010]; Request for Consultations by the European Union, Canada—Measures Relating to the Feed-in Tariff Program, WT/DS426/1 [August 16, 2011]). Wu and Salzman (2014) profile these and other cases.

24. Panel Report, Canada—Certain Measures Affecting the Renewable Energy Generation Sector, paras. 7.163–7.167, WT/DS412/R, WT/DS426/R (December 19, 2012).

25. Appellate Body Report, Canada—Certain Measures Affecting the Renewable Energy Generation Sector, WT/DS412/AB/R, WT/DS426/R (May 6, 2013).

26. The GATS classifies trade in services as occurring through four different modes of supply. Mode 1 is "cross-border trade" (e.g., a consumer in country A receives services from country B), mode 2 is "consumption abroad" (e.g., nationals from country A travel to country B to consume services in country B), mode 3 is "commercial presence" (e.g., a company of country A establishes an affiliate in country B to provide services in that country), and mode 4 is "presence of natural persons" (e.g., a national of country B moves to country A and supplies services within country A as a consultant or an employee).

27. The default rule does not apply if a Member has listed a relevant exemption from the MFN treatment obligation or if a Member has given "advantages to adjacent countries in order to facilitate exchanges limited to contiguous frontier zones of services that are both locally produced and consumed" (Article II[3]).

28. Countries may discriminate between services and service suppliers that are not "like." Thus, answering the question of whether services or service suppliers are "like" is a crucial part of the broader question of whether a measure violates the GATS' MFN treatment and national treatment obligations.

29. In theory, the national treatment provision could prevent governments from granting incentives to service suppliers located in their territories if similar supports are not provided to service suppliers located overseas and supplying services through another mode. However, as indicated by paragraph 15 of the Guidelines for the Scheduling of Specific Commitments Under the General Agreement on Trade in Services, the GATS' national treatment provision does not go that far: "There is no obligation in the GATS

which requires a Member to take measures outside its territorial jurisdiction. It therefore follows that the national treatment obligation in Article XVII does not require a Member to extend such treatment to a service supplier located in the territory of another Member." (Guidelines for the Scheduling of Specific Commitments Under the General Agreement on Trade in Services, para. 15, WTO Document S/L/92 [March 28, 2001]).

30. Panel Report, Canada—Certain Measures Affecting the Automotive Industry, para. 10.291, WT/DS139/R, WT/DS142/R [February 11, 2000].

31. Id. at para. 10.292.

32. As noted above, mode 1 is "cross-border trade" (e.g., a consumer in country A receives services from country B), mode 2 is "consumption abroad" (e.g., nationals from country A travel to country B to consume services in country B), mode 3 is "commercial presence" (e.g., a company of country A establishes an affiliate in country B to provide services in that country), and mode 4 is "presence of natural persons" (e.g., a national of country B moves to country A and supplies services within country A as a consultant or an employee).

33. More recently, the panel in *China—Certain Measures Affecting Electronic Payment Services* came to a similar conclusion, stating: "Furthermore, in the particular circumstances of this case, we do not see how our conclusion on 'likeness' of services could be different depending on whether EPS suppliers of other Members supply EPS through mode 1 or through mode 3" (Panel Report, China—Certain Measures Affecting Electronic Payment Services, para. 7.704, WT/DS413/R [July 16, 2012]). Although service suppliers based in different locations can be "like," the GATS—in footnote 10 to the national treatment provision—also recognizes that the article does not require "any Member to compensate for any inherent competitive disadvantages which result from the foreign character of the relevant services or service suppliers."

34. Article 1:3(c) defines a service "supplied in the exercise of governmental authority" as a service "which is supplied neither on a commercial basis, nor in competition with one or more service suppliers." As Krajewski (2003) and Lang (2004) have pointed out, this provision leaves many unanswered questions regarding the precise scope of the GATS.

35. Unlike the GATT, the GATS does not include an exception for measures "relating to the conservation of natural resources."

36. As used in this chapter, the ECJ includes two different courts, the General Court and the Court of Justice. Judgments of the General Court can be appealed to the Court of Justice.

37. If subsidies distort competition among EU firms in third markets, they can potentially constitute illegal State aid even if the subsidies don't actually affect intra-EU trade. This possibility was noted in paragraph 196 of the EC's *XXVIIIth Report on Competition Policy* (European Commission 1998).

38. Article 109 of the TFEU gives the European Council the authority to exempt certain types of aid from the requirements for prior notification and approval.

39. An *aid scheme* is "any act on the basis of which, without further implementing measures being required, individual aid awards may be made to undertakings defined within the act in a general and abstract manner and any act on the basis of which aid which is not linked to a specific project may be awarded to one or several undertakings for an indefinite period of time and/or for an indefinite amount" (European Council 1999).

40. Disclosures of tax relief may be treated differently than other types of State aid, with disclosures listing the range of tax relief granted, as opposed to the exact amount (European Commission 2014a).

41. The Regional Aid Guidelines are issued by the EC in order to facilitate and govern grants of State aid under Article 107(3)(a) and (c) of the TFEU. These guidelines are periodically revised. During the Ramboll and Matrix study, the 2007–2013 guidelines were in force.

42. *Aid intensity* is a measurement of aid that looks at the amount of the aid as a percentage of the total investment. EU law sets forth specific rules on how aid intensity is to be calculated and what levels of aid intensity are permissible. Those levels can vary based on a range of factors, including the location of the investment, the nature of the investment project, and the size of the beneficiary (European Commission 2014c).

43. There are some limits on these recovery orders. Recovery need not be done if it would violate a general principle of European Community law (Luengo Hernandez de Madrid 2007, 403–404).

44. There are only very exceptional circumstances in which it would be inappropriate for a court to order recovery of unlawful aid (European Commission 2009).

45. Occidental Petroleum Corporation and Occidental Exploration and Production Company v. The Republic of Ecuador, ICSID Case No. ARB/06/11 (October 5, 2012); Bayindir Insaat Turizm Ticaret Ve Sanayi A.S. v. Islamic Republic of Pakistan, ICSID Case No. ARB/03/29, Award (August 27, 2009).

46. As discussed in the text above, those types of requirements favoring locally established service providers may violate the GATS.

47. In Articles 12 and 13, the 2012 U.S. Model BIT, quoted above, requires only that the states consult with each other regarding issues arising under those articles and affirms that states may (but are not required to) "provide opportunities for public participation regarding" relevant matters. The obligations regarding labor and the environment are not subject to mechanisms for investor-state dispute settlement or state-state dispute settlement.

48. Agreement Between the Government of Canada and the Government of the Republic of Ecuador for the Promotion and Reciprocal Protection of Investments, Can.-Ecuador, art. VI(2), April 29, 1996, 2027 U.N.T.S. 195.

49. Agreement Between the Government of Canada and the Government of the Republic of Benin for the Promotion and Reciprocal Protection of Investments, Can.-Benin, annex II, January 8, 2014, 2014 Can. T.S. No. 2014/13.

50. Within the context of EU State aid law, there are detailed criteria regarding how to establish an incentive effect, which is required in order for the State aid to be allowed. This section uses the term more generally to refer to situations in which an incentive influences an investment decision.

51. Ioan Micula, Viorel Micula, S.C. European Food S.A, S.C. Starmill S.R.L. and S.C. Multipack S.R.L. v. Romania, ICSID Case No. ARB/05/20, Final Award (December 11, 2013). As of the time of this writing, that decision was being challenged through the annulment procedures available under the Convention on the Settlement of Investment Disputes Between States and Nationals of Other States, dated March 18, 1965.

52. Ioan Micula, Viorel Micula, S.C. European Food S.A, S.C. Starmill S.R.L. and S.C. Multipack S.R.L. v. Romania, 194–95.

53. Id. at 195.

54. Yukos Universal Ltd. v. The Russian Federation, Case No. AA 227, Final Award (Perm. Ct. of Arb. 2014), http://www.italaw.com/sites/default/files/case-documents/italaw3279.pdf.

55. Bilcon v. Canada, Case No. 2009–04 (Perm. Ct. of Arb. 2015), Award on Jurisdiction and Liability, 131–43, 177–79, http://www.italaw.com/sites/default/files/case-documents/italaw4212.pdf.

56. The parties to the latter treaty are Costa Rica, the Dominican Republic, El Salvador, Guatemala, Honduras, Nicaragua, and the United States.

57. According to Article 12.7(4), this provision does not apply to subsidies "granted as compensation for carrying out public service obligations and subsidies to the coal industry."

58. The disclosure and consultation requirements apply to subsidies affecting trade in goods as well as trade in services.

REFERENCES

Agreement on Subsidies and Countervailing Measures (SCM) (Marrakesh, April 15, 1994), 1869 UNTS 14.

Agreement on Trade-Related Investment Measures (TRIMS) (Marrakesh, April 15, 1994), 1868 UNTS 186.

Aguayo Ayala, F., and K. P. Gallagher. 2005. "Preserving Policy Space for Sustainable Development." *IISD Commentary*, 2–3.

Bhala, R., D. A. Gantz, S. B. Keating, and B. G. Simoes. 2013. "WTO Case Review 2012." *Arizona Journal of International and Comparative Law* 30: 207–419.

——. 2014. "WTO Case Review 2013." *Arizona Journal of International and Comparative Law* 31: 475–510.

Brewster, R. 2011. "The Remedy Gap: Institutional Design, Retaliation, and Trade Law Enforcement." *George Washington Law Review* 80: 102.

CCSI. 2015. "Investment Incentives: The Good, the Bad and the Ugly." *2013 Columbia International Investment Conference Report.* New York: Columbia Center on Sustainable Investment.

CETA. 2014. Comprehensive Economic and Trade Agreement (Canada-European Union), http://ec.europa.eu/trade/policy/in-focus/ceta/.

Consolidated Version of the Treaty on the Functioning of the European Union (May 9, 2008), 2008 OJ (C 115) 47.

Coppens, D. 2014. *WTO Disciplines on Subsidies and Countervailing Measures: Balancing Policy Space and Legal Constraints.* Cambridge: Cambridge University Press.

Dolzer, R. "Fair and Equitable Treatment: Today's Contours." *Santa Clara Journal of International Law* 12: 7–33.

European Commission. 1999. *XXVIIIth Report on Competition Policy 1998.* Brussels: European Communities. http://ec.europa.eu/competition/publications/annual_report/1999/en.pdf.

——. 2009. Commission Notice on the Enforcement of State Aid Law by National Courts. Official Journal C 85, 9.4.2009.

——. 2013a. Commission Regulation (EC) No 1407/2013 of 18 December 2013 on the Application of Articles 107 and 108 of the Treaty on the Functioning of the European Union to De Minimis Aid. Official Journal L 352, 24.12.2013.

——. 2013b. *State Aid Manual of Procedures: Internal DG Competition Working Documents on Procedures for the Application of Articles 107 and 108 TFEU*. July 10, 2013, rev. ed. Luxembourg: European Union.

——. 2014a. "State Aid Transparency for Taxpayers." *Competition Policy Brief*, issue 4 (May).

——. 2014b. Commission Staff Working Document: Common Methodology for State Aid Evaluation. SWD(2014)179 final.

——. 2014c. Communication from the Commission Amending the Communications from the Commission on EU Guidelines for the Application of State Aid Rules in Relation to the Rapid Deployment of Broadband Networks, on Guidelines on Regional State Aid for 2014–2020, on State Aid for Films and Other Audiovisual Works, on Guidelines on State Aid to Promote Risk Finance Investment and on Guidelines on State Aid to Airports and Airlines, Brussels. Official Journal C 198, 27.6.2014.

——. 2014d. European Commission Regulation (EU) No 651/2014 of 17 June 2014 Declaring Certain Categories of Aid Compatible with the Internal Market in Application of Articles 107 and 108 of the Treaty. Official Journal L 187, 26.6.2014.

——. 2014e. "Guidelines on Regional State Aid for 2014–2020." *Competition Policy Brief 14*. http://ec.europa.eu/competition/publications/cpb/2014/014_en.pdf.

——. 2014f. Memo, State Aid: Commission Adopts New General Block Exemption Regulation (GBER). 21.05.2014.

——. 2014g. Press Release, State Aid: Commission Exempts More Aid Measures from Prior Notification. 05.21.2014.

——. 2014h. State Aid SA.38517 (2014/C) (ex 2014/NN)—Implementation of Arbitral Award Micula v Romania of 11 December 2013: Invitation to Submit Comments Pursuant to Article 108(2) of the Treaty on the Functioning of the European Union. Official Journal, C 393, 7.11.2014.

——. 2013i. "State Aid Scoreboard 2014: Non-crisis Aid." http://ec.europa.eu/competition/state_aid/scoreboard/non_crisis_en.html.

——. 2015. Press Release, State Aid: Commission Orders Romania to Recover Incompatible State Aid Granted in Compensation for Abolished Investment Aid Scheme. 30.03.2015.

European Council. 1999. Council Regulation (EC) No 659/1999 of 22 March 1999 Laying Down Detailed Rules for the Application of Article 93 of the EC Treaty. Official Journal L 83, 27.3.1999.

General Agreement on Tariffs and Trade (GATT) (Marrakesh, April 15, 1994), 1867 UNTS 187.

General Agreement on Trade in Services (GATS) (Marrakesh, April 15, 1994), 1869 UNTS 183.

General Council. 2007. "Article 27.4 of the Agreement on Subsidies and Countervailing Measures—Decision of July 27, 2007." WT/L/691, July 31.

Green, A. 2006. "Trade Rules and Climate Change Subsidies." *World Trade Review* 5: 404–10.

Horlick, G. N. 2010. "WTO Subsidies Discipline During and After the Crisis." *Journal of International Economic Law* 13: 859.

Howse, R. 2010. *Climate Mitigation Subsidies and the WTO Legal Framework: A Policy Analysis.* Winnipeg: International Institute for Sustainable Development.

Johnson, L. 2014. "In New Filing, US Investor Alleges that Favourable Canadian Energy Pact Granted to a Korean Consortium Breaches NAFTA Chapter 11." *Investment Arbitration Reporter*, July 9.

Johnson, L., and L. Sachs. 2015. "International Investment Agreements, 2013: A Review of Trends and New Approaches." In *Yearbook on International Investment Law and Policy*, ed. A. K. Bjorklund. Oxford, UK: Oxford University Press.

Krajewski, M. 2003. "Public Services and Trade Liberalisation: Mapping the Legal Framework." *Journal of International Economic Law* 6: 341–67.

Lang, A. 2004. "The GATS and Regulatory Autonomy: A Case Study of Social Regulation of the Water Industry." *Journal of International Economic Law* 7: 801–38.

Luengo Hernandez de Madrid, G. E. 2007. *Regulation of Subsidies and State Aids in WTO and EC Law: Conflicts in International Trade Law.* Alphen aan den Rijn, The Netherlands: Kluwer Law International.

Peterson, L. E. 2014. "Brussels' Latest Intervention Casts Shadow Over Investment Treaty Arbitrations Brought by Jilted Solar Energy Investors." *Investment Arbitration Reporter*, September 8.

Ramboll and Matrix. 2012. *Ex-post Evaluation of the Regional Aid Guidelines 2007–2013, Final Report.* Luxembourg: European Commission.

Rubini, L. 2012. "Ain't Wastin' Time No More: Subsidies for Renewable Energy, the SCM Agreement, Policy Space, and Law Reform." *Journal of International Economic Law,* 15: 525–43.

SCM Committee, WTO. 2003. "Minutes of the Regular Meeting Held on 8 May 2013." G/SCM/M/46, July 23.

——. 2013. "Report of the Committee on Subsidies and Countervailing Measures." G/L/1052/Corr.1, adopted October 21.

Steenblik, R., and J. Simón. 2011. *A New Template for Notifying Subsidies to the WTO.* Geneva: International Institute for Sustainable Development and Global Subsidies Initiative.

Treaty Establishing the European Coal and Steel Community (April 18, 1951), 261 UNTS. 140. Expired by its terms July 23, 2002.

Treaty Establishing the European Economic Community (March 25, 1957), 298 UNTS. 3.

UNCTAD. 2012a. *Fair and Equitable Treatment.* Series on Issues in International Investment Agreements II. New York: United Nations Conference on Trade and Development.

——. 2012b. *Transparency.* Series on Issues in International Investment Agreements II. New York: United Nations Conference on Trade and Development.

US-CAFTA-DR. 2004. Central America–Dominican Republic–United States Free Trade Agreement, August 5, https://ustr.gov/trade-agreements/free-trade-agreements/cafta-dr-dominican-republic-central-america-fta/final-text.

Whitsitt, E. 2013. "A Modest Victory at the WTO for Ontario's FIT Program." *U.C. Davis Journal of International Law and Policy* 20: 75–103.

WTO. 2001. "Guidelines for the Scheduling of Specific Commitments Under the General Agreement on Trade in Services." WTO Document S/L/92, March 28. Geneva: World Trade Organization.

——. 2006. *Annual Report 2006*. Geneva: World Trade Organization.

——. 2014. *Annual Report 2014*. Geneva: World Trade Organization.

Wu, M., and J. Salzman. 2014. "The Next Generation of Trade and Environment Conflicts: The Rise of Green Industrial Policy." *Northwestern University Law Review* 108: 401–74.

CHAPTER 13

Conclusions

OUTSTANDING ISSUES ON THE DESIGN AND IMPLEMENTATION OF INCENTIVES POLICIES

Lise Johnson, Perrine Toledano, Lisa Sachs, and Ana Teresa Tavares-Lehmann

As we saw in the introductory chapter, in 2015 governments set landmark priorities and commitments to ensure long-term sustainable development. The United Nations adopted a set of sustainable development goals (SDGs) to set the post-2015 development agenda, including ending poverty and hunger; ensuring access to affordable, reliable, and modern energy; and promoting inclusive and sustainable economic growth. The Conference of the Parties of the UN Framework Convention similarly established a new binding agreement aimed at tackling the challenges of climate change. Implementing these global agreements will require the strategic and coordinated use of public and private resources. Public capital will need to support and catalyze private investment where it otherwise might not go at all or might not go with the speed and intensity required. Public capital will also be needed for critical and urgent public investments—for instance, in infrastructure and human capital.

Against that background, this volume suggests that careful investment policies are particularly crucial to guide the strategic and efficient mobilization of public and private resources for improved economic, social, and environmental outcomes. Investment incentives may play a useful role if they are strategically and thoughtfully designed and are based on a robust cost-benefit analysis.

However, the chapters in this volume have highlighted at least four deficiencies in the current use of incentives around the globe. Specifically, there is systematically a lack of transparency in the administration of incentives; most governments do not evaluate the costs or benefits of incentives, either ex ante or ex post; incentives are rarely designed strategically to promote particular behaviors in line with SDGs; and efforts to promote cross-jurisdictional cooperation or discipline to halt the race to the bottom are underdeveloped and patchy geographically.

LACK OF TRANSPARENCY

Very little is actually known about how many incentives governments are granting, to whom, for how much and how long, and in exchange for what. Anecdotally, we know that the scale of incentives is vast and growing, but most are given without fanfare or publicity. Moreover, most incentives schemes are discretionary (see chapter 7 by James), meaning that the lack of transparency may allow officials to use investment incentives to secure private gains, short-term victories, or powerful allies. The lack of transparency removes the ability of the public, business competitors, or even other agencies or branches within the government to scrutinize the use of incentives, much less hold officials accountable when incentives given are inconsistent with law, policy, or common economic sense. Thus, incentives can be "conceded despite the absence of any normative justification" (chapter 4 by Bellak and Leibrecht). Even when administered by well-meaning governments, the lack of transparency prevents analysis of the efficiency and effectiveness of incentives programs (chapter 2 by Tavares-Lehmann). Indeed, Krakoff and Steele show in chapter 6 that the transparency of incentives programs and their effectiveness are positively correlated.

LACK OF EFFECTIVE COST-BENEFIT ANALYSIS

As illustrated in part III, governments often grant incentives without sufficient ex ante or ex post evaluation of the actual costs and benefits of those measures. However, even when cost-benefit analyses are done, they often leave out important variables and considerations. First, as described in the chapters of part III, incentives are rarely evaluated holistically in the context of a jurisdiction's public policy objectives or SDGs; those chapters suggest some approaches and give examples of how incentives programs could be more strategically designed and evaluated by the granting jurisdiction.

Second, cost-benefit analyses do not take into account the losses suffered in incentives wars when one jurisdiction lures an investment away from another. Of course, the "winning" jurisdiction may suffer its own losses, through wasteful spending and redundant incentives, and the extent to which those are exacerbated by competition with other jurisdictions is also not captured in a standard cost-benefit analysis. As noted in chapter 6, for example, Washington State determined that, based on an estimated fiscal gain of $21.3 billion, it was worth giving Boeing $8.7 billion in incentives over fifteen years in order to keep the company's operations in the state. But even though the cost-benefit equation looks positive for that transaction, it does not account for how much of the $8.7 billion Washington would not have had to spend had there not been incentives competition from other states seeking to lure Boeing into their territories.

UNDERUSE OF BEHAVIORAL INCENTIVES

The majority of incentives programs are designed to influence a company's locational decisions and are focused on the traditional measures of an investment's impact: capital expenditure and the number of jobs. As chapters 8 and 9 argue in some detail, it is time to reorient investment incentives schemes from location-based schemes to those that will promote a jurisdiction's development objectives; this may very well include behavioral incentives that are designed not to affect a company's locational choice but rather to affect its strategic and operational profile. There has been some progress in that respect: chapter 4 describes the trend in the OECD toward research and development–focused incentives, tying investment incentives to preidentified policy objectives, such as innovation and technological progress. But these policy-oriented incentives schemes remain the minority. As the chapters of part III recognize, successfully using investment incentives to achieve more holistic sustainable development objectives requires significant planning and analysis, and more research, as discussed later on, is needed to identify and implement best practices in this area.

LACK OF DISCIPLINE ACROSS JURISDICTIONS

As described throughout this volume, the pervasive use of tax incentives has led to many cases of pernicious incentives wars—at the subnational level (for instance, in the United States, Canada, and Australia) and at the global level. In the absence of a comprehensive framework to limit incentives competition, individual jurisdictions are forced to compete with beggar-thy-neighbor policies. There is therefore an urgent need to review the successes and limitations of existing frameworks that regulate incentives policy and to consider how such cooperation could be improved and scaled up.

Part IV explores the efforts to date to regulate the use of incentives at the national and subnational levels (chapter 11) and the regional and international levels (chapter 12). Chapter 11 illustrates the attempts in Australia, Canada, and the United States to define and implement a regulatory framework, highlighting the fact that those efforts have often been weak or have fallen apart. So far, the most successful regional legal and policy framework to control incentives competition is that of the European Union (EU), as explained in chapter 12. In the EU, there has been a greater push toward transparency, a growing effort to monitor and evaluate the effectiveness of incentives, and an attempt to use past experiences to refine future policies. The EU also has attempted to prevent poaching and costly bidding wars and to ensure that, when incentives are used, they are sufficiently aimed to advance preapproved EU policy objectives, including, for instance, inclusive growth within its territory.

As explained in chapters 5 and 12, the EU system has limitations and gaps in coverage, and it has recently introduced more flexibility, which will require even stronger monitoring and enforcement to prevent those reforms from diluting the system's effectiveness. The EU framework also reveals some of the complexities and challenges inherent in designing a system of multijurisdictional regulation, including how deeply the regulation can reach (for instance, whether it would regulate subnational competition) and which factors to consider when designing the policy (for instance, whether to allow the use of incentives by less developed jurisdictions). The EU's framework illustrates at least some of the key ingredients for success, such as binding rules and enforcement mechanisms, while shedding light on some of the challenges that will have to be addressed by other regional or global attempts seeking to similarly regulate incentives.

FURTHER RESEARCH TO OPTIMIZE THE IMPACT OF INCENTIVES FOR SUSTAINABLE DEVELOPMENT

In addition to the core challenges outlined above, the chapters in this volume suggest a number of other important areas for further research in order to optimize the use and effectiveness of investment incentives for sustainable development.

First, further development of techniques for ex ante and ex post cost-benefit analyses is fundamental, as are additional (econometric, evidence-based) studies on how the effectiveness and efficiency of incentives vary based on their type, the granting jurisdiction, the industry, and the firm. As of today, as explained in chapter 10, assessing the redundancy of incentives—that is, the extent to which they were necessary to attract an investment or induce a particular behavior—can be exceedingly difficult, as it is nearly impossible to disentangle the role that the incentives play for the investor from the many other location- and company-specific factors. Designing an optimal incentives package that is effective but limits costs also requires an assessment of the attractiveness of competing jurisdictions (and their incentives), which is a daunting if not impossible task, complicated not least by the lack of data necessary to conduct relevant analyses.

Second, new and better ideas are needed on how granting jurisdictions can successfully tie their incentives programs to meeting performance targets or advancing sustainable development strategies without either discouraging investment or overburdening their administrative officials. This question includes the difficult task of establishing reasonable and realistic performance targets and sustainable development impacts that should be expected from the granting of investment incentives and that would be effective in changing investors' behaviors.

Finally, the possible contours of an international framework definitely deserve further exploration in order to ensure that framework's feasibility, desirability, and effectiveness. One important point in this context is the question of whether incentives mainly divert investment from one location to another or whether they are also effective in increasing total investment; both options have implications for an overarching regulatory framework. In terms of considering what such a global framework might look like, one would need to consider such issues as the rationale (e.g., whether collaboration is relevant because incentives divert investment geographically or because incentives competition causes all countries to lower their tax base), scope (e.g., whether poor regions should be excluded from incentives controls), investigation and enforcement mechanisms (e.g., whether individuals and civil society should be able to initiate complaints), and accountability mechanisms (e.g., what the roles of transparency and systemic evaluation are).

In exploring those issues and how to successfully resolve them, one should take into account the political economy animating the relevant actors.

Any solution is unlikely to succeed if no consideration is given to the different constituencies and their conflicting interests. Consider, for instance, the investment promotion authorities (IPAs) and the ministries of finance: any benefits in terms of increased investment are usually credited to IPAs while the costs of incentives are charged to the ministries of finance. Their opposing interests might generate some systemic inertia that will inhibit any collaborative solution, so we need to determine how to redesign the system to avoid falling into that trap. Where should the authority for granting incentives lie? Should decisions with respect to investments be made according to automatic criteria rather than allowing discretion to individuals or individual agencies? If IPAs are using incentives as marketing tools, could they be constructed in ways that do not reduce their effectiveness but that do reduce their cost? Which part of government should be "charged" with the costs—if they can be estimated? In addition to these considerations at the domestic level, similar issues of political economy would arise in the context of any international negotiations.

Tackling these outstanding issues will require improved multistakeholder dialogue, involving governments, academia, civil society, and the business community, with a view toward a shared understanding of the true drivers for global business, the types of investments and behaviors that contribute to sustainable development, and the regulatory framework and institutions that will be necessary to achieve such outcomes. This volume aims to contribute to that dialogue, and in light of the increased global rulemaking governing international investment, especially in support of the SDGs and the role of investment in financing development, it does so at a time when the need and opportunity for such dialogue are particularly ripe.

ACKNOWLEDGMENTS

This volume arose from the discussions at the Columbia Center on Sustainable Investment's Eighth Annual Columbia International Investment Conference on "Investment Incentives—The Good, The Bad, and the Ugly: Assessing the Costs, Benefits, and Options for Policy Reform," held at Columbia University in New York in November 2013. The editors are grateful to the discussions and insights from the conference participants and panelists, many of whom have authored individual chapters in this volume. The editors are also very grateful for the insightful comments and suggestions of Ted Moran and Lou Wells for their substantial improvements to the text. Ana Teresa Tavares-Lehmann further acknowledges that her research has been financed by Portuguese Public Funds through FCT (Fundação para a Ciência e a Tecnologia) in the framework of the project UID/ECO/04105/2013.

CONTRIBUTORS

CHRISTIAN BELLAK is an associate professor of economics at the Department of Economics, WU University of Economics and Business, Vienna (Austria). His research interests include international factor flows (foreign direct investment and migration) and economic policy related to multinational enterprises.

LOUIS BRENNAN is a fellow of Trinity College Dublin and a professor in the Trinity Business School. He previously served as director of the Institute for International Integration Studies at Trinity College. Louis has lived and worked in a number of countries in Asia and Europe and in the United States.

PHILIPPE GUGLER is director of the Center for Competitiveness of the University of Fribourg in Switzerland. He is chairman of the European International Business Academy (EIBA). He is editor-in-chief of the *Competitiveness Review*. He is also a member of the advisory boards of several academic institutes in Switzerland, Thailand, Italy, and the Netherlands.

ELLEN HARPEL is the founder of Smart Incentives, which helps states and communities make sound decisions throughout the economic development incentives process. She is also president of Business Development Advisors LLC, an economic development and market intelligence consulting firm based in Arlington, Virginia. Ellen speaks and writes frequently on incentive policies and programs for national audiences comprising economic developers, elected leaders and finance professionals.

SEBASTIAN JAMES is a senior economist in tax policy at the World Bank. Apart from taxation, he has worked in cross-cutting areas on investment policy and special economic zones. He has advised several developing countries on the design of their tax policy and tax administration. He authored a *Handbook of Tax Simplification* and his research on tax incentives has been published widely. He is a former Indian Revenue Service officer and has a PhD in public policy from Harvard University.

LISE JOHNSON is the head of investment law and policy at the Columbia Center on Sustainable Investment. She focuses on analyzing the contractual, legislative, and international legal frameworks that govern international investments, and that affect the positive and negative externalities generated by those investments. She received a BA from Yale University, a JD from University of Arizona, and an LLM from Columbia University.

JOACHIM KARL is chief of the Investment Policy Research Section in UNCTAD's Division on Investment and Enterprise. He worked previously at the OECD, at the Energy Charter Secretariat and at the German Ministry of Economics. He holds a PhD in international law from the University of Konstanz in Germany, and a master of public administration (MPA) from Harvard's John F. Kennedy School of Government. He has written numerous articles on European law and international investment issues, and was a lecturer at the German Federal Academy of Public Administration.

CHARLES KRAKOFF, managing partner of Koios Associates LLC and senior associate with Investment Consulting Associates, has 30 years of experience as an advisor to government and private sector clients on cross-border investment and trade. He has worked in over 60 countries, with a focus on emerging and frontier economies. He earned an MBA from Columbia Business School and a BA from Reed College.

MARKUS LEIBRECHT is associate professor at SIM University (UniSIM) in Singapore and a research associate at the Austrian Institute of Economic Research. He has published several articles on the determinants and economic effects of foreign direct investment. His current research focuses on the macroeconomic implications of fiscal policy and the drivers of economic reforms.

SARIANNA M. LUNDAN holds the chair in International Management and Governance at the University of Bremen in Germany. She has published widely in journals and books, and serves on several editorial boards, including the *Journal of International Business Studies*, *International Business Review* and *Global Strategy Journal*. She has also consulted extensively with the United Nations and the World Bank on issues related to the development impact of foreign investment.

FRANCES RUANE is an honorary professor at the Department of Economics at Trinity College, having stepped down from her role as director of the Economic and Social Research Institute in Dublin in September 2015. Earlier in her career she worked in Ireland's FDI promotion agency, IDA Ireland.

LISA SACHS is the director of the Columbia Center on Sustainable Investment, where she oversees the center's three areas of focus: investments in extractive industries, investments in land and agriculture, and investment law and policy. She received a BA in economics from Harvard University, and earned her JD and master of international affairs (MIA) from Columbia University.

CHRIS STEELE, COO of Investment Consulting Associates, has almost 25 years of business, economic development, and location strategy experience. He has previously worked at a small city planning firm, a global Big-Four consulting services firm and a world-class engineering and supply chain company. He has also led several major foreign direct investment, economic and community development projects. He holds a BA from Rutgers University and an MCRP from the University of North Carolina at Chapel Hill.

ANA TERESA TAVARES-LEHMANN is associate professor at Faculdade de Economia de Universidade doe Porto, researcher at the Center for Economics and Finance at Universidade doe Porto, head of Internationalization Programs at Porto Business School, head of InvestPorto, visiting professor in European and U.S. universities, and a consultant to international organizations and governments. She focuses on policies to attract inward investment and to promote internationalization. She holds an MA and a PhD in Economics from Reading University.

KENNETH P. THOMAS is professor of political science at the University of Missouri-St. Louis. He is the author of *Competing for Capital: Europe and North America in a Global Era* (Georgetown University Press, 2000) and *Investment Incentives and the Global Competition for Capital* (Palgrave Macmillan, 2011). He earned an AB in philosophy at Princeton University, an MA in political science at the University of Memphis, and a PhD in political science at the University of Chicago. He blogs at Middle Class Political Economist.

PERRINE TOLEDANO is the head of extractive industries at the Columbia Center on Sustainable Investment. She leads research, training and advisory projects on fiscal regimes, financial modeling, leveraging extractive industry investments in infrastructure for broader development needs, local content, revenue management, and optimal legal provisions for development benefits. She received an MBA from ESSEC in Paris, France, and an MPA from Columbia University.

JAMES X. ZHAN is senior director of Investment and Enterprise at UNCTAD, and editor-in-chief of the *UN World Investment Report* and the journal *Transnational Corporations*. He led the formulation of UNCTAD Investment Policy Framework for Sustainable Development and the establishment of the World Investment Forum. He has published extensively on trade and investment-related economic and legal issues.

INDEX

absorptive capacity of domestic companies: foreign investment and, 57; policy, 54; spillovers and, 56, 68, 87*n*10
accelerated depreciation: allowances for, 122; as fiscal incentive, 26; R&D and, 71; tax holidays and, 157, 161
accountability: government, 255; implementation and, 191, 196; leadership and, 245; mechanisms, 327; subsidies and, 11; transparency and, 31, 261
actionable subsidies, 270–75
administrative burden, 21, 186, 193
advance pricing agreements (APAs), 155–56
adverse selection market failure, 78–79
Africa: Sub-Saharan, tax incentives in, 158–59, *159*, 170; VAT exemptions and zero-ratings in, *165*, 165–66
after-care services, 35
agglomeration: effects of, 53; location choice and, 51–54
Agreement on Internal Trade (AIT), 145, 255–56
agricultural investments, 265
agricultural subsidies, 124
AIT. *See* Agreement on Internal Trade
allocation–related justification, for investment incentives, 64–65
Alcoa, 128–29, 131, 136, 138–39
Amazon, 156
APAs. *See* advance pricing agreements
Apple, 108, 155–156
attracting investment: effectiveness of, 6; FDI, 9, 56, 57, 67, 84; with fiscal and financial incentives, 56; IPAs and, role of, 35–37; locations and, 180–81; policies on, 54; state incentives and, 94; tax incentives for, 107
Austin, Texas, cost-benefit analysis in, 242–43
Australia: corporate relocation between states/territories in, 253–55; IICA and, 253–55, 260–61; regulatory mechanisms in, 11; state incentives in, 253; state/territory governing party, 254, *254*; subsidy competition in, 145
automatic incentives, 146

back-loaded incentives, 20
Bangladesh, tax incentives in, 170
BEATRs. *See* bilateral effective average tax rates
beggar-thy-neighbor policies, 10, 123
behavioral incentives, underuse of, 325
bidding war: in Australia, 253; in Canada, 256; in EU, 288, 326; interstate, 126, 129, 135, 145; intracountry, 8; jurisdictions engaging in, 2, 6; location and, 145; losses suffered in, 324–25; tax incentives and, 325–26; in U.S., 123, 126, 129, 135, 145, 257–59
bilateral effective average tax rates (BEATRs), 29
bilateral investment treaties (BITs): bilateral initiatives through IIAs and, 295–304; FDI and, 82–83; foreign investment protected by, 77; market failures and, 80–81; positive effects of, 82–83; U.S. Model, 302, 318*n*47
Bilcon v. Canada, 308
BITs. *See* bilateral investment treaties
Boeing: overbidding investment project and, 252; Washington, cost-benefit analysis, 240–41
Brazil, income tax rate in, 161
Burkina Faso, 161
Business Incentives Initiative, 245
business taxation, 107–8

California, cost-benefit analyses in, 239–40
California Competes tax credit, 239
Canada: AIT, 145, 255–56; bidding wars in, 256; *Bilcon v. Canada*, 308; CETA, 296, 310–11; Code of Conduct on Incentives, 255–57, 260; Crown Life Insurance relocation and, 252; Ecuador and, 304; *Mesa v. Canada*, 298–99; R&D investment incentives in, 72, *73*; regulatory mechanisms, 11
Canada-Autos case, 281
Canada—Renewable Energy/Feed-in Tariff Program, 315*n*6
Canadian value-added (CVA), 281–82
carried interest, 148*n*2
carryforward of losses: as fiscal incentive, 26; indefinite, 160; in OECD countries, 159; tax holidays compared with, 173*n*5
carve-outs, for subsidies serving certain policy objectives, 274–75
CBC. *See* Citizens' Budget Committee
Center for Regional Economic Competitiveness (CREC), Business Incentives Initiative, 245
CETA. *See* Comprehensive Economic and Trade Agreement
China: market-seeking investment and, 50–51; profitability-enhancing incentives in, 193
Citizens' Budget Committee (CBC), 138
clusters: FDI and new, 190; spatial, 53–54
Code of Conduct on Incentives, 255–57, 260
colocation: location choice model and, 52; resource exploitation and, 53; spatial, 53
Colombia, investments in tourism, 26

"Communication Concerning the Criteria for an In-Depth Assessment of Regional Aid to Large Investment Projects" (EC), 104
"Communication on Promoting Good Governance in Tax Matters" (EC), 107
communities: in cost-benefit analysis, 230; economic development strategy and, 231–32; state and municipal investment incentive effects on, 134–35
"Community Framework for State Aid for Research and Development and Innovation" (EC), 105
companies: employment in foreign-owned, 141, *141*; incentives and negotiation with, 136; relocation of, 253–57; tax holidays and, 157; tax incentives reforms and, 153. *See also* absorptive capacity of domestic companies
competition: CREC, 245; EC policy on, 109; for FDI, 179–80; FTA provisions on, 309–11; global race for investment, 6, government use of incentives and, 251–52; horizontal tax, mobile capital, 86*n*5; incentive, 8; interstate incentives, 145; for investment, 94; between jurisdictions, 2, 6, 8, 147; SD-related incentives and avoiding international, 223–24; state incentives, 145; subsidy, 145–46; tax, 27, 86*n*5. *See also* beggar-thy-neighbor policies; bidding war.
compliance: cost-benefit analysis and, 243–46; in EU, 293–94; ex post controls on, 289–90; with VAT, 164, 174*n*10
Comprehensive Economic and Trade Agreement (CETA): as mega-regional IIA, 296; subsidies in, 310–11
continuous subsidies, as cost-reducing incentives, 192–93
corporate relocation: within Australia, 253–55; within Canada, 255–57
corporate social responsibility standards, 225*n*4
corporate tax rate: EU, 27–28, 107–8; reduced, 26, 27; U.S., 28, 123–24
corporate welfare, 124
Costa Rica, 138
cost-benefit analysis: in Austin, Texas, 242–43; in California, 239–40; compliance and evaluation in, 243–46; cost of incentives and, 233; cost of new services and, 234–35; designing incentives programs and, 11; economic contribution and, 236–37; economic development and, 228–29, 243–45; effective, lack of, 324–25; in Erie County, New York, 241, *242*; examples and resources, 238–43; ex ante and ex post, 327; fiscal implications and, 232–35; good governance and, 245; implications of, 237–38; importance of, 7–8, 228–29, 246; investment promotion policy and, 65; in local government, 241–43; models and modeling

issues in, 235; in Montgomery County, Maryland, 241–42; new taxes and, 234; in practice, 238–43; project attributes and, 230–32; public spending and, 325; questions addressed by, 229; state government, 239–41; three-step approach to, 229–38; tools, 243; in Virginia, 239; in Washington, 240–41
cost-effectiveness analyses, investment promotion policy and, 65
cost-reducing incentives, 192–93
costs: ex ante, 80; expatriation, support of, 22; ex post, 80, 88*n*20; of FDI, 66, 192; Fixed Cost Aid (FCA), 108; of incentives, 7–8, 233; labor, 51; net additional cost test, 110; of new services, 234–35; of tax credits, 233; of tax incentives, 233; transaction, 50, 63, 66; transportation, location theory and, 52; VCA, 108
Cotonou Agreement, 312
creative subsidiary/product mandate, 38*n*3
CREC. *See* Center for Regional Economic Competitiveness
Crown Life Insurance, 252, 255
Cuno v. Daimler-Chrysler, 258
customs duty: relief and exemption regimes, 166–68, *167*, *168*, 174*n*14; tax incentives and, 155
CVA. *See* Canadian value-added

data on investment incentives: Impact DataSource, 243; transparency and, 29; UNCTAD, 3, 204, 207, 225*n*2
deductions: enhanced, 27; super-, 162
deficiencies in use of incentives, 323–28
Delaware, 28, 38*n*6
designing incentives: accountability and, 196; cost-benefit analyses and, 11; cost-reducing incentives and, 192–93; engagement-deepening incentives, 194; implementation mechanisms and, 194–95; principles of, 191–96; profitability-enhancing incentives and, 193; strategies for, 10–11; time frames and, 196
Development Indicators (World Bank), 187
disclosure: in SCM Agreement, 273–74; of subsidies, 273–74
discretionary approach to incentives, 195, *195*; bounded and level of discretion, 20; discretion in provision and application of tax incentives, 169
discrimination: level of, 19; nondiscrimination provisions, 280, 298–300
diversification, of investors, 18
dividends, tax rates on, 27
domestic content requirements, 301
duration of investment, locational incentives and, 56

Ease of Doing Business rankings (World Bank), 187
East Asian countries, tax losses and, 159–60

EATRs. *See* effective average tax rates
EC. *See* European Commission
EC—Aircraft dispute, 269–70
ECJ. *See* European Court of Justice
ECOFIN (Council of Economics and Finance Ministers), 107–108
economic contribution, of cost-benefit analysis, 236–37
economic determinants: of cost-benefit analysis, 229, 236–37, 243; economic development organizations (EDOs) and, 230–31; EU, 283, 286–87; goals and strategies, 231; improving outcomes and, 323; of investment incentives, 230; for SD incentives, 327–28; U.S., 239–43
economic development: cost-benefit analysis and, 228–29, 243–45; FDI and, 10, 179, 180, 186–87; holistic approach to, 201, 229; incentives, 228, 231, 238, 245–46; locational determinants and, 50, 188, 200; Louisiana Economic Development, 132; market-seeking investment and, 50–51; objectives, 233, 239, 244; programs, 245; Regional Aid Guidelines (RAG) and, 103–4; Rhode Island Economic Development Corporation, 133; strategy, 191, 229, 231–32, 239; in U.S., 132, 133, 142–44, 239–42
economic development organizations (EDOs), 230–32
economic equilibrium clause, 314*n*3
economic impact of investment, 236–37
economic openness policies, 54
Ecuador, Canada and, 304
education: cost of, 234; incentives related to, *214*; job training subsidies, 22, 23
effective average tax rates (EATRs), 29
effectiveness: assessing, 244–45; attracting investment and, 6; of cost-benefit analyses, 324–25; of incentives, 6–8, 327; of SD incentives, 219–22, *220*, 327; state and municipal incentives and, 143–46, 148*n*5; transparency and, 324, 326; in U.S., 137–46
effect of investment incentives, State aid intensity and, 292–93
efficiency: advantages, locations and, 182; economic, 105, 251; FDI and, 189; of incentives, 2, 6–8, 17, 327; of investment incentives, 147*n*1, 251; State aid and economic, 105; transparency and, 31, 324
efficiency-seeking investment: efficiency-seeking investors, 6, factor price differentials across markets and, 51; FDI, 7, 49, 182; locational determinants and, 51; motivations for, 46–49; redundancy and, 7
EFTA. *See* European Free Trade Association
emerging markets, 50–51
employment: FDI and growth in, 189; in foreign-owned companies, 141, *141*; incentive programs and, 142; job quality and, 231; job training subsidies and, 22, 23; relocation and, 252; urban, 202*n*9

endowment effects, 52–53
enforcement: in EU, 293–94; of regulations, 67, 260; of subsidies, 273–74; of treaties, 296
engagement-deepening incentives, 194
enhanced deduction, 27
environmental standards: attracting FDI and, 67; lowering of, 39*n*11; regulatory incentives and, 31–32, 301–2
EPZs. *See* export-processing zones
equivalence, in evaluation of incentives programs, 199
ERDF. *See* European Regional Development Fund
Erie County, New York, cost-benefit analyses in, 241, *242*
ESF. *See* European Social Fund
"Europe 2020 Strategy," 98
European Commission (EC): "Communication Concerning the Criteria for an In-Depth Assessment of Regional Aid to Large Investment Projects," 104; Communication on Promoting Good Governance in Tax Matters, 107; "Community Framework for State Aid for Research and Development and Innovation," 105; competition policy, 109; *EC—Aircraft* dispute, 269–70; GBER, 95–97; Global Entrepreneurship Monitor, 187; Innovation Scoreboard, 187; *Micula et al. v. Romania* and, 307; monitoring compliance and, 293–94; regulation of investment incentives and, 285; SAAP, 97; State aid policy of, 94–118, 284–295; TFEU, 94
European Court of Justice (ECJ), 285, 294
European Free Trade Association (EFTA), 22
European Regional Development Fund (ERDF), 23–24
European Social Fund (ESF), 23
European Union (EU), 94–118, 284–295; bidding wars in, 288, 326; CETA, 310–11; enforcement in, 293–94; evaluation in, 2, 288–95; GERD, 87*n*11; grants, 22; incentive policy in, effectiveness of, 108–13; incentives in, 94–115; MNEs in, 108; monitoring in, 2, 288–95; national courts in, 294; notification in, 288–95; policy on State aid and, evolution of, 97–99; regional State aid in, 103–5; regulation of investment incentives by, 2, 113, 313; regulation of investment incentives by, regional, 284–95; regulatory framework for State aid in, 95–97, *96*; SAM, 98–99; Singapore and, FTA between, 309–10, 312; state incentives in, 94; tax incentives in, 106–8; transparency in, 2, 288–95; TTIP, 224; types of State aid in, *99*, 99–102, *100*; use of investment incentives in, 9–10, 284–85, 311, 313
evaluation of incentives programs: clarity and, 199; consistency and, 198–99; cost-benefit analysis and, 243–46; equivalence and, 199; in EU, 2, 288–95; ex ante, 291; FDI

and, *197*, 197–200; focus and, 199; realism and, 199
ex ante: cost-benefit analyses, 327; costs, 80; evaluation, 291; provision of incentives, 20, 110
exceptions: IIAs, 303–4; for subsidies serving certain policy objectives, 274–75
expatriation costs, support of, 22
expectations, legitimate, 305–6
export contingency: de facto, 269–71; de jure, 270
export-oriented investment, 163
export performance and local content subsidies, 268–70
export-processing zones (EPZs), 26
export restrictions, 266–67
ex post: controls on compliance, 289–90; cost-benefit analyses, 327; costs, 80, 88*n*20; provision of incentives, 20, 110
externalities, 12*n*2, 86*n*4, 133, 147*n*1, 190, 193; environmental, 67
external market access, FDI and, 190–91

Facility for Investment Climate Advisory Services (FIAS), 6–7
"fair and equitable treatment" (FET) standard, 219, 221, 304–5
FCA. *See* fixed cost aid
FDI. *See* foreign direct investment
feed-in-tariff (FIT) program, 278
FET standard. *See* "fair and equitable treatment" standard
FIAS. *See* Facility for Investment Climate Advisory Services
financial contributions (see subsidies), 266
financial incentives: attracting investment with, 56; FDI and, 68; fiscal *vs.*, 131–32; government equity participation, 24; grants, 22; infrastructure subsidies, 22–24; as investment incentive, 21–24; job training subsidies, 22, 23; justification for, 55; loan guarantees, 24; loans, 22–23; money to organize missions, 24; for R&D, 69–77; reimbursement of, 22
firm-specific factors, locational determinants and, 50
fiscal incentives: accelerated depreciation, 26; attracting investment with, 56; carryforward of losses, 26; efficacy of, 28–29; enhanced deduction, 27; FDI and, 68; financial *vs.*, 131–32; government use of, 27; HQs and, 28; investment allowances, 26; as investment incentive, 21; investment tax credits, 26; justification for, 55; long-term capital gains, preferential treatment of, 27; popularity of, 25; for R&D, 69–77; reduced corporate income tax rates, 26; reduced tax rates on dividends and interest paid abroad, 27; role of, 6–7; for SD, 215–16; as share of GDP, 72; tax havens, 25; tax holidays, 25–26; zero or reduced tariffs, 27. *See also* tax incentives
FIT program. *See* feed-in-tariff program
fixed cost aid (FCA), 108

foreign direct investment (FDI): absorptive capacity of domestic companies, 68; agglomeration and, 51–54; allocation–related justification and, for investment incentives, 65; attracting, 9, 56, 57, 67, 84; benefits from, 189–91; BITs and, 82–83; competition for, 179–80; context for, 181–86; costs of, 66, 192; definition of, 4, 45–46; efficiency-seeking investment, 48–49; emerging, 185–86; evaluation of incentives and, *197*, 197–200; financial incentives and, 68; fiscal incentives and, 68; globalization and, 179; holistic approach to investment incentives and, 179–86; IIAs and, 78, 83; incentives program design and, 10–11; integrated regions and, emerging, 185–86; investment incentives defined by, 4; inward, 181, 197; IPAs and, 36–37, 39*n*14; locational determinants of, 12*n*8, 45–46, 49–51, 179–80; location and, 51–54, 181–91; market-seeking investment, 48; MNEs and, 45, 65–66, 182–84; motivations for, 45–49, 183, 184; objectives, 182; OECD Benchmark Definition of, 4, 46; policy, 10, 54–58; policy design, 10, 187, 191; political risk and, 81; positive impacts of, 12*n*2; potential supply of, 188; profitability-enhancing incentives, 193; promoting, 68; public policy and, 180; rationales for, 10, 180; R&D-related, 75–77; resources and, 188; resource-seeking investment and, 47, 182; SD and, 1, 212, *212*; from SMEs, 185; spatial balance and, 190; strategic asset-seeking investment, 47, 49; surplus of, dividing, 79, 88*n*19; sustainability, 83; taxation and, 29–30; taxes and, 29; tax incentives and, 154; technology and, 189; trade and, changing patterns of, 184; transaction costs of, 66; use of investment incentives and, 45, 180
foreign earnings, taxation on, 27, 124
France: non-crisis-related State aid from, 101–2; R&D investment incentives in, 72, *73*; Verdon Free Zone/Port, 163
free-trade agreements (FTAs): CETA, 310–11; EU-Singapore, 309–10, 312; SD in, cooperation for, 312
free trade zones (FTZs): consequences of, 186; investment legal framework and, 32; regulatory competition and, 31; resource-seeking investments and, 47; tax incentives in, 158–59; use of incentives in, 162
front-loaded incentives, 20
FTAs. *See* free-trade agreements
FTZs. *See* free trade zones

GATS. *See* General Agreement on Trade and Services
GATT. *See* General Agreement on Tariffs and Trade

GBER. *See* General Block Exemption Regulation
GDP. *See* gross domestic product
General Agreement on Tariffs and Trade (GATT), 275
General Agreement on Trade and Services (GATS): national treatment requirement, 280, 282–83, 316*n*29; nondiscrimination provisions in, 280; regulation of investment incentives, 279–83; trade classified in, 316*n*26
General Block Exemption Regulation (GBER): notice and approval rules exemption of, 288–89; State aid in, 95–97, *96*, 289
General Motors (GM), 134–36
geographically bound resources, 47, 53
geographic and spatial concentration of investment, 52
geographic information system (GIS), 235
GERD. *See* gross domestic expenditure on R&D
Germany, non-crisis-related State aid from, 101–2
GIS. *See* geographic information system
Global Entrepreneurship Monitor (EC), 187
global framework for investment incentives, 327
globalization: FDI and, 179; global value chains, 184; location and stage of, 187–88; measures of, 188
global value chains, location positioning in, 184, 188
GM. *See* General Motors
good governance: Communication on Promoting Good Governance in Tax Matters (EC), 107; cost-benefit analysis and, 245; emerging markets and, 50–51; policy influencing, 54; subsidy wars and, 257
governments: Australian state/territory, 254, *254*; cost-benefit analysis and importance to, 228–29; equity participation, 24; fiscal incentives used by, 27; of host countries, 79, 88*n*19; investment incentives used by, 1–2, 8, 251–52; investment-linked incentives and, 174*n*7; local, cost-benefit analyses in, 241–43; size of, 74; tax holidays offered by, 157; tax incentives and, 154–55, 172–73. *See also specific countries/regions*
grants: as cost-reducing incentives, 192; as financial incentives, 22; up-front, 192–93; U.S. government-provided, 124–25
greenfield investment, 45
green industrial policies, 275
green technologies, 277
gross domestic expenditure on R&D (GERD), 87*n*11
gross domestic product (GDP): fiscal incentives as share of, 72; growth, 50

Harris-Todaro type of rural-urban migration, 190, 202*n*9
headquarters (HQs): location of, 28; targeting of, 19
hold-up problem, 78–79. *See also* market failure

holistic approach to investment incentives: designing incentives programs and, 191–96; developing, 186; economic development stage of location and, 187–91; evaluation and, principles of, *197*, 197–200; FDI and, 179–86; regulation and, 314
horizontal aid, 103. *See also* State aid, EU
horizontal tax competition, 86*n*5
host-state characteristics, investment incentives and, 5
HQs. *See* headquarters

ICA. *See* Investment Consulting Associates
IIAs. *See* international investment agreements
IICA. *See* Interstate Investment Cooperation Agreement
ILO. *See* International Labor Organization
Impact DataSource, 243
implementation mechanisms: designing incentives programs and, 194–95; discretionary approach to incentives, 195, *195*; rule-based approach to incentives, 195, *195*; SD investment incentives and, 217–18
IncentivesMonitor, 148*n*7
Incentive Transparency Index, 142
income or price support, subsidy, 266–67
income tax: exemptions, 155, 160–61; incentives, 156–63, *157*; rates, 160–61
India: tax incentives in, 161; *US—Carbon Steel (India)*, 315*n*5
industry-specific agreements, 265
industry-specific subsidies, 267
inefficiency, allocative, 8
informAnalytics, 243
informational incentives, 308
information and technical services incentives: after-care services, 35; phases of investment project and, 34; rationale for provision of, 33; as type of investment incentive, 32–35
information asymmetry, 33
infrastructure subsidies, 22–24
innovation, State aid for, 105–6
Innovation Scoreboard (EC), 187
input credit method, 163
integrated regions, emerging, 185–86
Intel, 136–38, 148*n*6
interest: carried, 148*n*2; tax rates on, 27
internal market, regional aid and, 104
International Convention on the Simplification and Harmonization of Customs Procedures, 174*n*14
international investment agreements (IIAs): bilateral initiatives through, 295–304; economic rationale for, 78–81; empirical evidence and, 81–85; exceptions, 303–4; FDI and, 78, 83; FET standard in, 219, 221; heterogeneity of, 85; host country incentives and, 304–9; informational and promotional

incentives and, liability for, 308; investment incentives and, 296–97; investment incentive withdrawal challenged through, 222; market failures and, 78–80; mega-regional, 296; multilateral initiatives through, 295–304; nondiscrimination restrictions, 298–300; overview of, 295–96; performance requirements and, 300–301, 308–9; provisions, 295–96; race to the bottom and, 302–3; rationales for, 78–81; regulating incentives through, 298–304, 313; as regulatory incentive, 32; regulatory incentives restrictions and, 301–3; regulatory transparency requirements and, 303; SD-related investment and, 206; trends in, 81, *81*; TRIMs Agreement and, 300; use of, 63, 84–85
internationalized R&D, 66, 75
International Labor Organization (ILO), 31
international treaties, regulatory incentives and, 32
interstate incentives competition, 145, 257–60
Interstate Investment Cooperation Agreement (IICA), 253–55, 260–61
investment allowances, 26, 161–62
investment codes, tax incentives and, 170
Investment Consulting Associates (ICA), 139
investment incentive schemes, SD: designing, 207–12; factoring, 212–13; implementing, 217–18; monitoring effects of, 218–24
investment-linked incentives: governments and, 174*n*7; tax holidays and, 161
Investment Policy Framework for Sustainable Development (Policy Framework), 219
Investment Policy Monitor Database (UNCTAD), 204
investment promotion: for FDI, 68; IIAs and, 308; international, 122–23; policy, 65; SD, 204–17, *205*; strategies, SD in, 205–7
investment promotion agencies (IPAs): attracting investment and role of, 35–37; cost-benefit analysis and, 230–31; FDI inflows and, 36–37, 39*n*14; increased investment benefits and, 328; SD and, 205; UNCTAD survey of, 204, 207, 225*n*2
investment-related technical services, 34; investment-related information and business intelligence, 34
investment tax credits, 26
investor behavior: engagement-deepening incentives and, 194; influencing, 205, 219, 327; investment incentives and, 6, 17
investors: cost-benefit analysis and, 246; diversification of, 18; factors important to, 126; foreign, 33, 77–85; locational decisions of, 7; state and municipal investment incentives and, U.S., 126

investor-state contracts: regulatory incentives and, 31; specificity and, 269
investor-state dispute settlement (ISDS), 82, 222, 302; *Mesa v. Canada*, 298–99; *Micula et al. v. Romania*, 307
inward investment: FDI, 181, 197; incentives, 6, 9; policy and regulations of, 202*n*11
IPAs. *See* investment promotion agencies
Ireland: APAs used in, 156; attracting investments and, 56; incentives program, 148*n*6; National Linkage Program, 35; targeting and, 19; tax avoidance mechanisms, 173*nn*2–3; tax incentives in, 27–28; U.S. incentives and, 137–38
ISDS. *See* investor-state dispute settlement

Jamaica, tax reform, 153
Japan, R&D investment incentives in, 72, *73*
job quality, 231
job relocation, 252
job training subsidies, 22, 23
jurisdictions: competition between, 2, 8, 147; lack of discipline across, 325–26; national and subnational, 2–3, 252; in race to the bottom, 6, 8; tensions between, 8

key performance indicators (KPIs), 20
knowledge spillovers, 53
KPIs. *See* key performance indicators

labor: costs, 51; specialized, 53–54; standards, 31, 301–2; unskilled or semiskilled, 47, 51
laws: regulatory incentives and, 32; tax, 170–72
layering incentives, 241
least developed countries (LDCs), 276
liability: for informational incentives, 308; for promotional incentives, 308; for removing or reducing incentives, 304–8
liberalizing investment, SD and, 206
linkages: National Linkage Program, 35; policies to enhance, 55
loan guarantees, 24
loans: as financial incentives, 22–23; U.S. government-provided, 124–25
local government, cost-benefit analyses in, 241–43
local sourcing, policies on, 55
locational determinants: economic development and, 50, 188, 200; for efficiency-seeking investments, 51; for FDI, 12*n*8, 45–46, 49–51, 179–80; incentives, 8–9, 204; influence of, 7; investment duration and, 56; investment incentive definition and, 5; for investors, 7; market failures and, 6; for market-seeking investments, 50–51; MNEs and, 52–53; motivations for investment

and, 49; strategic asset-seeking investment and, 51; tax incentives and, 107; tax rates and, 30
locations, investment: agglomeration and, 51–54; attracting investment and, 180–81; bidding wars and, 145; comparing, 181–82; designing incentives programs and, 191–96; economic development stage of, 187–91; evaluation of incentives programs and, *197*, 197–200; FDI and, 49–54, 179–80; FDI and, context of, 181–86; FDI and, holistic approach to, 186; FDI and, potential supply of, 188; FDI benefits and, 189–91; globalization stage of, 187–88; HQs and, 28; incentives and, 5, 7, 126, 179; influencing, 7; integrated regions and, emerging, 185–86; location choice model for, 52–53; MNE motives and, evolving, 182–84; motivations for investment and, 57; policies regarding, 55; positioning in global value chains of, 184, 188; project attributes and, 230–32; R&D facilities and, 76–77; terminology and, 201; trade and, changing patterns of, 184; 1209 North Orange, 38*n*6
location theory (Alfred Marshall), 52–53
long-term capital gains, preferential treatment of, 27
Louisiana Economic Development, 132
Luxembourg, APAs used in, 156

macro stabilization–related justification, for investment incentives, 64
Malaysia, 161
manufacturing: investment in, 58*n*2; in U.S., 139, *139*
market distortions, 8
market failure: adverse selection, 78–79; allocation-based arguments for investment incentives and, 64–65; BITs and, 80–81; correcting, 65; IIAs and, 78–80; incentives provision by government and, 12*n*4; locational determinants and, 6; reason for, 86*n*3; spillovers and, 87*n*10; time inconsistency, 78–79; use of investment incentives and, 85–86
market growth, 181
market-seeking investment: FDI and, 182; growth of, 45; locational determinants for, 50–51; MNEs and, 52; motivation for, 48; strategic asset-seeking investment combined with, 51
market size, 50, 68, 126
measuring investment incentives, 29
megadeals: Alcoa, 127–28; largest, 129–31, *130*; questionable, 138–39; by state, *128*; 38 Studio, 129; in U.S., 126–29, *128*
Member States, EU: incentives granted by, 110; regional State aid granted by, 104; tax incentives in, 107; trade between, 111
merit goods or wants, 86*n*4

Mesa v. Canada, 298–99
Mexico, R&D investment incentives in, 72, *73*
MFN treatment obligation. *See* most-favored-nation treatment obligation
Micula et al. v. Romania, 222, 305–7
mining incentives, 173*n*4
missions, money to organize, 24
MNE. *See* multinational enterprise
models and modeling issues: cost-benefit analysis, 235; economic impact, 236–37
monitoring: in EU, 2, 288–95; investment incentive schemes and, SD, 218–24
Montgomery County, Maryland, cost-benefit analysis in, 241–42
most-favored-nation (MFN) treatment obligation, 280
motivations for investment: efficiency-seeking investment, 48–49; FDI, 45–49, 183, 184; locational determinants and, 49, 57; market-seeking investment, 48; multiplicity of, 37; resource-seeking investment, 47; strategic asset-seeking investment, 49, 183; tax incentives and, 161
multilateral initiatives, through IIAs, 295–304
multinational enterprise (MNE): efficiency-seeking investment, 48; in EU, 108; FDI and, 45, 65–66, 182–84; incentives tailored to, 198, 203*n*18; location choice and, 52–53; market-seeking investment, 48; motivations for FDI and, 45; motives of, evolving, 182–84; ownership advantages and, 65; purpose of incentives and, 18; R&D, 66, 75–76; R&D incentives for, 87*n*12; resource-seeking, 47; strategic asset-seeking investment, 47, 49; targeting and, 19; value-adding activities of, 57

National Governors Association (NGA), 251
National Linkage Program, 35
national treatment requirement, 280, 282–83, 316*n*29
negotiated incentives, 136, 146, 195
net additional cost test, 110
Netherlands, 156
NGA. *See* National Governors Association
nondiscrimination provisions: in GATS, 280; IIAs, 298–300
nonexcludability, 69
nonfiscal incentives, 146. *See also specific nonfiscal incentives*
no-raiding agreements, 11, 257–60
normative justification, for investment incentives, 67

OECD. *See* Organisation for Economic Cooperation and Development
OECD countries: tax incentives used by, 159; tax losses and, treatment of, 159–60; VAT exemptions and zero-ratings in, *165*, 165–66
OLI. *See* Ownership-Location-Internalization

Organisation for Economic Cooperation and Development (OECD): Benchmark Definition of FDI, 4, 46; investment incentives defined by, 3; R&D investment incentives and, 70
output growth, 189
overbidding, 252
overregulation, 284
Ownership-Location-Internalization (OLI), 65

Patent Box, 70–71, 162
patenting, 69–70
performance-based incentives: criteria for, 20–21, 327; for SD, 215
performance gap, 55–56
performance requirements: domestic content, 301; IIAs and restrictions on, 300–301, 308–9; incentives required for, 308–9
Pew Charitable Trusts: Business Incentives Initiative, 245; effectiveness of incentives evaluation, 142
poaching, of investments: of jobs, 256–57; use of incentives to, 254
policy: coherence of, 314; competition, of EC, 109; economic openness, 54; EU incentive, effectiveness of, 108–13; FDI and, 10, 54–58, 180; general investment incentive, 5; implications of investment incentives and, 4; incentives and, 1, 144, 146; incentives oriented towards, 325; on investment attraction, 54; investment promotion, 65; on investment retention and performance, 54; inward investment, 202*n*11; on local sourcing, 55; objectives, 274, 277, 324; postestablishment, 54–55; SD-related investment, 206–7, *208*; State aid, 97–99, 114; strategic decisions and inherent trade-offs, 17–21; subsidies serving certain, 274–75; tax incentives, 154; VAT and, 164
policy design: accountability and, 196; evaluation principles and, 197–99; FDI, 10, 187, 191; impact of incentives and, 45; outstanding issues on, 323–28; principles of, 196; tax, 164, 173
policy effectiveness: investment incentives and, 10; measurement of, *220*; regulations and, 325–26; of SCM Agreement, 276; State aid, 114; in U.S., 122
policy efficiency, 2, 8
Policy Framework. *See* Investment Policy Framework for Sustainable Development
political economy considerations, 67, 327–28
political income, 86*n*7
political risk, FDI and, 81
political stability, 88*n*22
politics, investment incentives and, *140*, 140–41
postestablishment policies, 54–55
PPPs. *See* public-private partnerships
preestablishment policies, 54
Prisoners' Dilemma, 8, 251

private creditor test, 110
private investment test, 109
private sector development policies, 54
profitability-enhancing incentives, 193
prohibited subsidies, 269–71
property tax exemptions, 127
psychic distance, 39*n*12
public expenditure, 86*n*2
public interest objectives: in EU-Singapore FTA, 310; investment incentives for advancing, 275
public-private partnerships (PPPs), 206
public procurement, policies on, 55
public spending: cost-benefit analysis and, 325; economic impact models and, 236–37; federal grant and loan programs, 125; limits of, 142

race to the bottom: IIAs and, 302–3; incentives competition creating, 11; regulatory, 31, 264; reigning in, 8–9, 324
RAG. *See* Regional Aid Guidelines
rates of return, spillovers and, 66
rationales: for FDI, 10, 180; global framework and, 327; granting investment incentives and, 63, 64; for IIAs, 78–81; informational incentives and, 33; of investment incentives, 64–68; policy, 3, 4; political economy considerations and, 67; provision of incentives and, 12*n*4, 17
rationalized subsidiary, 38*n*3
R&D. *See* research and development
R&D investment incentives: in Canada, 72, *73*; direct, 72–74; economic effects and implications, 72–74; empirical evidence on, 70–77; in France, 72, *73*; in Japan, 72, *73*; in Mexico, 72, *73*; for MNEs, 87*n*12; OECD and, 70; in South Korea, 72, *73*; in U.S., 72, *73*; use of, 63, 69–77, 162; volume and structure of, development of, *73*
realism, in evaluation of incentives programs, 199
redundancy of incentives, assessing, 6–7, 327
Regional Aid Guidelines (RAG): application of, 104–5; EC's review of, 290; evaluation of, 291–93; negative effects of aid and, 287–88
region-specific subsidies, 267–68
regulation of investment incentives: in Australia, 253–55; in Canada, 255–57; competition for investment and, 251–61; EU, 2, 113, 313; EU, regional, 284–95; FTAs and, 309–12; GATS and, 279–83; hard or soft, 2; host country incentives and, 304–9; IIA, 298–304, 313; informational and promotional incentives and, liability for, 308; international/supranational, 264–319; national/subnational, 251–61; overregulation and, 284; performance requirements and, 308–9; SCM Agreement, 266–77; state incentives and, 251; TRIMs

Agreement, 277–79; in U.S., 257–60; in WTO, 265–84, 313
regulations: Code of Conduct on Incentives, 255–57; enforcing, 67, 260; global, 11; IICA, 253–55; inward investment, 202*n*11; quality of, 88*n*23; restrictive, relaxed enforcement of, 67; SD-related investment, 207, *208*, *209*
regulatory frameworks: global, 327; international/supranational, 264–322; race to the bottom and, 8; for State aid, EU, 95–97, *96*, 108, 110–11
regulatory incentives: IIAs and restriction on, 301–3; international treaties and, 32; laws and, 32; for SD, 215; as type of investment incentive, 31–32
regulatory transparency, IIAs and requirements on, 303
reinvestment, policies on, 55
reliance, requirement of, 305–6
removing or reducing incentives, liability for, 304–8
renewable energy industry, 307
replica/multidomestic subsidiary, 38*n*3
research and development (R&D): accelerated depreciation in, 71; economic growth and, 69; engagement-deepening incentives and, 194; FDI related to, 75–77; financial and fiscal incentives for, 69–77; GERD, 87*n*11; government funding of business, *71*; incentives, *214*; internationalized, 66, 75; location of facilities for, 76–77; MNE, 66, 75–76; public, 75; State aid for, 105–6, *106*; subsidies, 271–72; tax credits for, 74; tax incentives for, *71*, 162
resources: exploitation of, 53; FDI and, 188; geographically bound, 47, 53; mining incentives, 173*n*4
resource-seeking investment: FDI and, 47, 182; MNEs and, 52; motivations for FDI and, 47, resource-seeking investors, 6
retaining investment, policies on, 54, 55
return-on-investment (ROI): analysis, 238; effectiveness of incentives and, 137
Rhode Island Economic Development Corporation, 133
risks: assessment, 232, of investment incentives, 132–37; political, FDI and, 81
ROI. *See* return-on-investment
Romania, *Micula et al. v. Romania*, 222, 305–7
round-tripping investment, 46
rule-based approach to incentives, 195, *195*
Ryanair, 108–9

SAAP. *See* "State Aid Action Plan"
SAM. *See* "State Aid Modernisation"
Sandals, Jamaica, 153
SCM Agreement. *See* Subsidies and Countervailing Measures Agreement
SD. *See* sustainable development
SDGs. *See* sustainable development goals

Senegal, tax incentives in, 170
sequential investment, 18
services: after-care, 35; investment in, 58*n*2; investment-related technical, 34; new, cost of, 234–35; suppliers, 282. *See also* information and technical services incentives
SEZs. *See* special economic zones
Singapore: attracting investments and, 56; EU and, FTA between, 309–10, 312; targeting and, 19
skills: development, incentives related to, *214*; new, FDI and, 190
small and medium-sized enterprises (SMEs): FDI from, 185; loans, 23
Smart Incentives, 238
SMEs. *See* small and medium-sized enterprises
social welfare, 67–68
South Korea, R&D investment incentives in, 72, *73*
spatial balance, FDI and, 190
spatial clustering, 53–54; colocation and, 53
special and differential obligations, 311
special economic zones (SEZs): duty relief in, 167; tax exemptions in, 26; tax holidays in, 26, 162–63; tax incentives for businesses in, 162–63
specialized labor, 53–54
specificity: enterprise-specific subsidies, 267; of investment incentives, 4–5; subsidy, 267–69
spillovers: absorptive capacity of domestic companies and, 56, 68, 87*n*10; investment incentives and generation of, 12*n*2; knowledge, 53; location choice model and, 52; market failure and, 87*n*10; policies to enhance, 55–56; rates of return due to, 66
Starbucks, 156
State aid, EU: analysis of, 108–9, 112–13; companies granted, 112; compliance with rules of, 293; crisis-related, 99, 102, *103*, 112; definition of, 285–88; de minimis regulation, 97; EC policy on, 114; effectiveness of, 112–13, 260–61; effect of investment incentives and, 292–93; "Europe 2020 Strategy," and, 98; exemptions, 111–12, 114; forms of, 286; in GBER, 95–97, 289; implications of, 293; for innovation, 105–6; intensity of, 292–93, 318*n*42; investment legal framework and granting, 285; legal framework of, 285–88; *Micula et al. v. Romania* and, 307; modernization of, 98–99, 112; non-crisis-related, 99–102, *100*, *101*, *102*, *103*; notification and approval rules for, 288; objectives justifying use of, 286–87; permitted use of, 285–88; policy, 97–99, 114; RAG and, 287; for R&D, 105–6, *106*; regional, 103–5; regulation of, 291–93; regulatory framework for, 95–97, *96*, 108, 110–11; tax incentives

and, 106–8; TFEU provisions on, 95, *96*, 110, 116–18; types of, *99*, 99–102, *100*
"State Aid Action Plan" (SAAP), 97
"State Aid Modernisation" (SAM), 98–99, 112
state and municipal investment incentives, U.S.: bidding wars and, 123, 126, 129, 135, 145, 257–59; communities and effects of, 134–35; cost-benefit analysis of, 238–43; effectiveness of, 143–46, 148*n*5; federal investment incentives and, 123, 125; fiscal *vs.* financial, 131–32; foreign firms and, 141, *141*; good practices for, 142–43, 147; importance of, 125–26; Incentive Transparency Index, 142; income and property taxes, 127; investors and, 126; manufacturing capital expenditures and, 139, *139*; megadeals, 126–31, *128*, *130*; net fiscal effects of, 146–47, 147*n*1; per capita, *140*, 140–41; politics and, *140*, 140–41; risks of, 132–37; state ranking of transparency and effectiveness evaluation for, 143, *143*; use of, 8, 10
state incentives: in Australia, 253; competition, 145; in EU, 94; politics and, *140*, 140–41; regulation of investment incentives and, 251. *See also* state and municipal investment incentives, U.S.
strategic asset-seeking investment: location determinants and, 51; MNE, 47; motivations for FDI and, 47, 49; strategic asset-seeking investors, 6
strategic decisions, policy makers', 17–21
subnational jurisdictions: incentives in, 2–3, 8; regulation of investment incentives, 251–61; subsidy use and, 252. *See also* government agreements; state incentives
Sub-Saharan Africa, tax incentives in, 158–59, *159*, 170
subsidiaries, types of, 38*n*3
subsidies: accountability and, 11; actionable, 270–75; adverse effects of, 271; agricultural, 124; in CETA, 310–11; competition, 145–46; continuous, 192–93; countermeasures, 315*n*19; de facto export contingency and, 269–70; disclosure of, 273–74; enforcement of, 273–74; exceptions or carve-outs for, 274–75; FTA provisions on, 309–11; infrastructure, 22–24; investment incentives as, 3, 5; job relocation via, 252; job training, 22, 23; loan guarantees, 24; policy objectives served by, 274–75; prohibited, 269–71; R&D, 271–72; region-specific, 267–68; review of, 273–74; SCM Agreement definition of, 266–67, 310; specificity of, 267–69; subnational government use of, 252; transparency and, 11; WTO provisions on, 110–11, 114

Subsidies and Countervailing Measures (SCM) Agreement: actionable subsidies and, 271–73; developing countries and, provisions for, 276; disclosure, review, and enforcement in, 273–74; exceptions or carve-outs for subsidies serving certain policy objectives, 274–75; key messages, 276–77; overregulation and, 284; prohibited subsidies in, 269–71; requirement of benefit and, 267; requirement of specificity and, 267–69; subsidy defined in, 266–67, 310; transparency and, 273; *United States—Large Civil Aircraft* dispute and, 271–73, 277

subtypes of investment incentives: financial incentives, 21–24; fiscal incentives, 24–30; information and technical services incentives, 32–35; regulatory incentives, 31–32

super-deductions, 162

sustainable development (SD): activities related to, identifying, 213–14; competition avoidance and, 223–24; FDI and, 1, 212, *212*; in FTAs, cooperation for, 312; ILAs and promoting investment in, 206; industries related to, identifying, 213–14; investment and, 1–2, 11, 225; investment barriers and, 206; investment incentives for, 326–28; investment incentives supporting, 1–2; in investment promotion strategies, 205–7; investment regulation and facilitation for, 207, *208*, *209*; investment-related action plans for, *209*; IPAs and, 205; policy options for facilitating investment in, 206–7, *208*; promotion strategy and investment for, 205, *205*; pursuing, through investment incentives, 215, *215*; synergies and, creating, 216–17; trade-offs of, dealing with, 216–17

sustainable development goals (SDGs), 1, 19, 323

sustainable development investment incentive: economic determinants for, 327–28; effectiveness of, 219–22, *220*, 327; industries eligible for, 213–14; optimizing impact of, 326–28; SD promotion and, 204–17; type of, selecting "right," *215*, 215–16

sustainable development investment incentive schemes: designing, 207–17; factoring, 212–13; implementing, 217–18; monitoring effects of, 218–24

Switzerland, attracting investments and, 56

synergy, SD and creating, 216–17, *217*

Tanzania, 162–63

targeting, level of, 19

tariffs: division of surplus and, 79–80; FIT program, 278; zero or reduced, 27

tax administration: APA and, 155; investment incentives discretion and, 168–70; tax provisions and, application of, 170

taxation: business, 107–8; FDI and, 29–30; fiscal incentives and, 24, 29; on foreign earnings, 27, 124; individual, 123–24; of MNEs, 108; in U.S., 28; worldwide system of, 27
tax avoidance mechanisms, 173*n*2–3
tax burdens, low effective, 87*n*8
tax competition: empirical evidence of, 27; in EU, 107, 286; horizontal, 86*n*5
tax credits: California Competes, 239; costs of, 233; investment, 26; for R&D, 74
taxes: cost-benefit analysis, 232–33; FDI and, 29; income, 127; infrastructure compared with, 12*n*8; new, estimating, 234; property, 127; reduced, 155; relief of, 318*n*40; state and municipal government, 127; withholding of, 173*n*2
tax expenditures, 24
tax havens, 25, 38*n*6, 46
tax holidays: carryforward of losses compared with, 173*n*5; eliminating, 40*n*15, 154; as fiscal incentives, 25–26; global, 156–57; government-offered, 157; investment-linked incentives and, 161; prevalence of, 157–58, *158*; in SEZs, 26, 162–63
tax incentives: for attracting foreign investment, 107; bidding wars and, 325–26; for businesses in SEZs, 162–63; competition over, 38*n*8; complications of, 155; costs of, 233; in EU, 106–8; evaluation of, 142; FDI and, 154; in free zones, 158–59; global, 153–74; governments and, 154–55, 172–73; granting, procedures for, 168–72, *172*; income, 156–63, *157*; investment codes and, 170; investment-linked, 161; in Ireland, 27–28; as motivation for investment, 161; policies, 154; as profitability-enhancing incentive, 193; provision and application of, discretion in, 169, *169*; for R&D, *71*, 162; reforms, 153; relevance of, 29–30; studies for, 30; in Sub-Saharan Africa, 158–59, *159*, 170; tax laws and, 170–72; transparency of, 173; in U.S., 107; VAT exemptions as, 165. *See also* fiscal incentives
tax laws, tax incentives and, 170–72
tax losses: carryforward of, 26, 159–60, 173*n*5; treatment of, 159–60, *160*
tax policy: fiscal incentives and, 25; in U.S., 28
tax provisions, fiscal incentives and, 24
tax rates: BEATRs, 29; corporate, 26–28, 107–8, 123–24; on dividends and interest paid abroad, 27; EATRs, 29; fiscal incentives and, 25; income, 161; locational factors and, 30; reduced corporate income, 26, 27
technical assistance, 34–35
technical services, investment-related, 34

technology: FDI and new, 189; green, 277; strategic asset-seeking investment and, 51
TFEU. *See* "Treaty on the Functioning of the European Union"
Third International Financing for Development Conference, 1
38 Studio, 129, 131–33
time frames, incentives programs and, 196, 232; modeling and, 235; project, 232; types of investment incentives and, 20
time inconsistency market failure, 78–79
TISA. *See* Trade in Services Agreement
tourism, investments in, 26
TPP. *See* Trans-Pacific Partnership
Trade in Services Agreement (TISA), 314
trade law: FTAs and, 312; interpretation and application of, 316; WTO agreements and, 313. *See also specific trade agreements*
transaction costs: FDI, 66; information for reducing, 63; institutional factors and, 50
Trans-Atlantic Trade and Investment Partnership (TTIP), 224, 296, 313
transfer pricing rules, 155
Trans-Pacific Partnership (TPP), 296, 313
transparency: accountability and, 31, 261; effectiveness of investment incentives and, 324, 326; efficiency and, 31; in EU, 2, 288–95; IIAs and requirements on regulatory, 303; in incentives administration, 323–24; lack of, 2, 323–24; regulatory, 303; SCM agreement and, 273; SD-related investment incentives and, 221; subsidies and, 11; of tax incentives, 173
transportation costs, location theory and, 52
"Treaty on the Functioning of the European Union" (TFEU; European Commission): Article 107 of, 103–5, 116–17, 286–87; Article 108 of, 117–18; Article 109 of, 118; Article 349 of, 114*n6*; competition for investment and, 94; exemption umbrella, 114; regulation of investment incentives and, 285; State aid provisions in, 95, *96*, 110
TRIMs Agreement: IIA and, 300; regulation of investment incentives and, 277–79
Triple Bottom Line tool, 243
TTIP. *See* Trans-Atlantic Trade and Investment Partnership
1209 North Orange, 38*n6*
types of investment incentives: effectiveness and efficiency of incentives, 6; financial incentives, 21–24; fiscal incentives, 24–30; information and technical services, 32–35; IPAs and attracting investment, role of, 35–37; purpose of incentives and, 17–21; regulatory incentives, 31–32; for SD, selecting "right," *215*, 215–16, *216*

UNCTAD. *See* United Nations Conference on Trade and Development
United Airlines, 135
United Nations, SDGs, 323
United Nations Conference on Trade and Development (UNCTAD): investment incentives defined by, 3; Investment Policy Monitor Database, 204; IPA survey, 204, 207, 225*n*2
United Parcel Service (UPS), 256–57
United States (U.S.): bidding wars in, 123, 126, 129, 135, 145, 257–59; corporate tax rate, 28, 123–24; economic determinants in, 239–43; economic development in, 132, 133, 142–44, 239–42; effectiveness of incentives, 137–46; federal investment incentives, 123–25; fiscal *vs.* financial incentives, 131–32; government agreements, 257–60; grants and loans provided by, 124–25; incentives in, 122–48; international investment promotion in, 122–23; Ireland's incentives and, 137–38; Louisiana Economic Development, 132; megadeals in, 126–29, *128*; no-raiding agreements, voluntary state, 257–60; policy effectiveness in, 122; R&D investment incentives in, 72, *73*; regulation of investment incentives in, 257–60; Rhode Island Economic Development Corporation, 133; risks of incentives and, 132–37; state incentives in, 132, 140, 144; subsidies, 124; taxation in, 28; tax incentives in, 107; tax policies in, 28; tax rates, 28, 123–24; TTIP, 224; use of investment incentives, 11. *See also* state and municipal investment incentives, U.S.
United States—Large Civil Aircraft dispute, 271–73, 277, 314*n*4
unskilled or semiskilled labor, 47, 51
up-front grants, as cost-reducing incentives, 192–93
UPS. *See* United Parcel Service
U.S. *See* United States
US—Carbon Steel (India), 315*n*5
use of investment incentives: cost-benefit analysis and, 324–25; deficiencies in, 323–28; discipline across jurisdictions and, 325–26; economic development incentives and, 228; in EU, 9–10, 284–85, 311, 313; FDI and, 45, 180; GATS and, 279–80; generalized, 67–68; global, 9–11; IAs and, 77–85, 298; international coordination in, 223; market failure and, 85–86; monitoring effective, 219; in OECD countries, 158, 160; performance requirements and, 300–301; policy and, 54; rationales and welfare impacts, 64–68; for R&D, 63, 69–77, 162; regulation and, 264–66, 271, 298; SCM Agreement and, 264–66, 271, 276; state and municipal, U.S., 10; targeted and precise, 158; transparency and, 2, 303, 324; TRIMs Agreement and, 277–78; in U.S., 11; widespread, 6, 39, 173; WTO rules and, 283–84

value-added tax (VAT): compliance with, 164, 174*n*10; exemption or reduction in, 155; exemptions under, 163–66, *165*; supply exemption under, 163; zero-rating under, 163–66, *165*
value-adding activities of MNEs, 57
variable cost aid (VCA), 108
VAT. *See* value-added tax
VCA. *See* variable cost aid
Verdon Free Zone/Port, 163
Virginia, cost-benefit analysis in, 239

wage subsidies, 22
Washington: Boeing and, 252; cost-benefit analysis in, 240–41
welfare: corporate, 124; impacts of investment incentives on, 64–68, 85; maximization of, 79; social, 67–68
withdrawal of investment incentives, challenging, 222
World Bank: Development Indicators, 187; Ease of Doing Business rankings, 187; FIAS, 6–7
World Trade Organization (WTO): Agreement on Subsidies and Countervailing Measures, 223, 266–77; duty relief and, 167; *EC—Aircraft* dispute and, 269–70; GATS and, 279; GATT and, 271, 275, 277; investment legal framework and, 284; regulation of investment incentives in, 113, 265–84, 313; subsidies and, provisions on, 110–11, 114; TRIMs, 277–279; *United States—Large Civil Aircraft* dispute and, 271–73

zero-rating, VAT, 163–66, *165*
zero-sum outcomes, 11
zero tariffs, 27